Women in Governing Institutions in South Asia

To
Members of South Asian Network for Governance Studies

PREFACE

South Asia, as Sobhan has argued, is united by a common thread of misgovernance. Several reasons may account for the lack of good governance in the region, of which the ineffectiveness of governing institutions, particularly parliament, civil service and local government, is very important. These institutions have had an asymmetrical growth, with the bureaucracy predating the other two. Parliament is the youngest among the three institutions of governance. These, however, share one attribute—all three can be considered as 'gendered' institutions. In fact, lack of gender balance in different governing institutions is one of the important reasons for their ineffectiveness. Different countries in the region have adopted measures in recent years to mainstream gender in these institutions, among other things, by adopting a policy of 'positive discrimination'. This has led to an increase in the number of women at different levels. Women have also fared well while competing with men for jobs/seats in different institutions. While it may take a long time to achieve gender parity, it is clearly evident that women are at least as capable as men in doing things that have traditionally been considered to be the 'preserve' of men. The change in gender composition of different institutions, however, has not taken place in a uniform way. Differences in the scope and scale of change are noticeable in different countries of the region; these can also be noticed in the same country over a certain period of time.

However, our understanding about the nature of change taking place in the gender composition of different governing institutions in South

Asia and its implications for empowering women is limited. The policy of inclusion adopted in different countries with a view to encouraging more women to come to the forefront has not received much scholarly attention. In particular, there is no major comparative study on the scope, implications, and limitations of the policies and/or measures used to mainstream gender in different governing institutions in the South Asian region. This volume seeks to redress this deficiency. It particularly tries to explore if there is any major relationship between descriptive representation and substantive representation of women in these three governing institutions and examines the factors that account for such relationship or lack of it.

Most of the papers included in this volume were earlier presented to an International Conference on Inclusive Governance in South Asia organized in Dhaka by Public Administration and Governance Research Network and the Department of Public Administration of the University of Chittagong, in collaboration with The Asia Foundation (TAF) and Southern University Bangladesh. I gratefully acknowledge the financial support of TAF, Southern University, UGC, University of Chittagong, YPSA, and Manusher Jonno Foundation. It would have been almost impossible to organize the Conference without such financial support. Several chapters—2, 3, 4, 5, 6, 9, 12 and 16—have been specially written for this volume. I am extremely grateful to the authors of different chapters who, despite their busy schedule, agreed to contribute to the volume. Colleagues from different parts of Bangladesh and abroad travelled a long way to attend the Conference; many of them also gladly agreed to review papers which the authors have found very useful. I appreciate their kind support and cooperation. Dr. Muhammad A. Hakim, UGC Professor of Political Science at the University of Chittagong read drafts of some of the chapters. I am grateful to him. I owe a special debt to Ms. Jerin Chaudhury for careful reading and extremely helpful editorial comments on the book. Special acknowledgements are due to Professor Drude Dahlerup of the University of Stockholm, Sweden; Professor Shirin M. Rai of the University of Warwick, UK; and Professor Ahmed Shafiqul Huque of McMaster University, Canada, for endorsing the book. Professor Huque also read drafts of Chapters 1 and 18 and made extremely useful comments. I am indebted to him. Finally, I am also grateful to members of the editorial team of Palgrave Macmillan, particularly to Warren Jemima and Beth Farrow, and to Jayanthi Narayanaswamy of Springer Nature, for their help and support in making the publication possible.

However, responsibility for accuracy of data and interpretation of facts and information in different chapters rests with individual author(s), and not with the publisher or the editor.

Chittagong, Bangladesh   Nizam Ahmed
February 2017

CONTENTS

Part IV   Conclusion

Abbreviations

A/L	Advanced Level
ADB	Asian Development Bank
AL	Awami League
ARC	Administrative Reforms Commission
BBS	Bhutan Broadcasting Service
BBS	Bangladesh Bureau of Statistics
BCS	Bangladesh Civil Service
BIGD	Brac Institute of Governance and Development
BNEW	Bhutan Network for Empowering Women
BNP	Bangladesh Nationalist Party
C & EG	Customs and Excise Group
C & TG	Commerce and Trade Group
CAS	Ceylon Administrative Service
CCS	Ceylon Civil Service
CIET	Community Information, Empowerment and Transparency
CP	Communist Party
CSB	Civil Service Board
CSO	Civil Society Organization
CSP	Civil Service of Pakistan
CSS	Civil Superior Service
CWC	Ceylon Workers' Congress
DC	Deputy Commissioner
DCT	Druk Chirwang Tshogpa
DE	Directly Elected
DFID	Department for International Development
DGP	Director General of Police

DM	District Magistrate
DMG	District Management Group
DoPT	Department of Personnel and Training
DPT	Druk Phuensum Tshogpa
DSP	Direct Seat Parliamentarian
DSWPs	Direct-seat Women Parliamentarians
DVA	Domestic Violence Act
ECB	Election Commission of Bhutan
ER	Elected Representative
EWR	Elected Women Representative
FAFEN	Free and Fair Election Network
FFs	Freedom Fighters
FGD	Focus Group Discussions
FIR	First Information Report
FPSC	Federal Public Service Commission
FSP	Foreign Service of Pakistan
GNI	Gross National Income
GoB	Government of Bangladesh
GoN	Government of Nepal
GoP	Government of Pakistan
GRAP	Gender Reform Action Plans
GSMNA	General Seat Member of National Assembly
HIS	Helvetas Intercooperation Swiss
IAS	Indian Administrative Service
ICS	Indian Civil Service
IDEA	International Institute for Democracy and Electoral Assistance
IFS	Indian Foreign Service
IG	Information Group
ILO	International Labor Organization
IMF	International Monetary Fund
IPS	Indian Police Service
IPU	Inter-Parliamentary Union
IRP	Interim Recruitment Policy
IRS	Inland Revenue Service
JHU	Jathika Hela Urumaya
JVP	Janatha Vimukthi Peramuna
KABIKHA	Kajer Binimoye Khaidda (Food for Works)
KII	Key Informant Interview
LFS	Labor Force Survey
LGB	Local government body
LGSP	Local Government Support Program
LSSP	Lanka Sama Samaja Party

MC	Municipal Councils
MDG	Millennium Development Goal
MEP	Mahajana Eksath Peramuna
MLCG	Military Lands and Cantonment Group
MNA	Member of National Assembly
MoGA	Ministry of General Administration
MoWA	Ministry of Women's Affairs
MP	Member of Parliament
NA	National Assembly
NCW	National Committee on Women
NCWC	National Commission for Women and Children
NGO	Non-governmental Organization
NHDR	National Human Development Report
NPAW	National Policy for the Advancement of Women
NRB	National Reconstruction Bureau
OBM	Open Budget Meeting
OECD	The Organization for Economic Cooperation and Development
OMG	Office Management Group
PA	Peoples' Alliance
PAAS	Pakistan Audit and Accounts Service
PAS	Pakistan Administrative Service
PC	Provincial Councils
PDP	People's Democratic Party
PG	Postal Group
PILDAT	Pakistan Institute for Legislative Development and Training
PML-N	Pakistan Muslim League -Nawaz
PMQT	Prime Minister's Question Time
PPP	Pakistan People's Party
PR	Proportional Representation
PRI	Panchayati Raj Institutions
PS	Panchayati Samity
PS	Pradesheeya Sabhas
PSC	Public Service Commission
PSCER	Parliamentary Select Committee on Electoral Reforms
PSP	Police Service of Pakistan
PTI	Pakistan Tehrik-e-Insaf
RENEW	Respect, Educate, Nurture and Empower Women
RG	Railways Group
RoP	Rules of Procedure
RSMNA	Reserved Seat Member of National Assembly
RSWPs	Reserved-Seat Women Parliamentarians

SC	Schedule Caste
SLAS	Sri Lanka Administrative Service
SLFP	Sri Lanka Freedom Party
SLMC	Sri Lanka Muslim Congress
SMS	Short Message Service
ST	Schedule Tribe
TNA	Tamil National Congress
TR	Test Relief
UN	United Nations
UNDP	United Nations Development Program
UNF	United National Front
UNO	Upazila Nirbahi Officer
UNP	United National Party
UP	Union Parishad
UPFA	United People's Freedom Alliance
USA	United States of America
UT	Union Territory
UZP	Upazila Parishad
VGD	Vulnerable Group Development
VGF	Vulnerable Group Feeding
WB	World Bank
WCP	Women Component Plan
WPC	Women's Parliamentary Caucus
ZP	Zila Parishad

List of Figures

LIST OF TABLES

EDITOR AND CONTRIBUTORS

About the Editor

Nizam Ahmed is Professor of Public Administration at the University of Chittagong, Bangladesh. He graduated with Honors and obtained a Master's in public administration from the University of Dhaka. He also has a master of social sciences (Administration) degree from the University of Tasmania, Australia, and a Ph.D. from the University of Melbourne, Australia. His fields of interest are legislative behavior, local government, party politics, and comparative administration. Dr. Ahmed did his postdoctoral research as a Commonwealth Fellow at the University of Hull, UK, and also at the State University of New York as a Senior Fulbright Scholar. He has authored/edited several books and published numerous articles in leading international journals. Professor Ahmed is the Chief Coordinator/President of Public Administration and Governance Research Network—Bangladesh and Secretary, South Asian Network for Governance Studies.

Contributors

Nishat Afroze Ahmed received her bachelor of international relations with Honors from the University of Chittagong. She has also an MA in international relations from the same University. At present she is working as a Lecturer in the Department of International Relations, University of Chittagong, Bangladesh.

Nighat Ghulam Ansari has obtained her Ph.D. from Utrecht University, the Netherlands, and currently working as Assistant Professor at the Institute of Administrative Sciences (IAS), University of the Punjab, Lahore, Pakistan. She did her MBA from Quaid-i-Azam University, Islamabad, and MPhil from IAS. She has 10 years of experience of working in the corporate sector and is associated with the teaching profession since 2006. She has published research papers in various national and international journals and presented papers in International Research Conferences. Her research interests include organization behavior and human resource management with a special focus on gender issues.

Bidyut Chakrabarty is Professor of Public Administration at the University of Delhi, India. After completing Ph.D. from the London School of Economics, Chakrabarty began teaching in Indian Institute of Management, Calcutta. He has taught at different universities outside India such as the University of Iowa, USA, University of Hull, UK, and Monash University, Australia. He became a professor at the University of Delhi in 1991 where he has built a special research group in public administration in 'the third world.' He held the Mahatma Gandhi Chair for Global Non-Violence at James Madison University, Virginia, USA, and India Chair at Hamburg University, Germany. Chakrabarty has published about 40 books and numerous articles in all major areas of political science.

Prakash Chand is Assistant Professor of Political Science at Dyal Singh College at the University of Delhi, India. He holds a Ph.D. from the University of Delhi. Dr. Chand has recently conducted post-doctoral research on environmental pollution, industrial relocations and labor rehabilitation in Delhi. He is the author (with Prof. Bidyut Chakrabarty) of *Public Administration in a Globalizing World* (Sage 2012). His research papers have appeared in various national and international journals. He received a Doctoral Fellowship from Indian Council for Social Science Research (ICSSR) and a Post-Doctoral Research Award from the University Grants Commission (UGC), India.

Nusrat Jahan Chowdhury is Associate Professor of Public Admini-stration at the University of Dhaka. She also taught in the Department of Public Administration, Rajshahi University and for a stint at Jahangirnagar University. She was awarded a Commonwealth Scholarship and received her Ph.D. in politics and international relations from the University of Auckland in New Zealand. She has published one book, contributed chapters to different books/volumes, and published articles in reputed local and international journals. Her research interests include peace and conflict issues in the Chittagong Hill Tracts, gender quotas and women's representation in politics, NGOs and women development, and public policy.

Sonam Chuki has Ph.D. in gender and politics from Queensland University of Technology, Australia. She has taught democracy, politics, and gender studies at the Royal Institute of Management in Thimphu for about 19 years. Sonam served as a commissioner at the National Commission for Women and Children (NCWC), Bhutan's only state agency which addresses women and children's issues. At present, she serves as a member for the gender advocacy team for Bhutan in the South Asian Region. Sonam has publications in gender and politics and is passionate about women's genuine empowerment. Currently, she works at the Royal Education Council in Paro, Bhutan.

Sangita Dhal is an Assistant Professor [in senior grade] and UGC post-doctoral fellow, Department of Political Science, Kalindi College, Delhi University, and has more than 14 years of teaching and research expe-rience in the field of public administration, public policy, gender stud-ies, and issues relating to governance. Her doctoral work from the Delhi University was on 'Grassroot Democratic Processes and Women: A Study of Panchayati Raj Institutions in Odisha.' Dr. Dhal has been a Member of Course Revision Committee for Public Administration and Public Policy in Delhi University and has contributed articles to several edited books and various reputed journals.

Sadik Hasan is Associate Professor of Public Administration at the University of Dhaka, Bangladesh. Previously, he worked as Associate Professor of Public Administration at the University of Chittagong, Bangladesh. He earned his Ph.D. in public administration from the University of Sydney, Australia, and Master of Public Administration

(MPA) from the University of Baltimore, Maryland, USA. He has published a number of research articles in reputed refereed journals and contributed chapters to several books. He is the author of *Women in Bangladesh Local Government: A Study of Gram Sarkar* (Dhaka 2007). His research focuses on e-governance initiatives in developing countries, e-transparency, South Asian Politics, Local Government, Women in South Asia, and NGOs.

Nasira Jabeen is the Dean of Faculty of Economics and Management Sciences and Professor and Director, Institute of Administrative Sciences, University of the Punjab, Pakistan. She has a postdoctorate from the University of Texas at Austin, USA, in gender and governance and a Ph.D. from the University of Stirling, UK. She also has a master of public administration (MPA) degree from the University of Southern California, USA. Prof. Jabeen has experience of working with many international developmental organizations. She has published widely in international and national journals. She is the Chairperson of National Curriculum Review Committee for Public Administration.

Ferdous Jahan is Professor of Public Administration at the University of Dhaka. She also worked as the academic coordinator of BRAC Development Institute (BDI) of BRAC University, Bangladesh, for several years. Jahan obtained a Ph.D. in political science in 2005 from the University of Pennsylvania, USA. She has authored journal articles on governance, development, and women's empowerment issues which have been published in renowned national and international academic journals. Dr. Jahan's current academic interests and research include religion and politics, pro-poor governance, public service, urban governance, and women's empowerment issues in developing societies.

Kunzang Lhamu obtained her master degree in public policy from the National University of Singapore. She is now the Director of the National Commission for Women and Children (NCWC), Royal Government of Bhutan (RGoB). Prior to this, she worked as the Chief of the Research and Evaluation Division (RED) of the Gross National Happiness Commission (GNHC), RGoB. She has spearheaded initiatives to institutionalize outcome management in Bhutan through development of the National Evaluation Policy and National Evaluation Protocol and Guidelines (currently in draft) and also is the Chair of the

Evaluation Association of Bhutan, which is in the process of being registered as a Civil Society Organization.

Kamala Liyanage is Senior Professor of Political Science at the University of Peradeniya, Sri Lanka. She has published more than 70 books, chapters in edited books, monographs, articles in refereed and non-refereed journals, and training modules on ethnic conflicts, gender issues, public administration, and international relations. She has been awarded several prestigious scholarships and fellowships such as Monbusho Scholarship, Commonwealth Fellowship, Fulbright Fellowship, and Japan Foundation Fellowship. Her research interests are comparative politics, ethnic conflicts and resolution, and gender studies. Dr. Liyanage is a human rights trainer and activist.

Umm-e-Farwa Mubasher is a Lecturer and Ph.D. Scholar (previously Research Scholar) at the Institute of Administrative Sciences, University of the Punjab, Lahore. She is currently working as a team member on a research project in the field of public sector governance and management, gender and governance and leadership. Her area of research in Ph.D. (management) is governance and human resource management.

M.A.F. Anwara Nilmi is a Temporary Lecturer of Political Science at the University of Peradeniya, Sri Lanka. She prepared a dissertation on The Role of Street Level Bureaucracy in Delivering Public Health Services in Sri Lanka in partial fulfillment of the requirement for the degree of bachelor of arts. Anwara worked as a Research Assistant in a project entitled 'Addressing Domestic Violence Through Antenatal Care in Sri Lanka's Plantation Estates: Contributions of Public Health Midwives' funded by the Research Council of Norway from 2013 to 2017.

Narendra Raj Paudel is Lecturer of Public Administration at Tribhuvan University, Nepal. His research interests include public policy implementation, development administration, and gender and health governance. He has authored two books and published a number of articles in reputed journals and chapters in edited volumes at home and abroad. He is the Managing Editor of *South Asian Journal of Policy and Governance*.

Shivani Singh is currently Assistant Professor of Political Science at Dyal Singh College, University of Delhi, India. She has published articles in various journals and presented papers in various national and international seminars on issues of contemporary relevance. Dr. Singh has contributed a chapter on MNREGA to a book on public policy co-edited by Prof. Bidyut Chakrabarty and Dr. Prakash Chand. She is the editor of *Governance: Issues and Challenges* (Sage 2016).

Maheen Sultan is one of the founders of the Centre for Gender and Social Transformation at the BRAC Development Institute, BRAC University, a regional center on research, teaching, and policy related to gender and social transformation. She is a development practitioner with over 30 years experience in a range of capacities, from direct program management to policy formulation. She has worked on issues of social development, local governance, civil society participation, and gender equality. Maheen is a member of *Naripokkho*, a Bangladeshi women's activist organization. She is co-editor of 'Voicing Demands: Feminist Activism in Transitional Contexts' (Zed Books: London, 2014).

Darshi Thoradeniya works as a visiting lecturer in the Department of History at the University of Colombo. She is the Colombo branch manager of the South Asia Institute, Heidelberg University since 2014. Darshi completed her Ph.D. in history of medicine at the University of Warwick in May 2014 on a Wellcome Trust Strategic Award. The title of her thesis is 'Women's Health as State Strategy: Sri Lanka's Twentieth Century.' She has published one chapter in a book titled *Women's Global Health: Norms and State Policies* published by the Lexington Books in the USA, and articles in international and local journals.

Punam Yadav is a Teaching Fellow in the Gender Institute and Research Fellow in the Centre for Women, Peace and Security at the London School of Economics. Prior to joining LSE, she was part-time Lecturer at the Centre for Peace and Conflict Studies, University of Sydney. Dr Yadav's research interests include gender, peace and security, gender and social transformation, gender and post-conflict reconstruction, gender and conflict-induced internal displacement, conflict sensitive program management, gender and development, gender and social inclusion, gender analysis, and gender planning and gender mainstreaming. She is the author of *Social Transformation in Post-conflict Nepal: A Gender Perspective* (Routledge 2016).

CHAPTER 1

Introduction

Nizam Ahmed

Women in South Asia, as in other regions of the world, constitute nearly half of the total population. According to one estimate, 48.4% of the South Asian population in 2014 were women. But they remain seriously disadvantaged vis-à-vis men in almost every respect. Women also lag behind their counterparts in other regions in Asia, particularly the Asia Pacific region and East Asia. A recent UNDP Report has observed that East Asia and the Pacific are pulling ahead of South Asia on most indicators of gender equality such as health, adult literacy, and economic participation.[1] The Report further observes that the divergence has become so magnified that today South Asia ranks close to or lower than sub-Saharan Africa, at the bottom of the heap. Gender inequity is particularly evident in representative politics as well as in the institutions of governance. Only 16% of women are represented in the parliaments in South Asia, which is less than the global average of 23.3% (IPU 2017).

South Asian women also lag behind in respect of their representation in the bureaucracy. In Southeast Asia, women have better representation in the bureaucracy than those in South Asia. In at least one country, Philippines, women surpass men in respect of representation in the bureaucracy; while in Thailand, the proportion of men and women in the civil service is almost equal. In only a few countries in South Asia

N. Ahmed (✉)
University of Chittagong, Chittagong, Bangladesh
e-mail: nijamuddin_ahmed@yahoo.com

© The Author(s) 2018
N. Ahmed (ed.), *Women in Governing Institutions in South Asia*,
DOI 10.1007/978-3-319-57475-2_1

do women have even one-third of representation in the civil service. In Nepal, for example, despite women-friendly and inclusive laws, women's representation in the civil service is still dismal. Only 15.8% of the total civil servants are women. The situation is more or less similar in Pakistan. South Asian women, however, fare better than their counterparts in Southeast Asia, East Asia, and the Pacific in local politics; they occupy between 24 and 36% of seats in local authorities.

The lack of female involvement and participation in different institutions of governance has several consequences. Haque (2003, p. 584) argues that the lesser representation of female citizens not only risks causing a legitimacy crisis for the government; it may also be seen as wastage of human resources from an economic standpoint as women are now better educated than in the past and have the potential to become assets. In the absence of a sizeable number of women at different levels of administrative hierarchy, there is a risk that they may be discriminated against in respect of the delivery of services. 'The male-dominated state bureaucracy may not adequately comprehend women's specific needs and problems—including special health care, child care, domestic violence, and so on—and serve them accordingly' (Haque, p. 584). Thus, in order to avoid gender-biased service delivery, there should be enough women in the public administration, so that their specific preferences can be better comprehended and presented, and that their needs would not be overlooked or neglected (Sun 2004).

The above observations are not intended to argue that the presence of an adequate number of women in different sectors and at different hierarchical levels will automatically help them take decisions that will benefit women, in other words, they will always be gender-aware and gender-responsive. There are doubts that more women in decision-making positions will be able to do much for women for various reasons, of which the following are important: first, most women have been socialized into traditional roles in a patriarchal society and have integrated these traditional values of inequality between women and men; second, women do not form a homogeneous group defined by their sex alone and as they are more likely come from the elite class, it is unlikely that they will challenge the interests of their class; third, women candidates do not always focus on women's issues alone during elections as it may cost them politically; and finally, since women in most countries do not have a critical mass in decision-making bodies, they will be less likely to confront the male leadership (Miranda 2005, pp. 3–5). This is, however, not to underestimate the capacity of women to make a change. Women can play the role of change agents in at least the same way as men, and one prerequisite is that they have adequate representation in different institutions of governance. But as stated earlier, women remain grossly under-represented in different institutions and there is a need for correcting the imbalance between men and women.

INCLUDING THE EXCLUDED

There is no 'one best way' of including the excluded in the governing process. However, one dominant way used to redress the imbalance in gender representation in different governing institutions is to adopt a policy of quota, i.e., setting aside a certain percentage of seats/posts for women. Quotas are of different types; these have advocates as well as detractors. Advocates of gender quotas point to evidence that quota reforms change the legislative arena by normalizing women's political presence, thereby generating new political cultures, broadening the mainstream political agenda, and causing both women and men to pay more attention to women's interests (Clayton et al. 2016, pp. 4–5). Detractors argue that the quota system undermines the principle of merit. It is also argued that quota reforms may create a backlash among male legislators who, in reaction to quotas and the influx of women, try to preserve power, close down spaces for women's substantive representation, and marginalize female newcomers (Clayton et al. p. 5). A United Nations report (2013) states that quotas themselves are insufficient unless accompanied by some other measures such as sanctions for non-compliance, candidates placed in winnable positions on party lists and party support.

Critics argue that the introduction of quotas for women does not always bring about positive results. As one analyst remarked on the experience of Bangladesh: 'Instead of contributing to women's political agency and autonomy, it accentuated their dependence in politics and reinforced their marginality' (Chowdhury 2002, p. 1). The real-world politics, however, does not appear to be as straightforward as Chowdhury's comments suggest. Those assessing the performance of women parliamentarians often consider modern western parliaments as a model without taking into consideration the characteristics of the contexts within which the role of women parliamentarians has evolved in those countries.

Most of the western and Nordic parliaments have followed the 'incremental track of representation,' to use Dahlerup and Freidenvall's terminology (2005), which implies that political representation of women will rise only after women are able to increase their resources (i.e., education and gainful employment). Without significant structural changes in society, the inclusion of women in political institutions will not lead to any long-term political empowerment of women. In contrast, most of the new nations in Asia and Africa have followed the 'fast track model of representation,' which provides for a sudden increase in the number of women in different institutions including parliament without providing much scope to them to express themselves. The main reason is that political representation often precedes economic empowerment of women in these countries.

Moreover, the quota system adopted by countries following the two representational discourses also varies substantially. Asian countries have preferred to have their quota provisions legislated, rather than expecting political parties to implement their own informal party quotas, as is done in Western Europe and some countries from the African continent (Ballington and Bylesjö 2000). Three major types of quotas have so far been used to ensure better representation of women: legislative quotas, party quotas, and reserved-seat quotas. Reserved quotas require setting aside a certain percentage of seats in a legislature/local body exclusively for women. Legislative quotas are mandatory provisions that apply to all political groupings that require a certain proportion of female candidates to address party selection, while party quotas are pledges by individual parties to aim for a particular proportion of women among their candidates to political office.[2]

Certain types of quota systems tend to be associated with particular regions. Reserved seats, for example, are the most widespread gender quota system used in South Asia (Rai 2005) and in the Arab region, while legal candidate quotas are the preferred system in Latin America and the Balkans. Party quotas or targets are generally preferred in liberal democracies such as the United Kingdom, Canada, Australia, and the Nordic region (McCann 2013). As Chowdhury's estimate (2015) shows, so far 28 countries have adopted the legislative quota, 61 countries have adopted party quotas, and 13 countries set aside (reserve) a certain percentage of seats for women. To date, reserved seats have produced the most favorable results in terms of increasing female legislators through guaranteed representation, provided that reservation is as high as 30%

or more (Tripp and Kang 2008; Krook 2009; Dahlerup and Freidenvall 2010).

Types of Representation

One thing which is clear is that the provision for quotas/reservation of seats for women in national and local politics (and also in bureaucracy) has led to some improvement in the 'descriptive representation' of women, although our understanding about their 'substantive representation' remains limited. The two types of representation—descriptive and substantive—were first expounded by Pitkin (1967) five decades ago. Pitkin also identified two other types of representation—formalistic and symbolic. Formalistic representation refers to the institutional arrangements (rules and regulations) that precede and initiate representation, while symbolic representation refers to the extent that representatives 'stand for' the represented with an emphasis on symbols or symbolization (Pitkin 1967). Compared with the formalistic and symbolic styles, the other two notions of representation have received much wider recognition.

Descriptive representation, according to Pitkin (1967), refers to the manner in which an individual representative 'stand for' the represented by virtue of sharing similar characteristics with the represented such as race, sex, age, class, occupation, gender, ethnicity, or geographical area. According to the descriptive perspective, electing more women serves a symbolic purpose of gender equality, and, moreover, a greater legitimacy is rendered to the political system (Iwanaga 2008, p. 3). Women in parliament bring new perspectives to the discussion of political issues, shaping an agenda that accommodates women's interests. The descriptive approach argues for increasing women's representation in legislative bodies so that it better reflects their proportion in society (Iwanaga, p. 3). Mansbridge (1999) argues that for African Americans and for women, both historically disadvantaged social groups, the entry of representatives into public office improves the quality of group deliberations, increases a sense of democratic legitimacy, and develops leadership capacity.

The extent to which a higher presence of women in national legislatures can be seen as a necessary condition to promote women's issues is difficult to ascertain. It is, however, often observed that having more women in elected office produces more women-friendly policies. In other words, the descriptive representation seems to have a direct effect on substantive representation. Substantive representation is considered important to incorporate women's interests and perspectives since they may espouse political issues that are either marginalized or excluded in legislative bodies that are dominated by men (Iwanaga, p. 4). Black (2013, pp. 4–5) refers to different studies to show that women politicians have been shown to assign more importance to the policy problems faced by women as a social group than their male counterparts, and second, using their personal experience as women, they are able to bring unique insights and innovative solutions to the policymaking process. Rahayu (2014, p. 9) explains the significance of women's representation in the following way: 'The presence of women in parliament is not solely to ensure women's representation ... the voices of women members during the decision-making process in parliament greatly contribute to the redefinition of political priorities, and introduce gender-related issues in the political discussion.'

Reingold (2006, pp. 4–5) observes that women's presence makes a difference in a deliberative body in at least two ways: first, female office-holders are more likely to take liberal positions [than men] on a wide array of issues such as gun control, social welfare, civil rights, environmental protection, community development, and public health and safety; and second, women in office are more likely to lend their support to such feminist proposals—or, more generally, to liberal proposals on 'issues of special concern to women' and women's political organizations. Research also shows that women, more often than men, take the lead on women's issues, no matter how broadly or narrowly such issues are defined. For example, 'women are more likely to express concern about such issues and take an active interest in them, often to the point where they consider themselves experts ... they are more likely to serve on committees relevant to women's issues, they are more likely to craft, introduce (sponsor or co-sponsor), and shepherd legislation addressing such issues' (Reingold, p. 6).

Some have, however, argued the link between descriptive representation and substantive representation is not as direct as is often assumed. Part of the reason is that female politicians may not always have a gendered awareness that influences them to act accordingly in specific ways. As Iwanaga (p. 5) observes: 'There are various differences among women politicians that may be found according to ideological, ethnic, religious, economic, social, and other differences ... there are male politicians who also advance women's interests and form alliances with women politicians in order to promote the interests of women.' In fact, where parties predominate, it is unlikely that women legislators will be able to do anything significant without the support of their male counterparts. 'If women and men MPs share similar attitudes and values, then it seems unlikely that the election of more women backbenchers has the potential to make any sort of substantive policy difference, whether through legislative votes, parliamentary activities, or influencing the policy process behind the scenes' (Lovenduski and Norris 2003, p. 86). Although gender, in general, is significant and does matter when constructing policy, women are more likely to promote women's issue policy when placed in positions of power, such as committee heads or chairpersons, or when their political party controls the majority vote (Peden 2015, p. 21).

Women's substantive representation depends on many factors, among which party is critically important. Research suggests that in the USA, Democratic female legislators are likely to promote women's issues more than their Republican counterparts. The way(s) women are recruited to the legislature is also critically important, so also is their number. There are suggestions that when the number of women legislators reaches the 'critical mass,' it is likely that women's issues will receive better attention than when their number does not satisfy the critical mass requirement (Thomas 1994). The concept of critical mass infers that the election of an adequate number of female politicians will result in governance more responsive to women (Grey 2002). There are differences of opinion on what makes a number adequate enough to make it really critical. The range varies from 10 to 40% (Childs 2004; Grey 2002)

Recent research, however, shows that critical mass is more a theoretical and popular expectation than a demonstrated effect (Grey 2002). Research also reveals that numbers alone cannot be seen as an adequate measure of the influence of women in a deliberative body (Crowley 2004; Carroll 2001; Sawyer 2002). In other words, relationship between numbers and outcomes is not always linear. How women (or male) representatives may choose to act, as Nazneen and Mahmud (2012, p. 31) observe, depends on contexts and opportunities for raising women's needs and gender equity concerns; identity and interests of the individual representatives; how representatives and others perceive 'women's issues'; and gendered nature of policymaking processes. What is important to know is what Dahlerup (1988, p. 206) calls 'critical acts.' These acts include the recruitment of other women, the introduction of quotas for women, and new equality legislation and equality institutions and depend crucially on 'the willingness and ability of the minority to mobilize the resources of the organization or institution to improve the situation for themselves and the whole minority group' (Childs and Krook 2008, p. 731). There are also arguments that a critical mass of women in parliament is more effective when there are strong links with women's movements and an effective national gender machinery exists (Nazneen and Mahmud, p. 31).

The two notions—critical mass and critical acts—are, however, not mutually exclusive; the former may be seen as a necessary, if not a sufficient condition, of the latter. Number matters, although it matters more in some than in other cases. Numbers make women visible; such visibility of women has some meaning in an institution almost dominated by the other sex. Quota systems have been viewed as one of the most effective and expeditious affirmative action policies in increasing women's participation and representation in both elective and appointive positions in public office (Iwanaga, p. 10). But different types of quota system used to increase the number of women are also likely to have differential impact. For example, as stated earlier, reserved-seat quota system allows more women to get elected to a deliberative body. Referring to the reserved seats in three South Asian countries—Bangladesh, India, and Pakistan—Rai (2005, p. 181) suggests that these have indeed addressed issues of the underrepresentation of women, as increasing numbers are joining local government institutions. There is some evidence that their involvement may lead to an increased participation of women in provincial and national-level politics (Rai, p. 181).

It is, however, assumed that women elected on a party quota system have better potential to play a proactive role than those elected from reserved seats. Part of the reason is that they are considered to be an integral part of the party-building process, and they have the scope to exert pressure (sometimes in collaboration with women's organizations outside) from within. On the other hand, women elected from reserved seats can rarely hope to play any major role as they often lack any independent base of power. In most of the cases, they remain disadvantaged vis-à-vis the party (leadership) and have to abide by party dictates.

Quota systems are inherently concerned with *quantitative* gains—fostering female involvement through increased physical ratios. However, to maximize the potential for women to make a meaningful contribution to the political sphere, the existing *qualitative* barriers to female engagement must also be identified and addressed (Bennett 2014). Besides, the reserved-seat system of representation can be seen as a step toward empowering women from above which mostly fails as women representatives do not have any real contact with the electorate. More importantly, women representatives often act as a broader state-building and regime-consolidating tool and are part of a larger project to reinforce patriarchal structures (Goulding 2009; Kuku 2009). However, the extent to which directly elected women fare better than those who are elected from reserved seats in promoting women's issues is difficult to ascertain.

WOMEN IN BUREAUCRACY AND POLITICS

Much of what has been described above can be noticed in local politics. Many countries have adopted a system of reserving a certain percentage of seats in local councils for women who, in some cases, have a larger constituency than their male counterparts and are elected in a much more competitive way than the latter. As at the national level, the introduction of the provision for reservations of seats for women in local councils has led to a large increase in the number of women in local government in many countries. The extent to which an improvement in descriptive representation at the local level has had any impact on substantive representation needs to be ascertained. In other words, whether the change in public policy aimed at increasing the number of women in local councils is a mere 'eye wash' or it can be seen as a step toward 'empowerment of women from below' deserves serious consideration. A common complaint—'representation without participation'—is widely heard in local government in many countries. The validity of this allegation needs to be probed. Many countries have also adopted a policy of reserving a certain percentage of positions in the civil service for women. As with other similar policies in politics and local government, the number of women in many civil services has increased with the implementation of this 'positive discrimination' policy, although the extent to which it has had any major impact on breaking the glass ceiling is difficult to ascertain.

In general, parliament, civil service, and local government have remained 'gendered' institutions in most of the countries of the world, notwithstanding the introduction of several measures to increase the number of women in these institutions in recent years in some countries. Glass ceiling is also widely noticed in both politics and bureaucracy.

In other words, there remains a major gap between descriptive representation and substantive representation in different governing institutions. South Asia provides a case where diversity in the representation of women can be widely found. Developments in different South Asian counties, however, have not taken place in any uniform way. Intercounty differences in the representation of women in different institutions of governance are noticeable in the region. The extent of such difference and its implications needs to be ascertained.

SCOPE AND STRUCTURE OF THE VOLUME

This edited volume probes into policies aimed at increasing the representation of women in various governing institutions, particularly parliament, civil service, and local government, in different South Asian countries where uniformity and diversity are both widely evident. The volume also seeks to explore the implications of uniformity and diversity for the substantive representation of women in these institutions. Different country papers seek to examine, among other things, the scope and limits of what can be called different 'positive discriminatory policies' adopted to promote women's representation, the extent to which the higher presence of women in different governing institutions, resulting from the implementation of quota policy, makes any difference in the process of policymaking, and the way men and women in different governing institutions look upon each other's role and adopt strategies for mutual adjustment. Most of the chapters in this book are revised versions of papers presented to an International Conference on Inclusive Governance in South Asia held in Dhaka in early May 2016. Different authors have revised and updated their papers in light of discussion in the Conference and comments of reviewers.

The volume is divided into three parts, with each part dealing with the issue of representation and participation of women in one particular governing institution. Part One focuses on the role of women in parliament. The aim is to see the extent to which an increase in the number of women MPs matters in lawmaking or oversight, to explore the way(s) male and female lawmakers perceive each other's role, and to identify the manner in which the two groups of lawmakers share parliamentary power and deal with the problem of mutual adjustment. Part Two deals with the issue of women's representation in the bureaucracy in different South Asian countries. Different chapters in this Part focus on several issues such as the structure of civil service, measures taken to mainstream gender in the civil service, attitude of men toward women, and problems faced by women civil servants to balance work and home roles. Part Three examines the extent to which women's higher presence makes any difference in local government policymaking including distribution of patronage and benefits, explores the way(s) male councillors perceive the role of women, and seeks to identify measures both groups of councillors take for mutual adjustment. The concluding part identifies the extent to which the policy of inclusion of women in different governing institutions in South Asia matters.

Notes

1. http://articles.economictimes.indiatimes.com/2010-03-09/news/27619587_1_gender-equality-south-asia-saharan
2. http://www.wikigender.org/wiki/debate-on-gender-quotas/. Accessed: January 20, 2017.

References

Ballington, J., & Bylesjö, C. (2000). Conclusion: Lessons learned from the Asian experience with quotas. In *The implementation of quotas: Asian experiences*. Quota Workshop Series, Stockholm: IDEA.

Bennett, C. (2014). *A gender agenda: The effectiveness of quota systems in increasing women's meaningful participation in politics*. Edited version of a paper written as part of Global Voices' UN Study Tour on Sustainable Development and Environmental Challenges. Available at http://www.internationalaffairs.org.au/a-gender-agenda-the-effectiveness-of-quota-systems-in-increasing-womens-meaningful-participation-in-politics. Accessed February 7, 2017.

Black, M. J. (2013). *Making the personal political: The role of descriptive and substantive representation in the war on women*. An Essay submitted to the Faculty of Wesleyan University in partial fulfillment of the requirements for the Degree of Bachelor of Arts with Departmental Honors in Sociology, Middletown, CT.

Carroll, S. J. (Ed). (2001). *The impact of women in public office*. Bloomington IN: Indiana University Press.

Childs, S. (2004). *New labor's women MPs: Women representing women*. New York: Routledge.

Childs, S., & Krook, M. L. (2008). Critical mass theory and women's political representation. *Political Studies, 56*, 725–736.

Chowdhury, N. (2002). The implementation of quotas: The Bangladesh experience—dependence and marginality in politics, In *The implementation of quotas: Asian experiences*. Quota Workshop Report Series, Stockholm: IDEA.

Chowdhury, N. (2015). *Gender quotas, reserved seats and women's representation in politics: A comparative study of Pakistan and Bangladesh.* Thesis, submitted in fulfillment of the requirements for the Degree of Doctor of Philosophy, The University of Auckland.

Clayton, A., Josefsson, C. & Wang, V. (2016). Quotas and women's substantive representation: Evidence from a content analysis of Ugandan Plenary Debates. Available at http://amandaclayton.weebly.com/uploads/2/5/7/1/25717216/cjw_pag.pdf. Accessed January 20, 2017.

Crowley, J. E. (2004). When tokens matter. *Legislative Studies Quarterly, 29*(1), 109–136.

Dahlerup, D. (1988). From a small to a large minority: Women in scandinavian politics. *Scandinavian Political Studies, 11*(4), 275–298.

Dahlerup, D., & Freidenvall, L. (2005). Quotas as a 'fast track' to equal representation for women: Why Scandinavia is no longer the model. *International Feminist Journal of Politics, 7*(1), 26–48.

Dahlerup, D., & Freidenvall, L. (2010). Judging gender quotas: Predictions and results. *Policy and Politics, 38*(3), 407–425.

Goulding, K. (2009). Unjustifiable means to unjustifiable ends: Delegitimizing parliamentary gender quotas in Tunisia, *Al Raida (The Pioneer), 126–127,* 71–78.

Grey, S. (2002). Does size matter? Critical mass and New Zealand's women MPs. *Parliamentary Affairs, 55*(1), 19–29.

Haque, M. S. (2003). Citizen participation in governance through representation: Issue of gender in East Asia. *International Journal of Public Administration, 26*(5), 569–590.

IPU. (2017). *Women in national parliaments.* Available at www.ipu.org/wmne/classif.htm4. Accessed April 28, 2017.

Iwanaga, K. (Ed). (2008). *Women's political participation and representation in Asia: Obstacles and challenge.* Copenhagen: NIAS.

Krook, M. L. (2009). *Quotas for women in politics: Gender and candidate selection reform worldwide.* New York: Oxford University Press.

Kuku, N. (2009). The quota system in Sudan: Parties perception to ways to enhance female political participation, *Al Raida (The Pioneer), 126–127,* 87–93.

Lovenduski, J., & Norris, P. (2003). Westminster women: The politics of presence. *Political Studies, 51*(1), 84–102.

Mansbridge, J. (1999). Should blacks represent blacks and women represent women? A contingent yes. *Journal of Politics, 61*(3), 628–657.

McCann, J. (2013). *Electoral quotas for women: An international overview.* Available at http://www.aph.gov.au/Parliamentary_Business. Accessed January 20, 2017.

Miranda, R. L. T. (2005). Impact of women's participation and leadership on outcomes. Available at http://www.un.org/womenwatch/daw/egm/eql-men/docs/EP.7_rev.pdf. Accessed February 7, 2017.

Nazneen, S., & Mahmud, S. (2012). *Gendered politics of securing inclusive development* (ESID Working Paper No. 13). Manchester: ESID.

Peden, R. (2015). *Female descriptive and substantive representation: A complicated correlation, undergraduate honors.* thesis, Department of Political Science, Indiana University. Available at http://polisci.indiana.edu/undergraduate/theses/peden.pdf. Accessed January 20, 2017.

Pitkin, H. (1967). *The concept of representation.* California: The University of California Press.

Rahayu, R. I. (2014). *The success and barriers to women's representation in South-East Asia: Between state policies, political parties and women's movement.* Jakarta: Partnership for Governance Reform.

Rai, S. M. (2005). Reserved seats in South Asia: A regional perspective. In Julie Ballington & Azza Karam (Eds.), *Women in parliament: Beyond numbers.* IDEA: Stockholm.

Reingold, B. (2006). *Women as office holders: Linking descriptive and substantive representation.* Paper prepared for presentation at the "Political Women and American Democracy" Conference held on May 25–27, University of Notre Dame, South Bend, IN. Available at https://rooneycenter.nd.edu/assets/11302/reingold_conference.pdf.

Sawyer, M. (2002). The representation of women in Australia: Meaning and makebelieve. *Parliamentary Affairs, 55*(1), 5–18.

Sun, Tsai-Wei. (2004). *Gender representation in politics and public administration: Taiwan and Asian countries.* Revised Version of a Conference Paper. Available at http://www.rchss.sinica.edu.tw/capas/publication/newsletter/N28/28_02_02.pdf. Accessed January 20, 2017.

Thomas, S. (1994). *How women legislate.* New York: Oxford University Press.

Tripp, A. M., & Kang, A. (2008). The global impact of quotas: On the fast track to increased female legislative representation. *Comparative Political Studies, 41*(3), 338–361.

United Nations. (2013). *The millennium development goal progress report 2013.* New York.

PART I

Women in Parliament

Alangkar or *Ahangkar*? Reserved-Seat Women Members in the Bangladesh Parliament

Nizam Ahmed and Sadik Hasan

Bangladesh has a unicameral parliament. It is composed of 350 members, of whom 300 are elected from single-member constituencies on popular votes, while 50 seats are reserved for women to be distributed among different parliamentary parties on the basis of a proportional system. The constitution, which came into effect on December 16, 1972, one year after independence, provided for reservation of seats for women for a

Research for this paper was carried out with funding from a DFID/ESRC Project entitled Parliament, Public Engagement and Poverty Reduction in Bangladesh and Ethiopia administered by School of Oriental and African Studies, University of London. The authors express their indebtedness to the Principal Investigator of the Project Professor Emma Crewe for her critical comments on the paper and suggestions for its improvement.

N. Ahmed (✉)
University of Chittagong, Chittagong, Bangladesh
e-mail: nijamuddin_ahmed@yahoo.com

S. Hasan
University of Dhaka, Dhaka, Bangladesh
e-mail: s.hasan@du.ac.bd

© The Author(s) 2018
N. Ahmed (ed.), *Women in Governing Institutions in South Asia*,
DOI 10.1007/978-3-319-57475-2_2

17

certain period of time. Initially, 15 seats were reserved for women to be elected by popularly elected members of parliament (MPs). The number of seats reserved for women increased to 30 in 1979, 45 in 2004, and 50 in 2010. The mode of election was changed in 2004 when the provision for proportional representation was introduced. Until the introduction of this amendment, the constitution provided for the election of (reserved) women MPs by those elected from general seats. This policy allowed the party winning a plurality of seats to claim all of the seats reserved for women. This 'winner takes all' policy caused serious resentment among women's organizations that not only sought a change in it but also demanded that parties make public commitments to nominate at least one-third of women candidates in general elections.

Reserved-seat women parliamentarians (RSWPs), numbering 30 in the 1980s, were once referred to as 30 sets of *alangkar* (ornament) by a popular national weekly on their election in 1986, which caused serious uproar and forced its editor to flee the country. Those elected to parliament in a similar manner a quarter-century later have claimed themselves to be the *ahangkar* (pride) of the nation. The two notions are different—one totally undermines the contribution of women representatives by relegating their role to a decorative one, while the later probably overestimates the potential role of women representatives. Both assertions need empirical probing. This chapter investigates the role of 'quota women'—those elected indirectly to the parliament—now numbering 50, using the notions of descriptive representation and substantive representation developed by Pitkin (1967). Empirical evidence shows that the 'quota women' are not as docile as people often tend to assume; they have, in fact, fared better than women elected on popular votes, referred here as direct-seat women parliamentarians (DSWPs), in performing parliamentary functions (see Ahmed 2013). Several factors, however, still discourage them from playing a major proactive role. This paper identifies those factors, based on a review of secondary literature and parliamentary records as well as in-depth focus group discussion with several women MPs, and examines their implications for empowering women in parliament.

PARLIAMENTARY RULES AND MP's ROLE DEFINITION

Formally, Bangladesh has a women-friendly parliament. The Bangladesh Parliament has more women members than many other legislatures. Bangladesh ranks 89th in terms of the representation of women in parliament worldwide.[1] Women also hold most of the important leadership positions including the positions of the Speaker, the Leader of the House, the Deputy Leader of the House and the Leader of the Opposition. Nowhere can one find a representative assembly as dominated by women, at least theoretically, as in Bangladesh. Such domination, however, is more formal than real, as we shall see later. Women face considerable difficulties to assert themselves, much more than their male colleagues, and RSWPs remain doubly disadvantaged, both in relation to their male colleagues and also women elected on popular votes.

The extent to which women parliamentarians or, for that matter, MPs as a group, can play a proactive role depends not only on their number, but also on several other factors of which three are important: the extent to which they understand the rules governing the operation of the House, their readiness as well as ability to use the rules, and their willingness to change the rules if they do not find these adequate to play a proactive role (Karam and Lovenduski 2005). Much of what is done in the parliament takes place in a structured way; to be able to influence any parliamentary decision is to understand the rules. No one, however, can expect an MP to have a good grasp of the rules overnight; it is a learning process which may take a long time for an MP to have mastery over rules. It depends largely on the age of the MP in parliament—her/his experience as a lawmaker. It is expected that the longer an individual works in an institution, the better is the prospect of learning the rules.

Experience, however, shows that there is no automatic relationship between the level of competence an MP possesses and his/her nature of activism in the parliament. The extent to which an MP is able to make his/her presence felt by others in parliament depends on many factors, of which knowledge about rules is only one, albeit an important criterion. Two other criteria—willingness and ability of members to be proactive—are critically important. Willingness is referred here as the motivation of members to do what is expected of them, while ability is referred mostly to their level of competence. Both are influenced by a number of variables such as the formal-legal status a parliament enjoys, the nature of the party system, and political culture. Legislatures do not exist in a vacuum; the very existence of a legislature is derived from a constitution (Olson and Norton 1996, p. 4). The constitution provides the basic framework, delineating the formal relationship of legislature with other organs of government, prescribing its formal scope of work and setting the guideline for regulating the behavior of members (Ahmed 2002). If the parliament remains seriously disadvantaged vis-a-vis other sources of power, its members, no matter how competent they are, will find it difficult to make any significant contribution.

Yet experience shows that the main hindrance to the willingness of an MP to use rules depends not as much on the constitutional system as on the type(s) of the party system a country adopts. An MP may find his/her role largely constrained even in countries where a parliament formally enjoys an 'exalted' status as in Bangladesh. The scope to work independently of party dictates is an important factor that will determine whether an MP will be willing to influence the parliamentary outcome in any significant way. If members are seen as delegates, the other personal attributes are unlikely to have any significant influence.

In Bangladesh, the constitution restricts floor crossing and prescribes a delegate role for the MPs. An MP who is elected as a nominee of a particular party cannot vote against her or his own party in the parliament. Nor can he/she abstain from voting defying party directives failing which he/she risks losing the membership of parliament. One can notice a high-level concentration of power/authority in the party's top leader. The Prime Minister, for example, has traditionally held the position of the Leader of the House, the Leader of the Parliamentary Party, and, most importantly, the head of the (organizational wing) party. Nothing moves within the parliament or outside of it without her concurrence. Those willing to use rules have to be careful before proposing any particular course of action. Any proposal to change the rules without the consent of the party leadership is fraught with risk; the latter may look upon this type of activity with suspicion.

On the whole, there exist serious impediments to the use of rules by MPs, no matter whether they are men or women; any attempt to change the rules appears to be risky. No one in Bangladesh now wants to be labeled as a 'reformist'; everyone wants to define his/her roles and responsibilities in a way that is not likely to challenge the status quo. This, however, does not mean that MPs always remain inert. What it perhaps implies is that there are limits to MPs aspiring to become policy advocates or parliament (wo)men, to borrow Searing's terminology (1994). Policy advocates are those who seek to initiate policy and/or to influence it. The government apparently enjoys monopoly over the policy process; it does not want to share this (power) with others, not even with MPs. Nor can one find any serious demand by the MPs for participation in the policymaking process. Nor do they have access to support and services needed to become policy advocates in Bangladesh.

If there is not much scope for the MPs to engage in policy debates, neither can they hope to become 'good' parliament men—those absorbed by the conduct of business in parliament (Searing 1994). Parliament (wo)men are focused on ensuring that the interest of parliament is protected. They spend most of their time in parliament and are not immersed in the process of representation. Reasons discouraging MPs to become 'good' parliament (wo)men in Bangladesh are many and varied; these range from time constraints and procedural difficulties faced by members, to negative attitude of government. Only a few MPs are full-time politicians. Most are business people (53.5% in the present parliament) who have to invest significant time to respond to the demands of their other roles. Career politicians do not have much scope to enter the parliament. Even if MPs are willing to be parliament men, they are likely to face various difficulties.

The parliament does not meet very frequently. The average number of sitting days per year (75) is exceedingly low, so also is the average length of each sitting day (3.32 h). In both respects, the parliament of Bangladesh lags far behind other parliaments.[2] Procedural constraints also discourage the private members to become parliament men. Most of the MPs (in Bangladesh and also elsewhere) thus want to become good 'constituency members'—those who do not look up but down (Saalfeld and Muller 1997, p. 10). Their priority is to provide services to their constituencies, either of a collective or individual kind. This does not imply that other categories of MPs lack constituency orientation. In fact, all MPs do some constituency work much of the time. However, compared with other categories of MPs, constituency members, as their names suggest, are more interested in promoting the interests of their constituents than other aspects of their multifaceted job.

RSWPs, however, remain disadvantaged in one important respect. They are not elected from any geographic constituency; rather, they owe their(s) election to party leaders. Theoretically speaking, they have better scope to become policy advocates or parliament women. Unlike the directly elected women MPs (DSWPs) who, as a matter of necessity, have to spend a large part of their time and resources to satisfy the needs and priorities of their constituents, RSWPs may try to specialize in higher-order activities (e.g., concentrating on policy/national issues). The way(s) MPs, particularly RSWPs, define their role and the manner in which their role definition differs with that of DSWPs will be explained in subsequent sections.

SCOPE FOR PARTICIPATION

Formally, men and women lawmakers in Bangladesh—no matter if they are directly elected or elected from reserved seats—enjoy similar powers, privileges, and facilities; both have an equal opportunity to perform different parliamentary functions, particularly lawmaking and oversight of the executive. The Rules of Procedure (RoP) do not discriminate one against the other. Although the lawmaking process in Bangladeshis is dominated by the government, as in other Westminster-style democracies, there is scope for private members to move bills and legislative matters. Rule 72 provides that any member other than a minister can seek to introduce a bill by giving 15 days notice in advance. A private member means a member other than a minister (Bangladesh Parliament 2007).

The RoP allows an MP to utilize several techniques to raise and popularize different issues and also to require the executive government to account for its actions. According to RoP, the first hour of every sitting is available for asking and answering of questions. An MP has the opportunity to ask questions that require an oral answer or written answer. There are also provisions for short-notice questions and supplementary questions. As in Britain, there also exists in the Bangladesh Parliament provision for Prime Minister's Question Time (PMQT). The Prime Minister now answers the questions of the MPs once a week (every Wednesday when the parliament is in session). MPs can also raise motions demanding the adjournment of the business of the House for the purpose of discussing a matter of recent and urgent public importance. They can also call the attention of a minister to any matter of urgent public importance (CAM) and ask for half-an-hour discussion (HHD) on a matter of public importance which has been the subject of a recent question, and the answer to which needs clarification on a matter of fact. Provisions also exist for short discussion (SD) on issues requiring immediate action, and an MP can make statements on matters of urgent public importance (SM). All these motions moved in the House require ministerial response. MPs can also move private members' resolutions demanding government actions, or/and support. Besides, the formal debates on the president's speech made at the beginning of each calendar year and, in particular, the debate on the budget speech by the finance minister in the middle of the year also provide for some scope to the MPs to scrutinize the activities of the government (Ahmed 2002, p. 108).

There are, however, certain limits to the use of different techniques. None of the motions can be moved without advance notice being given to the Parliament Secretariat. The various devices, however, are not subject to similar types of constraints. Thus, while questions (except PMQT) can be asked and call-attention motions moved in every sitting day except on the day the annual budget is presented, half-an-hour discussion and discussion for short duration can be held only twice a week. The latter, however, can be moved at short notice: two hours before the commencement of a sitting, while an MP who wants to ask questions to a minister has to give at least fifteen clear days notice. Besides, each technique is subject to certain other constraints; in particular, these have to satisfy a number of conditions before being accepted. These restrictions are, however, found not only in Bangladesh but also in the Westminster (House of Commons 2015) and the parliaments patterned after it (Kaul 1979). Different west European parliaments also impose many of these restrictions (Wiberg 1995). These are needed, among others, to ensure that the parliament maximizes its use of time. The way(s) women MPs in Bangladesh have tried to utilize different techniques will be explored in subsequent sections.

WOMEN IN THE PARLIAMENTARY PROCESS

As stated earlier, both men and women lawmakers formally have equal access to different parliamentary techniques. Reality, however, sharply differs with what is being written in the Rules Book. Women MPs lag far behind male legislators in moving private members' bills. According to parliamentary records, most of the private members' bills moved in the parliament between 1991 and 2015 (203) were initiated by 'male' parliamentarians. Women members so far moved only four bills—two in the fifth parliament and two in the seventh parliament. All except one have dealt with issues related to women. One of the bills provided for changing the composition of the parliament, reserving at least one-third (100) of the 300 seats for women. The other two women-related bills, which were moved in the fifth parliament, provided for replacing the arbitration of family disputes by an arbitration council headed by the local UP chairman by a *Munsif* Court. However, if not all bills moved by women MPs dealt with women's issues, neither can it be said that bills moved by male private members always lack any focus on women. Record shows that 'male' parliamentarians also have moved some bills that provide for better representation of women in parliament or to correct injustices inflicted on women. For example, the Domestic Violence (Prevention, Protection and Compensation) Bill, submitted by one Dhaka male MP to the Parliament Secretariat in 2009, provided for stringent punishment for those involved in violence. Such violence affects women more than the others.

Several 'male' members of the seventh and eighth parliaments moved private members' bills, proposing reinstatement of the provision for reserved seats for women and/or increasing the number of reserved seats and changing modalities for election. For example, one of the bills proposed for dividing the country into 30 zones for the purpose of electing the reserved-seat women parliamentarians, with directly elected MPs from each zone forming an electoral college for electing a woman parliamentarian. In contrast to the earlier system when an MP had 30 votes, the new system would allow an MP to cast one vote. Another bill by a 'male' MP provided for increasing the number of women MPs to 64, with each district electing a woman MP. Another MP moved a bill entitled The Oppression of Women and Children (Special Provision) (Amendment) Bill, 1997, providing for stringent punishment for those involved in oppression of women and children. All of these bills were moved by 'male' private members; none was enacted into a law.

An important bill was also moved by the Minister for Women and Family Affairs, a RSWP, which was subsequently made into a law. The law, entitled Domestic Violence Act (DVA), provides for preventing domestic violence and to provide protection to victims of violence. The bill originated in civil society. Usually, such bills do not have much prospect of success as these often lack government support. But the DVA case was different. Part of the reason was the strong commitment of the Minister who had links with CSO movements and was a staunch supporter of women's empowerment. She played an instrumental role in ensuring that the bill had an easy passage at different stages and succeeded in overcoming whatever resistance came from different sources.

Women MPs, however, have fared better in asking questions and raising other motions than in initiating legislation. On average, they asked 8% of the oral questions, 14% of supplementary questions, and nearly 13% of written questions in five parliaments (5, 7, and 8–10). Some differences in the nature of activism of MPs in different parliaments can be noticed. Of the five, the ninth parliament appears to be an exception. Nearly 19% of the oral questions and 25% of the supplementary questions in this parliament were raised by women MPs. Women members in the ninth parliament lagged behind their counterparts in the tenth parliament in respect of moving written questions in the House, and eighth parliament in raising supplementary questions. More written questions by women were also answered in this (9th) parliament than in earlier legislatures. Women MPs in the ninth parliament also fared better than their predecessors in moving different types of motions. More than a quarter of the statements made on matters of urgent importance and one-fifth of call-attention motions were moved by women MPs; the scope of activism slightly decreased in the tenth parliament, although it was much higher than what could be noticed in earlier parliaments (5th, 7th, and 8th parliaments) (Table 2.1).

Overall, women members in the eighth parliament trailed behind their counterparts in other parliaments in asking questions and moving other types of motions. The main reason was that it did not have many women members during the first three years of its operation. The 'quota' women in the eighth parliament were elected more than three years after its inauguration; hence, they did not have much time to play a

Table 2.1 Nature of women MP activism (1991–2015)

Parliament	No. and % of Women MPs	Questions asked[a] (% of total)			% of total questions asked	Other motions moved[b] (% of total)		
		Oral N = 402	Supplementary N = 315	Written N = 214	N = 931	CAM moved N = 364	SM N = 1820	SD held N = 5
5	34 (10.3)	4.8	10.2	5.2	6.6	12.2	9.4	4.4
7	38 (11.5)	5.1	8.9	3.4	6.2	14.8	17.1	11.1
8	52 (15.1)	1.5	28.2	1.1	2.0	7.1	5.5	0.0
9	70 (20.0)	18.7	25.5	6.8	15.8	21.1	25.6	0.0
10	71 (20.3)	13.3	14.6	22.3	16.0	25.8	17.6	0.0
Average	53	8.4	14.2	12.9	10.8	14.1	15.1	5.3

[a]Questions asked by women MPs in two sessions each of the fifth parliament (1991–1995), the seventh parliament (1996–2001), the eighth parliament (2001–2006), one session of the ninth parliament (2009–2013), and two sessions of the tenth parliament (2014–). Calculations have been made by the authors
[b]Motions moved by women MPs in the fifth, seventh, eighth, and ninth parliaments and first eight sessions of the tenth parliament. Calculations have been made by the authors
Source Ahmed (2013); Bangladesh Parliament (2014–15)

proactive role. Moreover, there were only a few directly elected women in the eighth parliament. On the other hand, as stated earlier, women in the ninth parliament showed greater enthusiasm in moving different types of motions. One of the important reasons was that the ninth parliament had the largest number of women members (70) until then, many of whom had long experiences in both parliamentary and party politics. The ninth parliament amended the constitution in 2011, increasing the number of RSWPs from 45 to 50.

An increase in descriptive description, which initially took place during the tenure of the eighth parliament, however, did not have much positive impact as the change came very late. On the other hand, the decision to elect reserved-seat women MPs immediately after the inauguration of the ninth parliament and the tenth parliament turned out to be advantageous from several standpoints. In particular, an early election of RSWPs helped them promote the cause of women better as they had more time to focus on different issues including those related to empowerment of women.

The change in descriptive representation has had some kind of positive impact. As stated earlier, following the change in descriptive representation, the number of motions moved increased substantially in the ninth and tenth parliaments. Those who were elected indirectly appeared to be more active than the popularly elected women MPs. Table 2.2 shows the nature of activism of the two groups of women MPs—DSWPs and RSWPs.[3] DSWPs trail behind the latter (RSWPs) in almost every

Table 2.2 Types of motions moved by two categories of women MPs (1991–2015)

Types of women MPs $N = 265$	Questions asked			Total questions $N = 931$	Other major types of motions moved		Total $N = 3115$
	Oral $N = 402$	Supplementary $N = 315$	Written $N = 214$		Call-attention moved $N = 364$	Statements made $N = 1820$	
DSWPs (22.6%)	11.2	7.2	15.4	10.8	6.6	4.6	7.4
RSWPs (77.4%)	88.8	92.8	84.6	89.2	93.4	95.4	92.6

Source Same as Table 2.1

respect. The percentage of questions asked and other motions moved by the latter is much higher than the former. The issue orientation of different types of motions moved by the two categories of women parliamentarians will be discussed in the next section.

ISSUE ORIENTATION OF MOTIONS MOVED BY WOMEN MPS

The RSWPs can be seen as more than onlookers as the discussion in earlier sections reveals; they fare better than women elected on popular votes and even 'male' MPs in moving different types of motions. Why do they fare better than others will be explained in a subsequent section. This section explores the behavioral orientation of the 'quota' women and compares it with that of their popularly elected counterparts. To ease comparison, issues raised and promoted by MPs, particularly women MPs, have been grouped into several categories. These are: issues that directly focus on women, women-related issues, economic issues, local development issues, national issues and problems, and others.

Table 2.3 shows the issue orientation of different types of motions moved by the women MPs. It reveals that women parliamentarians use call-attention motions more than the other techniques to popularize (directly) women and women-related issues; on the other hand, local level/constituency development issues find more prominence in Statements on Matters of Importance (71A), while questions deal mostly with national issues and problems as well as local development issues. What is, however, clearly evident is that less than one in ten motions directly focuses on women or deals with women-related issues. Women parliamentarians do not seem to be much keen to promote women's issues; to the contrary, they are apparently more interested in raising constituency-related issues than other matters.

One can also notice some differences in the issue orientation of the two groups of women parliamentarians. In general, RSWPs appear to be equally active in using different types of motions; their motions also focus on all different types of issues. This perhaps reconfirms an earlier assertion that RSWPs are not to be seen as mere *alangkar*; they play an important role in keeping the parliament alive. However, DSWPs outnumber the 'quota' women in moving motions aimed at promoting constituency interests. The difference is quite obvious. Those elected on

Table 2.3   Issue orientation of different types of motions

Categories of motions	Nature of issues raised						Total
	Directly focused on women	Women-related issues	Economic issues	Local develop-ment issues	National issues and problems	Others	
Questions N = 904[a]	7.7	3.3	1.6	44.5	28.7	14.2	100.0
Call-attention motions N = 364	11.3	4.9	0.8	34.1	11.8	37.1	100.0
Statement on matters of impor-tance N = 1820	7.6	2.7	0.8	52.4	10.2	26.3	100.0

Source Same as Table 2.1
[a]Issue orientation of 27 questions could not be ascertained

popular votes ignore their constituents and issues that interest them at their own peril. Since elections have become much more competitive in recent years than in the past, those who want to get reelected have to give special attention to what their constituents want.

On the other hand, those who owe their election to the parliament through parties and/or leaders (RSWPs) do not have to worry much about what local people think. Under the existing system, women elected from reserved seats do not have any territorial constituency; hence, they do not have to be as much concerned about the support of the locality as their directly elected colleagues. This is, however, not to argue that indirectly elected women totally neglect local development issues. Nearly half of the motions (except questions) moved by RSWPs focus on local issues. Like DSWPs, those elected indirectly also use more time and energy to promote local/constituency issues. The nature of activism of the two groups of MPs in highlighting different issues can be seen from Table 2.4.

Explaining Women MP Behavior

It has been observed that RSWPs appear to be comparatively more active, moving more motions on the floor of the House than the DSWPs. An average DSWP moved 0.4 call-attention motions, made 1.5 statements of urgent importance, and asked 1.9 questions. In contrast, a

Table 2.4 Issue orientation of motions moved by two categories of women MPs

Focus of motions (other than) questions	Types of motions							
	CAM 71 (N = 364)		71A (N = 1820)		68 (N = 5)		Questions (N = 904)	
	DSWPs N = 24	RSWPs N = 340	DSWPs N = 84	RSWPs N = 1736	DSWPs N = 0	RSWPs N = 5	DSWPs N = 102	RSWPs N = 802
Directly focused on women	8.3	11.2	2.4	7.8	–	14.3	9.8	7.5
Women-related issues	4.2	4.1	4.8	2.4	–	–	5.9	2.9
Economic issues	4.2	1.5	3.6	0.6	–	–	0.9	1.7
Local development issues	50.0	32.9	64.3	52.2	–	–	45.1	44.4
National issues and problems	12.5	14.1	13.0	11.2	33.3	14.3	28.4	28.7
Others	20.8	36.2	11.9	25.8	66.7	71.4	9.8	14.7
Total	100.0	100.0	100.0	100.0	100.0	100.0	100.0	100.0

Source Same as Table 2.1

RSWP moved 1.7 call-attention motions, made 8.5 statements on matters of urgent importance, and asked 3.9 questions between 1991 and 2015. Call-attention motions (CAMs) moved by RSWPs and urgent statements they have made also focus more on women's issues and women-related issues than those popularized by DSWPs. On the other hand, questions by DSWPs have greater women focus than those asked by RSWPs. Their motions also focus more on constituency issues than those moved by RSWPs. This difference, however, decreased substantially in the tenth parliament. Almost a similar percentage of questions asked by the two categories of women parliamentarians in the tenth parliament have dealt with constituency issues.

As stated earlier, directly elected parliamentarians often pay special attention to promoting the interests of their constituents. They usually spend more time and resources attempting to keep their constituents happy. Since MPs expect constituency work to yield more electoral payoffs than other activities, they are likely to engage in it (Ahmed 2015). In fact, constituency work is more important for reelection than is policymaking or oversight. As Fiorina (1977, pp. 43–45) has observed:

> By taking explicit stands on policy matters [in the USA], the member will make friends as well as enemies. In contrast, constituency work is not so controversial. Moreover, the members will have more difficulty to claim credit for his policymaking initiatives than for his constituency work because members of a legislature make policy collectively but perform constituency work individually. Finally, the benefits from constituency work are more immediate and concrete than policy outputs.

Effective member–constituent relationships also contribute to democracy by strengthening the people's connection to their government, and by providing 'real life' assessments of how government programs are actually working on the ground.

One can, however, notice that RSWPs are also no less constituency-oriented than those elected on popular votes. No RSWP has an independent constituency, but each of the 50 RSWPs is given responsibility for a certain number of constituencies, some in their home districts, and others in different districts. Yet experience shows that RSWPs tend to be at least as serious as their elected colleagues in visiting their home constituencies. As stated earlier, DSWPs appear to be less active than RSWPs in terms of raising different issues in parliament. Part of the reason is that only a few DSWPs are backbenchers in the real sense; most of them hold senior leadership positions in their parties or in parliament. They usually do not take part in parliament proceedings unless important issues find prominence.

As an example, reference can be made to the DSWPs in the current tenth parliament. Of the 16 DSWPs belonging to the ruling party (AL), only two can be considered as backbenchers in the real sense. Among the other 14 MPs, one is the Speaker, one is the Prime Minister and Leader of the House, one the Deputy Leader of the House, three are ministers, three are former ministers and now committee chairs, one is a whip and another one is a former whip, and two are committee chairs. The leader of the JP is the Leader of the Opposition in Parliament. These people generally do not take part in parliament proceedings. In fact, the four backbenchers moved almost all of the (AL) motions in the House.

The above observation is, however, not intended to idealize the role of the RSWPs, all of whom except one are backbenchers. As with DSWPs, most of the RSWPs do not play an active role in parliament, although it is difficult to identify the extent to which lack of preparedness or party restrictions account for this. Some RSWPs have observed that they are apparently needed to form quorum and to sustain the government; they are discouraged by leadership to play any proactive role. As one RSWP observed:

> Sometimes directives are issued from policy forums of the party asking [the MPs] to use offensive remarks against the opponents. To comply with such directives one has to forget [the value of] principles and morals and play the role of a 'quarrelsome' lady to keep the leaders of the party happy. If that can be done successfully, leaders are full of praise and commendation. If not, condemnations are forthcoming. To them, everything is alright if the party chief or members of the party policy forums are happy. Our responsibility is to 'say sir', 'yes sir' to everything. We have no other thing to do (*The Manabkantha*, January 8, 2017).

Another RSWP concurred:

> RSWPs are used to make the Sangsad glamorous and to overcome quorum crises ... As they are elected MPs as nominees of the party, they have to remain busy keeping senior leaders happy and doing what they want (*The Manabkantha*, January 8, 2017).

One RSWP once moved several amendments to a bill, some of which were also accepted. Yet rather than appreciating her role, the party secretary general subsequently criticized her for overactivism. Other RSWPs thus have learnt lessons from this example [not to be proactive] (*The Manabkantha*, January 8, 2017). Thus, an important reason prompting RSWPs to focus on constituency issues is their apparent 'inability' to raise legislative/policy issues in parliament. These constraints apply to almost all MPs, no matter if they are men or women, or directly or indirectly elected. Reference has been made to this structural constraint in an earlier section. Suffice it here to mention that the MPs in Bangladesh lack freedom to define their role independently of party control.

What is evident from the above is that the representation of women has improved—from 34 in 1991, to 71 in 2016, although it has not yet reached the 'critical mass' level, and data show an increase in the nature of activism of the MPs. However, such an increase in activism falls short of any major improvement in substantive representation of women. Several conditions still remain unfulfilled: willingness of women MPs to act together on behalf of women, their ability to cross party lines, if necessary, and scope for reaching out to male colleagues—conditions that are necessary to make descriptive representation meaningful. RSWPs face considerable difficulties in raising important issues. Even motions moved on issues related to women can be seen as negligible (8.8%).

Constraints Facing Women MPs

Members of parliament (MPs) in Bangladesh remain disadvantaged in several respects. Women are doubly disadvantaged and face more problems than their male counterparts while carrying out their business. In particular, RSWPs, who, as observed in earlier sections, fare better than the others in almost every respect, face obstacles from several sources. As an example, reference can be made to the opposition to the consideration of private members bills initiated by a RSWP in the fifth parliament. The bill, as stated earlier, provided for a minor change in the local arbitration process by replacing the chairman of the UP by a judicial official as head of arbitration council. Several ruling party MPs as well as ministers sought to resist the bill at almost every stage of the parliamentary process, arguing (erroneously) that the spirit of the bill was contrary to *Shariah*. They also observed that the bill, if enacted, would hurt the sentiments of the Muslim community. Farida

Rahman, a RSWP who initiated the bill, was not allowed to defend the bill.

Barrister Rabeya Bhuiyan, a RSWP, also moved a bill in the seventh parliament that was extremely important; it provided for reserving one-third of seats in parliament for women. The Commitee on Private Members' Bills and Resolutions (CPMBR) recommended the introduction of the amendment bill. But it never had the first reading. At one stage, it lapsed. However, the bill on domestic violence moved by the (then) Minister for Women Affairs, a RSWP, could become a law for several reasons, of which the special relationship of the minister with the Prime Minister was very important. Those opposing the bill were aware of this relationship. Moreover, the bill had a strong source of support among CSOs which the opponents could rarely underestimate.

RSWPs are also discriminated against in several ways. They are given less time to speak on the floor, and it is always difficult to convince the Chief Whip of the need for time to speak in the House. One RSWP attending the FGD referred to the difficulty of accessing the Chief Whip in the following way:

> Both men and women MPs are [formally] equal. But you're a woman, that's the problem. Women get less time [to speak] and are allowed to speak at less important time ... You've to turn to the Chief Whip [and whips] almost begging for time. But they will go to other (male) MPs and request: 'you speak', 'you speak' ... But women MPs, especially RSWPs, often go to the Chief whip and say, 'I want to speak'. The Chief Whip is all in all ... he decides who is to do what ... Our situation is vulnerable.[4]

Not all of those who want to speak are allowed time. Some are allotted time. For that, cautioned the RSWP, 'one needs to have a "special qualification" that we do not have. To be able to influence the decision of the Chief Whip, they have to do many things that we do not do or will never be able to do.'

RSWPs are also given less allocation for development. They receive one-third of the allocation that a popularly elected MP receives for test relief (TR) and food for works program (KABIKHA). Technically, a RSWP does not have a specified constituency to represent. However, she is given she is given responsibility for several upazilas(6/7), but does not receive any allocation for their development. On the other hand, a popularly elected MP is entitled to recommend infrastructural projects worth

TK. 40 million every year for his/her constituency to be implemented by contractors. Many other privileges and facilities granted to a directly elected MP are not given to RSWPs. For example, MPs are made chairs of governing bodies of high schools and colleges, but RSWPs are not allowed to be even members. Nor do RSWPs have any role to play in the working of local councils, particularly the Upazila Parishad (UZP) and Zila Parishad (ZP). Local government laws require different councils to mandatorily seek the opinion of the local MP before undertaking any activity and by local MP, people usually mean constituency MP. RSWPs are mostly ignored; they are not apparently considered to be MPs. One RSWP, in conversation with the authors, confirmed it. She observed:

> I'm a woman. I am addressed as a 'woman' MP, whereas a constituency MP is addressed as an MP. I am introduced in different functions as a reserved seat woman parliamentarian and people do it almost religiously. Like a man, I have been involved in politics and political activities for a long time. I am associated with all front organizations of the party. Despite having involvement with so many organizational activities, when I'm introduced in such a way I feel bad ... seriously bad.[5]

Patriarchy is widely evident. In fact, one of the greatest hurdles to the empowerment of RSWP is patriarchy. A national daily quotes a RSWP in the following way: 'It is really sad that many of our elected male colleagues do not look upon [us] with respect. Some of them tease us as parliament's "call girls." Prime Minister Sheikh Hasina is working for the empowerment of women. But many of her party MPs strongly believe in patriarchy—immersed in patriarchal values and beliefs.' (*Amader Shomoy*, March 3, 2016). Patriarchy is strongly entrenched in other institutions of the society—family, party, and even the judiciary. Narrating the difficulties faced in her early years in politics, one RSWP attending the FGD observed:

> My brothers and sisters were all good students. I also did extremely well in my SSC and HSC examinations securing a position in the merit list in the latter. When I started politics after getting admitted at the University of Dhaka, my brothers told my father: "She has become a liability for the family. We cannot face others for her ... people can see her pictures in the newspapers ... she has been spoiled. Abba (father), you do something; otherwise we [family] will be in trouble and such a good student's career

will be spoiled ... family members did not allow me even to attend any invitation. Now when they take pride saying that our sister is an MP, I try to scold them and make them responsible for torturing me mentally ... Only one male member in the family was my protector – my father. He always supported me and after my marriage, my father in law also defended me.[6]

Another RSWP attending the FGD also had similar experience when she was actively involved in Student League [a front organization of AL] politics in the 1990s. She used to live in a Dhaka University student hostel. Although one of her first uncles used to live in Dhaka, she did not have easy access to his house as she was involved in student politics. Her uncle used to remind her that her mother sent her money not for doing politics but for study. Whenever there was any unrest in the university or hostel and students were asked to leave hostels immediately, she used go to her friends' houses. Her uncle and aunt did not approve of her doing politics. Yet when she became an MP, her aunt called her seeking help to solve some problems. Other relatives also ask for help since she is an MP. But their mindset has not changed yet. Still now, many relatives or people in the so-called high societies do not want to accept them, although they readily seek to enjoy advantages.

RSWPs face opposition from various sources, for example, parties, DSPs, DSWPs, and hybrid politicians. Some RSWPs consider their election from the reserved seat as a stepping stone to be associated with mainstream politics—electoral politics. Their target, as some have observed, is to get elected on popular votes. Yet the task is not an easy one. Perhaps, the greatest challenge comes from DSPs, referred here as constituency MPs. They consider RSWPs as their main adversaries, rivals. One RSWP observed that her constituency MP does not visit the constituency very often. On the other, she spends much more time in the constituency than the DSP and has better links with the people. Yet, he is called the 'elected' and she as the 'reserved' MP. She finds it disgraceful when some people say: 'even though you are an MP, you are still not equal to him.' This hurts her.

RSWPs usually try to build a constituency with a view to preparing themselves for party nomination in the next election. This risks RSWPs becoming the target of attack by DSWPs. Many RSWPs spend more time in their own areas than DSWPs. Some consider the present DSWPs as their competitors and thus try to raise issues in parliament that concern the people of their own areas as a means to appeal to them for votes in the future. Usually, a RSWP is likely to face greater hostility from a constituency MP if both have responsibilities for the same constituency. Conflict between the two is likely to be inevitable in these constituencies than in areas where the two hold responsibilities for separate constituencies.

One national daily observed that a directly elected MP once threatened a RSWP from abroad when he came to know that the latter would attend a prize-giving ceremony in their constituency. He observed that the 'reservist' was not to be considered as an MP, so she should not be allowed to enter into the constituency. In fact, supporters of the MP attacked the function in presence of the RSWP; many children were wounded. Since then, the RSWP secretly visits the constituency when the constituency MP is not there (*Bangladesh Protidin*, February 4, 2016). Similar cases have been reported form other constituencies. One Dhaka MP used to take a female party leader with him wherever he used to go or whenever he held meetings. However, he started behaving differently after she became an MP. The two now consider each other as adversaries, not allies, as in the past. A RSWP, who was a directly elected MP in the last parliament, argued that the latter has better contact with the electorate than the former. The people of the constituency do not appear to be as enthusiastic now as they were during her last term as a directly elected MP (*Bangladesh Protidin*, February 4, 2016).

RSWPs observed that one must understand that they wanted to have a political career. Many of them have travelled a long way to reach this position. They are not political 'novices.' But the recent trend toward encouraging hybrids to join parliamentary politics is likely to cause one of the main threats to democratic consolidation in the country. In fact, those who have a glorious political past feel very threatened because of the quick rise of hybrids, especially daughters of ministers/MPs. As one RSWP observed:

> There are two trends in AL politics: daughters of ministers/MPs think that they are owners, and we're laborers. You've got two/three (seats of MP) – that's more than enough. We will get the majority because our fathers did it. In fact, we are now more concerned about our survival. Nomination is somewhat become secondary. Many have entered the parliament without knowing when to say 'Joy Bangla", "Joy Bangabadhu" ... many hybrids say that at the beginning of the speech; whereas those who have involvement with AL politics know that they have to end their speech by saying so.[7]

Many DSPs consider their parliamentary seats something like private properties; only they have the right to use it; and after their death, only their family members should be entitled to hold offices at any cost. In fact, dynastic succession and familial politics are widely noticed in Bangladesh; these have almost become part of the political culture. Most of the women parliamentarians have been nominated because of their family relations with parties to which they belong. As Jahan (2015, p. 119) has observed:

> Family connections are particularly important for women to gain leadership positions in political parties. Many women members of parliament get nomination as successors to their father's or husband's seats. In the ninth parliament, out of the 18 directly elected women MPs (with the exception of Hasina and Khaleda), more than half were dynastic inheritors.

Many of those who cannot be accommodated are assured of/given a place in parliament after elections. The change in the system of election to reserved seats now allows not only the ruling party but also other major parties to adopt this strategy.

Patriarchy, which is widely evident, works in various ways. One RSWP observed that she had held senior positions in a District Women AL for a long time. However, when she asked for a position in the district or upazila AL committee, people started saying that she could not leave the Mahila (Women) Awami League as if she was indispensable for its survival. Actually, it was intended to technically drop her from the race for MP. Two RSWPs observed that AL was probably the most gendered political party in the country. Even BNP was less gendered than the AL; it had three women district presidents/secretaries. Many Awami Leaguers even do not hesitate to ensure defeat of party women candidates so that they do not hold leadership positions. As an example, one RSWP attending our FGD referred to the last municipal mayoral elections. Seven women candidates for mayors were nominated by the AL in seven safe constituencies. But only two got elected; the rest were defeated. One of the important reasons underlying defeat was the support extended to opposition male candidates by many Awami Leaguers, a kind of 'unholy' alliance between two adversaries; the strategy was mostly intended to check the rise of female leadership.

Another important development to be noticed is that it is a fight not only between men and women. The RSWPS and DSWPs also consider each other as adversaries; one wants to prosper at the expense of the other. The latter do not want to act as mentors to the former; rather, there is some kind of serious competition between the two in some places. Like their male counterparts, women DSWPs are also keen to ensure dynastic domination than to act as role models for new generation of women party activists.

CONCLUSION

This chapter has tried to explore the role of RSWPs in Bangladesh. It shows that although they are not to be seen as *alangkar*, they cannot be considered as *ahangkar* either, however, not for their own failures or faults, but for defects of the context within which they have to work. An average RSWP appears to be more active, at least in terms of moving different types of motions in the parliament, than DSWPs, or even many direct-seat parliamentarians (DSPs). Their motions also focus on a wide variety of issues than those raised by other categories of MPs. However, they face considerable difficulties in charting out a political career for themselves; these problems risk making a RSWP an 'onlooker' in the long run or even a mere spectator, if not an *alangkar*.

Male parliamentarians do not appear to have a positive opinion about the role and performance of the RSWPs. Nor does the top party leadership appear to have an inclination to allow RSWPs to have a genuine political career. Experience shows that only a few RSWPs are given a second chance to become an MP. Nor can a RSWP realistically expect to be nominated to a general seat. The top leadership of the party (AL) has warned RSWPs not to try to create separate political spaces for themselves in their constituencies. The Prime Minster has made it clear that RSWPs will not be nominated to contest general seats.[8] This could be seen as a disincentive to those who want to choose politics as a profession. To some extent, it can also be seen as a triumph of patriarchy and familial politics over democracy.

NOTES

1. http://www.ipu.org/wmn-e/classif.htm. Accessed: October 24, 2016.
2. For example, in Pakistan the National Assembly must meet 130 days a year. In Britain, the House remains in session for 146 days a year. Each sitting day lasts about eight hours. The Indian Parliament meets, on an average, 100 days a year, with each sitting day lasting from 5.2 to 7.3 h.

3. RSWPs and DSWPs differ in a number of respects, e.g., age, income, and connection to power politicians. In this paper, we will focus mostly on their nature of activism in the House. Space limitations will not allow us to dwell on other differences between the two groups of women MPs.
4. FGD held on February 10, 2016.
5. FGD held on February 10, 2016.
6. FGD held on February 10, 2016.
7. FGD held on February 10, 2016.
8. (Ctn24.com., July 26, 2016).

REFERENCES

Ahmed, N. (2002). *The parliament of Bangladesh*. Aldershot: Ashgate.

Ahmed, N. (2013). *The Bangladesh parliament: A data handbook*. Dhaka: IGS.

Ahmed, N. (2015). The constituency role of the members of parliament in Bangladesh. *New Zealand Journal of Asian Studies, 17*(2), 41–59.

Bangladesh Parliament. (2007). *Rules of procedure of parliament of the People's Republic of Bangladesh* (As Modified up to 11 January 2007). Dhaka: Parliament Secretariat.

Bangladesh Parliament. (2014–15). *Summary of Proceedings of Tenth Parliament: Sessions 1–8*. Dhaka: Parliament Secretariat.

Fiorina, M. (1977). *Congress: Keystone of the Washington establishment*. New Haven, Conn: Yale University Press.

House of Commons. (2015). *Standing orders of the house of commons—Public Business*, London. Available at: https://www.publications.parliament.uk/pa/cm201516/cmstords/1154/toc.htm. Accessed 7 February 2017.

Jahan, R. (2015). *Political parties in Bangladesh: Challenges of democratization*. Dhaka: Prathoma Prokashan.

Karam, A., & Lovenduski, J. (2005). Women in parliament: Making a difference. In J. Ballington & A. Karam (Eds.), *Women in parliament: Beyond numbers*. Stockholm: IDEA.

Kaul, M. N. (1979). *Parliamentary institutions and practices*. New Delhi: National Publishing House.

Olson, D., & Norton, P. (Eds.). (1996). *The new parliaments of Central and Eastern Europe*. London: Frank Cass.

Pitkin, H. (1967). *The concept of representation*. California: The University of California Press.

Saalfeld, T., & Muller, W. (Eds.). (1997). *Members of parliament in Western Europe: Roles and behavior*. London: Frank Cass.

Searing, D. H. (1994). *Westminster's world: Understanding political roles*. Cambridge, MA: Harvard University Press.

Wiberg, M. (1995). Parliamentary questioning: Control by communication. In H. Doring (Ed.), *Parliaments and majority rule in Western Europe*. Frankfurt: St. Martin's Press.

CHAPTER 3

Women in Parliament—Entering the Public Male Domain in Bhutan

Sonam Chuki

Bhutan is a small developing country in South Asia, situated between the world's largest democracy, India, and the powerful emergent economy of China (Sherpa 2013, p. 42; Jha 2013, p. 1). Bhutan never experienced British colonial aggression as did the other countries on mainland South Asia and remained a sovereign state largely untouched as a result of its geographical isolation (Phuntsho 2013, p. 63; Sinpeng 2007, p. 34). The monarchy remained the established political system until March 2008 when the Fourth King decided to introduce democracy by decree (Turner et al. 2011). The King's devolution of executive power by decree was not driven by international pressure, economic crisis nor the citizen's movement for democracy (Turner et al. 2011, p. 185). The King personally travelled across the country and persuaded unwilling people to accept democracy before the new change gained its support. The majority conservative, politically passive and uneducated population supported the monarchy for they preferred 'the paternalistic style of governance' (Sinpeng 2007, pp. 40–41).

S. Chuki (✉)
Royal Education Council, Paro, Bhutan
e-mail: semthuen@yahoo.co.uk

© The Author(s) 2018   41
N. Ahmed (ed.), *Women in Governing Institutions in South Asia*,
DOI 10.1007/978-3-319-57475-2_3

Bhutan has a parliamentary system of government patterned mostly on the Westminster model. The Prime Minister is the head of the executive, while the parliament consists of the National Assembly (NA), the National Council (NC) and the King. Thus, the King remains one of the key actors in Bhutanese politics. There are 25 seats in the National Council or the Upper House. Five of them (eminent personalities) are nominated by the King and 20 elected from 20 districts. National Assembly or lower house consists of 47 members elected from 47 constituencies. Both houses have to meet at least twice a year; both also enjoy legislative powers, although money bills and finance bills originate in the NA. In case of disagreement between the two houses, a joint session is called to resolve the problem. The Constitution requires that elections to the National Assembly shall be by two political parties established through a primary round of election in which all registered political parties may participate. Funding for election campaign to registered political parties is provided by the Election Commission.

Elections to the parliament have been held twice: first in 2008 and second in 2013. The People's Democratic Party (PDP) won the elections in 2013, while Druk Phuensum Tshogpa (DPT) party, which was in power for 5 years (2008–2013), became the main opposition party. A study of Bhutan's first elections showed that at the national level, voter turnout for the National Council was 53% and for the National Assembly 79.3% (Sithey and Dorji 2009, p. 356). According to Sithey and Dorji (2009, p. 362), in the 2008 elections women constituted 51.8% of the total 186,431 cast votes in the National Assembly election. Women continue to outnumber men in voter registration and participation. According to the Election Commission of Bhutan (ECB), there were about 193,873 female registered voters against 187,917 male voters out of 381,790 registered voters for the primary rounds of the National Assembly elections held on 31 May 2013 (Dema 2013a, p. 1). Such numbers suggest that women are concerned about the political process and are eager to participate in the democratic process through voting. While men have traditionally been more active in public forums, they seem to take less interest in voting.

However, more female voters did not translate into the nomination and/or election of women to political office (Tremblay 2006). A total of 30 women candidates including two women party leaders contested the 2013 elections. The number of women elected to parliament is also very low. The existing patriarchal socio-culture does not seem to support women's participation in public decision-making in general and politics in particular. This can be traced back to the history of women's low status and subservient roles in the Bhutanese governance system. However, following the first democratic elections held in Bhutan in 2008, ten women were elected to the National Council and the National Assembly. They were entering a political space which was implacably masculine in its practices and processes. While these women approached the parliament with a sense of victory, their male colleagues were unwelcoming and sometimes intimidating because they had challenged and changed the norm for what it meant to be a politician in Bhutan. Within this dominant male environment, women had to carve out their position. Their involvement in the Council's and Assembly's Committees, and their voice and leverage during the process of legislation exposed the parliamentary milieu as masculine and not an easy work place for a woman. During the process of legislation, different dynamics between men and women parliamentarians were revealed.

The entry of women into the parliament also raised issues about furthering gender equity in the parliament. One method which has been embraced in some advanced Western democracies and a few developing democracies is seat reservation. However, such strategies are not widely welcomed in Bhutan. The women parliamentarians were also examined over their seemingly passive stance in the National Assembly and their leverage in the National Council. These women politicians are heavily scrutinized by the Bhutanese society as to their presence and activity in the parliament.

MASCULINE POLITICAL SPACE

Patriarchy is rooted in 'political, social, or economic forms, whether of caste or class, feudality, or bureaucracy, just as it pervades all major religions; it also exhibits great variety in history and locale' (Millett 2000, p. 25). Parliament is a patriarchal space. In Bhutan, the National Assembly is housed in a traditional *Dzong* (fortress) architectural design although it was built in modern times. Traditionally, *Dzongs* were a completely male space in terms of purpose, structure and functions although today the female workforce share its space with minimal practical needs like a separate washroom. The National Assembly building's structure is very formal and has a hierarchical ambience. A few women members are scattered around in a big hall amid a large male presence. However, the National Council is located in a less formal structure, a single storeyed modern building. The Council is less intimidating with members sitting quite close to each other in a semi-circular arrangement although the Chairperson has an elevated seat. The women members in the Council appear quite at ease during deliberations. Since renovation of the Assembly and Council buildings, modern washrooms for men and women are available, at least addressing basic practical gender needs. However, it is yet to be seen whether women will be permitted to breast-feed their children in these buildings.

The Bhutanese parliament's nature and structure exhibit masculine domination in terms of male supremacy. The fundamental masculine political culture, symbols and language are carried forward through the dominant Buddhist culture in the form of sword, scarves and boots which are largely a male prerogative. The parliamentary language, *Dzongkha*, is difficult for most women politicians to articulate their ideas in debate because they were not as proficient as most men. This is attributable to their less experience in the use of high-flown official *Dzongkha* in public debates.

Further, in Indonesia, Megawati Sukarnoputri, the daughter of the country's charismatic first President was accepted as the political candidate because she was the president's child and (Kwok 2014). In Bhutan the first cohort of ten women parliamentarians had to try and fit into 'ill-fitting' men's attire. During the process of trying the male political skin, the female body experienced more pressure because it is strikingly different from the presented masculine norm. 'Gender blindness has been the orthodoxy in political theory, even in radical critiques of liberal democracy' (Puwar 2004a, p. 14).

A young woman parliamentarian, who is also a mother, lived within the vicinity of parliament to attend to her young breast feeding child during the lunch hour. Two of her colleagues who were young mothers quickly returned home during short breaks to feed their children. Some advanced democratic countries still operate within the masculine model in parliament. In the UK, for example, breastfeeding was prohibited in the House of Commons in 2000 (Puwar 2004, p. 88, see also Puwar 2002, p. 129). In a similar vein, the Australian Parliament House had no child care room until 2009 but had a gym, pool and meditation room (Crawford and Pini 2010, p. 613; Crawford and Pini 2011, p. 93).

Moreover, opponents mercilessly blamed Edith Cowan, the first woman who was elected to parliament during her first campaign for abandoning her husband and children although she was 60 years of age then, and her husband was out campaigning for her (Sawer and Simms 1993, p. 82). This patriarchal attitude still appears to remain in contemporary Australia. Australia's first woman Prime Minister, Julia Gillard, was criticized for not being a 'natural woman' in terms of having no husband and children and therefore not being able to relate to average Australians (Kent 2010, pp. 227, 231). In addition, the Australian Broadcasting Corporation (ABC 2012) YouTube video revealed that former Prime Minister, Julia Gillard, faced misogyny and sexist comments from Tony Abbott, the then Leader of the Opposition.

WOMEN AND ELECTIONS

Entering the male political space, parliament, has not been easy for Bhutanese women (see Table 3.1). Wangmo, one of the senior woman members in the National Council, said that it is challenging for a woman politician to be included in party politics. Wangmo's experience is true for most women. During the 2008 elections, all four women in the National Assembly from the victorious DPT joined party politics with men's support. In 2013 general elections in the National Assembly, only three women were elected from the winning PDP. Although their tenure in office ended, the King re-appointed two former women Councillors as his eminent representatives in the National Council, which did not have a single elected woman representative.

Grey and Sawer (2005) argue that in Australia and New Zealand women's low representation in parliament and leadership roles within it for about half a century can be attributed to the male-driven political parties' 'gate keeping' function (Grey and Sawer 2005, p. 176). In the Bhutanese National Assembly, during the second parliamentary elections the number of women dwindled from four to three women out of 47 parliamentarians. However, the PDP government provided one of the ministerial berths to a

Table 3.1 Composition of Parliament of Bhutan

Parliament	2008		2013	
	Male	Female	Male	Female
National assembly	43	4	43	4
National council	19	6	23	2
Total	62	10	66	6

Source Chuki (2015)

woman. Thus, the country has its first woman Minister. Further, a woman candidate entered parliament when male member resigned after the 2013 general election. After the DPT's president's resignation (Wangchuk 2013a, p. 1), the DPT supporters nominated Dechen Zangmo, a woman entrepreneur from an influential local family.

Therefore, it was easier for women from influential families to obtain political nomination from male party gatekeepers (Dema 2013b, p. 1). A by-election was held on 9 November 2013. Dechen Zangmo won the elections. Hence, the number of women in the Assembly rose to four as in the first period of parliament and the percentage of women's representation increased to 8 from 7% with six females out of 72 members (BBS 2013j). When the opposition adopted Ministries and agencies based on the custom of shadow Ministers, Dechen Zangmo was given the responsibility for women and children issues (Dorji 2013, p. 1; Wangchuk 2013b, p. 1). In the traditional male-defined political arena, women's roles in both ruling and opposition parties appear to be relegated to conventional soft subjects (Puwar 2004, p. 89). These issues are considered less important when compared to 'hard' and significant issues such as 'foreign policy, economic or defense' (Puwar 2004, p. 89).

MEN AND WOMEN IN NATIONAL PARLIAMENT

In general, men and women parliamentarians are of view that they have a cordial personal and professional relationship. However, men and women differed on issues of ethics and moral values. Women participants in the research study generally perceived men to be more ambitious, publicity seeking, changing stances depending on situations and playing politics in a negative manner. Men were seen to accept pressure without upholding their principles either being diplomatic or crafty in their professional conduct. On the contrary, women remain steadfast, principled and consistent with their views in an erratic political environment. Women saw themselves to have less ambition than men and preferred working behind the scenes and meeting deadlines rather than emerging into the limelight. Women also felt that they were more easily accessible than most men.

There is a general view that men parliamentarians were more visible than women as the latter were not seen as often as men on television or heard on radio. Similarly, IDEA's recent study (2014a) showed that women focus less on media coverage during their election campaign than men. In Peru, for example, men spent'4.8 times more on media coverage than women' in their 2006 elections. Men put in time and effort for political marketing and therefore fare well at the polls (IDEA 2014). Yangden, a senior woman parliamentarian in the Council, stated that men are 'real' politicians implying a negative undertone. Yangden reiterated that she had no qualms about expressing her honest views about men to their face. Zhiwa, a young woman parliamentarian, and Wangmo, another senior woman parliamentarian in the Council, agreed with Yangden's views. Wangmo opined that women spent more time working and less time marketing themselves whereas men just did the opposite.

A study of gender in the Australian parliament confirms that men spent more time on self-promotion than women (Crawford and Pini 2011, pp. 91, 96). Shreejana, a senior woman member in the Assembly with more than a decade's work experience prior to joining politics, said that people find women politicians sensitive and approachable. Seven out of ten women parliamentarians said that women politicians were much more committed than men in supporting individual and collective voters' needs. They said that they ensure that all possible is done until the problem is resolved. They thought that men were casual about individual voter's problems.

The two youngest women parliamentarians felt that senior and veteran men, including an old Minister, undermined their capacity to address public policies. Pangchen, one of the young woman parliamentarians in the Assembly, stated that men tend to disapprove when women stress women's issues and sought men's support by including men's concerns. Deki, the youngest woman member in the Assembly, often lobbied one or two men for support and had them to convince the rest of the men when all four women in the Assembly failed to seek men's support. Thus, women tend to use a non-confrontational approach when seeking male support for a redress on issues that largely affect women.

Some men parliamentarians thought that women in the Council were more capable than women in Assembly. A single woman in the Assembly was named as capable but tough and emotional. The other three members were seen as passive participants. However, Kinga, an intellectual young male member, who is the Deputy Chair in the Council, saw men and women as people's representatives in parliament and had an equal amount of respect for them. Like Kinga, Lhendup, a senior male member in the Assembly, stated that he respected men and women as the people's representative irrespective of their gender. Tshering, a senior male member in the Council, thought that despite the abilities of women in the Council, they could not work as a team to address bigger women's issues. But, Kinga opined that women themselves take different stand on gender issues and that subjects are discussed on its merit and not on gender perspective.

Gender was given less importance than merit and capable women Councillors appeared to overlook women's issues and act in a gender-blind manner. However, women Councillors ensured inclusion of both 'he/she' in the Constitution during the first session of the parliament in 2008 when 'he' was used to refer to both male and female. A male DPT Minister in the Assembly claimed that Bhutanese politics was not yet tainted with the negative labels of politics and suggested that both men and women politicians were in the process of learning to deal with the complexities of politics. The Opposition Leader differed and said that several men and some women parliamentarians in the Assembly had poor conduct. He cited women parliamentarians in the Council as role models for aspiring women politicians. Both men and women parliamentarians labelled one senior, capable woman Councillor, who promoted women's issues, as a feminist in a negative sense.

Able women parliamentarians were cautious of openly promoting women's issues lest they be negatively termed feminist in the face of huge male dominance. Both men and women have very little understanding of feminism other than its association with women's issues. Hence in such a context, feminism seems to cause fury among the educated and influential elite. In a mature and much admired democracy like Norway, for example, there were a few women politicians who were feminist activists and men did not receive them well. Women faced difficulty in representing their sex (Bystydzienski 1995, pp. 93–95). In Australian party politics, women with strong feminist views face disappointment in a political environment where women's issues are sidelined (Sawer and Simms 1993, p. 208).

MEN AND WOMEN ON PARLIAMENTARY COMMITTEES

Both the National Council and the National Assembly have a set of committees related to key areas of governance. There were 15 different committees in the Assembly and seven in the Council during the first term of parliament. In the Assembly, two women served as Chairpersons of Education Development and Women and Children's Committees. The other three women participated in other committees as members.

All four women agreed that they learnt from their colleagues in small groups of different committees. In principle, women stated that equal opportunity is given to both men and women. However, one woman's Chairperson responsibility was given to a male member in the Ethics and Credential Committee even after her nomination as the Chair by her male colleagues within that committee and her full agreement to accept the position. The Speaker who approved the Chairpersons of different committees undermined the young woman legislator's age and limited work experience in being able to manage other senior members.

Women parliamentarians in the UK have needed to work hard to prove themselves continuously and experienced 'a double burden of doubt and representation' (Puwar 2004, p. 91). In Norway, most women politicians have experienced difficulties in influencing decisions in committees. However, men got into committees of their choice and could wield power and direct decisions (Bystydzienski 1995, pp. 86–87). Similarly, in Australia, men dominated economics and security-related committees and women occupied health and education committees (Crawford and Pini 2011, pp. 90–92).

Deki, the youngest woman member in the Assembly, did not chair any committees but was a member of Environment/Land, Urban Development and Poverty Reduction Committees. Despite her male colleagues' offer of Chairpersonship, she was apprehensive about her ability to meet the committee's objectives. Dawa, a young male member in the Assembly, was a member of Ethics and Credential and Public Accounts Committee. He said that he encouraged young women members to learn and improve their managerial capacity in the Assembly. He added that he found the senior woman member of the Council, who was Chairperson of the Joint Public Accounts Committee of parliament, to be a tough but balanced person.

As opposed to the Assembly, the responsibility of the Chairperson of all seven committees is rotated among 25 members including six women in the Council and appears democratic. The main reason was to provide equal opportunity to everyone. The Chair's main duty was to organize the meetings, identify issues and set the agenda. It was important as the entire sessions of the Council depended on the Chair's work. In the conduct of the meeting, there was very little difference between the Chair and members as everyone was treated equally and had equal amount of voice in the discussions. Wangmo, a senior woman Councillor, opined that Chairperson was just a title. Instead, the role was result oriented in nature and the Chair had to seek all members' support to get the work completed. She observed that a young Chairperson faced the challenge of gaining all committee members' support and often worked alone. But, Kinga, a young member in the Council, stated that he had no reservations against women chairing parliamentary committees.

The youngest woman member chaired a Committee whereas the oldest and the most experienced Councillor remained a member of the Committee. Women Chaired the Good Governance, Public Accounts, Legislative and Socio-Cultural committees based on a system of rotation. The Committees were important working bodies where most of the critical debates related to parliamentary agendas were discussed in great detail before the formal presentation and discussion in the Council and in joint sittings of the Council and the Assembly. It was in these small groups that women attempted to persuade their men colleagues on highly contested issues such as rape, child support in the case of divorced parents and domestic violence. Kinga and Yangden commented that the Council had a democratic spirit and an open-minded work culture. The men in the Council were also noted to be well-educated, experienced, worldly and therefore open to ideas and dialog.

The fine difference between the Council and Assembly was that the Council members were free of party affiliation and clear and confident about their stance. The Assembly members were guided by their party positions and restrained in taking individual stands. Further, all women in the Council thought that women from the Assembly lacked an open attitude of learning and were least prepared for the Joint Committee discussions. The experienced women thought that the two youngest women members in the Council exhibited an open attitude of learning and sought advice from senior and experienced men and women Councillors as and when required and built their professional capacity. There are now ten Committees in the Assembly. The former Women and Children's Committee was renamed as the Women, Children and Youth Committee. The new name appears broader in scope as it implies inclusion of not only women and children but also youth.

THE DIVERGENT VIEWS OF MEN AND WOMEN ON RAPE

Women parliamentarians in the National Assembly interviewed for this study stated that their men colleagues were usually supportive of gender issues because almost all of them had a family. There were times when they refused to support women's issues for they did not experience the same problems that women faced. Women had to make efforts to persuade them and win their support. Male parliamentarians were worried about serious penalties against male rapists who inflict irreversible pain on children and they seemed to identify with the perpetrator. Women did have the ability to address significant social issues like rape through strong preventative law.

Dema added that she was able to lobby and convince her sceptical male colleagues through evidence-based information from national and international perspectives. She said that she attempted to win the majority's support and ignored a few who had obstinate views that the majority's opinion was recognized in democracy. She also thought that her lobbying skills failed when the majority were against her views. Persuading skills seem challenging in a workplace with only four women, who were young in age and inexperienced, and 43 men, who were older in age and experienced, particularly, the ten seasoned Ministers.

Well-educated, experienced, worldly and articulate women in the Council made extra efforts to convince male members, including Ministers in the Assembly, during the discussion of rape in a joint sitting of parliament. Yangzom, the young member in the Council, noted that she and her colleagues in their Committee in which rape was discussed worked very hard to gather comprehensive information on rape registered in all the 20 Dzongkhag (District) courts, the Thimphu referral hospital's forensic unit and police and a comparative research on rape penalties from 15 different countries. She said that men members in the Council were convinced after listening to a well-researched argument with hard facts. She added that it is critical to garner men's assistance through conciliatory means while discussing sensitive women's issues like rape.

Zhiwa, a young woman politician, who was one of the King's eminent representatives in the Council, added that men politicians in the Council were convinced of and agreed to the need to make the rape penalty more a deterrent but some of male members in the Assembly argued that the rape penalty was too heavy. Zhiwa argued that there is no need to make another law if people behaved and rape does not take place. She added that male members including the Ministers in the Assembly argued against tough rape penalties. She thought that it was important to institute a stringent rape penalty because despite the awareness, rape occurred and a strong penalty would serve as preventative measure. It is interesting to note that gender alignment took place while discussing rape. Men parliamentarians identified with perpetrators and women with victims of rape during the process of discussion.

Women Seeking Support from Male Colleagues: The Domestic Violence Prevention Bill

Radical feminists view male sex and power along with domestic violence as an explicit manifestation of patriarchy (Millett 2000, pp. 23–26, Waters 2007, p. 253). The patriarchal social structure of masculine domination and feminine subjugation exposes women to violence. Despite the rise in domestic violence, women parliamentarians struggled to convince men. During the process of the Domestic Violence Prevention Bill enactment, Dema was the Chair of the Women and Children's Committee. She commented that she lobbied with her male colleagues and initiated ten rounds of Women and Children's Committee discussions in which she invited supporters and sceptics to comment on the contested clauses of the Bill. Further, the Women and Children's Committee met with the stakeholders in the government and civil society.

However, the study found that male members had reservations during the process of the Bill's discussion in parliament. The Speaker of the National Assembly, an old man, condescendingly expressed that there were only about 50–60 women instead of 250 women who were given permits to observe the discussion. Most men legislators spoke against the Bill. As recorded in the researcher's field notes from the parliamentary proceedings on 4 July 2012, some young male parliamentarians appeared insensitive to the rising domestic violence against women in the recent years, all of which had been covered by NCWC and RENEW's study, print and broadcast media. The author's observation of the parliamentary debate showed that out of four, three women supported the Bill. One was silent all through the discussion because of her limited *Dzongkha* language.

The institution of protection and social welfare officers to care for the victims in all 20 *Dzongkhags* (District) was the most important aspect of the Bill. This clause resembles the Indian 'The Protection of Women from Domestic Violence Act, 2005' for it has instituted protection officer in the Act (The Protection of Women from Domestic Violence Act 2005, p. 2). The protection officers are state government appointed public servants and authorized to carry out key functions related to protection of victims of domestic violence (The Protection of Women from

Domestic Violence Act 2005, pp. 4 and 9). However, in Bhutan's context, this clause became the point of debate and was not well received during the discussion of the Bill. Eight male members including an old veteran male Minister objected, stating that there was a conflict of interest with the police as the police looked after the cases related to domestic violence. They were insensitive about the existing culture of silence among the victims as many bore emotional trauma to save their family image. The victims sought police assistance as the last alternative when everything else had failed. In the hierarchical Bhutanese cultural context, people tend to listen to senior members in organizations including parliament. Although the Prime Minister did not share his views in the parliament, he supported the Bill in the cabinet. Also, three male Ministers spoke for the Bill.

After 2 days of detailed and heated discussion observed by many Bill supporters, who were mostly women, the National Assembly cast a vote on 5 July 2012. Out of 42 members present in the Assembly, 40 of them voted for the Bill, one abstained and one voted against the Bill. The Prime Minister's support helped to pass the Bill with a huge 'yes' vote. The existing literature on gender in masculine organizations points out that when women are a minority, they have the leverage to use their symbolic position to advance themselves (Yoder 1991, p. 187). On the contrary, in the National Council the Bill was well discussed in relation to critical issues and was easily passed.

SEAT RESERVATION IN THE PARLIAMENT

The topic of seat reservation or quota is an important aspect of current thinking on women and politics. The existing literature indicates that the concept of quota and its implementation is highly contested. In spite of the limitations of the quota system, past and recent research shows that gender quotas have been introduced in several countries around the world. According to International IDEA (2013), about 110 countries use quotas either 'voluntary, legislative or through reserved seats'. More than 60 countries have initiated gender quota in the past 15 years through constitution revision, electoral laws and party rules to allocate a certain number of party seats for women (Dahlerup and Freidenvall 2005, p. 26; Paxton et al. 2007, p. 269).

In Bhutan, since 2012 there has been public discussion about seat reservation to increase women's representation in parliament. The UN played an active role in quota debate. The topic of quota was discussed in UN Women organized workshop in 2012. There were views for and against a quota. Some key participants from the South Asian region supported quota. The workshop pointed to the need for deeper discussion on the quota issue following the first election and the lack of legislation to ensure minimum level of women's representation in the country (Zangmo 2012, p. 1).

Similarly, UNDP Bhutan initiated an e-discussion in 2012 on the scope of women's participation in politics in the 2013 elections. According to the author's participation, one view suggested seat reservation in parliament until a certain percentage of women in parliament is attained (Solution-Exchange Bhutan Discussion 27 February–19 March 2012, p. 3). The contested view argued for letting capable women exercise their own choice rather than asking government to encourage them as there were adequate numbers of able women in professional jobs who can be elected to office based on their capacity and help build confidence for all women (Solution-Exchange Bhutan Discussion 27 February–19 March 2012, p. 3).

Further, women's seat reservation in parliament was raised during the National Assembly elections of 2013. In those primary and general elections, the ruling party promised formulation of a legislation of 20% quota for women in all elected offices (PDP Manifesto 2013, p. 50). The DCT, one of the woman-led parties in the primary rounds also talked about introducing a quota. Krook (2011) argues that political elites pursue quotas for tactical reason (Krook 2011, p. 165) and appears true for Bhutan.

The interviewees saw quota as a highly contested subject. There were men and women respondents across a wide spectrum who argued for and against seat reservation. The reservation supporters argued for quotas as a time-bound short-term measure to include a critical mass of women in parliament to ensure an equal number of men and women until a level playing field is met. It was acknowledged that it was going to take a long time to equalize the men–women ratio in parliament if capability is the premise to include women. There was a recognition that it was important to balance men's and women's perspectives in dealing with societal issues in legislation.

Bhutan has a majority First-Past-The-Post electoral system. Similarly, in a BBS YouTube video (2014), Danish political scientist Dalherup argued that Bhutanese men enjoyed an 'indirect quota' privilege for in 38 out of the 47 constituencies women could not vote for women as there were no women candidates and without women's full participation democracy is incomplete. Tshendu, a young woman private documentary film-maker, involved in making award winning films on Bhutanese women leaders at local and national levels, viewed quota as an opportunity for women to be an elected local government representative in the face of their low education and patriarchal cultural beliefs. As for parliament, she opined that well-educated and capable women were against a quota more than men. The women party leaders share similar view.

Most interviewees did not support quota. Some respondents contended that the Constitution did not permit quotas. They also pointed to the fact that there is no blatant gender discrimination and a quota would not solve gender inequalities. Instead, equal opportunity must be ensured to access education and employment for women to exhibit their potential. They posited that there was no substantive evidence indicating that women cannot come into parliament without a quota, and strongly argued that women's abilities would be undermined and women's positions considered tokenism.

However, the ECB advocated for quota to enhance women's participation in politics after its study of two parliamentary and Local Government elections (Kuensel 2014a, b). Moreover, the need for quota re-emerged as an important resolution in the NCWC and Bhutan Network for Empowering Women (BNEW)'s 'National Consultation-Conference on Women in Politics in Bhutan' in 2014 (Lamsang 2014, pp. 1–3).

Conclusion

Women across the world participate in a structurally masculine political space and face difficulties in trying to fit into the male costume (Pateman 1989, p. 6). The IPU's current statistics state that women's representation in parliament at the global level is poor at 22% (IPU 2015). Closer to Bhutan, women's representation in parliament in some of the South Asian countries is single-digit figures. Bhutan falls under this category with 8%. Right from the process of being elected to parliament to their ability to influence the outcome of decisions within the parliament, women face challenges. In the Bhutanese context, women entered parliament with support from male party gatekeepers.

Despite their small numbers, the first cohort of Bhutanese women parliamentarians managed to convince their male colleagues to pass critical Bills related to women and children's issues. However, well-educated, experienced and worldly women who exhibited confidence were well received compared with young women who had little work experience prior to joining politics. Similarly, most men and some women politicians disliked feminist women politicians who promoted women's issues. Like women politicians in advanced democracies, Bhutanese women politicians were allocated soft subjects related to social affairs in parliament. Women parliamentarians were principled, committed and industrious. On the contrary, men were found to be good at political marketing and switching their political gear in tandem with an erratic political environment. Although contested, parliamentary seat reservation appears to be a way forward to improve women's representation in the Bhutanese parliament and the state efforts seem progressive toward this end. Seat reservation has enhanced women's representation in both mature and emerging democratic countries.

Women's entry to the Bhutanese parliament has ensured that change has occurred. The first ten Bhutanese women parliamentarians have demonstrated that it is possible for women to play a role in Bhutan's political life and move from the private to the public sphere. Despite the impediments which they faced due to the entrenched masculine values and practices, these ten women did pursue a legislature program and actively participated in parliamentary committee work. They were trailblazers and challenged the male hegemony of Bhutan's parliamentary system. They have shown other women that a political career and a role in the public space are possible for women in Bhutan.

References

ABC (Australian Broadcasting Corporation). (2012). *Gillard's misogyny speech goes global.* Available at http://www.abc.net.au/news/2012-10-10/international-reaction-to-gillard-speech/4305294. Accessed March 7, 2014.

Bhutan Broadcasting Service. (2013a). *DPT's dechenzangmo wins nanong-shumar by-elections.* Available at http://www.bbs.bt/news/?p=33728. Accessed November 10, 2013.

Bhutan Broadcasting Service. (2014b). *To pull women in politics?* Available at http://www.bbs.bt/news/?p=38690. Accessed April 4, 2014.

Bystydzienski, M. (1995). *Women in electoral politics: Lessons from Norway.* Westport: Praeger Publishers.

Chuki, S. (2015). *Women in politics in democratic transition: The case of Bhutan, unpublished.* Ph.D. thesis, University of Technology, Queensland.

Crawford, M., & Pini, B. (2011). The Australian parliament: A gendered organization. *Parliamentary Affairs, 64*(1), 82–105.

Crawford, M., & Pini, B. (2010). Gender equality in national politics: The views of Australian male politician. *Australian Journal of Political Science, 45*(4), 605–621.

Dahlerup, D., & Freidenvall, L. (2005). Quotas as a 'fast track' to equal representation for women. *International Feminist Journal of Politics, 7*(1), 26–48.

Dema, K. (2013a, September 28). Young lady to step in JYT's shoes. *Kuensel.*

Dema, K. (2013b, May 7). BKP down: But not out. *Kuensel.*

Dorji, T. (2013, December 5). Opposition adopts ministries. *Kuensel.*

Friedman, H. (1983). Local political alternatives for decentralized development. In G. S. Cheema & D. A. Rondinelli (Eds.), *Decentralization and development: Policy implementation in developing countries.* Beverly Hills: Sage.

Grey, S., & Sawer, M. (2005). Australia and New Zealand. In Y. Galligan & M. Y (Eds.), *Sharing power: Women, parliament, democracy.* Aldershot: Ashgate publishing limited.

IDEA (International Institute for Democracy and Electoral Assistance). (2013). *Women in the driver's seat of democratic politics.* Available at http://www.idea.int/gender/women-in-the-drivers-seat-of-democratic-politics.cfm?utm_source=Paloma&utm_medium=Newsletter&utm_campaign=International+IDEA+Newsletter+January-March+2013. Accessed 13.

IDEA. (2014). *Is it all about the money?* Available at http://www.idea.int/news/is-it-all-about-the-money.cfr. Accessed March 10, 2014.

IPU. (2015). *Women in national parliament: Situation as of 1st February 2015.* Available at http://www.ipu.org/wmn-e/arc/world010215.htm. Accessed March 27, 2015.

Jha, T. (2013). *China and its peripheries: Limited objectives in Bhutan.* Available at www.ipcs.org/pdf_files/issue/IB233-TilakJha-ChinaPeriphery-Bhutan.pdf. Accessed August 23.

Kent, J. (2010). *The making of julia gillard prime minister.* Melbourne: Viking.

Kenney, M. (2013). *Gender and political recruitment: Theorizing institutional change.* New York: Palgrave Macmillan.

Krook, M. (2011). Quotas for women in politics: Gender and candidates selection reform worldwide. *Journal of Women, Politics & Policy, 32*(2), 164–166.

Kuensel. (2014a). *Mistakes are to learn from.* Available at http://www.kuenselonline.com/mistakes-are-to-learn-from/UtxpuLQ_6Uk. Accessed January 20, 2014.

Kuensel. (2014b, April 2). Appointments. *Kuense.*

Kwok, Yenni. (2014). 'Indonesia's Elections Feature Plenty of Women but Respect Short Supply', Time World, April 8.

Lamsang, T. (2014, April 7). Women in politics meet recommends 20 to 50 percent quota in politics. *The Bhutanese.*

Millett, K. (2000). *Sexual politics.* Chicago: University of Illinois Press.

Pateman, C. (1989). *The disorder of women.* Cambridge: Polity Press.

Paxton, P., Kunovich, S., & Hughes, M. (2007). Gender in politics. *Annual Review of Sociology, 33*, 263–284.

PDP Manifesto. (2013, September 10). Youth and women. Available at http://pdp.bt/wp-content/uploads/2013/02/PDP-Menifesto-2013.pdf. Accessed September 10.

Phuntsho, K. (2013). *The history of bhutan*. New Delhi: Random House.

Puwar, N. (2002). Interview with carole pateman: The sexual contract, women in politics, globalization and citizenship. *Feminist Review, 70*, 123–133.

Puwar, N. (2004). *Space invaders: Race gender and bodies out of place*. Oxford: Berg.

Sawer, M., & Simms, M. (1993). *A woman's place: Women and politics in Australia*. Sydney: Allen & Unwin Pvt. Ltd.

Sherpem, S. (2013). Bhutan: Between two giants. *World Policy Journal, 30*(41), 41–44.

Sinpeng, Aim. (2007). "Democracy from Above: Regime Transition in the Kingdom of Bhutan." *Journal of Bhutan Studies, 17* (Winter): 21–47. Retrieved August 21, 2014, from http://www.bhutanstudies.org.bt/publicationsFiles/JBS/JBS_vol17/2.JBS17.pdf.

Sithey, G., & Dorji, T. (2009). *Drukyul decides: In the minds of Bhutan's first voters, the story of Bhutan's first democratic election*. Thimphu: TashiLoday and Bhutan Times Ltd.

Tremblay, Manon. (2006). "The Substantive Representation of Women and PR". *Politics and Gender, 2*: 502–511.

Turner, M., Chuki, S., & Tshering, J. (2011). Democratization by decree: The case of Bhutan. *Democratization, 18*(1): 184–210. doi:10.1080/13510347.2011.532626.

Wangchuk, S. (2013a, August 5). JYT submits resignation. *Kuensel.*

Wangchuk, S. (2013b, July 26) Meet the new cabinet. *Kuensel.*

Waters, M. (2007). Sexing it up? Women, pornography and third wave feminism. In Stacy Gills, Gillian Howie, & Rebecca Munford (Eds.), *Third wave feminism*. New York: Palgrave Macmillan.

Yoder, D. J. (1991). Rethinking tokenism: Looking beyond numbers. *Gender and Society, 5*(2), 178–192.

Zangmo, T. (2014, August 27). Gender discrimination may be deeply ingrained. *Kuensel.*

CHAPTER 4

Deepening Democracy in India: The Role of Women Parliamentarians and Their Challenges

Sangita Dhal and Bidyut Chakrabarty

In the aftermath of the Second World War, nations across the world experienced a host of path-breaking changes leading to positive transformations in the economic, social, and political spheres. The clamor for democracy, freedom, and economic development were complimented by the spread of liberal democratic values and ideas that touched the lives of millions of people. In the backdrop of this enabling post-war environment, women's empowerment became an indispensable outcome of a long drawn battle against gender inequality in the political domain. One witnessed a steady and healthy trend of democratization of the internal polity of the nation states across the globe, where women began to stake claim to their legitimate space in the political sphere. Both, in

S. Dhal (✉)
Department of Political Science, Kalindi College,
University of Delhi, New Delhi, India
e-mail: sangitadhal@hotmail.com

B. Chakrabarty
Department of Political Science, University of Delhi, New Delhi, India
e-mail: sanchitabidyut.chakrabarty@gmail.com

© The Author(s) 2018
N. Ahmed (ed.), *Women in Governing Institutions in South Asia*,
DOI 10.1007/978-3-319-57475-2_4

the western world as well as in the post-colonial states, political processes and institutions began to acknowledge the growing importance of women as a gender category, who had remained silent or underrepresented in the political space despite their numerical strength, which has a critical significance in democracy. Thus, the growing demand for democracy, equality, and justice in the last century led to the establishment of rule of law based on constitutionalism that paved the way for greater participation of women in the political and decision-making processes. The inclusive character of participatory democracy, which ensures equitable representation, is considered to be an ideal model for delivering justice to women and other underprivileged categories of people, who are jostling for space in the political sphere (Dahlerup 2006).

Women as a gender category have encountered systemic disabilities woven around sociopolitical structures of dominance and deprivation in the past (Beauvoir 1988, Wharton 2006). However, today women are gradually proving to be an indispensable part of every sphere of life ranging from family to the larger domains of politics and economy. It appears that women today are gradually recapturing the lost space in the social, economic, and the political spheres, which was historically denied to them due to a variety of factors, most importantly, patriarchy and its various forms of expression such as domination and subjugation (Walby 1997, Menon 1999). Nations across the world have realized the importance of women who contribute toward national development and economic growth in various capacities. India is a classic example of such a society that embarked on the path of democracy and constitutionalism after independence. It is an evolving democracy, where though slowly, but steadily woman are attaining political and economic empowerment through participation in the political processes and institutions (Kumar 1998).

This paper attempts to examine the nature and scope of women's role in the larger political landscape of India and tries to unravel the critical aspects linked to their assertion in the political structures, institutions, and policymaking processes. It will also try to analyze the historical and present roadblocks that prevented women from entering into the so-called male bastion, which is evident from the small percentage of their overall representation in the Parliament. The study includes important women parliamentarians from diverse backgrounds, representing different political parties and their role in the legislative processes and policymaking. The paper will also delve into the critical area of gender quota in politics, wherein the demand for 33% reservation to women in

Parliament and state legislatures will be discussed. Last but not the least, there will be an attempt to understand whether women's political participation and representation in the Parliament and legislatures has any bearing on the overall question of gender equality and gender justice, which will lead to their empowerment and emancipation in the society.

Conceptual Framework

Despite the sacred objective of the Constitution of India to lay the foundation of a just and equitable society, where men and women shall enjoy equal status, the reality is that despite 70 years of independence, our democratic polity reveals an entirely dismal picture. Social stereotyping and violence at the domestic and societal levels are some of the manifestations of this deep-seated system of patriarchy. Discrimination against girl child, adolescent girls, and women persists in every walk of life. Women are denied the rights and opportunities that are available to men both in the public and in the private domain (Jaggar 1983). Though the Constitution grants equality to women and also empowers the state to adopt measures of positive discrimination in favor of women, the actual implementation of the state's agenda runs into problem when confronted with the structures of patriarchy from the grassroots level to the topmost structures of administration. Annie Mascarene, the first woman MP from Kerala who was elected to the First Lok Sabha as an independent candidate from Thiruvananthapuram constituency in 1952, lamented the fact that women were not given their political dues in independent India (Forbes 1998). Though India has witnessed the robust functioning of the formal representative institution of the Parliament since several decades which mirrors the highly pluralistic social order, the proportion of female representation has been relatively less as compared to the male representation (Mehra and Kueck 2003).

The Feminist Perspective

Feminist idea aims to recreate society, culture, and politics in non-patriarchal forms and holds that participation in public life is a key to advancing the status of women, gaining access to power and equal rights. Committed to social progress and emancipation of women, activists of women movements all over the world demand the end of patriarchal domination, which is regarded as the root cause of gender inequality in the society

(Pitkin 1971, Eisenstein 1994, Millet 2000). They maintain that equality of sexes requires radical transformation of power structure in the society. Mary Wollstonecraft, one of the early feminists, advocated women's education, which would enable them to be autonomous decision-makers and economically independent of men. Radical feminists like Zillah Eisenstein and Kate Millet demanded more powers for women in the decision-making process and their access to state resources, benefits, and protection. Millet promotes the concept of gender equality through equal rights and proper job opportunities within the existing system. These women activists support the process of modernization as it is democratic and egalitarian and thus beneficial for wom (Kimmel and Aronson 2011).

Modernization is also associated with gender equality as it provides women various opportunities for employment, which would not only empower them socially but also enrich them financially. Melissa Williams (1998) advocates political representation in legislative bodies for historically disadvantaged groups like women to combat systemic discrimination. According to Williams democratic states should undertake special measures to include historically marginalized groups in representative bodies whose perspectives would be excluded without the special measures. Most of current demands over democracy revolve around the need for more meaningful political presence (Phillip 1993), equal representation (Kymlicka 1996), and political inclusion of the excluded groups (Young 2000), and this situation can become a reality only when all members of the community are treated with equal concern (Dworkin 1978).

Changing Social Paradigms

In heterogeneous societies, there is a multiplicity of different and conflicting interests. Often there are particular interests and needs of women which would be inadequately represented in a political system dominated by men. Equal right to vote has not been able to deal with this problem of unequal representation of women in representative bodies. Changing the gender composition of elected assemblies is a major challenge to the social arrangement which has systematically placed women in a subordinate position. Young (2000) argues that in large-scale societies representation and participation mutually require each other for politics to be deeply democratic and representative. The issue of political presence was also linked to the idea of participatory democracy which would enable equitable representation. It is heartening to see that there is political will emerging to have more women in public life.

Although the changes appear to be slow, the increasing presence of women in Parliaments across the world is a positive trend for their political empowerment. The 73rd constitutional amendment act in India, has resulted in empowering women with increased political participation at the grassroots level. Various studies have revealed that increasing women participation in the local bodies has improved their functioning to a significant extent. Elected women representatives at the local level are making a difference in shifting the focus of development policy by highlighting basic needs issues such as water, food security, education, and livelihood (Datta 1998; Jayal and Nussbaum 2003). It was expected that the Act would overcome the centuries-old inhibition among women and encourage them to gradually shoulder responsibilities in the Legislative Assemblies and National Parliament.

The National Policy for the Empowerment of Women addresses several important commitments of the 12th Five Year Plan and the other policies relating to empowerment of women. The goal of this policy is to bring about the advancement, development, and empowerment of women at the various levels by creating a society where women work as equal partners in all spheres of life and develop a framework to ensure equal rights and opportunities for women. The principle of gender equality expressed in the Indian Constitution in its Preamble, Fundamental Rights, Fundamental Duties, and Directive Principles, supports this noble objective.

However, there still exists a wide gap between the goals enunciated in the Constitution, legislations, policies, plans, programs, and related mechanisms on the one hand and the situational reality of the status of women in India on the other. Therefore, the conceptual framework of analysis of this paper will be based on a thorough examination of the gap between the pious objectives of the constitutional democracy, which was established after independence and the achievements of the Indian Republic in the past seventy years in delivering gender equality and justice. The broad framework of the study will revolve around the question of women's political representation and their empowerment within the broad structures of parliamentary democracy in India.

POLITICAL EMPOWERMENT OF WOMEN

The issue of women's historical under-representation in political institutions has been addressed through the use of gender quotas in many countries. In spite of its controversial nature, this constitutional and legal provision that increases women's representation is fast becoming an acceptable enabling tool in the world today. Women's political under-representation is substantially rectified through the introduction of gender quota. This is being effected through constitutional amendments and changing electoral laws (electoral gender quota) in many countries in recent times. Apart from gender quota, in many countries, national political parties are setting aside fixed number of seats exclusively meant for women candidates as part of their inner-party democratic measures. Thus, the core idea behind the quota systems is to recruit women into political positions and to ensure that women are not only mere tokens in political life.

In India, the first significant step toward political empowerment of women at the grassroots level through gender quota was the introduction of 33% reservation of seats for women in the Panchayat bodies—the grassroots political institutions. It has been nearly 25 years since this landmark legislation was brought into effect in 1993 through the 73rd Constitutional Amendment, but we are yet to see any significant change in the plight of women in terms of their political empowerment. At the national level, the debate over gender quota in the Parliament and State Legislative Assemblies has remained inconclusive and controversial, as there appears to be no consensus on the issue. As a consequence of this lack commitment and political will to bring gender quota in politics, our democratic institutions have remained highly skewed in terms of gender representation.

Though women are highly underrepresented in the Parliament, their contributions are noteworthy as they have taken exemplary parliamentary initiatives to raise issues concerning women's interests at large. For example, Rajkumari Amrit Kaur, Cabinet Minister for Health (1952–1957) played an exemplary role in introducing health and family planning programs. The most noteworthy contribution was the establishment of All India Institute of Medical Sciences (AIIMS) in New Delhi apart from introducing BCG vaccination program on large scale during her tenure. Mrinal Gore (member Lok Sabha, 1980) was fondly addressed as *Paaniwali Bai* (the water-woman advocate) and was famous for mobilizing women to protest against chronic water problems in various parts of the country. As an activist also she raised the issue both inside and outside the Parliament. Other women Member of Parliament (MP) who have taken up significant parliamentary initiatives were Phulrenu Guha, Renuka Ray, Geeta Mukherjee, Jayanti Patnaik, who have raised several questions and private members Bills which proves that these women members were conscious of their responsibilities and duties as people's representatives. However, due to weak numerical strength, they have fallen short of achieving their objectives in the Parliament.

GENDER QUOTAS: FAST TRACK MECHANISM FOR WOMEN'S POLITICAL REPRESENTATION

Electoral gender quota, as a fast track measure for women's empowerment in various countries, has opened up enormous opportunities and political space for women to make a difference in the national, regional, and local governments (Dahlerup 2006). As Shireen Rai has rightly observed that the reservation of seats has begun to turn the wheels of political fortune for the "silent majority" (Rai 2005). Grassroots studies have revealed that wherever women have taken up the leadership roles, there has been a positive focus on utility-oriented expenditure and the focus is on the basic issues such as housing, sanitation, and health. Political environment provides the best chance to ensure equality of opportunity because in the long run, greater representation of women in politics translates into greater empowerment of women and increases their presence in other fields too (Phillips 1993). Women's movements in India are drawing strength from the prevailing international environment and are using it as an opportunity to press their long-standing demands. The changing nature of the global milieu demands a qualitative improvement of the image of the nation-state; hence, every state today is striving to portray an image that is acceptable to the global community in the era of globalization and economic integration (Forbes 1998).

IMPACT OF WOMEN'S MOVEMENT ON WOMEN'S REPRESENTATION

Given the historical legacy of colonialism and the challenges of the post-colonial state in the developing countries, contemporary women's movements have focused on the creation of a conducive environment for women to enter the public space. These movements are generally identified with the goals of realizing social and economic rights of women. It also has to be meaningfully integrated with contemporary issues such as women's social rights, political empowerment, rights of ethnic minorities, disabled and environmental protection in the new global era. Women's movement was one of the burgeoning efforts within the society demanding for drastic changes in the functioning of government, the planning process and the development strategies. Woman Parliamentarians like Smt. Pramila Dandavate passionately championed the cause of abolition of the dowry system and played an effective role in the passing of the Anti-Dowry Bill. She also suggested for the establishment of Anti-Dowry Commission on the lines of National Commission for Women.

The demand for women's representation is considered to be important as it identifies itself with several important issues relating to the notion of social justice and idea of empowerment which is expected to address women's historical exclusion from political institutions and processes. In an attempt to make gender equality a reality, women's movements had to struggle for making universal political rights a reality, fighting against the idea of gendered perspective in political institutions. However, the issues of patriarchy, caste, region, community, and religion continue to divide women and get reflected in the nature of local politics. Subordination of women at home, political space, and workplace still continues to hinder the progress toward an egalitarian society. It is still a far cry, where women enjoy equal status in a society that is egalitarian and ensures equity and justice to all (Hewitt and Rai 2010).

Committee on the Status of Women in India (CSWI)

The Committee on the Status of Women in India was set up on September 22, 1971, by a Resolution of the Ministry of Education and Social Welfare to make a comprehensive examination of all questions relating to the rights and status of women in the country. The first Status of Women Report, prepared under the Chair of Dr. Phulrenu Guha and editorial guidance of Vina Mazumdar, was submitted to the Minister for Education and Social Welfare on January 1, 1975. It was an important year, coinciding with the first ever United Nations' *International Women's Year* in 1975. The Committee had the mandate to examine the constitutional, legal, and administrative provisions that had bearing on the social, educational, and employment status of women during the last two decades. The Committee recorded that in spite of constitutional and legal equality, women's status in every sphere of life had remained unequal with persistent disparities. Although many laws had passed in the intervening period to remove these disabilities, they have had little impact. The Committee had therefore recommended the establishment of statutory, autonomous Commissions for women at the Center and the State levels with the mandated objective of collecting information regarding trends in social organization, which affect the rights of women and an evaluation of the existing policies, programs, and laws that have a bearing on the status of women.

It also recommended eradication of polygamy in Muslim personal law, the enforcement of provision against bigamy under the *Hindu Marriage Act*, to make offenses under the *Child Marriage Restraint Act* cognizable and appointment of special officers, compulsory registration of marriages as recommended by the United Nations, amendment of the *Dowry Prohibition Act 1961*, improvement of laws of divorce including addition of cruelty and desertion as grounds of divorce in the *Hindu Marriage Act*, changes in personal laws relating to inheritance, particularly to bring legislative measures to cover Christian women of Kerala under the *Indian Succession Act* as a step to unify the law. It also recommended women's rights to matrimonial property and establishment of Family Courts among other enabling measures (Saxena 1999).

The CSWI also revealed that although women were participating in increasing numbers in economic and political activities and in the process of change, they were necessarily not the actual beneficiaries and were becoming the victims of under-representation along with the other marginalized sections of the society. In units of local self-government, rural women rarely get directly elected, instead co-opting and nomination was the standard practice. With the publication of the Report in 1975, a demand for the representation of women in the Panchayat bodies by reservation rather than by nomination was voiced and reiterated. This Report of the Committee thus proved to be a landmark in the decades that followed which still serves as a sacred document and guiding principle for generations of policymakers to achieve women's emancipation. The debate on political representation concerning women has been how to encourage women to actively participate and in large numbers to the panchayat (local administrative bodies) at the various levels (National Perspective Plan For Women 1988).

Prior to 1993, women had very little space in the political environment at the grassroots level. There was a lack of interest to contest elections and participate in any kind of political activities as politics was considered to be the male preserve. As a result, the Parliament passed the 73rd Constitutional Amendment Act in 1992 which reserves one-third seats for women in the panchayat bodies. This measure unleashed a process of tremendous mobilization and democratic grassroots governance as millions of women have been elected to the local bodies every term which has enhanced political empowerment among the rural womenfolk. However, the number of women contesting elections at the national level is still very low compared to men. The number of women contestants increased from 45 in 1957 to 70 in the year 1977 and rose to all time high in 1996 with 599 women contestants in the Lok Sabha elections, this figure came down to 274 in 1998 and rose to 668 in the sixteenth Lok Sabha elections. In contrast, the number of men contesting elections has always been higher in number as compared to women. In 1957, the number of male contestants was 1,474 which increased to 7,583 as compared to only 668 women contestants in 2014 general elections. Though more than 93% of the total contestants are men, interestingly the percentage of women winning elections has always been higher than men in the present times.

The percentage of men who won elections in 1952 was 26.05%, whereas women were 51.16%. In the year 1999, 12.3% men won the elections out of the total male contestants and 17.3% women won out of the total female contestants. In the fourteenth Lok Sabha elections, 12.6% female contestants won the elections. Despite more percentage of women winning elections, political parties deny tickets to women candidates presuming that they are not capable of winning elections. Many factors are responsible for this state of affairs. History of freedom movement shows that a large number of women participated in freedom movement. But after that it went on decreasing. The gender justice and equal opportunity ideology of the Nehru-Gandhi era has lost its importance significantly in the present times. Gender roles have become major obstacles in women's political empowerment. Traditional division of labor, illiteracy, economic barriers, the type of electoral system, lack of sufficient training etc. has been keeping women away from politics. Apart from this, elections have become a very costly affair. Women are unable to collect large amount of money required to fight elections. Systemic inequalities, discriminatory practices, and unequal power relations have become major obstacles for women's meaningful representation and participation in the areas of political decision-making (Basu 2010).

Representation of Women in Parliament Since Independence

The first Lok Sabha had only 2–3% women members which included Masuma Begum, deputy leader of Congress Party who later became the Minster of Social Welfare, Renuka Ray who was a veteran social worker, Durgabai Deshmukh prominent Gandhian and the Chairperson of

Central Social Welfare Board, who all have made noteworthy contributions in the Parliament. The sixth Lok Sabha in 1977 witnessed less proportion of women in Parliament at mere 3.5%. Although the number of women MPs increased from 59 to 61 under the present NDA government, it still remains far below the global average of 21.3%. In a recent study conducted by the Inter-Parliamentary Union (IPU), India is placed at 111th position in the list of 189 countries having women representatives in Parliament. Even the lesser developed neighbors of India such as Pakistan, Bangladesh, and Nepal have around 20, 19, and 30% women members in their respective Parliaments (Shankar and Rodrigues 2011).

Table 4.1 shows the total representation of women members in the first to the sixteenth Lok Sabha which reveals that men have monopolized representation in the Parliament and women are victims of political underrepresentation despite constituting half of the population. Women leaders account for just 11% of the 543 parliamentarians, while 89% of seats are being represented by men. Ironically, this is the highest number of women MPs elected to the Lok Sabha in the history of the country, although by a small margin, according to a report by PRS Legislative Research, New Delhi. The percentage of women parliamentarians in the Lok Sabha in

Table 4.1 Women representation in various Lok Sabha

General election	Year	Total members in Lok Sabha	Women members	% of Women in Lok Sabha
First	1952	499	22	4.41
Second	1957	500	27	5.4
Third	1962	503	34	6.76
Fourth	1967	523	31	5.93
Fifth	1971	521	22	4.22
Sixth	1977	544	19	3.49
Seventh	1980	544	28	5.15
Eighth	1984	544	44	8.09
Nineth	1989	517	27	5.22
Tenth	1991	544	39	7.17
Eleventh	1996	544	40	7.35
Twelfth	1998	545	44	8.07
Thirteenth	1999	545	44	9.02
Fourteenth	2004	552	47	8.5
Fifteenth	2008	543	59	10.86
Sixteenth	2014	545	62	11.41

Source Ministry of Statistics and Programme Implementation, Government of India, 2015

relation to the total number of seats in the various general elections has considerably increased from around 5% in the 1950s to 11.4% 2014. The presence of women in the upper house has been slightly higher—72 as compared to the 62 women members in the fourteenth Lok Sabha— probably due to indirect election and nomination of women members.

Among the States, Uttar Pradesh has the highest number of women MPs (12) in the sixteenth Lok sabha; it is followed by West Bengal (7) and Madhya Pradesh (6). Delhi, Meghalaya, Karnataka, and Tamil Nadu have one seat each. In 12 states, women do not have any representation in the Lok Sabha. Among the parties, the Indian National Congress has the highest number of women MPs (24), while BJP ranks second with 13 women MPs. Although the present Lok Sabha has the largest number of women, India still has to be more accommodating to induct more women MPs so that issues concerning them get more prominence and are raised frequently in Parliament.

EDUCATIONAL QUALIFICATION OF WOMEN MEMBERS

Education is one of the enabling factors of deepening democratic liberal values and traditions, which eventually compliments the process of healthy nation-building. Many women members in the 1950s and even 1970s were drawn from the freedom movement. Women members in 1990s had impressive educational attainments. Dr. Suguna Kumara held MBBS, MD, DGO, DCH degrees, Dr. Prabha Thakoor had a doctorate degree as was the case with Professor Rita Verma. While the proportion of the representation of women members in the House did not undergo significant changes most of them were better endowed educationally in the 1990s. The women members of Rajya Sabha, most of whom had high educational attainments, played a meaningful role in the proceedings and debates of the House. The Upper House has elected three women members as the Deputy Chairperson: Smt. Violet Alva (1962–1969), Dr. Najma Heptulla (1985–1998), and Smt. Pratibha Devisingh Patil (1986–1988). Some of them with their background in the struggle for freedom and participation in representative institutions had added luster to the debates and discussions of the House.

The women members having professional background relating to social work and upliftment of women and weaker sections were in an advantageous position to champion the cause of the downtrodden. In this context, the role of Smt. Margaret Alva has been exemplary who being in the Ministry of Personnel sought on many occasions to improve the working conditions of the women employees. Late Ms. Jayalalitha, who symbolized the true meaning of woman power, was the member of Rajya Sabha for 5 years (1984–1989) during which she actively participated in the proceedings of the House on pertinent contemporary issues such as dowry prohibition, land acquisition, and national anthem. Many of the women members with a distinguished career in the profession of law and journalism articulated the interests of common people with great compassion. The nominated women members possessing special knowledge or professional experience and being relatively free from the political affiliations have driven home their stand with vigor and courage. This has been facilitated by the fact of their nomination which makes them the representatives, not of any State or Union Territory but of the whole nation. Their exemplary performance has not only brought them laurels but also raised the prestige of the Council of States (Rajya Sabha Secretariat 2003).

Parliamentary Initiatives of Women Members

In a multi-party democracy, women do not express their opinion independent of their party line. It is rare in Indian politics that individual MPs express their personal opinion contrary to the view of the party they represent. In other words, it is a well-established norm that in the Indian party system MPs are expected to toe the party line. Rarely women MPs have been found taking unanimous stand on issues other than gender specific ones. This also is limited to voicing opinion only and not pressing for legislation. However, it is wrong to assume that young women parliamentarians today are unable to register their presence on the floor of the Parliament as compared to their earlier counterparts. They need to be given the reasonable time to become mature and effective parliamentarians. Earlier women who chose to enter politics made it their be all and end all who lived and breathed politics. For them being in politics is like being in a job they are committed to. It is no longer about being in a man's world and usurping his territory; hence, the aggression that used to be the hallmark of the earlier women parliamentarians is no longer a requirement for the younger breed.

Many questions of the women members expressed on the floor of House pointed to the finer emotions of mercy, compassion, and love reflecting the nobler aspects of life. For instance on April 5, 1953, Smt.

Violet Alva asked a question as to whether the Government knew about the way in which monkeys exported by India are being used. She was particularly keen to know whether such monkeys were used for medical research or conducting experiments in atomic energy establishments. Smt. Rukmini Devi Arundale a nominated Member of the House through her questions drew attention to vivisection of monkey without anesthesia and preservation of wildlife. Such concerns reflected one of the predominant issues covering rights of animals and advocating kindness to animals which are now being taken up by many environmentalists throughout the world.

The Eighth Lok Sabha (1984) for the first time appointed Smt. Chandra Tripathi as the Chairperson of the Estimates Committee who discharged her responsibilities in a fair and just manner. Ms. Mamta Banerjee too played a noteworthy role in the eighth Lok Sabha who spoke on various pertinent issues with regard to rehabilitation of displaced persons and unemployment. In the Sixteenth Lok Sabha, women MPs like Jyotirmoi Sikdar, Poonam Mahajan (BJP), and many others have proved that though politics was considered to be a male terrain, women are also trying to reclaim their political space through representation. However, on most occasions, we can see instances where the women MPs toe the party line, though there have been exceptions like Kanimozhi Karunanidhi (DMK), Supriya Sule (NCP), and the lesser known Tejaswani who are very articulate and passionately taking up issues and fighting for causes. Kanimozhi has taken astounding initiatives to promote and revive the classical literature and heritage of Tamil Nadu. For most women parliamentarians, it was not difficult to maintain an amicable family and work life balance and ensure that both are attended to in the best possible manner.

The above account provides the broad range of issues raised by women members in Rajya Sabha through the various parliamentary mechanisms of question hour, half-an-hour discussions, and short notice questions. The range of pertinent issues raised through the relevant questions, the level and depth of discussions generated by it, and information provided to them by the Government to each such question amply proves the noteworthy role played by the women members in the highest forum of democracy.

WOMEN REPRESENTATION IN THE STANDING COMMITTEES

Both the Houses, individually as well as jointly, work in smaller groups in the various Committees. This enables small groups of members to intensively view and look at certain issues and make relevant recommendations to the appropriate House for legislation as well (Singh 2015). In the Sixteenth Lok Sabha, a cursory glance at the composition of the Standing Committees involved in policy framing would reveal that women MPs are in microscopic minority except for Committee on Empowerment of Women (Chairperson—Bijoya Chakravarty) has all 20 women MPs from Lok Sabha and out of 10 Rajya Sabha MPs, eight are women MPs and rest two MPs are men. This committee has submitted various reports on women's issues which have impacted women's lives in a significant manner.

Important Standing Committees on Finance and Railways have no women representatives whereas Standing Committee on Agriculture is represented by one woman MP, Smt Raksha N. Khadse out of the total 31 MPs. The Standing Committee on Chemicals and Fertilizers is represented by seven women MPs out of total 31 MPs (22.5%). In order to promote substantial progress and development in the rural and urban areas, on September 5, 1998, the Committee on Members of Parliament Local Area Development Scheme was set up under the headship of Deputy Chairperson Dr. (Smt.) Najma Heptulla, in the Rajya Sabha which was possible due to the constant pressure of women parliamentarians. Leader of the Opposition in the Lok Sabha Smt. Sushma Swaraj (BJP) and presently External Affairs Minister has been keen on raising issues related to women reservation bill.

Changing the gender composition in representative bodies cannot guarantee that women's needs or interests will be addressed. In many departmental standing committees of the Parliament, women composition is very insignificant because they are culturally thought to be lacking traits such as leadership qualities, objectivity, and expertise and the like, which are treated as masculine traits. Though various legislations have tried to remove the structural barriers in order to promote gender equality and combat gender discrimination at workplace, one cannot be blind to the fact that men in reality continue to dominate the upper tiers in the political processes as well as administrative organizations.

REFLECTION OF GENDER SENSITIVITY IN THE PROACTIVE SOCIAL LEGISLATION

In recent years, the empowerment of women has been recognized as the central issue in determining the status of women. The 73rd and 74th Amendments (1993) to the Constitution of India have provided for one-third reservation of seats in the local bodies of Panchayats and Municipalities for women, laying a strong foundation for their participation in decision-making at the local levels. It is in this context the issue of women's empowerment gains importance. Empowerment as a social process challenges the fundamental imbalances of power distribution and power relations between individuals in societies. This movement is aimed at achieving social equality, which can be achieved through disempowering some structures of power which have inherent class, caste, and gender biases.

Empowerment as a political process has larger social repercussions since it challenges the fundamental imbalances of power distribution in the family and society. Empowerment of women would definitely help in liberating themselves from the clutches of traditional bondage and exploitation. Thus, it can be seen as a means of creating a new social environment in which women can take decisions and make choices of their own, either individually or collectively. The following social legislations have a strong feminist content which contributes to the women's empowerment in the long run.

1. Pre-Conception and Pre-Natal Diagnostic Technique Act, 1994 providing for the prohibition of sex selection by any person by any means before or after conception and the prevention of its misuse for sex determination.
2. Mahatma Gandhi National Rural Employment Guarantee Act [MGNREGA], 2005 guaranteeing 100 workdays per year at minimum wage which benefits about 50 million people mostly of whom are women has an enduring effect in boosting rural income and wage rates.
3. Prohibition of Child Marriage Act, 2006 which is intended to prohibit the practice of child marriage and ensure that this evil practice is eradicated from the society.
4. Protection Against Domestic Violence, 2005 is primarily meant to provide protection to the wife or female live-in partner from

domestic violence at the hands of the husband or male live-in partner or his relatives.

5. Amendment To Hindu Succession Act, 2005 provides for giving equal rights to sons and daughters in the property of parents and abolishing the concept of widow's estate under which a woman was never a full owner but was one for life only.

6. The Sexual Harassment of Women at Workplace [Prevention, Prohibition and Redressal Act], 2013 seeks to protect women from sexual harassment at their place of work through the grievance committee set up at the workplace.

7. National Food Security Act, 2013 provides for granting special benefits to pregnant women and lactating mothers such as maternity benefit of not less than Rs. 6000 and access to adequate quantity of quality food at affordable prices.

A large share of the credit for these social legislations goes to the initiatives taken by the women parliamentarians in both the houses of the Parliament. However, there is a need for creating a level-playing field for women representatives to contribute effectively and meaningfully in the legislative processes of the Parliament. They can be effective when their number is increased and their voice is multiplied. The lack of their numerical strength creates hindrance in so far as raising diverse issues concerning women's interests

Concluding Observations

Politics in India is still dominated by men at all level of participation, and women have not been given a respectable share of the political domain, although they constitute almost half of the electorate. Women are still not getting a share equivalent to men in decision-making process. Their aspirations and needs are not adequately reflected in our legislatures as their representation remained abysmally low. The average women representation in the Lok Sabha from 1952 to till date is 6%, and in the Rajya Sabha, it is 9%. The power of the national Parliament can be strengthened with substantial women's political representation and progressive legislation through increased participation of women in the public sphere as vital stakeholders that will improve the quality of politics.

Women's representation in the Parliament, while important on the grounds of social justice and legitimacy of the political system, does not easily translate into improved representation of women's varied interests. While we cannot assume that more women in public offices would mean a better deal for women in general, there are important reasons for demanding greater representation of women in political life. First is the intuitive one: the greater the number of women in public office, articulating interests, and seen to be wielding power, the more the gender hierarchy in public life could be weakened. Second and more important, we could explore the strategies that women employ to access the public sphere in the context of a patriarchal sociopolitical system. These women have been successful in subverting the boundaries of gender and in operating in a very aggressive male-dominated sphere. Their experiences could be good learning examples for other women of Indian society.

Political will, inclusive development, restructuring power relations, and administrative efficacy are significant instruments of the desired change that the policymakers are aspiring to accomplish today. The women parliamentarians must take initiatives to design gender friendly policies to enhance the capacity of women and empower them to meet the negative socioeconomic impacts which arise from the globalization process. Constant pressure exerted on the patriarchal system of dominance through women's movements and assertion of democratic rights based on the principles of equality and justice through legal, political, and constitutional means is going to be the game changer in the twenty-first century for rural, urban, and tribal women.

References

Basu, Amrita. (2010). Gender and politics. In Niraja, G. Jayal & Pratap, B. Mehta (Eds.), *The oxford companion to politics in India*. Oxford: Oxford University Press.

Dahlerup, D. (Ed.). (2006). *Women, quotas and politics*. New York: Routledge.

Datta, B. (1998). *And who will make the chappatis: A study of all-women panchayats in Maharashtra*. Calcutta: Stree publishers.

De Beauvoir, S. (1988). *The second sex*. London: Picador.

Dworkin, R. (1978). *Taking rights seriously*. Cambridge, MA: Harvard University Press.

Eisenstein, Z. R. (1994). *The color of gender: Reimaging democracy*. Berkeley: University of California Press.

Forbes, G. (1998). *Women in modern India*. Cambridge: Cambridge University Press.

Hewitt, V., & Rai, S. (2010). Parliament. In Niraja, G. Jayal, & Pratap, B. Mehta (Eds.), *The oxford companion to politics in India*. Oxford: Oxford University Press.

Jaggar, A. (1983). *Feminist politics and human nature*. Brighton: Harvester Press.

Jayal, N., & Nussbaum, M. (2003). *Gender and governance: An introduction*. New Delhi: Human Development Resource Centre—UNDP.

Kimmel, M. S., & Aronson, A. (2011). *The gendered society reader*. New York: Oxford University Press.

Kumar, R. (1998). *The history of doing*. New Delhi: Kali For Women.

Kymlicka, W. (1996). *Multicultural citizenship*. New York: Oxford University Press.

Mehra, A. K., & Kueck, G. W. (Eds.). (2003). *The Indian parliament: A comparative perspective*. New Delhi: Konark Publishers.

Menon, N. (Ed.). (1999). *Gender and politics*. Delhi: Oxford University Press.

Millet, K. (2000). *Sexual politics*. New York, NY: Columbia University Press.

National Perspective Plan for Women. (1988–2000) AD. Department of Women and Child, Government of India.

Phillips, A. (1993). *Democracy and difference*. Cambridge: Polity Press.

Pitkin, H. (1971). *The concept of representation*. Berkeley: University of California Press.

Rai, S. M. (2005). Reserved seats in South Asia: A regional perspective. In Julie Ballington & Azza Karam (Eds.), *Women in parliament: Beyond numbers*. IDEA: Stockholm.

Rajya Sabha Secreatariat. (2003). *Women members of rajya sabha*. New Delhi.

Saxena, K. S. (1999). *Women's political participation in India*. Jaipur: Sublime Publications.

Shankar, B. L., & Rodrigues, V. (2011). *The Indian parliament: A democracy at work*. New Delhi: Oxford University Press.

Singh, M. P. (2015). *The decline of the Indian parliament*. London: Routledge.

Walby, S. (1997). *Theorizing patriarchy*. Oxford: Basil Blackwell.

Wharton, A. S. (2006). *The sociology of gender*. Oxford: Blackwell Publishers.

Williams, M. S. (1998). *Voice, trust and memory: Marginalized groups and the failings of liberal representation*. Princeton: Princeton University Press.

Young, I. M. (2000). *Inclusion and democracy*. Oxford: Oxford University Press.

CHAPTER 5

Women in the Parliament: Changing Gender Dynamics in the Political Sphere in Nepal

Punam Yadav

Although women in Nepal have had the right to vote since 1951 and they have been actively involved in various movements, the political sphere remained male dominated until recently. The first woman parliament member was elected in 1958. However, despite women's early engagement and their active participation in various political movements, women's presence in the parliament remained significantly low even after the establishment of democracy in 1990. The first democratic election was held in 1991, and only seven women, out of 205 parliamentary seats, were elected. The second election was held in 1994. Despite the mandatory provision for at least 5% women's representation, less than 5% women candidates were given a chance to stand in the election by the political parties. Although women's candidacy increased to 6.3% in the third election in 1999, only 5.85% won the election. Therefore, even though there were some efforts made to ensure women's representation in politics, their participation did not exceed 6% until 2008, and even then, those who were in the parliament were excluded from

P. Yadav (✉)
London School of Economics and Political Science,
Centre for Women, Peace and Security, London, UK
e-mail: punamy@gmail.com

© The Author(s) 2018
N. Ahmed (ed.), *Women in Governing Institutions in South Asia*,
DOI 10.1007/978-3-319-57475-2_5

decision-making processes. Moreover, most of the women who were elected or given the opportunity to run in the election were either high-caste women or the close relatives of male politicians such as their wives, widows, or daughters (see Yadav 2016; IDEA 2011). A career in politics was out of reach for the overwhelming majority of Nepali women.

Nepal saw a significant increase in women's participation in politics in 2008. Women won 33% of the seats in the first Constituent Assembly (CA) election held in 2008. It was a historic achievement and a radical transformation in the political sphere of Nepal. Currently, women are appointed in various key positions. The president of the country, Speaker of the Parliament, and the chief justice are all women. In this chapter, I aim to analyze the complex, multifaceted, and nonlinear nature of the lived experiences of women parliamentarians in Nepal. This chapter also aims to examine whether women's increased presence in the parliament has made any difference to the political sphere, especially in regard to making key legislative changes. It also aims to shed light on the changing gender relations within the political sphere, with a particular focus on the ways in which male and female lawmakers perceive each other. This chapter is based on my in-depth interviews with 32 women parliamentarians in Nepal. The fieldwork was carried out between May and June 2011 and December 2016 and January 2017, with CA members from both the first and second Constituent Assemblies.

HISTORICAL CONTEXT

Although the political history of Nepal has been well documented, at least for the past 300 years, with a detailed history from the 1950s (see Whelpton 2005; Singh 2013), women are almost completely absent from these records. To be able to see women's contribution in politics, one has to look at the literature on women's movements in Nepal, which demonstrates that women were not just discouraged from participating in politics, but that their contributions were also not recognized.

Despite the suppressive culture, the historical evidence suggests that women have taken various leadership positions in the past, especially during the Shah dynasty between the period of 1786 and 1951. Likewise, women have also played significant roles in various political movements (see IDEA 2011). However, their right to vote was only established in

1951 by the Interim Constitution of Nepal. The 1959 Constitution, which also guaranteed these rights, however, only survived for a year as the King Mahendra assumed all the power, dismissing the parliamentary system in 1960. He introduced the party less *panchayat* system and endorsed a new Constitution in 1962, which banned all the political parties (Whelpton 2005). The rights of citizens were significantly compromised (IDEA 2011). Although women had the right to vote, there were a lot of discriminatory provisions in the 1962 Constitution: for example, women could not pass their citizenship on to their children, children could only acquire citizenship from their father, and women did not have the right to inheritance.

The 1962 Constitution was a reflection of the society of that time. Women were seen as secondary citizens. Their identity was linked to their husbands or their fathers. They had limited mobility and were constrained from participating in any movements. Women who went out and participated in politics were seen as "bad" women. Therefore, they were confined within the four walls of their homes, and the scope of their engagement in public life was very limited. However, despite all these sociocultural restrictions, women started getting organized on a small scale. The first women's rights organization was formed in 1917 in Siraha District, which was called the Nari Samiti (the Women's Committee) (Acharya 1994; IDEA 2011). This movement was against the authoritarian regime of Ranas, who ruled the country for 105 years, from 1846 to 1951. The aim of this women's movement was to educate girls, so that they could fight against the Rana regime. As a result of this movement, the first girls' school was established in 1936. Likewise, a more organized effort, the Nepal Mahila Sangh (the Nepal Women's Association) was established in the same year under the leadership of Mangala Devi Singh to create awareness of the discrimination against women (Acharya 1994; IDEA 2011). They also advocated for women's right to vote. The Nepal Women's Association also raised awareness of other suppressive cultures and traditions, such as early marriage and polygamy (IDEA 2011).

The women's movement was getting stronger. However, after the establishment of democracy in 1950, various political parties were formed and each political party had its own women's wing, which meant that women's movement was fragmented by different political views. Women were not included in any of the leadership positions after the establishment of the first democracy in 1950 despite their active engage-ments in pre-democratic movements against the Rana regime (Acharya 1994). For instance, a 35-member Advisory Assembly was formed after the fall of the Rana regime, and all of them were men. However, women started protesting from outside the Assembly, and as a result, when the second Assembly was formed in 1954, four women were included (Acharya 1994). Shahna Pradhan became the first elected member of the Kathmandu Municipality by standing in the election in 1952. Likewise, Kamal Rana became the first Vice Chair of the National Assembly in 1952 and Dwarika Devi Thakurani became the first woman minister in 1959 (IDEA 2011). She was the only one who won the election, out of the 15 women candidates who stood in the election in 1959. This democracy was short-lived as King Mahendra took over all the power in 1960, which also impacted the women's movement (IDEA 2011). Although it halted the political movements, women were active and still operated underground.

The second democratic movement, which is known as the first People's Movement (*Jana Andolan I*), was launched in 1990 with the aim of establishing a multiparty democracy. The movement started on February 18, 1990, under the leadership of Sahana Pradhan. The move-ment was successful, and the democracy was established that year. The 1990 Constitution was progressive and saw women and men as equal cit-izens. This Constitution also guaranteed equal pay for equal work.

Despite some progress in the status of women, women's participa-tion in the parliament remained minimal until 1990. However, after the establishment of democracy in 1990, the social and political space became flexible and open to women, which meant that women could easily get together and advocate for women's rights. Nepal also ratified several conventions on women in the 1990s including the Convention on the Elimination of All forms of Discrimination Against Women (CEDAW). The women's movement particularly became stronger after the ratification of CEDAW in 1991. The *Muluki Ain 2020* (National Code 1963), which gave more rights to sons over daughters and did not give the right to daughters to inherit parental property, was amended in 2002. Through the 11th and 12th amendment bills (also known as the Gender Equality Bill 2006), the government of Nepal abolished many such discriminatory provisions from the *Muluki Ain 2020* and guaran-teed women's rights, including their right to abortion.[1] Even though this was a progressive step, it still did not guarantee the full rights to daughters. Although women had the right to inheritance, they had to return their parental property if they get married. In the country where marriage is almost universal, this kind of provision shows a strong influence of patriarchy even in the legislative body.

Despite discriminations and continuous backlash, women's interest and participation in political movement kept increasing. One of the successful examples of women's political participation is the Maoist movement, which is also known as the People's War. The Communist Party of Nepal, Maoist, launched its People's War in 1996 (see Hatlebakk 2010; Cottle and Keys 2007). Although the 1990 revolution established a democracy, power remained in the hands of a few elites (Thapa and Sharma 2009). Discrimination based on gender, class, caste/ethnicity, religion, and region continued (Thapa and Sharma 2009). Moreover, people were frustrated with the unstable democratic government of the 1990s, which failed to fulfill the promise they had made to people. Therefore, people started joining the Maoist movement. In addition to various other reasons, women particularly joined the Maoist movement to fight against gender-based discriminations (see Frieden 2012; Thapa 2012; Yadav 2016). There are various estimates as to how many women were in the People's War; however, according to the majority of sources, women's participation in the Maoist movement was 33–40% (see Yami 2007; Aguirre and Pietropaoli 2008).

Women's participation in the Maoist movement changed the whole political landscape of Nepal. Women did not just prove they are no less than men within the Maoist party but also influenced women's movement outside (see Yadav 2016). The 10-year-long period of civil war in Nepal was a peak period of political consciousness. People were curious about the rapid and unpredictable political developments. It was also a necessity of that time to keep themselves updated about politics as the whole country was impacted by the war. The news of bombings, killings, and arrests had become like "a new normal." For their own safety, it was necessary to take interest in political developments. Therefore, women, even though they were not educated or had no political background, started taking interest in politics.

The gender equality discourse within the Maoist party also influenced the outside discourse. It is important to note that the women's movement was getting stronger outside the Maoist party as well, and this had influenced the decisions made by the government. For example, the government amended several gender discriminatory provisions in the *Muluki Ain 2020* (National Code 1963) due to the lobbying of women's rights activists and civil society organizations (see 11th and 12th amendment bills for more details about the amendments). Moreover, the government also started recruiting women into the Nepal army to counter the Maoist, which was a historic step as women were not considered for combat roles before. The Nepal Armed Police Force also started recruiting women. The Civil Service Act 1993 was amended in 2007 and guaranteed 33% of seats for women in civil services.

While the People's War was still ongoing, King Gyanendra took over all the power from the democratic government and formed his own government in 2002. Angry with the King's move, political parties started getting together. They formed a political alliance called the Seven Party Alliance (SPA) and launched the second People's Movement (known as *Jana Andolan II*).[2] The Maoists also supported this movement. Women's participation in this movement was also remarkable. The second People's Movement was successful. The People's War also ended in 2006 by signing of the Comprehensive Peace Agreement (CPA). Women's participation in the parliament increased after the success of the second People's Movement. Out of 330 members of the interim parliament in 2006, 17% were women. This interim parliament passed a bill to include 33% women in all state organizations, which was formalized by the Interim Constitution 2007, a historic step that paved the way for women's participation in the Constituent Assembly election, which took place in 2008.

FIRST CONSTITUENT ASSEMBLY (CA) AND WOMEN

For the first time in the history of Nepal, nearly one-third (32.78%) of women became the CA members. This was possible through the multiple electoral processes that were adopted to ensure the proportional representation of the discriminated groups, including women (IDEA 2011).[3] The first CA election was significant in many ways. Women who were elected or nominated to be CA members were not only from political, elite families but also represented various caste, ethnicity, class, and educational backgrounds. Most of the women CA members (35.7%) were from indigenous (Janajati) groups. Likewise, just over two-fifths (22%)

were from Brahmin, around 16% from Madhesi, and 11% from Dalits. Chhetris were around 11%, and other castes were around 2%. There was a good representation from various religions as well: over 57% identified themselves as Hindus, around 9% were Buddhist, and nearly 3% were Muslims, whereas over 26% said they did not follow any religion.

The age range of these CA members also varied. Although most of the CA members were below 35 years of age, the ages that were represented were between 28 and 78 years, which suggests that a lot of young women joined politics. These CA members held different educational status and backgrounds. Nearly one-fifth (17.9%) of women had no formal education (see IDEA 2011; Yadav 2016). Likewise, others had completed secondary school (24.5%) and above (14.8%). Although most of them were married, 7.7% were unmarried and 15.3% were widowed/single, which also includes war widows (see IDEA 2011). Those who were married not only to politicians, but also to farmers and businessmen.

Out of 197 women CA members in the first CA, only 26 had experience of being members of the parliament. The majority of the CA members did not have any experience of the parliament, and for some of them, politics was a fresh start. One of the CA members said, although she was helping her father when he was in politics, she never had thought that she would one day become a legislator. There were various reasons and circumstances surrounding their decision of joining politics (see IDEA 2011; Yadav 2016). Some of them started their political career from their student life, whereas others started by being involved in various movements such as the Maoist movement, Madhesh movement, and other ethnic conflicts, which erupted after the Comprehensive Peace Agreement in 2006. Moreover, some women became active in politics only after the death of their husbands. Sunita Kumari Mahato[4] shared how she joined the Maoist movement:

My father was in politics. He was communist but in the United Marxist Leninist (UML) party. When I got married, my husband's whole family was in the Communist Party of Nepal – Maoist. My husband encouraged me to join the [Maoist] party but I didn't because the situation was very difficult at that time. It was an armed struggle and the Maoists were operating from underground. I had to take care of my son and family. Therefore, I started teaching in a school as a secondary school teacher. The Maoist movement escalated. The government announced an emergency situation in 2058 BS (2002). My husband's name was on the most wanted list. I was arrested from the school. I told them I was just a teacher, not in the party; they released me after three days. However, they came every now and again to my house, looking for my husband and tortured me and my family. One day, my husband came home to do some party's work but he was arrested by the army along with his other friends. They were lined up and killed ... After my husband died, I became whole timer [fulltime in politics] in the Maoist party. I was in the women's committee, then took the lead in the teacher's committee and also became a Central Committee Member and then I was nominated a CA member.

Ramrati Ram joined politics in a different circumstance. She was from a lower caste. They were discriminated by the higher-caste people. She wanted to fight against the discrimination, and for this reason, she said she joined politics. Likewise, for some, their political journey started by being involved in various political and ethnic movements. Whatever their reasons for joining were, all of the women CA members wanted to bring social change.

Second Constituent Assembly Election

The first CA was dissolved on May 27, 2012, after it failed to deliver the Constitution even after 4 years. The second Constituent Assembly election was held on November 19, 2013. This time only 30% women were elected or nominated for the CA. Although it was less than the first CA, it was still much higher than what it used to be. This time the women in the CA felt different. They could not form a Women's Caucus, which meant that they could not raise a collective voice. The women's movement within the parliament was not as strong as the first CA.

Onsari Gharti Magar[5], the Speaker of the Parliament, said,

> Political parties did not allow women to gather in one platform. Women are discouraged from being united on women's issues. It is not like the first CA. Women politicians who were at the forefront in the first CA for women's issues, the party has sidelined them. That's why now women's voice is weaker in the parliament. We are now trying to form an informal Caucus through which we will again be able to bring women's issues to the table.

Although the women's movement seemed to have weakened in the second CA, or it can be said that it is not as aggressive as it was in the first CA, they are still pushing their agenda.

AFTER THE PROMULGATION OF THE NEW CONSTITUTION

The most controversial Constitution of Nepal was finally endorsed on September 20, 2015, which led to civil unrest. The Madhesis, women, and other discriminated groups started protesting against the discriminatory provisions in the Constitution (see Jha 2015; Haviland 2015). The new Constitution was somewhat progressive in relation to women's rights, as violence against women (VAW) based on any cultural, religious, or traditional practices was criminalized and women were given equal rights to inheritance. Likewise, it also reserved a 33% quota for women in all state organizations. However, it has several discriminatory provisions. One of the major problems with the new Constitution is the citizenship rights.

The citizenship is the main basis on which to claim anyone's rights. The current citizenship provisions are discriminatory not just to women, but it has a larger impact. Although the Constitution says "No Nepali citizen shall be denied the right to acquire citizenship," it categorizes citizenship into two categories: citizenship by descent and naturalized citizenship, and marriage seems to be the basis for citizenship. The following arrangements have been made in the new Constitution 2015:

- Article 11.2b: Any person whose father or mother was a citizen of Nepal at the birth of such person can acquire citizenship by descent.
- Article 11.5: A person born to a Nepali citizen mother and having his/her domicile in Nepal but whose father is not traced shall be conferred the Nepali citizenship by descent, provided that in case his/her father is found to be a foreigner, the citizenship of such a person shall be converted to naturalized.
- Article 11.6: If a foreign woman married to a Nepali citizen so wishes, she may acquire naturalized citizenship of Nepal.
- Article 11.7: In case of a person born to a Nepali woman citizen married to a foreign citizen, he/she may acquire naturalized citizenship of Nepal as provided for by a federal law if he/she is having the permanent domicile in Nepal and he/she has not acquired citizenship of a foreign country.

While a woman married to a Nepali man can acquire a Nepali citizenship if she wishes to, the same does not apply to a woman married to a foreign national. Likewise, a Nepali man may confer citizenship to his child if his wife is a foreigner, but the same rule does not apply to Nepali women. The Nepali woman has to establish that the father of her child is Nepali. If the mother is unable to prove that her husband is Nepali, or if her husband denies their relationship, her child may not be able to obtain a citizenship. Moreover, for women, their children need to be born in Nepal, whereas this does not apply to the children of a Nepali man. This raises a question: What happens to trafficked women, migrant women, and others whose children are born in other countries?

The absentee population has doubled since 2001, from 0.762 million to 1.92 million in 2011. People who were not in the country during the census are called absentees. Nearly half (44.81%) of the absent population is from the age group of 15–24 years (CBS 2011). On the one hand, Nepali women have the right to marriage, which includes the right to marry of one's own choice, whether the spouse is a Nepali or a foreigner. But the Constitution is silent about foreign men married to Nepali women. According to a report prepared by the UNHRC in 2011, there were 800,000 stateless people in Nepal. With the current provision and increasing mobility of people, globalization, and media, this number is likely to increase and the impact of this discriminatory provision will not only be on women or girls but also on men.

I asked a few CA members about why, despite the significant presence of women in the CA, they were not able to advocate for women's equal rights to citizenship. Rekha Sharma, Minister of General Administration, said, "it was a patriarchal mindset that led to this decision. The provisions in the new Constitution are the reflection of male domination and patriarchy in our society." Kamala BK, who was nominated as a CA member in the second CA, said, "when we raised our concern about the citizenship issue, we were told that it is not about women ... it is a question of national sovereignty." She further added, "the political leaders were afraid of India; because of the open border with India, they were scared that it would be misused." Onsari Gharti Magar added to that saying,

> They [male politicians] may be right about protecting the national interest. However, they need to think beyond the box. They need to come up with an alternate solution if the open border is a problem. In this globalized world, there is increased movement of both men and women. They should have analyzed the consequences properly before coming up with such a conservative policy.

Women CA members also said that there were different opinions about the citizenship in different parties. Since it was seen as a national issue, not as a women's issue, women CA members were not allowed to comment on it. Therefore, they said, even when they were there, they could not do anything.

LIVED EXPERIENCES OF WOMEN CA MEMBERS

Women have made significant contributions to the success of various democratic movements in Nepal, such as the democratic movements of 1950, 1979, 1990, 2006, the Madhesh movement in 2007, and various other political movements. However, women's political participation only increased after the first CA in 2008. Women in the first CA represented various castes, ethnic groups, and religions. They came from different regions with very different cultural backgrounds. It was a very unique opportunity to see such a diverse group of women in the parliament. Women who had never been to school or did not have any formal education had become CA members. They were working with women who already had established political careers. Likewise, women who started their careers as combatants were also now part of the legislative body. Since these women came from different backgrounds, their lived experiences of being in the legislative body also varied. They had both positive and negative experiences.

For some, it was their first visit to the capital city, so they found it difficult to navigate their way through the city, whereas for others, because they could not read or write, it was difficult for them to understand what was going on in the parliament. Likewise, even for those who had a long political career, they said it has been easier for them to be in the leadership position now than before as women were more easily accepted as leaders, which was not the case before. Puspa Bhusal[6] said, "If you are a man, you can easily be accepted as a leader, but for women, you have to prove first that you can be a leader. The situation is much easier now."

I asked the Speaker of the Parliament about her experience of being in such a high-level position in a male-dominated institution, and she said:

> People were suspicious about me when I was elected as the Speaker of the Parliament, especially men. The Prime Minister was blamed for nominating me for this post. The Prime Minister came and said to me, 'I gathered all the courage to nominate you and you will now have to prove

it.' I got huge support from women. When I became the Speaker, many women came to congratulate me. Men also came but with their families ... they also brought their daughters with them. I see that as a change. These young girls will be inspired and will take an interest in politics and may become like me one day.

Rekha Sharma, Minister of General Administration, had a similar experience. She said,

It is certainly easier now than before. However, we still need to prove ourselves ... we need to prove that we can do the job. The first couple of months are about proving ourselves and creating an environment that people will accept us as a leader. When I was appointed as a minister, the first month was very difficult ... staff and Secretary did not see me as a Minister ... they saw me as a 'Woman Minister'. Although things have changed now, we still need to prove ourselves that we are good at work, whereas men never have to prove anything.

Most of the CA members I interviewed said, although they had to work hard to establish themselves in the position, their life has transformed. They also said that because of their new subject position, their status in their family as well as in society has improved.

Women CA members also said that because of their involvement in politics, especially after becoming a CA member, their confidence levels have increased. Kamala BK said, "I can put my agenda clearly now, I can express my views in public and in the party meetings. I feel one has to get the opportunity to change themselves or develop themselves."[7] Onsari Gharti Magar said, "I have set a role model. Before they [people] thought only lawyers can be the Speaker of the Parliament but now after I have done well in this role, every woman sees herself becoming the Speaker of the Parliament one day." Women CA members also expressed that they feel more comfortable with the women Speaker of the Parliament. Kamala BK said, "When there was a male Speaker of the House, we never went to his office but now, we do not hesitate to go to her office." She also said that having a woman in leadership makes a huge difference. She said,

Now we have the woman President. She invited all women CA members to celebrate *Teej* and 16 days of activism against GBV (Gender based Violence). This happened for the first time in history. When women are in leadership, they give us respect and recognition. If there was a man, this would not have happened.

HAS WOMEN'S INCREASED PARTICIPATION MADE ANY DIFFERENCE?

Nepal ranked 17th best in the world in regard to the number of women in the parliament.[8] Because of the critical mass in the parliament, women in Nepal have been able to secure a 33% reservation quota for women in every sector. After the first CA election, women were able to form a Caucus in January 2009. Women CA members from all parties were the members of this Caucus. Usha Kala Rai, ex-President of Women's Caucus,[9] said,

> The Women Caucus was there since 2058 (2001) but it wasn't active. The Caucus is made up of 19 political parties. It has been active since the CA [the first CA]. Basically, this is a pressure group for women's related issues. There is no limitation to its work ... everything that is related to women falls under the mandate of this Caucus. Women from this Caucus are representing various Constitution-drafting committees, we identify issues in the Caucus and the relevant person takes those issues to their committees to discuss and incorporate in the Constitution.

Usha Kala Rai drafted a document during her presidency, which listed all of the women's issues, and handed over to the Constitution drafting committees. The Women's Caucus was a very good platform where they could discuss women's agendas, putting aside all the ideological differences. Diversity among these women CA members also meant that they had knowledge and experience of different groups of women in Nepal.

The first CA was historic also in a sense that it brought many women into decision-making levels. Despite some resistance and hesitancy by the male members, women kept pushing their agendas (Yadav 2016). There were nine bills approved within three years, between May 2008 and May 2011. Women played a crucial role in the approval of these bills. Their involvement in the approval of the Domestic Violence Bill, 2009, was crucial. This bill was tabled for a long time. Because of the critical mass of women in the CA, this bill was approved and also the Domestic Violence and Punishment Act was passed in 2009, which includes laws making domestic violence, which is defined as "physical, mental, sexual, and financial violence, as well as behavioral violence, as domestic violence," illegal (IDEA 2011, p. 77).

In addition to this, they also participated in the passing of other bills such as the Caste Discrimination and Untouchability Bill and Financial

Bill (IDEA 2011). Since these CA members were responsible both for their constituencies and the legislative parliament, they were involved in various development projects, such as infrastructure development, drinking water projects, education, and health. Shanti Devi Rajbansi, from the first CA, said that she brought several development projects to her constituency.

These women CA members were able to negotiate on various women's issues individually or through the Caucus. They are still fighting for the proportional representation of women in every sector. They raised concerns about any kind of discrimination based on gender and have also been advocating for the implementation of international acts, laws, treaties, and conventions on the rights and protection of women. Recently, they were also able to pass a bill on rape which allows more time for women to report it, and it also has increased punishment for those who commit rape crimes.

Forty percent women's representation at the local government bodies is mandatory now. However, women CA members also shared their concerns that women are accepted in some positions and not in others. Women's presence in decision-making level is still low. Kamala BK said, "There are 11 legislative committees, only two women are in leadership roles. These are the committees that will pass the laws for implementation of the Constitution. Therefore, women's presence in these committees is extremely important." She also highlighted that, "Although there are 172 women representatives in parliament, there is only one woman full minister and 2 deputy ministers."

Kamala BK, who became a CA member only in the second CA election, said, "in the first election, CA women pushed the inclusion agenda. They advocated for increasing women's representation. Now we would like to push it from 33 to 50% but we are also advocating to increase women's participation in the decision roles. Gradual changes have taken place. We now have the woman President and woman Speaker. We are trying to empower more women at local levels, too."

Onsari Gharti Magar also added:

> It has been difficult to challenge the patriarchal mindset. They [men] have been very clever, which reduced the number of women in the second CA. They first called for reserved seats. All qualified women were selected in the reserved seats. When they asked for nominations for the direct election, all the strong women candidates had already been selected for the

reserved seats, that's why women who stood in the election did not win and, as a result, women's participation in the second CA was reduced to 30%. They played a very clever game with women.

She also added:

Although we have achieved quite a lot within a small amount of time, implementation is still a challenge. For instance, a woman from Jumla district can't come to the Supreme Court in Kathmandu to report her domestic violence case. First of all, she might not know about it. Even if she did, she will not be able to seek the legal service because she will not have enough resources to access these services. Recently, two young girls died while in *Chhaupadi*[10] home. If they were aware about the consequences, these girls would not have died. But they have no education and they accept it as a social norm. Although dowry is illegal, it is still being practiced in Terai. Therefore, we need to focus on the implementation of the law and I tell everyone that we need to start from our home.

Moreover, she also mentioned that, "although women have the right to inheritance now, it will take time to fully implement. There is a perception that girls are someone else's property. People also believe that giving property to daughters is not practical as she will have to move to someone else's house and it will break up the relationship with their brothers, so although the Constitution has guaranteed their rights, it will take a long time before it is practiced as normal."

Moreover, women parliamentarians also commented on the unwillingness of the male leaders to give up. They said they are discussing with the male leaders for the rotational leadership, but men do not want to give up their positions. They also said that the provision to bring more women into local leadership will produce more women leaders in the long run.

Women CA members of the second CA also said that if the Constitution was adopted by the first CA, it would have been more inclusive and better for women. Rekha Sharma said, "the first CA was strong in women's issues. No one would have dared to say no to any of the women's agenda but it is different now. Women are not allowed to organize for women's issues. All main political parties have internal disputes. Women have not been able to come as strong as it was in the first CA."

Despite all these hurdles, women have been pushing their agenda. They are in the process of forming an informal Women's Caucus. Onsari Gharti Magar is taking the lead, and she believes that there will soon be a Women's Caucus.

CONCLUSION

If a man is unsuccessful then it is only about that one man but if a woman is unsuccessful, the entire community is unsuccessful. So I always say, a man is just one man but a woman is a whole community. Therefore, women have to prove themselves (Onsari Gharti Magar).

Women's presence in the parliament has significantly increased in Nepal since 2008. Women who have been involved in politics certainly have benefitted from this increase. Their lives have changed. They are more confident. Because of their involvement in politics and various leadership positions, they have become role models for many other women. The political sphere is no longer only men's space. Women have been able to participate in and influence many important decisions, and they are still trying to make women's position better. They have advocated for various legal reforms. Although initially for some women CA members it was a challenge to enter into a male-dominated space, slowly the political sphere has transformed into a more friendly space for women. The perception about these women CA members has also slowly changed.

The new Constitution has been promulgated. The main aim of these parliamentarians is to make that Constitution work and have all the provisions in the Constitution to be converted into laws and policies. The fight for proportional representation, which is increasing women's participation to 50%, is still ongoing. Women have been in many key positions. However, women parliamentarians are still experiencing patriarchy and male domination. Although their presence in politics has increased, their presence in decision-making positions remains low. However, women parliamentarians are determined to keep pushing their agendas.

NOTES

1. See 11th and 12th amendments of *the Muluki Ain 2020* for details about the new provisions. The 11th amendment bill is available at http://nepal.ohchr. org/en/resources/Documents/English/other/2009/March%2009/1.

Country%20Code%20amendment.pdf and 12th amendment bill (Gender Equality Act) is available at http://evaw-global-database.unwomen.org/en/countries/asia/nepal/2006/gender-equality-act-2006.

2. See Routledge, Paul (2010) for more details about the People's Movement II 2006.

3. The demographic data of the women CA members presented in this section are mostly taken from a report published by IDEA International in 2011.

4. Interview with Sunita Kumari Mahato, member from the first CA, interviewed on May 27, 2011.

5. Interview with Onsari Gharti Magar, member in both first and second CA and the Speaker of the Parliament, interviewed on January 2, 2017.

6. Interview with Pushpa Bhusal, member in both first and second CA, interviewed on May 27, 2011.

7. Interview with Kamala BK, member in the second CA, interviewed on December 27, 2016.

8. See http://www.ipu.org/wmn-e/classif.htm...

9. Interview with Usha Kala Rai, member of the first CA, interviewed on May 27, 2011.

10. *Chaupadi pratha* is practiced in the Western hills of Nepal. Women and girls are seen impure during their menstruation and are therefore required to sleep in a cowshed. A lot of women and girls have lost their lives because of this practice. There has been a lot of campaign against this practice. However, it is still being practiced in some parts of the country. For more details about *Chaupadi* system, see UNRHCO (2011). *Chaupadi in the Far-West. Kathmandu:* UN Resident and Humanitarian Coordinator's Office. Also see Chapagain, B. (n.d.). Shackles of the Chhaupadi System, *Astitwa*. Retrieved October 20, 2015, from http://www.astitwa.com/index.php/shackles-of-the-chhaupadi-system

REFERENCES

Acharya, M. (1994). Political participation of women in Nepal. In Barbara J. Nelson & Najma Chowdhury (Eds.), *Women and politics worldwide*. New Haven and London: Yale University Press.

Aguirre, D., & Pietropaoli, I. (2008). Gender equality, development and transitional justice: The case of Nepal. *The International Journal of Trasitional Justice, 2*(3), 356–377.

Central Bureau of Statistics. (2011). *Population census 2011*. Kathmandu: Government of Nepal.

Cottle, D., & Keys, A. (2007). The Maoist conflict in Nepal: A Himalayan prediction? *Australian Journal of International Affairs, 61*(2), 168–174.

Frieden, J. (2012). A donor's perspective on aid and conflict. In S. V. Einsiedel, D. M. Malone, & S. Pradhan (Eds.), *Nepal in transition: From people's war to fragile peace*. Cambridge, USA: Cambridge University Press.

Hatlebakk, M. (2010). Maoist control and level of civil conflict in Nepal. *South Asian Economic Journal, 11*(1), 99–110.

Haviland, C. S. (2015, September 19). Why is Nepal's new constitution controversial? Retrieved February 4, 2017 from http://www.bbc.co.uk/news/world-asia-34280015.

IDEA. (2011). *Women members of the constituent assembly: A study on contribution of women in constitution making in Nepal*. Kathmandu. Full report available at http://www.idea.int/publications/women-members-of-the-constituent-assembly/index.cfm.

Jha, H. B. (2015, September 24). Nepal's new constitution: An analysis from the Madheshi perspective. Retrieved February 4, 2015, from http://www.idsa.in/idsacomments/NepalsNewConstitution_hbjha_240915.

Muluki, A. (2020). (General code 1963) The Government of Nepal, available at http://www.equalrightstrust.org/ertdocumentbank//muluki-ain.pdf.

Routledge, P. (2010). Nineteen days in April: Urban protest and democracy in Nepal. *Urban Studies, 47*(6), 1279–1299.

Singh, M. M. (2013). *Forever incomplete: The story of Nepal*. New Delhi: Sage.

Tamang, S. (2009). The politics of conflict and difference or the difference of conflict in politics: The women's movement in Nepal. *Feminist Review, 91*, 61–80.

Thapa, D. (2012). The making of the Maoist insurgency. In S. V. Einsiedel, D. M. Malone, & S. Pradhan (Eds.), *Nepal in transition: From people's war to fragile peace*. Cambridge, USA: Cambridge University Press.

Thapa, G. B., & Sharma, J. (2009). From insurgency to democracy: The challenges of peace and democracy-building in Nepal. *International Political Science Review, 30* (2), 205–219. The Muluki Ain (General Code) Retrieved February 6, 2017 from http://nepalconflictreport.ohchr.org/files/docs/1963-04-12_legal_govt-of-nepal_eng.pdf.

UNRHCO. (2011). *Chaupadi in the far-West*. Kathmandu: UN Resident and Humanitarian Coordinator's Office.

Whelpton, J. (2005). *A history of Nepal*. Cambridge: Cambridge University Press.

Yadav, P. (2016). *Social transformation in post-conflict Nepal: A gender perspective*. London and New York: Routledge.

Yami, H. (2007). *People's war and women's liberation in Nepal*. Kathmandu: Janadhwani Publication.

CHAPTER 6

Who Speaks for Women in Parliament? Patriarchy and Women MNAs in Pakistan

Nusrat Jahan Chowdhury

It is now widely recognized that women's presence is must in the political institutions to represent women's views and interest that are different from those of men who constitute the majority group in these institutions. Women's presence is an effective way of making men more aware about women's different sets of needs, sensitizing them about the experiences and deprivation of women and imparting different norms and standards in political institutions. The presence of more women in this process means more possibilities to bring changes in these institutions for ensuring equality and democracy. Thus, the demand for increasing women's descriptive representation in parliament, a situation where legislators share ascriptive similarities with population subgroups, is linked with the expectation of women's substantive representation, a situation wherein legislators take policy actions that serve their population subgroups (cited in Schwindt-Bayer and Mishler 2005, p. 407). Substantive representation is comprised of acting for or voicing women's interests, needs and expectations. Such expectation and link between descriptive and substantive representation have prompted many countries to adopt

N.J. Chowdhury (✉)
University of Dhaka, Dhaka, Bangladesh
e-mail: nusrat3@hotmail.com

© The Author(s) 2018
N. Ahmed (ed.), *Women in Governing Institutions in South Asia*,
DOI 10.1007/978-3-319-57475-2_6

and implement different mechanisms such as gender quota to increase the number of women in the national parliaments.

The experience of increased presence of women in parliament, however, has produced a mixed result in terms of women's substantive outcome. Research shows that with the increasing presence of women, issues important to women are raised more frequently in the legislative institutions and female politicians do contribute to strengthening women's issues in important decision-making bodies (Celis and Childs 2008; Lovenduski and Norris 2003; Swers 2002). Women MPs work for women and children in constituencies, committees and parties (Childs 2004). Women, as different scholars argue, act for women on the basis of gender consciousness (Dahlerup 1988; Thomas 1991). However, notwithstanding the general recognition that women's larger presence makes a difference in terms of promoting women's issues, there is little evidence to demonstrate that women have been able to change pervasively masculine cultures and norms of politics (Kittilson 2005). In some instances, women have refrained from opposing bills that have disproportionately and negatively affected women; they have even voted along party lines for bills that affected women's rights and interest (Bauer 2008; Tripp 2004). In some cases, women intentionally have distanced themselves from representing or supporting women's issues in a bid to fit with the dominant male style and environment (Rahman 2004; Childs 2002).

The feminist analysis reveals that institutional context where women MPs are present and act is crucial to understand their substantive representation. The formal and informal institutions of society and politics have a gendered structure (Krook and Mackay 2011). These institutions largely undermine the presence of women or the integration of women's views (Acker 1990). The gendered parliamentary institution affects women's substantive representation in varying degrees and manners (Kenny 2013; Krook and Mackay 2011). Despite the increase in the number of women, the timing, rules and norms of political institutions, working environment and arrangements, allocation and membership of important parliamentary committees and other important positions remain male dominated (Dalton 2008; Ross 2002). Women in such historically male-dominated institutions are considered as 'space invaders' (Puwar 2004, cited in Dalton 2008, p. 4); they experience marginalization (Bochel and Briggs 2000). Evidence indicates that women are met with negative reactions or even sanctions if they are 'too' feminist (Dahlerup 1988, p. 294).

Women parliamentarians elected through quota face an additional but different set of challenges in such gendered institutions. In many cases, demeaning status and labels are used to stigmatize, marginalize and delegitimize women elected through the quota system (Bilal 2006). The 'quota label' in some cases may influence women to disavow their association with what are considered to be a 'narrow' set of female concerns (Childs 2004) or vote against legislation that would promote women's rights (Tripp 2004) or to be less willing allies to their female-friendly colleagues (Schwindt-Bayer 2006). In other cases, quota women's agency to act for women is further decreased by indirect election and the absence of constituency (Tinker 2004).

With such reality of parliament and women parliamentarians, this chapter examines and analyzes the role of women Members of the National Assembly (MNAs) in Pakistan. It also explores the challenges they face in male-dominated institutions. Pakistan adopted and implemented a quota system, reserving a number of seats for women in national and provincial assemblies. At present, 60 seats are reserved for women in the National Assembly. In addition, several women have been elected to the NA on popular votes. This chapter compares and contrasts the nature of activism of general- and reserved-seat women MNAs in Pakistan. It specially seeks to examine whether indirect election and gender quota label impact on women's substantive representation.

Ideally, one would not expect Pakistani women MNAs to play any major proactive role in parliament. Part of the reason is the existence of a patriarchal belt where a 'culture against women' is deeply rooted and established in Pakistan. Patriarchs often use legislation to limit women's autonomy and to control women outside the private domain (Moghadam 1992). The masculinist informal norms and practices have also been institutionalized in the legal system in the name of religion to control the life and sexuality of women (Mumtaz and Shaheed 1987). In addition, feudal and tribal dimensions of Pakistani society have further strengthened the process of subjugating and controlling women in the name of religion, honor and tradition. In such sociocultural context, patriarchy is traditionally institutionalized in politics that pose several challenges for women politicians in general and women parliamentarians to act for women in the parliament, party and constituency.

Yet, as evidence shows, Pakistani women parliamentarians have fared better than their counterparts in other countries in the South Asian region. Why and how women parliamentarians in Pakistan seek to promote issues that interest women in parliament mostly remain unexplored. This chapter is likely to fill this gap. Two primary methods, content analysis of debates of the 12th National Assembly (2002–2007) and 13th National Assembly (2008–2013) and interviews with several women MNAs, were conducted for the purpose of exploring the reality of substantive representation of Pakistani women parliamentarians. Content analysis was important to locate whether women MNAs speak in reference to the women's issues which they themselves identified as women's issues during interviews. Women legislators' speeches in the parliamentary debates are as important as any of their acts (Childs and Krook 2012). Any speech of women legislators that referred to any of these issues was counted as an act of substantive representation (SR). Interviews provided an important source to understand the personal experiences and challenges of women MNAs.

This chapter is organized into the following sections. Section two provides a brief account of descriptive representation, examining the background of the introduction to the quota system, its working and limitations. Section three explores the nature of substantive representation, identifying the activism of women MNAs in the legislative field and their issue orientation, while Section four tries to answer the main question raised at the beginning: Who speaks for women? Section five explores the differences in issue orientation of reserved-seat lawmakers (RSMNAs) and directly elected lawmakers (DE/GS MNAs), while Section six makes an overall assessment of the role of women MNAs. Section seven identifies the main barriers to substantive representation. Section eight concludes the chapter.

Women in Pakistan Parliament

Pakistan has a bicameral parliament. The National Assembly (NA) of Pakistan, the lower House, is composed of 342 members, of whom 282 are elected on popular votes for five years and the rest (60) are reserved for women which are distributed among different parties according to the proportion of 'general' seats they hold in parliament. The Senate, the upper House, has 104 members. Senators are elected indirectly by members of provincial assemblies for six years; half of them retire after every three years, and 17% of the seats in the Senate are reserved for women.

Over the years, the representation of women in the NA has increased significantly: from 4% in 1972 to 11.1% in 1988, and to 23% in 2008. Women's representation dropped below 2% in the 1990s primarily due to the absence of the reserved-seat provision. But following the reintroduction of the reserved-seat system, the number of women in the NA increased significantly. Such increase could be noticed in both categories. The number of directly elected women increased from 3 in 1988 to 13 in 2002 and to 18, in 2008. Similarly, the number of seats reserved for women had a threefold increase in the last two decades, from 20 in the 1980s to 60 now.

The provision for reserved seats has significantly contributed to an increase in the number of women in the NA. However, the reserved-seat women legislators do not have a geographical constituency to represent. Predominantly, male political actors play the decisive role in the election of women to reserved seats (Bari 2010). On the other hand, each woman elected on popular votes has, like her male counterpart, a specific geographical constituency. So it is important to understand to what extent indirectly elected quota women and directly elected women MNAs can act for women, differences in their role performance and challenges they face in such gendered institutional context.

SUBSTANTIVE REPRESENTATION OF WOMEN IN NATIONAL ASSEMBLY

As stated above, the number of women members in the NA has increased over the years. To understand the dynamics and diversity of representation, attempts have been made to identify the role of women MNAs in both the legislative and non-legislative arenas. The next subsection focuses on the legislative orientation of the women MNAs.

Women MNAs as Lawmakers

Women in Pakistan have historically remained more disadvantaged than their counterparts in other countries in the region. Until recently, not many women-friendly legislation could be found in Pakistan. As Shah (2011) has observed: 'The legislative history of Pakistan's National Assembly suggests that in terms of introducing women-specific issues in Parliament, the performance of male parliamentarians has historically remained extremely low. Perhaps more worrying from feminists' standpoint is that popularly elected female members often behave like surrogate men.' The situation is, however, changing somewhat in recent years, with more women-related issues now finding prominence in parliamentary behavior. In particular, reserved-seat women MNAs have played a major proactive role in popularizing women-related issues. They appear to be equally active in moving legislation aimed at promoting women's interests and raising other women-related issues. This section focuses on the nature of women MNA activism in the legislative field, while other issues will be dealt with in the next sub-section.

Reserved-seat women MNAs have moved and supported a large number of private members' bills that deal with women's rights and issues; some of these bills have been enacted into laws. They have also initiated measures for the repeal of many discriminatory laws. They moved 42% of the private members' bills in the 12th NA and 70% in the first three years of the 13th NA (Shah 2011). In the 12th NA, reserved-seat women legislators of both the ruling and opposition parties played a critical role in the enactment of a law aimed at repealing honor killing. The legislation, The Protection of Women (Criminal Laws Amendment) Act 2006, declared honor killing as a 'cold-blooded' murder (WPC 2010). It provided for amending two ordinances of the Hudood Law: Zina and Qazf. The Women Protection Act 2006 moved all the provisions of Zina Ordinance back to the Pakistan Penal Code including rape and gang rape. This Act protects women as they can no longer be arrested and imprisoned on just the mere accusation of Zina (Mehdi 2010). It blocked the path of false FIRs in the cases of Zina because after the enactment of new law it becomes difficult for the people to wrongly implicate the people on the charges of adultery or Zina.

In the 13th NA, women MNAs initiated and helped the passage of several bills aimed at protecting women's rights. Some of these bills were: The Prevention of Anti-women Practices (Criminal Law Amendment) Bill 2008, National Women Commission Bill 2008, The Criminal Law (Amendment) Bill 2009 (on sexual harassment), The Prevention of Harassment at Work Place Bill 2008, The Reproductive Health Care Right Bill 2009, and The Acid Crime and Prevention Bill 2010. Pakistani women MNAs also actively spoke in support of Reproductive Health Care Rights Bill 2009 that provided comprehensive reproductive healthcare services, particularly to women in remote areas and marginalized groups. Other important bills moved/supported by women legislators were: National Commission on the Status of Women Bill 2012 and Women in Distress and Detention Fund (Amendment) Bill 2010. The National Commission on the Status of Women Act has afforded the Commission new financial and administrative autonomy and therefore better scope to investigate women's rights violations (Jamal 2012).

Through the submission of many women-related bills and speaking and voting for their passage in the House, women legislators advocated women's inheritance, legal and reproductive rights. They also spoke for the passage of bills that afforded protection, support and legal action for victims (UN Women 2010). The passage of the Domestic Violence Bill submitted and supported by women from all the parties brought domestic violence within the purview of the state which had previously been considered as a domestic issue and therefore was excluded from state jurisdiction. The number of times women legislators, especially reserved-seat women, spoke for these bills indicates that Pakistani women made an impact in relation to feminist legislation and acted to ensure the protection of women's human, social and legal rights.

WOMEN AS CHAMPIONS OF WOMEN'S ISSUES

Women parliamentarians not only fared better than male legislators in moving private members' legislation in the NA; they also outdistanced the latter in raising other issues. For example, in the 12th NA, they asked 27% of the total questions, moved 30% of the total calling attention notices and 24% of the resolutions and raised 8% of the adjournment and privilege motions (Shah 2011). They performed much better in the 13th NA. Table 6.1 shows the performance of reserved-seat (RS) MNAs and general-seat (GS) MNAs in raising different women-related issues in the House.

Table 6.1 A comparative view of numbers of Pakistani general-seat and reserved-seat women MNAs and their representation of women's issues

National assembly	General-seat women		Reserved-seat women	
	% of women representation	% of total intervention made	% of total women	% of total intervention made
12th (2002–2007)	18.0	6.0	82.0	94.0
13th (2008–2012)	22.0	11.0	78.0	89.0

Source Developed by author based on content analysis of the parliamentary debates

In the 12th NA, GS women MNAs constituted 18% of the total (women) members but made only 6% of the total interventions. On the other hand, RS women MNAs made 94% of the interventions, although they constituted 82% of total women MPs. Similar situation could be noticed in the 13th NA. Women legislators spoke on several issues including violence against women, honor killing, forced religious conversion of minority girls, kidnapping and gang rape of minor girls, increased incidence of kidnapping and acid violence on women. They raised their voice against the apparent discrimination of reserved-seat and opposition MNAs in terms of allocation of time during the debates and development funds. They made formal complaints to the Speaker for discrimination against RSMNAs. Women also raised and spoke about women and children-related issues such as the increase in the number of incidents of child abuse, acts or practices that hindered girls' education and increased child labor, which were highlighted in their speeches.

Several other issues, for example, law and order, increase in the prices of daily necessities, and the plight of flood-affected people was also raised and discussed by women MNAs. Women also raised issues that affected women disproportionately, such as the rapid increase in HIV and Aids, human trafficking and provisions for disabled persons. They also expressed their concerns on women's rights issues, drawing the attention of the House to issues such as preventing women from casting the vote and the violation of women's rights in the Swat Valley by the *Taliban*. The representation of these issues indicated that women were critical of government's failure and unwillingness to protect women's political and civic rights.

Table 6.2 Women-related issues raised by reserved-seat and general-seat women MNAs

Issue Areas	12th Parliament N = 159		13th Parliament N = 171	
	RS MNAs	GS MNAs	RS MNAs	GS MNAs
Violence against women,	26	11	16	5
Women and legal system	27	3	58	6
Women and politics	17	1	1	–
Women and material interest	6	–	5	–
Women and children	1	–	21	3
Women's right issues	11	1	18	1
Women and society	52	3	34	3
Total	140	19	153	18

Source Developed by the author from the content analysis of daily bulletins of 12th and 13th national assembly of Pakistan

WHO SPEAKS BETTER FOR WOMEN?

Generally, women MNAs speak for promoting and safeguarding women's rights and interests more than others. In the 12th National Assembly, as one estimate shows (Shah 2011), only 17 (6.3%) of the National Assembly's 269 male members stood in support of their female colleagues or individually initiated the issues of women's rights. The findings relating to the attitude of GSMNAs are similar. RSMNAs played an instrumental role in raising and popularizing women's issues in the House. As Table 6.2 shows, they were more active than the GSMNAs in almost every respect.

Table 6.2 shows that the representation of women's issues by the GS women members remained low in each National Assembly. This is not surprising as general-seat women's lower contribution to overall representation of women's issues corresponded to their lower presence. GS women, despite having more autonomy and independence compared to RS women, spoke less for women and on critical issues. The analysis clearly shows that RS women MNAs brought on the floor those issues that were responsible for the subordinate status of women in Pakistan. RSMNAs presented their views and perspectives with arguments, experience and relevant data. Women legislators devoted their time and efforts to present the situation and needs of general Pakistani women.

EXPLORING THE DIFFERENCES

RSMNAs, as the discussion above shows, surpassed their general-seat counterparts in terms of legislative performance on women's issues. This finding is not unusual and is consistent with the earlier findings of civil society organizations such as PILDAT, FAFEN and Aurat Foundation that among the most active 25 female parliamentarians in the 12th National Assembly, only two were general-seat women (Mirza and Wagha 2009). The reason for this apparent difference in the substantive representation of general- and reserved-seat women stems mostly from differences in role perception and the institutional context. General-seat women may find it beneficial and practical to invest more of their political time and effort on attending constituents' claims than speaking for women. Most of the general-seat women in Pakistan, as their bio-graphic data reveals, were from feudal backgrounds and elected in the male member's constituency. They did not face the complex process of a formalized nomination process, nor had experience of discrimination in political parties.

In addition, most of the general-seat women had no previous experience of social and women rights activism. More importantly, they lacked any experience of politics and/or knowledge of women's issues. A Pakistani reserved-seat female legislator mentioned that there were some general-seat women who did not do anything. The most effective starting point for knowledge is one's own experiences, and the lack of personal and political experiences of general-seat women impacts their feelings, willingness and effectiveness to speak for women (Jones 1993 cited in Reingold 2000, p. 34). Moreover, in the institutional and political contexts of Pakistan, women elected to general seats find it difficult to be publicly identified with women's issues because it might be detrimental to their future political career.

Feminist institutionalists argue that women seeking to be both accepted and effective in politics encounter assimilative pressures to conform to the established male behavioral norm in the gendered cultures of the institutions (Puwar 2004, p. 77 cited in Franceschet 2011, p. 65). Sometime women in such masculinist institutions deny their gender identity and try to fit in with the dominant male styles. Some women under the pretext of being national leaders ignored women's issues. Some argue that they are like the biological females who act as a social man (Sorenson 1984 cited in Acker 1990, p. 139). Such a tendency by female leaders to deny their gender identity and consciousness is dubbed 'The Margaret Thatcher syndrome' (Rahman 2004; Shaheed 2002).

Contrary to this perception of general-seat women, reserved-seat women confirmed that they considered themselves as the representatives of women and were responsible for voicing women's concern in the political process. Their responsibility was not confined within a specific geographical constituency like those women in general seats. This difference in role perception and responsibility arises from their election to reserved seats that confer a special mandate to improve the representation of women as a group (Schwartz 2004). Mandates emerge over the quota campaign as a result of arguments that female representatives are needed in order to present perspectives of women which are different from those of men (Childs and Krook 2012). Such expectation translated into an informal norm and impacts on reserved-seat women's representation of women.

Moreover, reserved-seat women are constantly reminded of their responsibility to women constituents, to use their political time and presence to pursue important issues of women (Bari 2010; Dahlerup 2009). Thus, reserved-seat women's perception of being a representative and their representative acts shape the prospects for the substantive representation of women. Reserved-seat legislators in Pakistan claimed that reserved-seat women do better work than many directly elected female legislators.

Explaining Women MNA Activism in Pakistan Parliament

Despite the differences in role perception between general- and reserved-seat women, data indicate that representation of women's issues increased in the 13th NA compared to 12th NA. Several factors contributed to an increase in the representation of women's issues. These were: the appointment of a female Speaker, the formation of a women's caucus, the presence of more experienced women, the entry of highly educated professional women and grassroots political activists with a background in social activism. Accordingly, women's voices got stronger with the presence of an experienced woman Speaker who gave women MNAs encouragement and opportunity to speak their mind (Ebrahim 2009).

The role of the Speaker was significant in the formation of the Women's Parliamentary Caucus (WPC) and its continued effort to act for protecting and ensuring the rights of Pakistani women.

Women's Parliamentarian Caucus (WPC) was instrumental in the formulation and passage of different women-related bills in the 13th NA. Notwithstanding differences in party affiliation and/or intellectual orientation, women MNAs in the WPC adopted an all-party approach while discussing different issues. The WPC provided women parliamentarians space and motivation to act for women. It also worked as a training ground for newcomers where they learned about legislative procedures from the experienced MNAs. It facilitated women's substantive representation in the 13th NA and increased commitment to support bills that benefited women. It also confirms that women do introduce and support women-related bills more when there is an increased number of women or when there is a women's parliamentary caucus (Thomas 1991).

Also, more experienced women entered the 13th NA due to the re-election of several women legislators of the 12th NA. They were experienced in the legislative procedures and the lawmaking process. Women of this group were more active in representing women's issues when compared to other reserved-seat and general-seat women (FAFEN 2012). It provided women legislators the opportunity to continue their work on women-related bills, some of which they had initiated in the 12th NA. In addition, background profiles reveal that many grassroots-level political workers and social rights activists were elected to reserved seats. These women were familiar with Pakistani women's issues and the discriminations they faced, and were willing to use the floor of the parliament to seek redress.

BARRIERS TO SUBSTANTIVE REPRESENTATION

While the data indicated increased and active representation of women, there were also valid data and example that indicate that not all women act or speak for women. It is likely that some women are less effective and willing than others to act for women. Almost 42% reserved-seat women and 70% general-seat women in the 12th NA, and 35 and 53% general- and reserved-seat women MNAs, respectively, in the 13th NA did not voice concerns for women. Interview data reveal that the willingness and ability of MNAs to act are circumscribed by a set of personal and institutional factors. Such factors include: formal and informal norms of political institutions, gender quota and indirect election, party discipline and affiliation, and lack of support system.

The Pakistan legislature is infused with patriarchal, feudal and tribal norms, and women legislators complained of not being taken seriously, not only by male colleagues but also by the Speaker of the National Assembly who, on several occasions, ignored the notices of women and allocated less time to them to speak (PILDAT 2006). In the 12th National Assembly, women's opportunity to participate in the legislative process was curtailed and not a single woman member was put on the list of the Panel of Chairmen (Mirza and Wagha 2009). Experiences of marginalization and invisibility in the masculinized space like legislative institutions constrained and sometimes discouraged women from speaking for women (Dalton 2008). Women legislators mentioned that their male counterparts were not supportive of reserved seats and were suspicious about the formation of the WPC.

Women MNAs also experienced a lack of support from their own party members and male colleagues while raising issues related to women's interests. Sometimes women legislators were either expelled from the party or criticized for promoting women's concerns and initiating cross-partisan networking. Kashmala Tariq, a reserved-seat legislator and a woman activist, was expelled from the party (PML-Q) due to her outspoken nature and the anti-woman mind-set of the party (Sahi 2008). Dr. Fehmida Mirza, Speaker of the 13th NA and three times directly elected MNA, was criticized for being 'Women's Speaker only,' for her support to women legislators in promoting women's issues and for her role in the formation of the caucus (PILDAT 2013). For general- and reserved-seat women MNAs, the political context is similar, if not exactly the same.

Feminist scholars argue that institutions created by men in response to the interests of elites often function to constrain the behavior of women (Browne 2014). It was observed that in Pakistan, whenever women wanted to raise issues of mutual concern, parties or party leaders were always there to impose their own political priorities which usually conflicted with the larger agenda of gender equality (cited in Saeed 2010). Women legislators faced resistance from their male colleagues during the passage of women-related bills. Women members of the ruling party failed to incorporate two positive amendments in the Criminal Law Amendment Act (on honor killing) due to strong resistance from some quarters in the government and party (Mirza 2011). The Prevention of

Anti-Women Practices Bill 2011 and its standing committee had faced significant resistance to pass the bill (Khan 2011). The main opposition women MNAs faced was from male members of their own or opposition parties who tried to ignore them in the legislative process or block any legislation to ensure women's access to gender rights, goods and services (Imtiaz 2011).

Moreover, according to informal conventions, senior members and leaders of the parties and parliaments are given priority in the conduct of business and appointment to important positions of the parliament. Most of the senior members are obviously male. Women's junior status limits their access to the formal position of institutional power which, in turn, constrains and discourages women from taking any initiative to speak or participate in debates (Swers 2002). In some cases, women were sexually harassed and felt pressured to give sexual favor to leaders in powerful positions in the parties and legislatures (Bari 2010, p. 380).

Available evidence indicates that women legislators in Pakistan were ignored, marginalized and victimized in political institutions. Their efforts to act for women were further limited by constitutional rules to control the freedom of legislators. Thus, the masculinist formal and informal norms and practice constrain women legislators to voice women's concerns and affect their ability to act for women. Although the 'quota' MNAs play a more proactive role than the GSMNAs, in the Pakistani institutional context they experience greater marginalization and invisibilization than the general-seat women and demeaning statuses are attached to them. In fact, quota label, indirect election and the lack of a constituency are likely to diminish reserved-seat women's capacity to represent claims (Reyes 2002).

The indirect election and reserved-seat status were used by male leaders and parliament members to make women legislators invisible in the legislative process. In the 12th National Assembly of Pakistan, female reserved-seat legislators were ignored during debates on important national issues and were not even provided with the minutes of the meetings despite repeated requests. RSMNAs were only allowed to speak for two to three minutes with repeated interruptions to wind up (Mirza and Wagha 2009). Reserved-seat women MNAs were even termed as 'political show girls' by some of their male colleagues.

RSMNAs confided that they were often reminded of their election and positions. Male members regarded them as 'not real politicians' since they had no constituency and their election was dependent on the favor of the party leadership (Bari 2010). Also, due to reserved-seat status, women were more vulnerable to party pressure and disciplinary actions. Women legislators stressed the informal institutions and norms regarding the status and position of reserved-seat women in parliament. What is evident is that the reserved-seat label reduces women's ability to act for women and build solidarity with constituents. However, not all are equally affected by this label. Those having strong professional, personal and political credibility were able to resist being labeled as 'token' lawmakers and succeeded in working for women. But those who were 'junior' political party workers without any leadership or organizational experience and also lacked strong feudal or political family connections were most often affected by the reserved-seat label. Many RSMNAs experienced triple jeopardy due to their gender, their reserved-seat status and their lack of leadership support or connections.

The substantive representation of women is also influenced by the extent of party discipline. Party discipline is the rule, whereby the members of a political party take a common public stand on a given issue (Tremblay 2003, p. 230) and have a tendency to prevent women working across parties (Mackay 2001). However, in the context of a weakly institutionalized authoritarian party structure, what influences the capability of women to speak for women is party affiliation. As women are both individuals and politicians with their own political beliefs and views, they are also like male party candidates, who represent that party's policies and programs (Bochel and Briggs 2000; Phillips 1995). Pakistani political parties are weak and dynastic in nature; these are also disciplined in practice. The cross-party networking among women MNAs in such an environment is viewed with a lot of suspicion. Party practices, if not rules, discourage their MNAs from working closely with their counterparts in other political parties (Bari 2010). Women legislators who disregard party rules are subject to disciplinary action, and reserved-seat women MNAs are more vulnerable to party discipline in Pakistan. Reserved-seat women legislators who have tried to act independently or disregard party directives risk losing the prospect of re-election.

However, apart from adhering to party rules, female legislators' affiliation with the party ideology in some cases also influenced women to act against women's interest or to remain inactive. For example, women parliamentarians, Dr. Farida Ahmed and Ms. Samia Raheel Qazi, of MMA strongly condemned and rejected the Protection of Women (Criminal Laws Amendment) Bill 2006, due to their party affiliation and ideology.

Sometimes, female legislators weigh the party's position and their own future career prospects as a parliamentarian. The ruling party's (PML-Q) female legislators in the 12th National Assembly opposed opposition member Sherry Rahman's motion on 'The Introduction of a Bill to Provide for Elimination of Gender Discrimination.' The bill proposed that one-third of women must be recruited in the Federal Public Service Commission and that equal pay be paid for equal work to women in line with the International Labor Organization's Convention No. 100 (Bari 2010).

In the 13th NA of Pakistan, pro-women legislators like Nafisa Shah, Bushra Gohar and Shazia Mari remained silent on Nizam-e-Adl Regulation (Zubeida 2009), the aim of which was to impose *Sharia* laws in the Swat Valley in the North West Frontier Province of Pakistan. Sharia courts would interpret civil rights according to Islamic scriptures which would render women invisible and enable unprecedented violence to be inflicted on them (True et al. 2013). However, female lawmakers were silent on raising the implication of *Sharia* law on the lives of women (Zubeida 2009). It is evident that women legislators like their male counterparts have to act within parameters set by the party leaders and rules. Party affiliation remains important in light of its role in providing access to political patronage (Goetz and Hassim 2003). Such attitudes and practices of the parties also limit the effectiveness of the presence of women to work for women and determine whether substantive representation can take place.

Political institutions can facilitate or hinder the substantive representation of women by providing different levels of resources to initiate women-related activities or research (Franceschet 2011). As legislative business is a complex process, it takes time to learn the rules and apply them. The inexperience of new women legislators in participating in the legislative business is multiplied by the absence of institutional support systems for women. This is a characteristic of underdeveloped institutional contexts. Many of these newly elected women were political party workers and professionals but they lacked knowledge about the complex process of legislative business. There was no system of training in place for these women, nor mentors for newcomers to learn the legislative rules and procedures. In such institutional environments, new women legislators became invisible in the legislative process almost immediately. In particular, the lack of gender expertise, research staff and gender disaggregated data posed difficulties for women to raise gender-related issues in parliament. In Pakistan, elected representatives continued to work without office space and assistance (Bari 2010). As such, the lack of institutional support systems limited the effectiveness and willingness of women to act for women in the legislative process or to initiate women-related activities.

CONCLUSION

Women's representation in the parliamentary arena shows that with the presence of more women, representation of women's issues increased and therefore confirms the relationship between female representatives and representation of women. Data also reveal that reserved-seat MNAs in both parliaments (12th and 13th) represented women better than those elected from general seats; they also made major contributions to promote women's issues. Not only could one see an increase in the number of issues raised and discussed by women MPs; there was a qualitative shift in the nature of issues moved. Several factors such as the [positive] role of the female Speaker, the formation of a women's caucus, an increase in the number of experienced women MNAs and the presence of feminist activists as lawmakers caused this shift in the nature of representation. However, women MNAs could not always represent women the way they wanted mostly because of the informal and formal rules and norms, party discipline, gender quota label and indirect election and the lack of an institutional support system. It is evident that women's substantive representation does not depend solely on the number of women elected but on the presence and complex interactions of institutional and individual-level factors. These factors intervene in the process of substantive representation of women. These findings indicate that the relationship between descriptive and substantive is not deterministic but complicated (Childs 2006).

REFERENCES

Acker, J. (1990). Hierarchies, jobs, bodies: A theory of gendered organization. *Gender and Society, 4*(2), 139–158.

Bari, F. (2010). Women parliamentarians: Challenging the frontiers of politics in Pakistan. *Gender, Technology and Development, 4,* 363–384.

Bauer, G. (2008). Elected gender quotas for parliament in East and Southern Africa. *International Feminist Journal of Politics, 10*(3), 348–368.

Bilal, G. (2006). *Revisiting reservations.* Islamabad: Friedrich Naumann Foundation.

Bochel, C., & Briggs, J. (2000). Do women make a difference? *Politics, 20*(2), 63–68.

Browne, E. (2014). *Elected women's effectiveness at representing women's interests.* Accessed April 12, 2014. Available from http://www.gsdrc.org/docs/open.

Celis, K., & Childs, S. (2008). Introduction: The descriptive and substantive representation of women—new directions. *Parliamentary Affairs, 61*(3), 409–425.

Childs, S. (2002). Hitting the target: Are labor women mps acting for women? *Parliamentary Affairs, 55*(1), 143–153.

Childs, S. (2004). *New labour's women mps: women representing women.* London: Routledge.

Childs, S. (2006). The complicated relationship between sex, gender and the substantive representation of women. *European Journal of Women's Studies, 13*(1), 7–21.

Childs, S., & Krook, M. L. (2012). Labels and Mandates in the United Kingdom. In S. Franceschet, M. L. Krook & J. Piscopo (Eds.), *The Impact of Gender Quotas,* New York: Oxford University Press.

Dahlerup, D. (1988). From a small to large minority: Women in scandinavian politics. *Scandinavian Political Studies, 11*(4), 275–298.

Dahlerup, D. (2009). *What constitutes successful substantive representation of women? theoretical and methodological problems in the study of women's substantive representation,* Paper presented in the World Congress of the International Political Science Association, July 11–16, Santiago de Chile.

Dalton, E. (2008). *A masculinised party culture: Obstacles facing women in japan's liberal democratic party,* Paper presented at the 17th Biennial Conference of the Asian Studies Association of Australia, July 1–3, Melbourne.

Ebrahim, Z. (2009). *Women in parliament push for space.* Accessed December 2, 2012. Available at http://ipsnews.net/news.

FAFEN. (2012). *Report on the performance of female parliamentarians during the fourth parliamentary year of the 13th national assembly,* Islamabad.

Franceschet, S. (2011). Gendered institutions and women's substantive representation: Female legislators in Argentina and Chile. In M. L. Krook, & F. Mackay (Eds.), *Gender politics and institutions: Towards a feminist institutionalism,* NY: Palgrave MacMillan.

Goetz, A. M. and Hassim, S. (2003). Introduction: Women in Power in Uganda and South Africa. In A. M. Goetz and Shireen Hassim (Eds.), *No shortcuts to power: african women in politics and policymaking.* London: Zed Books.

Imtiaz, H. (2011). *In pakistani politics, it's still a man's world, the South Asia channel 19 July.* Available at http://afpak.foreignpolicy.com. Accessed March 14, 2012.

Jamal, S. (2012). Pakistani Women Legislators Outperform Men. *The Pakistan Observer*, November 22.

Kenny, M. (2013). *Gender and political recruitment: Theorizing institutional change*. London: Palgrave Macmillan.

Khan, S. (2011). Women-specific bills passed: Fourteen-year jail term for acid-throwers. *The Express Tribune*, December 12. Accessed October 14, 2013. Available at http://tribune.com.pk.

Kittilson, M. C. (2005). In support of gender quotas: Setting new standards, bringing visible gain. *Politics & Gender, 1*(4), 638–645.

Krook, M. L., & Mackay, F. (Eds.). (2011). *Gender politics and institutions: Towards a feminist institutionalism*. London: Palgrave MacMillan.

Lovenduski, J., & Norris, P. (2003). Westminster women: The politics of presence. *Political Studies, 51*(1), 84–102.

Mackay, F. (2001). *Love and politics: Women politicians and the ethics of care*. London: Continuum.

Mehdi, R. (2010). The Protection of Women (Criminal Law Amendment) Act, 2006 in Pakistan. Accessed 22 November 2014. Available at http://droit-cures.ultrevues.org/2016.

Mirza N. (2011). Seven Pro-women Laws in Seven Years. *Legislative Watch, 38*.

Mirza, N., & Wagha, W. (2009). *A five year report on performance of the women parliamentarians in the 12th national assembly (2002–2007)*. Islamabad: Aurat Foundation.

Moghadam, V. (1992). Patriarchy and the politics of gender in modernizing societies: Iran, Pakistan and Afghanistan. *International Sociology, 7*(3), 35–53.

Mumtaz, K., & Shaheed, F. (1987). *Women of Pakistan: Two steps forward, one step back?*. Islamabad: Vanguard.

Phillips, A. (1995). *The politics of presence: The political representation of gender, ethnicity and race*. Oxford: Clarendon Press

PILDAT. (2006). *Fifth meeting of parliamentary consultative group on women's issues*. Islamabad: PILDAT.

PILDAT. (2013). *Citizen's report: Five years of the 13th national assembly of Pakistan*. Islamabad: PILDAT.

Rahman, S. (2004). *Dialogue on the first year of increased women's representation in the parliament: lessons, Reflections and the Way forward*. Islamabad: PILDAT.

Reingold, B. (2000). *Representing women: Sex, gender, and legislative behavior in Arizona and California*. Chapel Hill: University of North Carolina Press.

Reyes, S. (2002). Empowering women elected through quotas: The Pakistani experiment. In *The Implementation of Quotas: Asian Experiences*. Stockholm: IDEA.

Ross, K. (2002). Women's place in "male" space: Gender and effect in parliamentary contexts. *Parliamentary Affairs, 55*, 89–201.

Saeed, M. (2010). Pakistan: Breaking the Glass Ceiling. Accessed March 9, 2011. Available at http://content.undp.org.

Sahi, A. (2008). I was punished because I dared to speak against a Makhdoom. *Newline*, August 7. Accessed October 27, 2013. Available at http://www.newslinemagazine.com.

Schwartz, H. (2004). *Women's representation in the Rwandan parliament*. Master's thesis, Department of Political Science, Gothenburg University. Accessed May 10, 2011. Available at http://www.quotaproject.org.

Schwindt-Bayer, L. A. (2006). Still super madres? gender and the policy priorities of latin american legislators. *American Journal of Political Science, 50*(3), 570–585.

Schwindt-Bayer, L. A., & Mishler, W. (2005). An integrated model of women's representation. *The Journal of Politics, 67*(2), 407–428.

Shah, S. A. (2011). Women's Role in Legislation. *The Dawn*, September 18.

Shaheed, F. (2002). *Imagined citizenship: Women, state and politics in Pakistan*. Lahore: Shirkat Gah.

Swers, L. M. (2002). *The difference women make: The policy impact of women in congress*. Chicago: The University of Chicago Press.

Thomas, S. (1991). The impact of women on state legislative policies. *The Journal of Politics, 53*(4), 958–976.

Tinker, I. (2004). Quotas for women in elected legislatures: Do they really empower women? *Women's Studies International Forum, 27*, 531–546.

Tremblay, M. (2003). Women's representational role in Australia and Canada: The impact of political context. *Australian Journal of Political Science, 38*(2), 215–238.

Tripp, A. M. (2004). The changing face of Africa's legislatures: Women and quotas'. In *The implementation of quotas: African experiences*, Stockholm: IDEA.

True, J., Niner, S., Parashar, S., & George, N. (2013). *Women's political participation in Asia pacific: Report for United Nations department of political affairs*. New York: Social Science Research Council.

UN Women. (2010). *Convention on the elimination of all forms of discrimination against women*. Accessed May 23,2011. Available at http://www.undp.org.

Zubeida, M. (2009). Pakistan: Why the silence of women parliamentarians on the passage of 'nizam-i-adl' regulation? *South Asia Citizens*. Accessed April 15, 2013. Available at http://www.sacw.net.

CHAPTER 7

Gender Inclusive Governance: Representation of Women in National and Provincial Political Bodies in Sri Lanka

Kamala Liyanage

Inclusive governance implies bottom-up decision making, having all concerned people at every level of governance participate (Beall 1996, p. 3). Inclusiveness is a core value of democratic governance, in terms of equal participation, equal rights, and treatment. It implies that all people including women, poor, and ethnic minorities also have the equal rights similar to men, rich and ethnic majorities to participate meaningfully in governance and influence decisions that affect them (UNDP 2007, p. 1). It also recognizes that all citizens are entitled to take an interest in public issues and to address them. Equitable representation in governing institutions is essential to the building and sustaining of democracy. The achievement of democracy presupposes a genuine partnership between men and women in the conduct of the affairs of society in which they work in equality and complementarily, drawing mutual enrichment from their differences (Inter-Parliamentary Union 2014, p. 4).

K. Liyanage (✉)
University of Peradeniya, Peradeniya, Sri Lanka
e-mail: imiyakamala@yahoo.com

© The Author(s) 2018
N. Ahmed (ed.), *Women in Governing Institutions in South Asia*,
DOI 10.1007/978-3-319-57475-2_7

117

The arguments for inclusion of women in political decision-making bodies are many and diverse. For example, the presence of women in elected bodies strengthens the legitimacy of equal rights and ensures equal opportunities and promotes gender inclusive governance. It also assures that women as a group have a leader who protects and shares their interests and represents and enriches the experiences of women in the decision-making process. There may also exist scope for better allocation of public funds including subsidiaries for childcare, and efficient delivery of basic services. Women's presence is likely to encourage qualitative changes in women's lives, create opportunities to build women's leadership skills, contribute to the change in the nature of political institutions and political culture, and create more women-friendly political environment. The political women also serve as important role models, which may inspire other women to involve themselves in politics (Rule and Zimmerman 1994; Phillips 1995; Dahlerup 1988, 2007; Sawer 2000).

Today, in many countries including Sri Lanka, there is an increased political awareness, higher voter turner out, and active participation at election propaganda among women but their representation in the elected bodies is pitifully low. In Sri Lanka, women constitute 51.9% of the total population and their achievements in all fields including life expectancy are remarkable. Despite the fact that women are almost on par with men in every sphere of life, they have been marginalized in higher decision-making levels. Article 12(2) of the Sri Lankan Constitution (1978) affirms equal rights to men and women. In 1980, Sri Lankan government accepted the UN International Covenant on Civil and Political Rights of 1966. In 1981, Sri Lanka became a signatory to the Convention on Elimination of All Forms of Discriminations against Women (CEDAW). The Women's Charter—Sri Lanka (1993, 2: 1)—affirms equal rights to men and women in politics. Thus, equal political rights including right to representation of Sri Lankan men and women have been guaranteed by national as well as international laws.

But there exists a major gap between what is written in the Constitution and the ground reality. Electoral politics still remains a preserve of men and women mostly remain 'invisible.' This paper focuses attention on the underrepresentation of women in national and provincial political bodies in Sri Lanka. It seeks to explore a number of issues such as women's political rights, their role as voters, party members, activists, and leaders, and also their role and performance as elected representatives at national and provincial levels. The paper also identifies and explains factors that account for women's exclusion from elected bodies in Sri Lanka. The data for this study has been derived from four researches conducted in 1994, 1998, 2010–2012, and in 2015–2016.[1] During this period, 29 female politicians (including a woman Prime Minister, President, two presidential candidates, and 12 Ministers, one Governor of a Provincial Council (PC), three Deputy ministers) and 42 male leaders (two Prime Ministers, 17 Ministers, two Governors of PCs, and 7 Deputy Ministers) at the national and provincial levels and 19 party officials (all four women party leaders, seven women members—party Executive Committees, four male General Secretaries, two male Deputy Leaders, and two Treasures) were interviewed. In addition, 23 Focus Group Discussions (FGDs) with party activists, members of women's wings and selected voters in 14 districts were conducted.

CONSTITUTIONAL DEVELOPMENT AND EVOLUTION OF POLITICAL PARTIES IN SRI LANKA

There have been three constitutions in Sri Lanka: the 1947 Soulbury Constitution, the First Republican Constitution of 1972, and the Second Republican Constitution of 1978. The Soulbury Constitution which consisted of the Ceylon Independence Act, 1947, provided a Westminster or a parliamentary cabinet model of government to Sri Lanka. The Governor General, the House of Representatives (101 members), and the Senate (30 members) exercised legislative power under this constitution. The First Republican Constitution, 1972, provided a unicameral legislature, a nominal president and a cabinet of ministers headed by a Prime Minister. The simple majority system was used as the electoral system to elect parliamentarians under these constitutions. The Second Republican Constitution, 1978, which was a mixture of the French, American, and British government models established an Executive Presidential system with a unicameral legislature (225 members) and a cabinet headed by the President. This constitution introduced a form of multi-member proportional representative system for parliamentary and presidential elections (Wilson 1979). Under the 13 Amendment to the 1978 Constitution, nine Provincial Councils were established and below the provincial level, there are elected 18 Municipal Councils, 42 Urban Councils, and 270 *Pradesheeya Sabhas.*

The Lanka Sama Samaja Party (LSSP) was established in 1935 in Sri Lanka as the first political party and the Communist Party (CP) followed it by founding in 1943. From 1947 to 1952, the United National Party was the dominant party in electoral politics in Sri Lanka and after that, a two-party coalition system emerged in which the UNP and the SLFP alternatively established governments (Kearney 1983). At present, there are 68 registered parties in Sri Lanka and they can be divided into four main categories such as major/dominant parties, old and new left parties, ethnic parties, and smaller parties.

WOMEN'S PRESENCE IN POLITICS

One of the important characteristics that set apart Sri Lanka from its neighbors is that it recognized equality of men and women in politics much earlier than the latter. The Donoughmore Constitution, which came into effect in 1931, granted franchise to men and women on the same terms and conditions, and Sri Lankan women became the first to enjoy franchise among the Asian countries (Mettananda 1981; Jayawardena 1986). There have been 15 general elections in Sri Lanka and the percentage of voter turnout has increased with each election from 55.5% in 1947 to 86.7% in 1977 and since then it has been around 65–70% even during the civil war period (Liyanage 1992, p. 17). Though there is no official gender-disaggregated data on voting in Sri Lanka, there is a strong perception that men and women have equally voted or women have voted more than men at general elections since the mid-1960s (de Silva 1995, p. 84).

Women not only vote in large number in Sri Lanka but also participate in different party-related activities both as party members and leaders. The Sri Lankan parties do not have clear records on their party membership and the way of granting membership differs from one party to another. According to a survey done by Women's Bureau of Sri Lanka, the membership of women in different parties varies from about 20 to 30% (Women's Bureau 1984). One survey (Kiribamune 1998) illustrates that 33% of men and 25% of women own party membership cards. However, although women do not obtain membership cards as frequently as men, many of them generally attend party meetings where the decisions taken by party's inner circles are presented. This study illustrates that the majority of women members of different parties generally come from rural areas and their main interest in attending party meetings is to 'enjoy the event' by going out or to obtain some material support. Many female party activists said that they contributed a lot to their parties mainly during the elections, but blamed them for exploiting women and ignoring them immediately after the elections.[2]

Women members appear to be active in mobilizing voters, but not in making decisions or interest articulation. Like other patriarchal institutions, parties also place women in a subordinate position and exploit them in a clever manner to achieve their political goals. In almost all parties in Sri Lanka, the female segment of the Central or Working Committee is very small. Women constitute 13.5% and 12.9% of members of the Working Committee and the Executive Committee, respectively, of UNP. 7.4% of the Central Committee members of SLFP, 3.0% of LSSP, and 5.0% of CP are women. SLMC and the JVP do not have any women in their highest policymaking bodies. In none of the parties has the post of General Secretary been ever held by a woman. Very few women represent the middle level of the party structures too.

The few women who have reached the top in party hierarchies have attained these positions by virtue of their kinship to male heirs. The emergence of Sirima Bandaranaike, Chandrika Kumaratunga, Srimani Athulathmudali, and Farial Asraff in political leadership roles represents a paradox in Sri Lanka's patriarchal culture that is best explained by their linkages to male authority. The political value of some of these women lies in their symbolizing the former leaders in the absence of direct male heirs capable of taking their places. The transformation of Mrs. Bandaranaike and Athulathmudali from housewives to party leaders underscores their potential as unifying forces against the backdrop of serious party internal crises. Thus, inheritance has legitimated their leaderships.

Many interviewees[3] did not have a clear understanding about the importance of the inclusion of women in the party structures. Some female MPs even said that they could not remember the total number of female members of the Central/Working Committee of their parties. This demonstrates the lack of interest in their party structures and inclusion of women in them. Two female leaders emphasized boldly that it was their 'inherent' right to represent higher committees since they had been contributing actively to their parties. One female MP described how her father took initiatives to establish a political foundation for her and since then how she has been contributing to her party. Also, she expressed her unhappiness regarding a gender quota to increase women's representation in elected bodies.[4] Her point was that general women who have no political experiences or ambitions should not be pushed by others (*meant NGOs*) to political bodies.

Sri Lankan political parties, notwithstanding differences in ideology and structure, have not done anything to address the issue of underrepresentation of women in politics. Women are underrepresented at top levels of all parties, and the male leaders have been successful in protecting the patriarchal nature of these structures. Very few women MPs demonstrated their 'genuine' interest in increasing women's representation. The behavior pattern of the majority of women MPs shows that once they enter party politics, they too become 'male politicians' or they just serve as symbols of their husbands or fathers. Some women leaders have occasionally demonstrated their opposition and anger toward the proposal for including more women in political bodies.

Very few leaders of the parties whether female or male have illustrated their genuine interest and commitment to address the issue of including more women in elected bodies. Both female and male leaders are reluctant to initiate a sound discussion on this issue or to convince some of their leaders to recognize its importance. The reasons for this are the perceived fear and threat among leaders of parties regarding a possible internal dispute over this issue and a division of the party. The fear of losing the 'popularity' of party leaders among the second level ranks by challenging the patriarchal party structure was seen as a major barrier by many female candidates. It is obvious that many men who have established their power bases are not ready to give up their positions. According to a Provincial leader: 'in granting election nominations, first we have to consider the sitting members of the elected bodies, then the family members/relatives and/or close associates/friends of leaders, some unsuccessful candidates in previous elections, strong supporters of the party and some young men. Finally, there is no vacancy for women—that is the reality.' Even in the National List, though women's names were included several times, after the elections, they disappeared without the notice of the particular candidate and men were appointed to the Parliament. In 1999, two women were elected to the Uva and North Central Provincial Councils but they were pushed out and their seats were given to two men.

One can clearly understand this factor by analyzing the changes of status of present prime minister regarding a relevant proposal presented to him. Another factor that hinders women's access to parties is men's patriarchal attitude towards women mainly as 'protectors and decision makers'. A statement made by a former male minister and sent to the Ministry of Women's Affairs at a national event where all female MPs, women's activists and concerned individuals gathered, states that 'men can represent women in an effective way, therefore it is not necessary to have women members to represent their own interests' clearly reveals such beliefs'. He further observed: 'I believe I am the most suitable person to be the Minister of Women's Affairs because my mother is a woman, and my wife is a woman, I have four sisters and three daughters and have looked after around 400 working women, as a manager of a garment factory'.[5] This depicts the general belief of many male political leaders, that it is their 'hereditary' rights/duty to represent and look after women.

Party politics has become a lucrative and competitive income generating avenue in Sri Lanka. Therefore, securing nomination is very competitive and difficult even for a man. Generally, parties have their own priorities to give nominations, and women are not given any space in that. This has been practiced by parties to satisfy mainly the male associates of leaders. In case if they are unhappy or disappointed, many men cross over the party or else create internal disputes. Since many leaders do not want to face such challenges, they are hesitant to exclude men and to include women. The long-standing experiences of men in using power, the patriarchal party structures, negative attitude of party leaders toward women's inclusion in political bodies, and lack of financial ability also have become major barriers to women aspiring to join party politics and/or assume leadership roles.

The low level of inner party democracy also has become another obstacle. Several case studies show that though some national leaders have recognized the importance of the issue, the local leaders do not allow women to come out of their shells. In case where there is a little space, the local leaders push their family members, mainly a man, if not available a woman. National leaders often try to avoid conflicts due to the fear of breaking down of parties by keeping quiet or just by listening to the local leader.[6] Also, the lack of courage, willingness, and commitment of party leaders at least to initiate a discussion on this issue can be identified as another barrier to accommodating women.

The authoritarian nature of some party leaders too has negatively influenced individuals who plan to initiate discussion about changing such conservative traditions or challenging the party structures. Such vocal persons have been marginalized/expelled from the party by the leaders in the past. These incidents have not only provided negative precedence but also created fear and suspicion among women's minds than men in the middle level of party hierarchies. Furthermore, ethnic parties such as SLMC, CWC, and JHU do not show any support to increase women's representation, probably due to their ideological stances and inability to find sufficient number of capable or qualified women for party positions and election nominations. This factor has been used as a main 'excuse' by both major parties for more than two decades in objecting to any relevant proposal for increase in women's representation.

WOMEN AS CANDIDATES IN GENERAL AND PROVINCIAL ELECTIONS

In Sri Lanka, it is difficult to give an accurate number of women contesting elections due to lack of gender-segregated data. In general, the percentage of women candidates is very low. As Table 7.1 shows, it varied from 0.3 in 1947 to 9.5 in 2015. The maximum percentage of women nominated in national elections between 1947 and 2004 was in 1965—3.2. However, the situation changed quite significantly in 2015 when more than 6000 candidates contested the elections, of which more than 500 were women, who represented parties and independent groups. Even in 2015, there were 81 (2.2) women to 3653 men candidates nominated only by parties. Among the parties, JVP fielded 4.3% women in 2015, and the United Lanka People's party the highest (33.3%). The two main coalitions led by major parties fielded only around 1.9% of women candidates. Ethnic parties such as SLMC and JHU have never nominated a single woman at any general election. In 1994, the two main parties nominated women as their presidential candidates. Although the UNP did not initially plan to field a woman candidate, it did so after the assassination of the official candidate—Gamini Dissanayake (Liyanage 1998).

The percentage of women candidates nominated by all the parties and independent groups for Provincial Council elections in 1989 was 2.8. The percentage, however, increased in subsequent elections—3.5 in 1993, 3.7 in 2004, and 4.5 in 2008. Generally, stiff competition among the aspiring candidates is widely noticed during the nomination process. It is often said that a candidate cannot win an election without a 'base support,' a well-known name, and money. According to some women

Table 7.1 Total candidates nominated and the percentage of women in general elections (1947–2015)

Candidates	Year of election														
	1947	1952	1956	1960 March	1960 July	1965	1970	1977	1989	1994	2001	2004	2015
Total	360	305	249	899	393	493	437	756	672	692	738	624	3653
Women	3	10	7	11	7	16	13	20	13	20	20	17	81
Women (%)	0.8	3.3	2.8	1.2	1.8	3.2	2.9	2.6	1.9	2.9	2.7	2.7	2.2
Women elected	3	2	4	3	3	6	6	10	12	10	11	11	13

Source Calculated by the author from data related to general elections 1947–2015—nominations given by parties only and nominations of independent groups are not included. 2010 data is also not included activists, 'although there is a selection criterion, in practice it is done on some "hidden" factors such as financial ability, family and individual connections of the candidate with party leaders.'

Among 34 women who were nominated by political parties, between 1947 and 1994 general elections in Sri Lanka, 25 had or have come from political families and they were nominated as substitutes for a father's, husband's, or a brother's vacant seat.[7] This study demonstrates that many younger men are supported by senior male political leaders to get nomination but many younger women are not supported by women leaders. One vocal female activist emphasized that there are not many women in the higher level of parties with leadership qualities, and skills to influence the party leaders. However, according to some male party leaders, there are not many women with leadership skills to merit nominations.

WHY SO FEW NOMINATIONS?

The study has identified several factors which have hindered women representation in political bodies. In Sri Lanka, generally major parties with strong electoral support and ability to win the elections do not nominate women. Therefore, difficulty in obtaining nomination has become a major barrier for women to represent in political bodies. According to experiences of many women politicians, men always push out women and help other men to get nominations or to be party office bearers. Such men use various strategies such as spreading rumors, emphasizing on their 'weaknesses,' threatening, blocking their opportunities to establish close associations with leaders, and discouraging to do so. Some local women who have been trained and pushed by several women's organizations failed to secure party nominations though they had worked years for their parties. Although they joined smaller parties or independent groups, it is extremely hard to win the elections.[8] Almost all studies done on this issue have shown that due to nepotism, gender stereotypes, gendered socialization process, gendered roles, relations, and identities, patriarchal nature of party structures, political violence, and lack of financial and muscle power, women are at a disadvantage (de Alwis 1995; Leitan 2000; Liyanage 1996, 1998, 1999, 2000, 2005, 2012; 2013; Kodikara 2009).

Generally, parties select winnable candidates and in the Sri Lankan political culture, women are not considered as strong, popular, and winnable candidates. Because the candidates' popularity depends on the material benefits they distribute, the way they attend public events and demonstrate their power. According to the gathered information, many male candidates spend around 30–40 lakhs of Rupees on election propaganda to distribute materials among voters. Some respondents pointed out that 'even if women candidates have funds they do not distribute materials and alcohol etc. similar to men, because they are generally thrifty.' They believe that this is due to the different socialization process undergone by men and women.

Many male political leaders interviewed view politics as a 'masculine' activity and women are not suitable for it. The majority of respondents considered political violence such as threatening women candidates, not allowing to organize meetings, following by motor bicycles, destroying their posters and properties, spreading rumors on them, and attacking their family members/supporters as main obstacles to women's active political participation. Moreover, many men generally do not encourage women by appreciating their political activities because they want to undermine and place them in subordinate positions. As a result, many women do not develop their self-confidence.

Sri Lankan women are generally socialized to be shy, naïve, polite, and peaceful; therefore, many women do not want to challenge the male political domain in an aggressive manner because they do not want themselves to be considered 'unfeminine' by the society. Almost all relevant studies have illustrated that the existing political culture of Sri Lanka, mainly violent nature of election propaganda, aggressive campaigns, 'gift—distributing,' male-dominated decision making in parties, late-night 'drinking' parties, informal networking, and character assassinations, has pushed women into disadvantaged positions (CENWOR 1995; De Silva 1995; Kiribamune 1998; Kodikara 2009; Liyanage 1996, 1998, 1999, 2000, 2005, 2013; Samarasinghe 2000; Wickramasinghe and Kodikara 2012).

Many voters also do not consider women as suitable representatives. They compare the characteristics given by the society to women with those of men and vote for male candidates who possess 'masculine' leadership characteristics. The majority of voters measure the level of the leadership by using very traditional sociopsychological indicators. This is due to two main reasons: First, women are socialized in a different manner and they believe that it is natural for them to behave as 'women' or in a 'feminine' way. But the society still believes that such 'feminine' characteristics and behavior are not appropriate for a political leader. Second, the majority of women are not given opportunities to play leadership roles; therefore, they have not improved their skills compared to men or up to the level of the expectations of the society.

Lack of women's visibility in political forums, mainly on electronic media, lack of competence in delivering public speeches, and organizing attractive propaganda meetings and lack of bargaining skills have been considered by the voters as 'negative or weak points' of women. Thus, masculine nature of party politics, the violent political culture, and some conservative attitudes toward women have influenced to worsen this situation. Lack of nation-wide strong and established women's campaign to lobby for women's representation too has been identified as a major barrier in this regard. Though some women's organizations and few individuals genuinely take interest in this issue, some of their activities are short-term, project-based or are confined to election periods, and no continuity is seen until achieving the final goal. The majority of women's organizations also lack strong lobbying skills, resources, and abilities in organizing nation-wide campaigns/demonstrations.

WOMEN'S ROLE AS ELECTED REPRESENTATIVES

The number of women elected to the national legislature has varied. Only 3.0% of the total members in the first Parliament elected in 1947 were women. The percentage decreased to 1.9 in 1960. It increased up to 3.8% in 1970 and after that it has been increasing very slowly. However, since 1989, this percentage has ranged between 4.0 and 5.8%. It was only in the 1977 parliament that the percentage of women's representation increased up to 6.5%. Until 1977, women elected as MPs belonged to left-of-center parties. After that, the majority of women parliamentarians have come from either the UNP or the SLFP. At the 2010 general election, the UNP nominated one woman and the UPFA two women to the Parliament from the national list. Between 1947 and 2010, there were/have been 23 women parliamentarians from the UNP, 26 from the SLFP, or PA and UPFA coalitions, three from the LSSP, and one from the CP and two from the JVP.

However, the total number of women remains very low and since the 1980s, it has never exceeded 13 (Table 7.2). There have been only five Tamil women MPs (UNP—3 and TNA—2) and two Muslim women (SLFP led PA/UPFA—1 & JVP—1). In the 2015 general election,

Table 7.2 Elected women according to political parties: 1947–2015

Political Parties	Year of election													
	1947	1952	1956	1960 March	1960 July	1965	1970	1977	1989	1994 N = 225	2001	2004	2010	2015 N = 224
LSSP	1	1	1	1	2		4							
CP		1												
UNP				1		4	1	9	4	4	4	3	5	7
SLFP/PA	1					1	1	1	8	5	5	8	8	5
UPFA														
MEP	1		2			1								
Jathika Vimukthi Peramuna			1	1	1									
TNA											2			
JVP										1				1
Total	3	2	4	3	3	6	6	10	12	10	11	11	13	13

Source Calculated by the author—General election results 1947–2015

11 women (6—UNP/UNF, 5—SLFP/UPFA) were elected and one from each UNP and TNA has been appointed from the national list. There are two Tamil Women among them (1—UNP, 1—TNA). The percentage of women Provincial Councilors in 1989 was 2.8%. In 1993, it was 4.7%, 1999—3.2%, 2004—5.0, and in 2008/09—4.8.

Even when nominated to contest, it would appear that women do not have equal opportunities with men at an election. All women MPs and Provincial Councilors interviewed said that they had to face various difficulties during elections. The organizational structure of parties makes no allowance for the special difficulties faced by women. Therefore, one can easily agree with Jayawardena's (1986, p. 129) statement made two decades ago: 'Women's representation in the national legislature has never been more than 4%, and participation at local government levels has also been insignificant. The few women who have successfully contested and made a name for themselves in the political process have generally entered politics as a result of a death of a father or husband, inheriting, as it were the male's mantle power, even after completing more than five decades after receiving universal suffrage.'

Women MPs do not have the same opportunities as men for participation at policymaking levels. From 1947 to 1956, there was not a single woman in the UNP Cabinet. The first woman appointed as a Cabinet Minister—Wimala Wijewardene, Minister of Health (1956–1959), came from the *Mahajana Eksath Peramuna* (MEP). Mrs. Bandaranaike headed the SLFP cabinet as the world's first woman Prime Minister (1960–1965) but did not include any other women in her cabinet. The situation did not change during her premiership between 1970 and 1977. One woman was included in the 1977 UNP Cabinet; this practice had been followed by the UNP until 1994. In 1989, one woman was appointed as a Cabinet Minister and three were appointed as Ministers of State by the UNP. In 1991, two more UNP women were appointed as ministers not in the cabinet. There was one woman in both Cabinets and three Deputy Ministers of PA coalition in 1994 and 1997. In 2000, there were three women in the Cabinet headed by Chandrika Kumarathunga. In 2016, among 92 such ministerial positions there are seven women (7.6%). Under the UPFA government, there was a woman Governor of the Provincial Council and at present there are two women Governors.

Generally, women ministers in Sri Lanka play a minor role since they are given 'soft' portfolios—those related to women, children, youth, social services, health, teaching hospitals, local government, or rural development; these are also considered as 'less influential' or 'feminine.' Except when a woman is the head of government, they have never been appointed to the more 'powerful' ministries that deal with the budget, foreign affairs, or armed forces. However, few women Ministers who were/are in 2001, 2004, 2010, and 2015 cabinets had/have been assigned slightly different portfolios, such as transport, highways, electricity and power, land, plan implementation, and foreign employment, and it may be considered as a new trend toward changing the traditional mindsets of male political leaders.

The information gathered illustrates that majority of women ministers perceive themselves and are perceived by male party leaders as being in the right place only when dealing with problems mainly related to their lives.[9] Thus, similar to the party hierarchies, at the top level of government also the majority of women representatives has not played powerful roles and just followed the policies of their male heirs. Therefore, they have not questioned about or not challenged the patriarchal nature of political structures. Even leaders such as Mrs. Bandaranaike and Chandrika Kumaratunga did not pay any serious attention on political empowerment of other women or changing the male-dominated party structures. Women Parliamentary Caucus, formed in 2006 with the objective of initiating and promoting legislation on women's issues, mostly remained ineffective possibly due to the paucity of women representatives and the lack of party support (Wickramasinghe and Kodikara 2012, p. 805).

The Parliamentary Caucus formed in 2006 with all 13 women MPs as members had several discussions with party leaders, women activists, and academics and presented three recommendations to the Parliamentary Select Committee on Electoral Reform (PSCER): (a) one of every five National List nominees be women; (b) create multi-member constituencies in comparatively large electorates to have two nominations—one for a man and one for a woman; and (c) in a mixed system of representation which combines the simple majority and the proportional representative system, every third person in the party electoral list should be a woman. The PSCER, in its Interim Report made public in 2007, made two recommendations: First, political parties should include provisions in their policies to ensure nominations of women candidates in order to guarantee better representation of women in Parliament, Provincial Councils, and local government bodies; and second, necessary legal provisions be formulated to make it mandatory that every third candidate nominated by a party secretary from the National List be a woman candidate (Interim Report of the Parliamentary Select Committee on Electoral Reform, June 5, 2007).

The Local Authorities Elections (Amendment) Bill, presented to the Parliament in 2010, provided that 25% of the total number of candidates and additional persons whose names appeared in each nomination paper might consist of women and youth. The Bill was passed by the Parliament in 2012 but without any mention on gender quota or a special provision to ensure women's political representation. In 2013, a private member Bill was brought by a female opposition MP providing for the amendment of the Local Authorities Elections Ordinance. It proposed that women and youth should, respectively, have 30 and 20% nominations in each local election. However, the MP was not allowed to move the bill on the ground that it did not have the prior approval of the Attorney General (Gomez and Jayawardena 2014). Nor do women always speak for women when there is an opportunity to do so. During the debate around the Prevention of Domestic Violence Bill in Parliament in 2005, many women MPs did not speak at all on the issue—signaling clearly that they did not consider themselves as representatives of women's or gender issues, and through extension, perhaps even women as a sex/gender (801). Some women MPs also did not support abortion when parties allowed free votes on the issue in Parliament (Wickramasinghe and Kodikara 2012, p. 803).

PARTIES AND GOVERNMENT: TOWARD REDEFINING ROLE

It is widely recognized that there exist widespread restrictions on the empowerment of women in Sri Lanka. Both the government and the mainstream parties have apparently followed a policy biased toward men, while women have often been sidelined for various reasons as explained earlier. In recent years, some change in the attitude of both can be noticed. Since 2000s, both major parties have been reiterating their commitment to increase women's political representation. Wickramasnighe and Kodikara (2012) mentioned that there is no doubt that they have discursively recognized the problem of women's under representation as evinced by their political rhetoric, going to the extent of committing to increasing women in politics in their election manifestoes. Yet, concrete action continues to remain elusive (Wickramasnighe and Kodikara 2012). When questioned about ensuring women's representation, both major parties have given similar excuses. According to them, 'these are not demands of general women and they are just the interest of elite or middle class, urban women. Sri Lankan women have gained many achievements, they are a "privileged" group and enjoy equal status with men and as a Buddhist country women are considered as the "center" of the family.'

During the ethnic conflict of Sri Lanka, both parties gave the priority to find solutions to the ethnic issue as the most important task of the nation but not to this issue. The socialist parties in Sri Lanka emphasize that they treat men and women equally and do not consider women's issues as special issues. Some changes in the attitude of government toward the empowerment of women are also noticeable. In 2015, immediately after the Presidential elections, the Ministry of Women's Affairs and the NCW appointed a Sub-Committee to prepare a proposal to increase women's political representation. When the Committee presented the proposal to the Prime Minister (March 6, 2015), he vowed to resolve this issue observing that: 'the issue related to women's political representation has been dragging for last three decades and this time we should definitely find a solution to this issue.' He promised to discuss it with other party leaders and then to present it to the Cabinet. Minister of women's Affairs and another female leader of the UNP, who did not win the 2015 general elections, took much interest in preparing and presenting this report to the Prime Minister. The Cabinet approved in 2015 a proposal to amend the Provincial Councils Act No 2 of 1988, providing that at least 30% of total candidates included in nominations list submitted by parties and independent groups should be women.

The MoWA and the NCW under the UNP government prepared a Women's Rights Bill with the support of women's groups and both major parties pledged to make it a law. However, the Bill has been languishing for many years due to many obstacles. As Gomez and Jayawardena (2014, p. 5) mention 'in this particular instance, governments have been reluctant to translate their unenforceable policy declarations into actual law.' Nor does the government appear to be very keen to translate its commitment for the empowerment of women into action.

For example, at a national event organized to commemorate the International Women's Day (March 8, 2015, in Anuradhapura), the Prime Minister reiterated his commitment to resolve the issue of women's underrepresentation in politics. Yet, after two days, at a similar event (March 10, 2015, at the Bandaranaike Memorial International Centre, Colombo), organized by the Parliamentary Women's Caucus, the Prime

Minister emphasized that 'it is extremely hard to increase women's representation since men do not like to give up their positions.' As an alternative, he suggested to increase the total number of representatives of all elected bodies and office bearers of parties in order to give a space for women because men are not ready to give up their 'established positions.' This clearly shows that his 'fear of a possible threat' may have come from opposing groups. At a recent meeting, when the Prime Minister was inquired about the 20th amendment to the Constitution and the inclusion of women's demand he said that 'affirmative action should be introduced at the local level and not at the national level.'

This shows that on one hand, the leaders are reluctant/hesitant to challenge the male-dominated power-base of parties and on the other hand, women's lobbying is not strong enough to shake this power-base. These experiences illustrate that lack of sensitivity, lack of genuine interest, and lack of commitment of party leaders in increasing women's representation in their party hierarchies and elected bodies. All governments have mainly targeted rural women or poor women in plantation, garment, and migrant workers' industry. The study shows that the male as well as female leaders of the parties whether democratic or socialist have used electoral democracy in a clever manner to improve women's socioeconomic status in a way to obtain their efficient contribution to the family as well as the economy but to exclude them carefully from important public positions and to maintain and strengthen the patriarchal nature of the private and public spheres.

CONCLUSION

This study concludes on two contradictory situations, the active role of women as voters and party members and a very low representation in the elected bodies of Sri Lanka at the national and provincial levels. Therefore, women have been excluded from key governing institutions and pushed into the second-class citizens. Despite the fact that Sri Lanka has had seven decades of independence and democracy, politics still continues to be dominated by men thereby causing constraints for women to participate actively in governance. As a result, Sri Lanka has not yet achieved gender inclusive governance according to its political dimension. To achieve gender inclusive governance, it is necessary to challenge the patriarchal dominance of the political bodies and for that intervention, there should be a well-organized women's movement as well as interim measures such as the affirmative action or quota system.

Notes

1. The author is grateful to the NORHED project on Democracy and Governance, University of Peradeniya for granting a fund to undertake research (Oct. 2015—Sep. 2016) on 'Inhibiting or Increasing Women's Representation: Role of Political Parties in Sri Lanka.' Some information gathered for this study has been used to compile this chapter.
2. FDGs—members of Women's Wings—UNP & SLFP—2015.
3. Interviewed—29 female and 42 male political leaders at national level (1994–2015).
4. Interviewed—female MP—1998 and in 2009, meeting of the Parliamentary Women's Caucus.
5. The researcher delivered the key note address on 'Importance of Increasing Women's Political Representation' at this event organized by the Women Media.
6. The information received from interviews conducted with male and female candidates and mainly local-level political leaders before and after the 2011 local elections.
7. The researcher interviewed 21 women out of these 34 women candidates (2001–2016).
8. Seventy-nine women, aspiring to run for local election 2011 in the Central Province, were trained or supported by Women for Peace and Good Governance (WPGG). Though party leaders were influenced in various ways, only 31 women were given nominations, mainly by smaller parties. Among the 48 candidates whose nominations were rejected, 32 joined minor parties or independent groups to obtain nominations, but only ten woman won the election (UPFA—5, UNP-2, SLMC—1, *kandurata Janatha Peramuna*—1, and Ceylon Workers Congress—1).
9. During the period between 1994 and 2016, the researcher has interviewed 19 male and 12 female Cabinet, Non-Cabinet, or State Ministers and six female Deputy Ministers.

References

Beall, J. (1996). Urban governance: Why gender matters. Available at www.ucl.ac.uk/dpu-projects/drivers_urb_change/urb_society/pdf_gender/UNDP_Beall_gender_matters.pdf. Accessed April 5, 2016.

Center for Women's Research (CENWOR). (1995). Women, political empowerment and decision making: Report of a workshop No. 55. Colombo: Center for Women's Research.

Dahlerup, D. (1988). From a small to a large minority: Women in Scandinavian politics. *Scandinavian Political Studies, 11*(4), 275–298.

Dahlerup, D. (Ed.). (2007). *Women, quotas and politics.* London: Routledge.

de Alwis, M. (1995). *Gender politics and the 'respectable lady Unmaking the nation: The politics of Identity and History in Modern Sri Lanka* (pp. 137–157), P. Jeganathan & Q. Ismail (Eds.). Colombo: Social Scientists Association.

De Silva, W. (1995). Political participation of women in Sri Lanka 1985–1995. In *Facets of change: Women in Sri Lanka 1986–1995.* Colombo: Centre for Women's Research.

Gomez, S., & Jayawardena, K. (2014). *State's response to gender equality and women's demands for reform in legal, institutional and public spheres,* Colombo: Social Scientists' Association. Available at http://www.unp.lk/index.pup/proposedconstitution/English. Accessed March 28, 2015.

Inter Parliamentary Union. (2014). Universal declaration on democracy. Available at www.ipu.org/cnl/-e/161-dem.htm. Accessed on March 21 2016.

Jayawardena, K. (1986). *Feminism and nationalism in the third world.* London: Zed Books.

Kearney, R. N. (1983). The political party system in Sri Lanka. *Political Science Quarterly, 98*(1), 17–33.

Kiribamune, S. (1998). *Women and politics in Sri Lanka: A comparative perspective.* Kandy: International Centre for Ethnic Studies.

Kodikara, C. (2009). *The struggle for Equal Political representation of women in Sri Lanka.* Colombo: Ministry of Child Development and Women's Empowerment and United Nations Development Programme.

Leitan, T. (2000). Women in political Participation and Decision making. *Post Beijing Reflections: Women in Sri Lanka 1995–2000* (pp. 116–127). Colombo: Center for Women's Research.

Liyanage, K. (1992). *Women in national politics: A comparative study between Japan and Sri Lanka.* Colombo: CENWOR.

Liyanage. K. (1996). Pary women: Their role in Sri Lankan Politics. *Pakistan Journal of Women's studies,* Vol. 3:3 pp. 13–32.

Liyanage, K. (1998). Women in political parties: The Sri Lankan experience. In S. Kiribamune (Ed.), *Women and politics in Sri Lanka: A comparative perspective.* International Centre for Ethnic Studies: Kandy.

Liyanage, K. (1999). Electoral system and women's representation. In L. Fernando, & D. Kneitschel (Eds.), *New Electoral system for Sri Lanka.* Colombo: Friedrich Ebert Stiftung.

Liyanage, K. (2000). Sri Lankan Women: Gender, Citizenship and Political Representation. *Sambhavana* (Vol. 1, July–Dec, pp. 151–181).

Liyanage, K. (2005). Women in Local Self-governance in Sri Lanka: Dilemmas and Challenges. In M. Perera, & R. Chandrasekera (Eds.), *Excluding women* (pp. 123–144). Colombo: Social Scentisists Association.

Liyanage, K. (2013). *Women's representation in local governments in Sri Lanka: Challenges and expectations.* Colombo: Fedrich Ebert Stiftung.

Liyanage, P. (2012). *Women in politics in Sri Lanka: The left movement.* Colombo: CENWOR.

Mettananada, T. (1981). *Votes for women 1923–1931—Universal Franchise 1931–1981: The Sri Lanka experience.* Colombo: Department of Information.

Phillips, A. (1995). *The politics of presence.* Oxford: Clarendon Press.

Rule, W., & Zimmerman, J. F. (Eds.). (1994). *Electoral systems in comparative perspective: Their impact on women and minorities.* Westport, CT: Greenwood.

Samarasinghe, V. (2000). Subverting patriarchy? Leadership and participation of women in politics in South Asia. *Ethnic Studies Report, 18*(2).

Sawer, M. (2000). Representation of women: Questions of accountability. In Paper presented at IPSA Conference, Quebec. Aug 1–5.

United Nations Development Program (UNDP). (2007). *Towards inclusiveness governance: Promoting the participation of disadvantaged groups in Asia Pacific.* Bangkok: UNDP Regional Centre.

Wickramasinghe, M., & Kodikara, C. (Eds.). (2012). Representation in politics: Women and gender in the Sri Lankan Republic. In Asanga Welikala and Vikalpa Pratipatti Kendraya (eds.) *The Sri Lankan Republic at 40,* Colombo: Center for Policy Alternatives. Available at http://www.worldcat.org/title/sri-lankan-republic-at-40-reflections-on-constitutional-history-theory-and-practice/oclc/835799089. Accessed April 4, 2015.

Wilson, A. J. (1979). *Politics of sri Lanka, 1947–1979.* London: Macmillan.

Women's Bureau of Sri Lanka. (1984). *Impact of the UN decade for women in Sri Lanka.* Colombo: Women's Bureau.

PART II

Women in Civil Service

CHAPTER 8

Balancing Work and Family: Women in Bangladesh Civil Service

Nishat Afroze Ahmed and Ferdous Jahan

Bangladesh, one of the world's top 10 most populous countries with around 160 million people, has graduated from a low-income country to lower-middle-income country status, based on its US$1190 per capita gross national income (GNI) in 2015. Equally impressive is the substantial decline in the incidence of poverty. Between 2000 and 2010, the number of people living below the poverty line of US$1.90 per day (2011 purchasing power parity) fell from 44 million (33.7% of population) to 28 million (18.5% of population). The country has also made remarkable gains in human development indicators over the past decades. It has experienced substantial improvements in key education, health, nutrition, and population outcomes, including several health-related MDG targets. However, Bangladeshi women have not been doing well. They continue to be disempowered on the economic front relative to men. Data from the Bangladesh Bureau of Statistics (BBS) 2015 and the Labor Force Survey (LFS) of 2013 show that only

N.A. Ahmed (✉)
University of Chittagong, Chittagong, Bangladesh
e-mail: nishat_abha@yahoo.com

F. Jahan
University of Dhaka, Dhaka, Bangladesh
e-mail: jahan70@gmail.com

© The Author(s) 2018
N. Ahmed (ed.), *Women in Governing Institutions in South Asia*,
DOI 10.1007/978-3-319-57475-2_8

one-third (33.5%) of eligible women were in the labor force in 2013 compared to the vast majority (over 80%) of eligible men (ILO 2016).

With regard to women's employment in public sector, most of the women employees are found in directorates/attached offices (91.4% in 2010), while only 0.6% work in ministries and divisions. The majority of working women, however, hold subordinate positions; only a few occupy class i positions. However, there has been a steady increase in the representation of women in the higher civil service of Bangladesh (BCS cadres) over the years. For example, the percentage of women qualifying to join (28) different BCS cadres increased threefold in one decade—from 10.7% in 1994 to 30.2% in 2004. Women also performed better than men in the 32nd BCS examination; more than 55.0% of the total candidates qualified to join the civil service were women. The percentage of women at mid-level and senior level also increased from 8.5 in 1999 to 15.0 in 2006 and 21.0 in 2011 (Sultan and Jahan 2016; BBS 2012).

Notwithstanding such increase, women still lag behind men in their participation in civil service. Despite equal opportunities guaranteed by the Constitution and 10% reserved quota for women in civil service, the overall rate of participation of women is still low. The question remains why do we see low participation of women in civil service despite having favorable economic and social development as well as pro-women affirmative recruitment policies. Most scholarly articles and research concentrate on inter-bureaucratic structural and cultural constraints while trying to answer this question (Sultan and Jahan 2016). This article argues that both intra-organizational and intra-household relationships and gender norms put women in a delicate situation when they enter the civil service. Balancing family and work often becomes too difficult for women that results in discouraging women to enter and excel in civil service.

Based on empirical research, this chapter identifies problems women at work in Bangladesh face and strategies they adopt to overcome such problems, particularly to balance work and family roles. Data for this study were collected from both primary and secondary sources. Secondary sources included review of books, articles, research monographs, and reports published in newspapers and magazines. For collecting primary information, a questionnaire survey was undertaken in January–February 2016. Structured questionnaires were administered among 53 women officials of different cadres in the Bangladesh Civil Service (BCS). Respondents belonged to the following cadres: administration, health, education, livestock, and forest. We also interviewed some women working in the civil service to check their views on how they cope with demands of combining work and family. The chapter is organized into eight sections. The following section tries to identify a framework for discussion of the issue of balancing home and family role. Section three provides a statistical account of the entry and advancement of women in the civil service, while section four explores the reasons underlying this development. Opportunities and constraints faced by women working for the government are explored in the next two sections. Two types of constraints—work-related and home-related—have been identified, and the way they deal with these constraints has been explored in section five and section six, respectively. Section seven identifies and explains the way(s) working women seek to balance work and family roles, while section eight concludes the chapter.

WORK–FAMILY BALANCE: A FRAMEWORK FOR DISCUSSION

Balancing work and family life is a critical challenge in most countries of the world, and current social trends are making its integration more laborious (Chinchilla et al. 2010, p. 7). It is now conventional wisdom that working women everywhere play multiple roles; such roles often conflict, causing further stress and inconvenience. Although women have taken on employment outside the home, their household duties have usually remained more or less the same. Several expressions such as double duty, double day, second shift, or double burden (Beaujot and Liu 2005; Berk 1985; Hoschchild 1989) have been coined to describe this phenomenon. Handling of many things at a time very often causes stress. Double-day work invariably implies double burden, and many women fail to deal with this problem in an effective manner. There are, however, counter arguments that multiple roles may be a source of well-being. Rodin and Ickovics (2005, p. 279) argue that being involved in multiple roles expends possible resources and rewards such as different sources of self-esteem and social support. Dissatisfaction in one role may not create any serious stress as a more rewarding role may create a balance (Rodin and Ickovics, p. 279).

Central to the literature of working women is the issue of how they balance work and family roles. Available literature shows that the two roles—work and family—often conflict. Such conflicts, however, do not affect different categories of women in the same way. Herman and Gyllstrom (1977) observe that married women experience more work–family conflict than that of the unmarried ones. Some studies have found that parents of younger children experience more conflict than do parents of older children (Beutell and Greenhaus 1980), while large families are seen as more prone to work–family conflict than small families (Keith and Schafer 1980). Beutell and Greenhaus (1982) also argue that women whose career orientations are dissimilar from those of their husbands experience relatively intense conflict between home and non-home roles. Work–family conflict is also associated with the amount of time an employee spends in work place (Keith and Schafer 1980). There is a possibility of conflict in case of employees working overtime or are engaged in strenuous jobs. Ambiguity and/or conflict within the work role have been found to be positively related to work–family conflict.

There is no 'one best way' to deal with the problem of double-day work. As women face the demands of combining work and family, they develop strategies for organizing their lives and accomplishing many tasks (Zarra-Nezhad et al. 2010; Ajaz et al. 2015). Such strategies differ from one country to another. In the UK, for example, although women sometime rely on relatives/friends, the main method used is to turn to formal childcare arrangement and prioritization (White 1999). Working women in the USA, Germany, and France also follow similar strategies to cope with the problem. Pocock (2003) has observed that Australian women balance work and family life mostly by doing part-time jobs. Brazil provides a deviant case. Working mothers in Brazil get a generous 4–6 months leave, and they even have the option to work part time until their child becomes a year old. Smith and Converse provide a succinct account of the way working women try to balance work and home roles, although the extent of success is difficult to measure. As they observe:

> While paid employment takes priority in scheduling time, women do negotiate with their employers and adapt their work hours when necessary, to make themselves available for their families. Working mothers often use weekends to catch up on household chores from the previous week and prepare for the coming week. Sometimes they lower their expectations of what absolutely must be done and reduce their housework so that they can spend free time with their families, and they ask their partners and children to share with the load. Double day work provides many time management challenges for women (Smith and Converse 2012, pp. 1–2).

Working women in developing countries, while facing similar, if not the same, problems, often have to follow somewhat different strategies to balance the conflict. Part of the reason is the lack of options available to women in developing countries, and partly because of sociocultural factors. Research shows that family has traditionally provided an important source, enabling working women to deal with the problem, particularly in Asian societies. As Chinchilla, Herras, and Torres have observed: 'Family has been the fundamental building block of society for centuries. Families contribute to society and personal well-being in the private sphere, as well as create social capital for companies and for the community' (2010, p. 9). The support structure immediately given by family to working mothers in the developing countries is one of the most important sources to help reduce stress both at work and at home when compared to working women in Western countries.

However, although the family takes precedence in highly collectivistic societies, it is also recognized that paid work is crucial to ensure decent lives for family members or at least to make ends meet (Caparas, p. 139). It is often the failure to recognize the latter (by family members) that leads to conflict. The dilemma facing policymakers is to evolve ways to make work and family as allies (Chinchilla et al. p. 10), not adversaries. No simple prescription can be made. However, responsibility tends to lie more with employers than with family as the most significant determinant of work–family conflict is found in the work domain (Warner and Hausdorf 2009), not at home. What is immediately needed is the introduction of family supportive strategies [by employers] (Rimi 2014, pp. 88–89), although it is difficult to prescribe any standard formula for such support. It will vary depending on the geographic region or culture. As Chinchilla et al. (2010, p. 10) have argued:

> In cultures where large extended families are the norm, child-care needs will not be the same as those in cultures where there is less family centeredness ... Countries with high-quality educational systems and good transportation infrastructures will have different work-family needs than those with poorer systems.

However, although the involvement of extended family can be seen as a support (as well as a strain) for working parents, the availability of family supportive strategies, for example supportive work cultures, supportive supervisors, and family-friendly benefits, may be seen as important prerequisites to make work and family as 'allies.' No universal strategies can, however, be found or suggested as the needs, problems, and priorities of working women may vary from one culture to another. What is nevertheless observed is that a combination of inside (family support) and outside support (family supportive strategies) may be seen as an important way of helping working women balance work and home roles.

WOMEN IN BANGLADESH CIVIL SERVICE: FROM 'MINIMAL' TO 'MARGINAL' REPRESENTATION

Bangladesh emerged as an independent country on December 16, 1971. The new nation began with 399,839 officers and employees, which included 48,000 armed personnel (Ahmed 1986, p. 153). The Interim Recruitment Policy (IRP), announced in early 1972, provided for reserving 30% of posts for freedom fighters (FFs), 40% as district quotas, 10% for affected women, and 20% to be recruited on the basis of merit in the case of class i positions. In other cases (non-gazetted), recruitment would be done on a district quota basis. The quota system was revised in 1976 when provisions for reserving 10% of regular posts for women were introduced in the Constitution. Following a 1985 revision, the provision for reserving 10% of posts for affected women was abolished, but the general women quota was retained. Half (5%) of the 10% of quota, so long reserved for affected women, was now earmarked for merit, and the other half (5%) was allocated to the women from small ethnic communities. There is no merit quota in case of recruitment to class iii and class iv positions. Since 1976, women have joined the higher civil service (BCS cadres) on a regular basis. The percentage of women candidates has also increased over the years, so also has their performance (Table 8.1).

Initially, it was difficult to fill up the 10% of posts that was reserved for women. But now women not only have surpassed the permissible limit; more women now join the service on the merit quota (Table 8.2). Initially, women were not allowed to join the police service and some other services, partly for their physical strength and partly for the technical nature of the cadres. The IRP did not apply to technical posts, posts of defense services and to such other posts as may be considered unsuitable for women by the concerned ministry (Khan, p. 40). No such restriction, however, exists now. As a result, more women now join the civil service.

Table 8.1   Performance of women candidates

Name of BCS exams	Eligible women candidates (%)	Candidates qualified in preliminary test (%)	Candidates qualified in written test (%)	Candidates recommended (%)
28th BCS Exam	31.02	20.85	21.48	30.59
34th BCS Exam	32.35	23.96	25.29	35.63

Source PSC (2014, 2015)

In recent years, as Table 8.3 shows, more women have also succeeded in moving upward in the hierarchy, holding senior positions in greater numbers in the Secretariat, the nerve center of administration and policymaking. Such success can be noticed at all levels—from Assistant Secretary to the level of Secretary (Table 8.3). This implies that that the attitudes of senior men toward women in the civil service are gradually changing. This is partly as they too have wives and daughters engaged in professional work (Sultan and Jahan 2016, p. 159).

However, there is better scope for promotion at the lower level than at the higher level. At more senior levels, as Sultan and Jahan (2016, p. 157) argue, 'there is a feeling that women might not be skilled as men in "maintaining the liaisons" and networking, which are necessary to secure promotions.' Lack of 'enough' exposure or 'visibility' is also a problem (Sultan and Jahan, p. 157).

Table 8.2   An overview of BCS examinees notified in the gazettes (by sex)

Name of BCS exams	Male	Female	Total
5th BCS Exam 1984	678 (89.3)	81 (10.7)	759 (100.0)
16th Sp BCS Exam 1994	873 (69.8)	378 (30.2)	1251 (100.0)
25th BCS Exam 2004	2029 (74.5)	693 (25.5)	2722 (100.0)
26th BCS Exam	703 (66.1)	360 (33.9)	1063 (100.0)
27th BCS Exam	2417 (74.6)	822 (25.4)	3239 (100.0)
28th BCS Exam	1520 (69.4)	670 (30.6)	2190 (100.0)
30th BCS Exam	1622 (68.0)	763 (31.99)	2385 (100.0)
32ndBCS Exam	752 (44.9)	923 (55.1)	1675 (100.0)
33rd BCS Exam	5252 (61.7)	3255 (38.3)	8507 (100.0)
34th BCS Exam	1400 (64.4)	765 (35.6)	2175 (100.0)

Source Karim (2008), PSC (2014, 2015)

Table 8.3 Breakdown by sex of male and female officers at middle and senior levels (1999–2011)

Position	2011		2006		1999	
	Men (%)	Women (%)	Men (%)	Women (%)	Men (%)	Women (%)
Secretary	96.1	3.9	98.4	1.6	98.0	2.0
Additional secretary	94.8	5.2	100.0	0.0	98.2	1.8
Joint secretary	90.2	9.8	93.2	6.8	98.5	1.5
Deputy secretary	88.1	11.9	88.3	11.7	98.6	1.1
Senior assistant secretary	79.8	20.2	84.3	15.7	91.0	9.0
Assistant secretary	74.1	25.9	77.3	22.7	85.7	14.3
Total	79.0	21.0	85.0	15.0	91.5	8.5

Source Sultan and Jahan (2016)

EXPLAINING THE DEVELOPMENT

There is no 'one best way' of explaining the steady increase of women in the civil service. A number of factors account for it, of which the affirmative action policy (quota system) is the most important. In particular, in the early years of the civil service, women could not even fill up the vacant seats. Now they perform so well that, as Khan has argued (2015, p. 148), 'quota system is likely to be an obstacle rather than a special facility for them.' The Constitution not only provides for granting women and men similar rights and opportunities; it also allows the state to make special provisions for women and other disadvantaged groups in public employment (GoB 2011). Gender issues now find prominence in different government policies and programs. Special allocations for women's development have routinely been made in different development plans. The Government of Bangladesh (GoB) declared the National Policy for the Advancement of Women (NPAW) on March 8, 1997. It has addressed 14 different and relevant issues where employment and administrative empowerment of women were given special emphasis (GoB 1998).

Several provisions have been made in different legislation for a woman-friendly work environment; these have had some beneficial effects, especially in terms of encouraging women to join the civil service and to stay in it. For example, women undergoing training at BPATC are now allowed to have infants and their attendants live with them at their hostels; this policy helps women ease tension and concentrate more on work/studies. The period of maternity leave has been increased, and paternity leave introduced. Legislation/rules requiring the setting up of childcare centers for children up to 6 years of age, separate wash rooms for women at work place, and punishment for improper behavior with women colleagues have also been introduced (Sultan and Jahan, p. 160). In addition, several other factors such as education, educated and progressive family background, economic necessity, the introduction and expansion of the Internet services, and the resulting modernization of the society have effectively contributed to the increase in the representation of women in the civil service (Ahmed 2016). However, women still face problems and uncertainties that largely hamper their entry and advancement in the civil service. These are explained in subsequent sections.

Working Women in Bangladesh: Opportunities and Constraints

The scope of female employment, as stated earlier, has increased considerably over the last few decades. More women now compete for jobs, and many of them do it successfully. In one sense, they have managed to intrude into what was once considered to be the 'preserve' of men. Those who join the service come from diverse backgrounds. Joining the service is seen as a means to achieving many higher order goals. Motivations for joining the service vary. For example, among the 53 women civil servants, almost all stated that job security (96.2%) and better social prestige (98.1%) have been the prime reasons for joining the service. Another important reason that attracts women to the civil service is the availability of various facilities such as childcare, maternity leave, and provisions for housing and transport. Only a few (16.9%) join the civil service to avail the scope of exercising power. The women officials, almost all of them, have the inclination to serve the public. Officials have a strong desire to continue in the service unless anything serious happens. No one has expressed any serious dissatisfaction with the way they do things in their organizations. Only two out of 53 BCS officials expressed any desire to leave the service.

This, however, does not imply that they can always work in a problem-free environment. In fact, women routinely face many problems and constraints, some of which are insurmountable. These problems can be categorized into two broader groups—work-related and family-related—and are discussed separately in the next two subsections.

PROBLEMS AT WORKPLACE

The main problems that working women face at their workplaces include gender discrimination, overwork, misbehavior of colleagues, and sexual harassment. More than three-quarters of the interviewed respondents considered gender discrimination as more pronounced than any other problems except overwork which tops the list. Misbehavior of colleagues is also a very serious problem. This section identifies reasons that account for these problems, while the next will identify strategies that women officials adopt to cope with these problems and their effectiveness.

Gender discrimination According to the interviewees, women are deprived of their promotions, they are given a different job title, and they are prevented from training opportunities, or posted to less important positions, or/and transferred to very risky positions. Women are also scrutinized more harshly than men; such harsh scrutiny might have some kind of negative impact on their promotion to higher positions. Fifty-three percent of the respondents who were discriminated against on the basis of their gender in their workplaces were posted to less important positions and also scrutinized more harshly than men, whereas about 38% observed that they were deprived of participating in training programs. Reasons for such discrimination are many; these range from jealousy of male colleagues and organizational biases toward men, to their ability to do things in a better way than their male colleagues. Majority of them stated that their organization was biased toward males.

Sexual harassment Sexual harassment—any unwelcome sexual behavior which is offensive, intimidating, or humiliating (Mahtab 2012)—is at least as prevalent as gender discrimination, if not more, in work places. Women who are perceived to be more vulnerable, physically weak, and lack connections with high-ups in the society have been subjected to various forms of sexual harassment. Men even harass their female colleagues if they see that the latter are more capable than they are at work or outside and also use harassment as a weapon for taking revenge against women with whom they have any kind of problems. Nearly one-third of the respondents (31%) stated that they were at least once sexually harassed at their workplaces. Half of the (8) senior officials experienced sexual harassment. Married women officials with children experienced more sexual harassment than those without children. Women at the workplaces are sexually harassed by their male colleagues (senior, junior, and same level) and even outsiders/non-employees. Sexual harassment could be found in various forms.

The dominant modes of sexual harassment that women respondents faced were suggestive comments/jokes, perpetrators using foul or hostile language, benefits made conditional on sexual favors, and the act of staring or leering by male counterparts. Those experiencing sexual harassment observed that the perception and stereotyped gendered characteristics that the society creates and assigns them for being a woman make them vulnerable to sexual harassment. Among other reasons, the respondents stated that as they could not shout when something wrong was being done and their apparent physical weakness gave the perpetrators a chance to harass them. Two respondents in the study found that their beauty and attractiveness were responsible for the harassment they had to undergo.

Misbehavior of colleagues Working women face two other major problems: misbehavior of colleagues and overwork. Male colleagues working at the same level misbehave more than those who are at the senior or junior levels in the workplaces of the women respondents. This does not mean that the high-ups in the organization always behave properly. Twenty-five percent of the women officials complained that their bosses were among those who misbehaved with them in the office. More than 71% stated that male colleagues misbehaved with them while 29% complained about their male seniors. The interviewed respondents experienced misbehavior of various kinds that ranged from verbal abuses, avoidance and spreading of rumors, to passing on bad comments about one's family. Jealousy and the perception that prevailed among the male employees that women were vulnerable were the prime causes of misbehavior.

The majority of the married respondents with children stated that their colleagues misbehaved with them first as they were women and thus vulnerable and also as they came from families with no strong educational or cultural background. On the other hand, married respondents with no children believed that their colleagues perceived them to be vulnerable due to their gender and also considered them as strong competitors and thus wanted to oust them from the office. The jealousy of male colleagues for their female counterpart's achievement is quite natural as males in our society have grown up with the perception that women are less capable and knowledgeable than they are. So when they realize that they lag behind their female colleagues in terms of capability and efficiency, they become jealous which is reflected in their misbehavior. Male colleagues, driven by their ego and self-interest, often intentionally misbehave with their female colleagues at workplaces with the aim of driving out the latter, who are more competent, from their offices.

Overcoming Problems at Workplace

Women civil servants adopt a number of strategies to cope with problems and challenges at workplace. The extent to which such strategies and tactics actually work depends upon a number of factors. For example, those who experience gender discrimination often seek to fight against the injustice, while some prefer to remain silent. None of the respondents preferred to quit jobs to overcome the problem of gender discrimination at their workplaces. About one-fifth of the civil service officials stated that they found no change in the behavior of perpetrators, despite the adoption of several strategies to change their attitude and orientation. Those who faced sexual harassment used different coping strategies which included doing nothing but keeping silent due to fear of stigma, lodging complaints with higher authorities, threatening to file law suit, mobilizing women colleagues to fight against harassment, and trying to avoid perpetrators and other strategies. The majority of the respondents mobilized women colleagues to fight against harassment, and also some chose the safe way of avoiding their perpetrators.

However, when asked whether they slapped their perpetrators, none of them answered in the affirmative which meant they did not want to create any further hassles in their future. The outcome was also positive for most of the respondents as their perpetrators were seen to realize their mistakes and tried to mend their way of behavior. However, it has been observed that two of the married respondents with children were still harassed by their perpetrators. To overcome the problem of misbehavior of colleagues, the respondents adopted a number of strategies.

These included lodging complaint with higher authorities, abusing the culprits verbally, and avoiding the persons misbehaving with colleagues. The majority of the respondents (57.1%) extended their hand of friendship and making colleagues realize their faults. Also, the same percentage of respondents chose the strategy of avoiding their misbehaving colleagues. Only a few (14.3%) chose to complain to higher authorities.

The outcome of the strategies adopted to correct the misbehavior of the respondents is slightly better. Sixty-four percent of the sample respondents believed that their colleagues had become more understanding, 28.5% found no change in misbehavior, while 10.7% reported an increase in misbehavior of colleagues at their workplaces. However, the proportion of married women who had no children and whose colleagues had no change in their bad behaviors was more than the unmarried and also the married officials with children.

CHALLENGES AT HOME

Working women in Bangladesh, as in other countries, are burdened with the dual responsibility of managing both work and family at the same time. It is seen that married women are mostly caught up in this dilemma that ultimately creates stress in their lives and affects their efficiency and effectiveness at work. Though both men and women work in the same workplace, it is perceived in our society that a woman would do all the household chores before going to and after coming back from work. However, nowadays many women prefer nuclear family to joint family to enjoy privacy in their personal lives and to avoid 'interference' which is often noticed in the latter (extended family) . Such a decision has both advantages and disadvantages. Women staying in joint families, if fortunate enough, get relief from the worries of looking after their children when they are at work. But the contention between women and their mothers-in-law that prevails still in today's society apparently takes away energy from women and intensifies their level of stress. Explained below are some of the important problems that the sample respondents faced in their homes.

Managing household chores Women have been traditionally assigned the responsibility of managing the household chores, whereas men are supposed to work outside and earn for the family. The household chores range from cooking, cleaning, and looking after the family members, to addressing their needs, shopping, and keeping minute details about the household. More than half of the respondents in the study replied that they themselves did the household chores (54.7%). In many cases (60.4%), they depended on maidservants in managing the household chore. Working women thus still have to do various household chores before going to office and after returning home from a long day's work. Such dual responsibility causes stress among many women employees. Women respondents, who have to do the household chores after working for 8–10 h a day, become exhausted which eventually affects their level of efficiency at work the next day. It is to be stated here that 32.1% of the sample respondents worked for 8–10 h in the office, while 22.6% worked for more than 10 h. The majority of respondents in the sample, however, lived in extended families. This may be regarded as beneficial to the respondents as their work at home is likely to be shared by other family members.

Looking after children Working mothers are bound to worry for the children they leave behind at home while they are at work. Women officials depend upon more than one source for taking care of their children when they and their husbands are away from home. Thirteen out of the 29 respondents who had children relied on their in-laws for taking care of their children during their absence. Also, 10 relied on maidservants, while eight took help from their parents. Parents and in-laws of women employees are often seen as one of the most reliable, constant, and comfortable sources when the question of taking care of children in their absence arises. None of respondents having children chose the option of daycare centers for taking care of their children. Most of the respondents stated that they did not find having children a barrier to their career development probably for the reason that they had access to dependable sources of taking care of children. Some of them considered having children while building a career was one of the important challenges that working women faced. So if this is a challenge, it means that they do not want to speak out clearly that they are burdened by the dual responsibilities of childcare and workplace in case they hurt their family members or they betray with the unwritten ethics of motherhood.

Managing husband and other members of family One of the important means of reducing overload by a working woman is to seek support from others in the family, especially husband. Working women who have supportive and cooperative husbands can perform their dual responsibility of managing home and work more easily than those who lack such support. Nearly half of the respondents in the sample observed that their husbands were very supportive and cooperative; eight found their husbands to be supportive, and another eight considered their husbands to be supportive but not always. Husbands' support can come in various forms, of which mental support and inspiration are more important than sharing of household chores and looking after children as one can find in developed countries. Some husbands, however, do not like the idea of their wives staying outside at work for long hours. They are more comfortable with the idea that their wives should be confined to the boundaries of home and take care of their children and family members.

The above observations are not intended to imply that the sample women officials did not face problems at home. In fact, facing problems with husbands, such as arguments and clash of opinions regarding decisions, contention with in-laws, especially with mothers-in-law, and irritation created by mismanagements of chores by servants are nothing new in the daily lives of working women in our country. The majority of respondents, when asked if they had any problem at home, answered in the affirmative (20 out of the 39 respondents acknowledged that they had problems at home), while married respondents with children reported that they experienced more problems than the others. The major problems that women faced at home were arguments with husbands and hostility in interpersonal relationships at home. The most dominant method used by the women officials to solve their problems at home was keeping calm and discussing the problems with other family members to reach a solution.

BALANCING WORK AND FAMILY

The environment and culture in which women are born and brought up largely decide the way they will view different challenges confronting them and the manner they will respond to such challenges. The strategies working women adopt to cope with challenges also depend on the type of support structures to which they have access to. Bangladesh is considered to be a collectivist society. Although the culture of individualism is on the rise, it still remains at its infancy. Earlier research (e.g., Hofstede 2005) revealed that Bangladesh scored a low 20 on the dimension of individualism, implying that the culture of collectivism still remains strongly entrenched in the family structure of the country. This can be seen as a manifestation of the way(s) people value their relationships with their families, both immediate and extended, and their commitment to defend the tradition of collectivity. The Bangladesh society combines patriarchal tradition (of giving special importance to masculinity) and collectivistic values, both creating obstacles as well as providing a support structure for women at work.

For coping with challenges at home, women adopt several strategies that are different in nature and effect than those found in Western societies. In extended families, responsibilities for doing household work are shared by many. Unmarried women mostly depend upon parents who readily support their working daughters having a relaxed evening that their counterparts in other countries can rarely expect. For balancing between work and home, working married women adopt various methods as Table 8.4 shows.

The majority of the respondents (79.2%) said that they took support from their family members and relatives to balance their work and home roles. Almost 57% stated that their husbands also supported them in the sharing of works. Among other strategies to balance work and family life, respondents negotiated the flexibility of work hours with their boss (18.9%); some refrained from doing their office work at home (30.2%) and took support from maidservants and drivers (37.7%). Only one respondent did not know how she could balance her office and family work.

Support from servants is one of the dominant methods of coping with challenges. Servants are in great demand nowadays. With the gradual expansion of the low/non-skilled jobs in formal sectors (mainly

Table 8.4 Ways to balance work and home roles

Balance between work and home	BCS officials (%) N = 53
Take support from family members and relatives	79.2
Support from husband in the sharing of work	56.6
Flexibility of working hours negotiated with boss	18.9
Not doing office work at home	30.2
Support from maidservants, drivers, and daycare centers	37.7
Outings on the weekends	35.8
Dont' know	2.5

the ready-made garments sector), maidservants are in short supply now. There is thus an unequal competition among working women for hiring the services of maidservants. In fact, a short supply of maidservants causes some kind of concern among working women. Although they can, in many cases, depend upon their elderly parents or in-laws to look after their children or ensure the safety of the house, servants are needed to do household chores that require physical strength. Yet having servants at home becomes a source of concern and irritation as in most of the cases servants cannot be seen as very trustworthy or dependable. So, a strategy adopted to cope with one major problem can become a source of another major challenge. The dilemma thus continues. There remains the risk of disrupting family life.

It has been observed that 25 out of the 29 married women officials with children resorted to the tactic of taking support from their family members and relatives and seven out of the eight unmarried officials and nine out of the 15 married officials who had no children also chose the same strategy to balance work and family. From this observation, we can understand that those who are unmarried have to rely on their parents and siblings, while those who have children need the support from their parents and also their in-laws to manage their household chores while they are away at work and also when they come back home after a long hectic day. Women who had children were more in number than those who had no children when it came to the strategy of taking support from their husbands in the sharing of work.

Unmarried women officials were more comfortable in negotiating the flexibility of working hours with their boss rather than their married counterparts. It has also been observed that the proportion of married women officials who had no children preferred outings on the weekends rather than those who had children. Probably, the main reason is that the latter could not afford to go for outings as frequently as the former partly for financial reasons and mostly because such a strategy might hamper the education of their children. A greater proportion of married women officials having children relied on taking support from maidservants as well as parents/in-laws because depending on one source was likely to create problems rather than solving them. Not doing any office work at home in order to balance responsibilities arising from home and work was a strategy that was less used by all of the respondents.

Yet the respondents apparently were adamant to retain their job rather than quit in the case of serious conflict between work and home.

Working women planning to quit in case of conflict is extremely negligible (9.43%). An absolute majority of respondents observed that the strategy they would adopt if they were required to choose between staying in a job and disrupting family life would depend upon the situation, i.e., they would try hard to resolve the problem before taking any action. This implies that the working women are determined to balance work–home needs and priorities.

CONCLUSION

This chapter has explored the way(s) women in the Bangladesh Civil Service seek to balance work and family roles, a task which is very difficult to accomplish. On the whole, one can notice that the number of women in the higher civil service has increased manifold over the decades. Such increase can be attributed to different factors: increase in education of women, government policies aimed at encouraging women's education and employment, adoption of international conventions, and growing awareness among women about their rights facilitated by women's movements and NGOs. But the facilities and privileges granted to women do not keep pace with this increase. The problem compounds as male colleagues often do not want to consider women as equals. The former have a tendency to consider the latter first as women, then as colleagues. This kind of attitude and behavior creates tension among working women. As a means to ease tension, many women turn to the 'safest' source—the family—for support, which is usually forthcoming. But in the absence/ineffectiveness of stable family support structures, women find it extremely difficult to cope with challenge of balancing the two roles—family and work. Measuring balance is, however, difficult.

Our data reveal that working women in Bangladesh are strongly supported by their families, especially by parents and in-laws, which is common in different south Asian countries. Unlike in the West where extended families are a rarity, most of the people in the south Asian region have collectivist orientation. Extended families are very common in south Asia which are valued, although some changes are forthcoming in the family structure under Western influence. People are more committed toward their own groups in south Asian countries, whereas individualistic values reign the West. The support structure immediately given by family to working mothers needs to be nurtured rather than being allowed to be disrupted that one can notice in Bangladesh and also other countries now. Family disintegration is taking place in Bangladesh, as in other countries, at a much faster rate than in the past. While economic reasons and attitudinal change may be seen as important factors causing disintegration, working women often face uncertainties in career building because of worries of leaving children alone and/or to the care of 'unreliable' people. Disintegration, however, causes a different type of stress that ultimately affects work spirit and accomplishment. Notwithstanding limitations, family still provides a very dependable source of balancing the conflicting roles.

Yet, as observed earlier, family may be a necessary but not a sufficient condition of balancing the conflicting roles. In fact, involvement of extended family may sometime be seen as a strain for working parents. What is needed is to have strong family supporting structures as work-to-family conflict is more common than family-to-work conflict. As stated in an earlier section, the government has introduced several important work/family-friendly legislation which, if properly implemented, should create an enabling environment for working women. Experience, however, shows that enforcement of such legislation is a major problem in Bangladesh (as in other developing countries). Although the right to maternity has been enforced by the government, many provisions of different women-friendly legislation remain unimplemented.

For example, The Bangladesh Labor Act, 2006, requires an organization employing more than 40 women to arrange childcare facilities for children up to 6 years of age, near the workplace, with adequate light, space and fresh air (Sultan and Jahan, p. 160). The law is mostly honored in the breach. Rarely can one find these facilities in different organizations; wherever exist, these are of so low quality that working women often feel discouraged to use these. Similarly, The Government Servants Discipline and Conduct Rules 1979, Section 27 on the conduct or behavior toward female colleagues, states that 'no government servant shall use any language or behave with his female colleagues in any manner which is improper and goes against the official decorum and dignity of female colleagues' (Sultan and Jahan, p. 160). Our findings, as stated earlier, reveal that many women officials almost routinely face sexual and other types of harassment, but the perpetrators are rarely punished. The provisions of the 1979 Rules thus remain ineffective. What is needed most is to ensure that the provisions of the various women-friendly legislation introduced so far are implementled properly.

References

Ahmed, N. A. (2016). *Women at work in Bangladesh: A comparison of the challenges in the public and private sectors.* Thesis submitted to the Department of International Relations, University of Chittagong in partial fulfillment of the requirement for the degree of Master of Social Sciences, Faculty of Social Sciences.

Ahmed, S. G. (1986). *Public personnel administration in Bangladesh.* Dhaka: Dhaka University.

Ajaz, S., Mehmood, B., & Kashif, M. (2015). Impact of work-family conflict on female intent to quit: Descriptive study of commercial banks of Faisalabad, Pakistan. *International Journal of Academic Research in Accounting, Finance and Management Sciences, 5*(4), 74–83.

BBS (Bangladesh Bureau of Statistics). (2012). *Statistical year book of Bangladesh 2012.* Dhaka: Ministry of Planning.

Beaujot, R., & Liu, J. (2005). Models of time use in paid and unpaid work. *Journal of Family Issues, 26,* 924–946.

Berk, S. (1985). *The gender factory: The apportionment of work in American households.* New York: Plenum Press.

Beutell, N. J., & Greenhaus, I. H. (1980). Some sources and consequences of inter-role conflict among married women. In *Proceedings of the Annual Meeting of the Eastern Academy of Management.* Vol. 17 (pp. 2–6).

Beutell, N. J., & Greenhaus, J. H. (1982). Inter-role conflict among married women: The influence of husband and wife characteristics on conflict and coping behavior. *Journal of Vocational Behavior, 21,* 99–110.

Chinchilla, N., Heras, M., & Masuda, A. (2010). *Balancing work and family: A practical guide to help organizations meet the global workforce challenge.* Amherst: HRD Press.

GoB (Government of Bangladesh). (2011). *The constitution of the people's Republic of Bangladesh.* Dhaka: Ministry of Law and Justice.

GoB. (1998). *Women's development policy,* Dhaka: Ministry of Women and Children Affairs.

Herman, J. B., & Gyllstrom, K. K. (1977). Working men and women: Inter and Intra-role conflict. *Psychology of Women Quarterly, 1,* 319–333.

Hochschild, A. R. (1989). *The second shift.* New York: Avon Books.

Hofstede, G. (2005). *Cultures and organizations: Software of the mind.* 2nd Ed. New York: McGraw-Hill.

International, Labor Organization. (2016). *Bangladesh—labor force survey 2013.* Retrieved from file:///Users/macbookair/Documents/Google%20Drive/WB%20STC%20work/Whispers%20to%20Voices/ddi-documentation-english-1045.pdf.

Karim, M. R. (2008). Women in Bangladesh civil service: Vulnerability and challenges. Paper presented at the 12th World Congress of Rural Sociology, Goyang, KR. 6–11 July Retrieved from http://www.irsa-world.org/XII/papers/1-2.pdf.

Keith, P. M., & Schafer, R. B. (1980). Role strain and depression in two-job families. *Family Relations, 29*, 483–488.

Khan, A. A. (2015). *Gresham's law syndrome*. Dhaka: UPL.

Mahtab, N. (2012). *Women, gender and development: Contemporary issues*. Dhaka: AHD Publishing House.

Pocock, B. (2003). *The work/life collision: What work is doing to Australians and what to do about it*. Sydney: Federation Press.

Rimi, N. N. (2014). Achieving balance in work-family conflict through the influences of family supportive HRM: A conceptual framework for the organizations of Bangladesh. *International Journal of Business and Innovation, 1*(3), 80–99.

Rodin, J., & Ickovics, R. (2005). The role of gender in workplace stress: A critical literature review. *Health Education Journal, 64*(3), 271–288.

Smith, S., & Converse, D. (2012). *Double day work: How women cope with time demands*. Florida: Institute of Food and Agricultural Sciences. Retrieved November 30, 2016, from http://edis.ifas.ufl.edu.

Sultan, M., & Jahan, F. (2016). Openings and resistances. In N. Ahmed (Ed.), *Public policy and governance in Bangladesh*. London: Routledge.

Warner, M. A., & Hausdorf, P. A. (2009). Understanding work-to-family conflict: The role of organization and supervisor support for work-life issues. *Organization Management Journal, 6*(3), 130–145.

White, J. M. (1999). Work-family stage and satisfaction with work-family balance. *Journal of Comparative Family Studies, 30*, 163–175.

Zarra-Nezhad, M., Moazami-Goodarzi, A., Hasannejad, L., & Roushani, K. (2010). Occupational stress and family difficulties of working women. *Current Research in Psychology, 1*(2), 75–81.

CHAPTER 9

Women in the Bhutanese Bureaucracy

Kunzang Lhamu

Since the launch of the First Five Year Plan (FYP) in 1961, the Royal Government of Bhutan (RGoB) has followed a gender-neutral approach in the formulation and implementation of its policies, plans, and programs. A review of the 5-year plans indicates evolution from a Women in Development (WID) approach from the Fifth FYP (1981–1987) to a gendered approach in the Tenth FYP (2008–2013). The country ratified the Convention on the Elimination of all Forms of Discrimination Against Women (CEDAW) in 1981, without any reservations. The Gender Pilot Study 2001, the first study on gender conducted in the country by the erstwhile Planning Commission, renamed as the Gross National Happiness Commission, and the Central Statistical Office, renamed as the National Statistics Bureau, found that gender disparities existed in education/literacy, employment and decision making. Today, 15 years on, these issues are still valid areas of concern. The Sixth FYP states that Bhutan's full human potential, as well as ensuring that the whole population benefits from development, requires special efforts to involve women in development."

The Ninth FYP (2002–2007), in its chapter "Women, Children and Gender" stated the Government's commitment to promote wider

K. Lhamu (✉)
National Commission for Women and Children (NCWC), Thimphu, Bhutan
e-mail: klhamu@ncwc.gov.bt

© The Author(s) 2018
N. Ahmed (ed.), *Women in Governing Institutions in South Asia*,
DOI 10.1007/978-3-319-57475-2_9

representation of women in decision-making bodies as well as in the civil service. In recognition of women's integral role in development, the government allocated women-specific resources and proactively recognized woman's integral participation in development through the establishment of the National Commission for Women and Children (NCWC) in 2004 for coordinating and monitoring women-related activities. The National Plan of Action for Gender (NPAG) was developed coinciding with the Tenth FYP and highlighted seven critical areas for action: good Governance; economic Development (focus on employment); education and training; health; aging, mental health and disabilities; violence against women; and prejudices and stereotypes.

The Eleventh FYP (2013–2018) marked the beginning of concerted efforts made in mainstreaming gender into the policy and planning processes. The plan included a separate National Key Result Area "Gender Friendly Environment for women's participation" emphasizing gender mainstreaming as a key crosscutting issue in the development plans and also identifying it as a necessary consideration in the pursuit of Gross National Happiness (GNH). Gender responsive key performance indicators were included and Gender Responsive Planning and Budgeting (GRPB) implemented as a key tool for gender mainstreaming.

As part of implementing the government commitment to ensure gender equality as enshrined in different five year plan documents, the government has introduced several legislative measures. The Labor and Employment Act of Bhutan, 2007, for example, governs all labor and employment matters of the country and has provisions to protect and prohibit all forms of discrimination relating to labor and employment. The Act provides for ensuring a conducive working environment for women and specifically includes requirements such as a sexual harassment protocol and flexible working hours for pregnant and nursing women. The need for enacting such a law became imperative as the number of women in the civil service has increased over the years.

This chapter examines the status of women in the civil service in Bhutan. It explores a number of issues such as the gender composition of the civil service and reasons accounting for an increase of women [in the civil service]. The paper also tries to identify the measures taken for mainstreaming gender in the civil service, particularly ensuring a gender-friendly environment. The chapter begins with a short introduction to the civil service in Bhutan.

THE CIVIL SERVICE IN BHUTAN

The Constitution of the Kingdom of Bhutan 2008, in Article 7 (8), provides Bhutanese citizens with the right to have equal access and opportunity to join the public service. Article 9 (17) commits that "the state shall endeavor to appropriate measures to eliminate all forms of discrimination and exploitation against women, including trafficking, prostitution, abuse, violence, harassment, and intimidation at work, in both public and private spheres." Furthermore, Article 7 (11) states that "a Bhutanese citizen shall have the right to equal pay for work of equal value." The responsibility for ensuring the state's commitment rests with the Royal Civil Service Commission (RCSC). As Article 26 (5) of the Constitution states: "The Royal Civil Service Commission (RCSC) shall, in the interest of promoting merit, productivity and equity, ensure that uniform rules and regulations on recruitment, appointment, staffing, training, transfers, and promotion prevail throughout the civil service." The RCSC is the central personnel agency of the RGoB and is responsible for instituting an apolitical, professional, and meritocratic civil service.

According to the RCSC Annual Report 2015–2016, the total number of civil servants is 26,928 as on 30 June 2016. While efforts are being made to maintain "a small, compact and efficient" civil service, there is concern over the existing ratio of 1:28 civil servants to citizens. The cumulative growth of the civil service between September 2003 and June 2016 is 78.92%. The annual growth rate has declined to 0.85% in 2016 compared to 1.68% in 2015 and 5.31% in 2014. Rationalization of agencies, freezing of non-critical positions and redeployment of staff were the main reasons for the decreased annual growth.

The Bhutanese civil service is comprised of five main categories:

i. Executives at the leadership/management (EX1–secretary; EX2–director general; EX3–director)
ii. Specialists at the technical (ES1; ES2; ES3)
iii. Professional and management (P1–Chief; P2–Dy. Chief; P3–Sr. Officer; P4–Officer; P5–Asst. Officer)
iv. Supervisory and support (SS2; SS3; SS4; S1; S2; S3; S4; S5)
v. Operational (O1; O2; O3; O4; O5)

The largest group is represented by the professional and management category (49%), followed by supervisory and support category which makes up 43% and the executives and specialists representing leadership positions in the bureaucracy account for only 1% of the total civil service strength. As per the Report, the median age of civil servants is 34 years with 25% younger than 29 years and 25% of civil servants older than 40 years. The median age range for females is 25–29 years and 30–34 years for males, indicating that on average female civil servants are younger than male civil servants.

REPRESENTATION OF WOMEN IN CIVIL SERVICE: TRENDS AND PATTERNS

Out of a total of 26,928 civil servants, 17,417 are males (64.7%) and 9511 are females (35.3%) as on 30 June 2016. The number of female civil servants has increased fourfold—from 2180 to 9511 over the past 20 years. The Civil Service Statistics December 2015 indicates that among the Major Occupational Groups (MOG), the highest numbers of female Civil Servants are in the Education and Training Services with 3392 constituting 12.75% of the total Civil Servants and 36.75% within the MOG. There are 1451 female employees in general administration and support Services constituting 5.45%, medical and health services have 1292 females constituting 4.86%, architectural, engineering and land services have 661 females constituting 2.46%, and finance and audit services have 505 female employees constituting 1.90% (Table 9.1).

At the leadership level, i.e., the executives and specialists category, there are 253 civil servants (forming 0.94% of the civil service) with 228 males and 25 females. Females comprise only 10%, showing a huge gender gap at the decision-making level. However, at the P1 level, which is the level from where executives/specialists are selected, the gender gap is slightly lower and females comprise 20% of civil servants in this category (Table 9.2).

The highest proportion of civil servants 48.62% is at the professional and management level with 13,093 civil servants as of June 2016. This category has 4843 females and 8250 males. The support and supervisory level makes up 42.98% of the civil service followed by the operational category with 7.46%. In the support and supervisory, out of 11,574 there are 7042 males and 4532 females, while under the operational category, out of 2008, 299 are females and 1709 are male. The support and supervisory category has the highest proportion of females at 39% (the closest to the target set in the National Plan of Action for Gender 2008–2013 (NPAG, 2008–2013).

Table 9.1   Civil servants by gender—trend over the past 20 years

Year	Male	Female	Total
1996	11,386	2180	13,566
1997	10,901	2271	13,172
1998	11,164	2378	13,542
1999	10,972	2723	13,695
2000	10,748	2897	13,645
2001	11,036	3222	14,258
2002	10,760	3505	14,265
2003	11,143	3982	15,125
2004	11,718	4396	16,114
2005	12,290	4800	17,090
2006	13,092	5257	18,349
2007	13,308	5499	18,807
2008	13,957	5891	19,848
2009	14,590	6523	21,113
2010	15,453	7059	22,512
2011	15,730	7421	23,151
2012	16,053	8222	24,275
2013	16,862	8444	25,306
2014	17,328	8992	26,320
2015	17,383	9228	26,611
2016	17,414	9511	26,925

Source RGoB (2016)

Table 9.2   Gender profile of executives and specialists by position level

Sl. No.	Position/level	Female	Male	Total
1	ES1	1	1	2
2	ES2	1	29	30
3	ES3	12	57	69
4	EX1	1	27	28
5	EX2	1	54	55
6	EX3	8	56	64
7	CO	1	4	5
Total		25	228	253

Source RGoB (2016)

EXPLAINING THE TREND

Representation of women in the civil service is gradually increasing. Women now account for 35.3% of the total civil service, which is an increase of 77% over the last 10 years. Female representation in the civil service has been increasing due to the enabling and non-discriminatory environment provided by the Constitution and the Civil Service Act of Bhutan, 2010, which provides for safe and healthy working conditions to perform duties and equal opportunities for employment in the civil service.

Furthermore, the Government's policies in the social sectors have also contributed to women's increased participation in the civil service. The literacy rates for females, though lower as compared to males, have increased over the years from 46% in 2006 to 55% in 2013. The net primary enrolment ratio for girls was estimated at 96% as compared to 95% for boys in 2013. At the primary education level, national survival rate for girls is 79.4%, which exceeds that of boys (78.3%). At the secondary level (VII–X), girls make up more than half (51.9%) of the total enrolment. Girls' participation at the public higher secondary level (XI–XII) has increased from 32% in 2002 to 45.5% in 2013. Girls make up for 50.1% of the total enrollment in private secondary schools (VII–X). The increasing number of female teachers at all school levels have helped boost girls' enrollment and retention, by creating a conducive environment and also serving as role models (female teachers constitute 37% of the primary school teachers, 47% in the lower secondary schools, 44% in the middle secondary schools, and 34% in the higher secondary schools).

The Comprehensive School Health Program has helped to bring about substantial changes in hygiene, and the availability of iron supplements, school health coordinators, school guidance counselors, and gender-friendly school facilities has succeeded in retaining girls in schools. The provision of hostel facilities and midday meals has also helped in enhancing girls' enrolment and retention in the remote areas.

The Continuing Education (CE) program, which was launched in 2006, was targeted at providing opportunities for in-service persons who had discontinued their secondary studies for various reasons. As of 2013, a total of 2077 learners (1013 males and 1064 females) are enrolled in the CE program compared to 148 learners (78 males and 70 females) in 2006. The government does not restrict pregnant or married girls from continuing their education but are encouraged to continue their education by the school and institutes. The traditional belief that prevailed in the past, that women are better caregivers, also prevented women from joining or pursuing professional careers, which was further exacerbated by the lack of child care facilities in the workplace.

The NPAG, 2008–2013, had set the target of increasing women's representation in the civil service to 40% of the total strength, which indicates that the target has not been achieved even three years past the target year. Although the reasons for this may require a deeper assessment, the decline in girls' participation at the higher level, lower performance of girls in science and mathematics, and the lack of child care facilities in the work place could be contributing factors for the target not being met.

The higher proportion of female civil servants at the lower levels signifies that as younger women are entering the civil service, we can expect increased numbers in the higher levels in the future years. The low participation of women at higher levels can partly be attributed to the late start in education and the lower literacy rates for women. The general literacy rate across all ages for females was 55%, which is lower to that of males at 72% in 2013. The Gender Parity Index stands at 1.01, which indicates that for every 100 boys there are 101 girls at the primary school level.

As per the NPAG, 2008–2013, women's lower representation at the leadership levels may be explained by the late participation of women in the education process. Assessing from the trend, the increase of female civil servants at the highest levels of bureaucracy is seen to be slow and may require targeted support/interventions.

Barriers to Gender Mainstreaming in Bhutanese Civil Service

Since 1961 with the beginning of planned development in Bhutan, the country has concentrated its efforts on improving the standards of living of its people and fulfilling the spiritual, economic and emotional well-being of the people. The philosophy of Gross National Happiness (GNH), propounded by His Majesty, the Fourth King of Bhutan, provided the guiding principle and the basis on which development took place. The development framework emphasizes the achievement of sustainable development and self-reliance and places the individual at the center of development. Such an approach creates a conducive environment for promoting gender equality and mainstreaming it, into the development processes and outcomes.

However, the country, in the past, has always adopted a gender-neutral approach to development whereby equal opportunities were provided for women and men without assessing their different situations and needs. So while the RGoB is committed to promoting people's equal participation in development, it may be recognized that providing of equal opportunities alone is not adequate to achieve equality of outcomes or gender equality. It is important that consideration is given to institutions, mechanisms, and processes that enable women and men to participate in the development arena and become equal partners in nation building. This could include, among others, providing a gender-friendly environment in workplaces through establishment of child care crèches; reviewing selection practices (for work and training) and terms and conditions of employment to remove potential biases; instituting gender-friendly practices and frameworks to address the lower representation of women in committees/boards and providing incentives to encourage women to take up leadership positions; and instituting temporary special measures in areas where gender gaps are higher. As such, the different needs, constraints and interests of both women and men need to be understood and incorporated into the development process.

Toward an Assessment

The unequal status of women and their lack of opportunities are often taken for granted and are considered normal. The gender inequalities deeply rooted in families, communities, and individual minds, remain largely invisible and underestimated. In case of Bhutan, Bhutanese women are in a relatively better position compared to many neighboring countries in the region mainly due to gender-neutral public policies, legislation, and Buddhist values, inherent in the fabric of Bhutanese society.

While there has been notable progress in the area of reducing gender gaps in Bhutan, there are disparities in many important areas of development such as:

i. Low female representation in decision-making positions in governance (Judiciary, Executive, Legislative, and Local Governance)
ii. Higher female unemployment rate (urban overall: 6.8% with female at 9.5% against 5.3% male; and rural overall: 2.8% with female at 2.7% against 2.9% for male)
iii. Low female participation in economic activities
iv. Low female enrollment in tertiary education, implying higher dropout rates after completion of secondary education
v. Low female enrollment in technical and professional fields

According to the findings of the Gender Pilot Study, Bhutan 2001 (www. gnhc.gov.bt/wp-content/uploads/2011/05/rep_gpsr.pdf), an interesting difference or stereotype in governance was evident, where men tended to dominate the public domain and were involved in macro-level decisions, while women were in the private sphere. Women perceived men to be more capable of making decisions at higher levels. As such, despite positive indicators, as per the study women believed in that men were better equipped to understand and participate in the matters of governance and decision making in the public sphere.

The same study found that though women were active in village meetings, their participation declined as the level of governance became higher especially at the national level. There was a perception among women that the men better made important decisions as they were more literate and more experienced in pubic dealings. Women felt that "they are not taken so seriously." Some women felt that, "there were no women leaders in their community." While women recognized the value of meetings at the higher levels, they found extensive travel and night halts as major constraints for attending meetings outside their community. In addition, the burden of household and farm work coupled with long and inflexible hours of both public and political work, prevented women from participation in governance.

In a 2010 study on attitudes of Sherubtse College students—a leading tertiary education institute—male respondents (58%) were of the view that men made the best leaders while females (78%) tended to think capacities were equal (Tshomo et al. 2010). Men attributed the under-representation of women to lack of toughness, leadership qualities, and drive. The limited number of women in leadership roles also seems to have affected how women's capacities are perceived.

When it comes to women in the bureaucracy, the findings from the above study, explain to a large extent the lower representation of women in the civil service especially in decision-making positions. Despite an enabling policy environment, women are still under-represented due to the need to balance work/careers and family life. There are distinct gender stereotypes that are embedded in families, communities and individual mindsets, which are subtle but largely affect women's participation. The Study on Gender Stereotypes found that 44% of survey respondents believed that Bhutanese culture considers women as inferior to men. These are apparent in proverbs referring to men being superior to women, family habits, and household norms and expectations where the women always has the role of the caregiver, community and institutional practices, and through images and advertisements.

A 2010 study, which focused on the attitudes of students in one of the oldest colleges in Bhutan (Sherubtse College), found that while 48% of women viewed discrimination against women as a serious issue, only 29% of men though it was very serious or somewhat serious. The lower literacy levels of women, attitudes and stereotypes, lower self-esteem, the triple burden (reproductive, productive, and caregiving responsibilities), and the lack of a conducive environment for empowerment of women are the various constraining factors as per the Study Report on the Participation of Women in the Local Government Elections, 2011 (RGoB 2011).

Toward a Gender-Friendly Environment in the Bureaucracy

Although equal opportunities exist for both sexes in terms of recruitment, promotion and, scholarship in the civil service, women's participation in the civil service is lower than men. It is recognized that some of the constraining factors, which deter women's participation in the civil service, are the lack of gender sensitive rules and regulations especially pertaining to working mothers. As part of the reforms initiated in 2015 to enhance and sustain women's participation in the civil service and create gender-friendly work conditions, the RCSC in consultation with key agencies reviewed the Bhutan Civil Service Rules 2012 (BCSR 2012).

With effect from March 2016, the maternity leave has been extended from 3 months to 6 months, and the paternity leave increased from 5 to 10 days. The provision on baby feeding hours from 12 pm to 2 pm for 12 months was increased to 24 months to promote healthy breastfeeding till the child attained 2 years of age. In addition, government agencies have been encouraged to establish Crèche facilities with standard child safety and well-being measures and guidelines for the pre-school children (1–3 years) of their employees. This has further been strengthened by the inclusion of two mandatory indicators in the Annual Performance Agreement 2016–2017 of all the sectors: (i) timeline by which childcare center (crèche) for the employees is provided and (ii) timeline by which the internal framework to address gender issues at workplace developed. Annual Performance Agreements are signed between the Prime Minister and all Government Ministries, autonomous agencies, and local governments. The setting up of the Civil Service Support Desk for addressing issues such as sexual harassment faced by civil servants, further supported actions being made toward providing a gender-friendly environment in the civil service.

CONCLUSION

Although women are not well represented in the civil service especially at the executive levels, the representation of women in the civil service continues to grow owing to the enabling and non-discriminatory environment provided by the Constitution of Bhutan. Safe and healthy working conditions for the performance of duties and equal opportunities for employment in the civil service are provided as per the Civil Service Act of Bhutan, 2010. Conditions that facilitate women's enhanced participation in the civil service have been put in place in the form of extended paid maternity leave, increased breastfeeding duration, and the mandatory establishment of workplace crèches. Further, the extension of paternity leave underlines the fact that men are equally responsible for child rearing. The BCSR 2012 also prohibits sexual harassment at workplaces.

REFERENCES

BCSR. (2012). *Bhutan Civil Service Rules and Regulations*. Thimphu: Royal Civil Service Commission.

RGoB (Royal Government of Bhutan). (2001). *Gender pilot study, 2001*. Thimphu: Gross National Happiness Commission.

RGob. (2008a). *Study on gender stereotypes and women in governance*. Thimphu: National Commission for Women and Children.

RGoB. (2008b). *National plan of action for gender (NPAG) 2008–2013*. Thimphu: Gross National Happiness Commission and National Commission for Women and Children.

RGoB. (2011). *Study report on the participation of women in the local government elections*. Thimphu: Election Commission of Bhutan.

RGoB. (2013a). *Eleventh five year plan guidelines and eleventh five year plan volume 1 (2013–2018)*. Thimphu: Gross National Happiness Commission.

RGoB. (2013b). *Information brochure*. (5th ed.). Thimphu: Royal Civil Service Commission.

RGoB. (2015). *The civil service statistics*. Thimphu: Royal Civil Service Commission.

RGoB. (2016). *Annual report (July 2015–June 2016): State of the royal civil service*. Thimphu: Royal Civil Service Commission.

Tshomo, T., Angmo, T., & Patel, S. (2010). *The Gender Divide in Bhutan: Opinions on the Status of Women Split along Gender Lines Among College Students*. Research paper by members of Sherubtse College, Royal University of Bhutan.

CHAPTER 10

Women in Civil Service in India

Shivani Singh

The Indian Civil Service, by and large, has remained a male preserve due to a complex set of socioeconomic and ideological factors. The composition of civil service is at odds with the gender make-up of the society they represent which reveals that certain voices are being silenced or suppressed. The scene is, however, undergoing slow and steady changes in view of the socioeconomic churnings that India has recently witnessed. Besides sustained movements opposing gender discrimination, the prevalent political authority seems persuaded to raise voice against sociopolitical practices supportive of gender inequality. Although this campaign is gaining strength day-by-day, it cannot be said to have completely uprooted the sources of prejudices against women being considered equal for all practical purposes. The question that women are asking is very simple: why should women not be a part of the decision-making processes that impact them? Despite the promise of universality and equality, women have remained on the margins of decision-making and public office.

The main objective of this chapter is to highlight reasons underlying the low representation of women at all levels of the government and identify factors that cause gender inequalities in the civil service. It also

S. Singh (✉)
Dyal Singh Evening College, University of Delhi, Delhi, India
e-mail: 85ganapati@gmail.com

© The Author(s) 2018
N. Ahmed (ed.), *Women in Governing Institutions in South Asia*,
DOI 10.1007/978-3-319-57475-2_10

explores factors that discourage gender mainstreaming in the civil service. This chapter argues that despite not having completely achieved its goal, the campaign for women empowerment appears to have created a mind-set in support of gender equality which is also evident in the changing texture of Indian Civil Services in view of the growing number of women in responsible positions in the administration.

THE STEEL FRAME IN INDIA

Modern civil service in India is essentially a British creation. The Indian Civil Service (ICS) provided the foundation of what Lloyd George called the "steel frame" of British rule in India. There were three categories of services—All-India, central, and provincial—in British India. Among the different services, the ICS, an All-India service, was the most important. It was the sole repository of power (Morris-Jones 1964, p. 23). The nationalist leaders did not have any positive opinion of the ICS. Nehru once characterized the Indian Civil Service as "neither Indian, nor civil, nor service" and argued for its disappearance in independent India. There was, however, no serious break with the past in post-partition India. The threefold classification of services found in British India was retained. The steel frame, now represented by the Indian Administrative Service (IAS), has also continued and retained its class character even in independent India. Alexander (1998) observed that the new civil service, after independence, was the continuation of the old one, with the [only] difference that it was now to function in a parliamentary system of government under elected political leaders.

The civil service in India is heavily colored by status and rank consciousness. Despite the popular image of the Weberian notion of bureaucracy as the most rational and efficient form of organization, it has been found in real life mirroring the prejudices of the larger society. Even within the bureaucracy, not much attention has been paid to minority or gender issues. Thus, the "merit myth" of bureaucracy has been questioned by many critics. However, the issues of inequalities of power and status existing within bureaucracies never attracted the concern of scholars until recently. The so-called bureaucratic rationality has in reality worked in such a way that women have been judged unfavorably as potential members of the bureaucracy. It has been argued that a "discourse of bureaucracy" with emphasis on rationality, objectivity, and impersonality ran alongside a "discourse of domesticity" that stressed emotional and familial values.

Historically, bureaucratic principles, as opposed to the domestic sphere, came to be associated with males and maleness and served to exclude women from the bureaucracies or to confine them to the lower levels (Bhattacharya 2000). In British India, women were disqualified from holding Class I posts in various departments under the control of Governor-General-in-Council. They were eligible for Class II posts and the clerical services. In independent India, despite the constitutional guarantee of "equality before the law" and "equality of employment opportunities," the number of women and underprivileged sections in the civil service has been abysmally low. In 1983, the government of India's high-power panel on minorities, the Gopal Singh Committee, reported that the percentage of Muslims in the civil service was far behind in proportion to their population. This stands against the principles of inclusive governance.

Thus, although the Muslim population in the country is almost 12% of the total, their representation in the country's highest services stood at only 3.15% between 1981 and 2000 (Najiullah 2006, pp. 688–689). Similarly, of the 3284 officers in the Indian Police Service recruited during the same period, only 120 were Muslims. This is the general trend of Muslim representation in the service all over India with slight variations (Najiullah, p. 689). There has not been much improvement in the representation of Muslims over the last 20 years. Equality of opportunity, as a principle, does not take into account the claims of structurally disadvantaged groups (Mohanty 2000). Different reasons are attributed to the poor representation of Muslims in the civil services in India. Although Muslim leaders often consider it as a prejudice against them, observing that their access to the professions is deliberately blocked because of their faith, a recent research (by a Muslim scholar) reveals that "the low level of participation of Muslim students in the CS examinations rather than their probability of being selected is the major cause for low representation of Muslims in these services." A second factor that inhibits Muslim participation is that "Muslim girls are performing well in many areas but they are not encouraged to attempt the civil service (CS) examinations" (Patel 2014).

However, one positive trend noticed over the last few years, as evident from examination results, is that the civil service is becoming representative in terms of caste, tribe, regions, and ability. The number of physically challenged successful candidates has increased over the years—from 34 in 2012 to 53 in 2014 (Jain 2015). A differently able candidate even topped the merit list in 2014. In terms of the geographical profile of the successful candidates, the results over the recent years confirm a pan-India distribution. The 25 toppers in 2013 list were spread across 11 states; in 2014, the top 25 candidates came from 15 states (Patel 2014).

The family background of top 25 candidates shows diverse representation from all walks of life with their parents being a farmer, teacher, businessman, government servant, doctor, advocate, professor, and civil servant (PTI 2013). Candidates from OBC, SC, and ST also perform well nowadays; no seat in those categories remained vacant in 2014, although nearly 100 posts in the General category remained vacant. Women also succeeded in increasing their representation, although they still constitute a distinct minority.

The above observations, however, are not intended to argue that the situation has changed drastically. Continuity with the past is still widely noticeable. The experience of the last few years shows that there is less representation of students from low-income groups and rural backgrounds. Even among the backwards, SCs, and STs, the economically well-to-do are joining the civil service. A case in point is that of *Meenas* and *Negis* of the north that dominate the services among the STs. These communities are economically better equipped than their counterparts. Rural–urban differences are also widely evident. Available information shows that candidates from urban areas are in an advantageous position. For example, the number of urban male candidates is higher than their female counterparts; the number of urban female candidates is higher than their rural female counterparts; the number of rural male candidates is higher than their rural female counterparts; the number of urban male candidates is higher than their rural male counterparts; and the number of urban female candidates is higher than rural male counterparts.

WOMEN'S REPRESENTATION IN CIVIL SERVICE: TRENDS AND PATTERNS

The national movement for independence from British rule pioneered the participation of women in public life. In the civil disobedience movement launched by Mahatma Gandhi in 1930, more than 17,000 participants were women. A major reason for women being drawn into the

Table 10.1 Performance of women candidates

Year	Total candidates		Candidates selected		Percentage of total	
	Male	Female	Male	Female	Male	Female
2012	208,569	62,873	753	245	75.5	24.5
2013	241,726	76,458	861	261	76.7	23.3
2014	NA	NA	950	286	76.9	23.1

Source Jain (2015); UPSC Annual Reports

independence movement was the nature of Gandhi's personality which inspired confidence not only in women but also their predominantly male guardians who allowed their women folk to join his movement.

Nevertheless, in India, women are generally treated as subjects or recipients of policy decisions rather than full participants in them. The representation of women is very low at the top level where policies are framed. For example, the number of women holding higher positions—Secretary, Additional Secretary, and Joint Secretary—is very small. In 1951, the Indian Administrative Service recruited its first woman officer, and it was not before 1972 that the first woman joined the Indian Police Service. Until then, women were not considered physically fit for jobs like police and army. Women working in the central government were around 3% until the early seventies. The percentage doubled in the late 1980s and early 1990s when women constituted 6.6% of the total workforce in the union government.

In the case of the Indian Foreign Service and Indian Police Service, the share of the women was a meager 1.6%. According to the statistics of the late nineties, the proportion of women in central government was approximately 7.6%. Out of this, 98% were in Group C and D posts. The position of women in higher civil service was equally bleak —10.45% in the IAS, 3.4% in the IPS, and 3.18% in the IFS. In recent years, women have performed extremely well, topping the merit list for four succeeding years. The percentage of women joining the civil service has also increased. Although there has been a slight slid in recent years, the share of women can be seen as quite respectable compared to earlier situation. The top position in Scheduled Tribe (ST) and Scheduled Caste (SC) was also been secured by women candidates in 2012 (Table 10.1).

However, as Jain has observed, although women remain on top in UPSC results, they [still] fail to break male stranglehold in the overall merit list. For every 20 male IAS officers, there are only three female officers.[1] Since 1974, India's steel frame has incorporated only 687 women compared to more than 3000 men.

FACTORS ENCOURAGING WOMEN TO JOIN THE CIVIL SERVICE

The celebration of the Women's Development Decade and the growth of women's movement in different parts of India have generated a good deal of literature on the women's question. From a situation where women have been usually confined to the roles of housewife and mother or in the traditional occupation of teaching, nursing, and other social work, modern Indian women are trying to enter into diversified spheres of activity which were earlier considered exclusively male domains. The number of women officials in civil service, although compared unfavorably with men, has increased over the years. One of the important reasons is the quest for status. Among the inequalities, most noticeable in contemporary societies are the inequalities of income, occupation, and education, and inequalities inherent in the distribution of power and authority which manifest themselves in relation to domination and subordination. Status factor has become pertinent for women in India. In particular, status is concerned more with esteem and prestige rather than with wealth and power. Therefore, to acquire power, status, and respectability in society, girls have found civil service a viable option.

Status in ancient India was governed by the concept of ritual purity. Even today, among high caste Hindus, women may be said to be the custodians of the purity of the house and its members and of ritual. Their considerable concern for the material and spiritual welfare of the household is believed to depend on the meticulous observance of the purity-pollution rules and the periodical performance of ritual. Feminine preoccupation with rituals provides them power over men (Srinivas 1978). With changing times, status and power are associated with financial independence. However small is the proportion of urban educated women, the fact is that they have jobs that give them both regular incomes and social esteem. Therefore, personal career growth, security of job, financial independence, respectability in society, bright career prospects, and to acquire power and status in society are the factors that are encouraging women to join civil service in large numbers.

Among the higher castes, a girl was trained to be wife and daughter-in-law, and success or failure in both the roles reflected the credit or discredit of her parents. Now to counter this, girls are inspired to join civil service to protect the self-esteem of their parents. In many cases, the absence of a son compels parents to motivate their daughters to fulfill the role of son by joining civil services. Also, the cost of urban living has made both males and females realize that two incomes are better than one. Family members influence women to become bureaucrats since it saves parents from paying dowry and solves the marriage problems of their daughters.

However, while individual/family factors are important in influencing more women to join the civil service, there are other reasons, particularly "positive" government policies, that have contributed to the process. The Fifth Pay Commission recommended several measures to encourage more women to join the civil service which were accepted by the government. These include:

- Provision of common rooms and toilets for women.
- Quality crèches and day care facilities for children, preferably in the office campus.
- Flexi-timing for women employees.
- Part-time employment for women when their children are very small.
- Raising the age of recruitment for women to 35 years.
- Increase working women's hostels.
- Priority allotment of accommodation for women and assured housing for married women employees.
- Grant of paternity leave for 15 days.

The Ministry of Personnel has also adopted several measures to make women interested in the civil service. Some of the important measures include:

- Introducing guidelines for the posting of husband and wife at the same station.
- Allowing cadre change in respect of members of the All-India Service on grounds of marriage.
- Attempting to create harassment-free work environment by issuing guidelines for dealing with instances of sexual harassment.

- Adopting measures aimed at creating awareness pertaining to job opportunities in civil service among women.
- Creations of more schools and counseling centers in rural areas.
- Alleviation of poverty among girls.
- Changes in social attitudes of parents.

A focal point has also been set up in the Department of Personnel and Training to deal with all women-related issues in the civil services. The Department has been running a number of courses for gender sensitization of all government officials—to change male attitudes so that they learn to share the household and childcare duties.

PERCEPTION OF MALE AND FEMALE OFFICIALS IN THE CIVIL SERVICE

This section seeks to explore the perception of male and female officials toward each other's role and their relations. Male officers believe in gender stereotyping because they feel that women lack the competence to handle portfolios like Finance, Defence, and Home. Therefore, they should be preferred for "soft ministries" like Social Welfare, Culture, Women and Child Development. Male officials also believe that informal visibility of women officials is low and they lack networking abilities. Male officials are apprehensive about the mobility of women, which is a prerequisite in civil service. The general interpretation of male civil servants is that because of multiple roles as wives, mothers, and daughters, women are unable to render due attention to the demands of their job.

One pertinent problem is that male officials feel uncomfortable to work under a woman boss and sometimes do not want to accept a woman boss. Male officers are of the opinion that women often misuse laws. Till the time male seniors are sympathetic to their cause, women officials get along with them smoothly. The moment they are reprimanded for dereliction of duty or denied place of posting or designation of their choice, they immediately complain against their male seniors. Also, contrary to the general perception, women officers too have been found to indulge in acts of financial malpractices and corruption. For example, one former Uttar Pradesh woman official has been convicted for corruption and given imprisonment.

Women in authority find themselves in double mind due to the perceptions of men regarding qualities that a civil servant should possess which are unsuitable for women. If they behave like women, they are perceived as unsuitable leaders. If they behave like leaders, they are perceived as domineering and undemocratic by the male officials because of masculine culture of the organization. Women officers believe that unlike their male colleagues, they avoid an unholy alliance with political leaders. Also, they are not always eager to twist and bend before political leaders to get their choice of top postings. The male officers develop close proximity with the political leaders to further their careers as well as use their proximity to political power to aggrandize themselves. Women, by and large, keep themselves insulated from political pulls and pressures, thereby leading to visible improvement in governance.

Women officers believe that more women in civil service will lead to the improvement in the quality of governance because women are efficient managers. They manage household expenses with a limited budget; also, they are capable of responding to needs and priorities of the elders, children, and the spouse, thus making them more sensitive in nature. This quality enables them to deal with their colleagues at office and also the public at large with greater perfection. Women feel that they are competent enough to face the challenges of civil service. They believe that they are more humane, accessible, less aggressive, and less prone to corruption. More women in governance would help in improving the status of women in society. Women officials feel that they possess unique qualities as they are assertive and persuasive, more willing to take risks, more empathetic, and have strong interpersonal skills. One of the significant results of, for instance, success in the IAS is the fact that young women get posted as Collectors at district headquarters. Traditionally, the Collector was regarded as the lord of his district, and it is something of a cognitive revolution for villagers to find that they are being governed by a woman and a young one (Srinivas 1978).

BARRIERS TO GENDER MAINSTREAMING IN INDIAN CIVIL SERVICE

Despite the steady increase of women in the civil service, adequate representation is still lacking. The reasons cited for low proportions of women in Indian Civil Service vary from lack of motivation to lack of facilities.

As Jeanne (1988) observes: "If women are ambitious, they lack necessary education; where they get education, they often gain access to jobs less prestigious and less powerful than those of men. When they enter the public services, they are blocked in promotions and upward mobility, where they get high positions, they are neglected or discriminated against." Overall, several barriers—structural, administrative, political, and social—discourage women to enter the civil service and/or to remain in it. These barriers are explained below.

STRUCTURAL BARRIERS TO GENDER MAINSTREAMING

Individual human beings are unequally endowed both physically and mentally. Much of what an individual does in life and a great deal of what she can do depend on her place in society. Therefore, inequality among sexes can be traced to basic structural phenomena such as class, status, and power which are found to exist in all societies (Beteille 1988). The representation of women in civil service shows an increasing trend but the increase is not substantial. The increase is also not proportionate to the increase in education levels of women.

One pertinent reason is that education is not taken by women to build a career in civil service; graduation is mostly meant to get good grooms. Another reason is social background of civil service candidates which is tilted toward a small section of the society which is rich and powerful. The majority of the selected candidates are from public and missionary schools which provide education to a microscopic minority. Similarly, women who qualify in the civil service are elite within elite (Barik 2004). There is less representation of women from the rural background and from low-income groups because they cannot afford to take classes in expensive coaching centers.

In view of the well-entrenched structural impediments toward women empowerment in general, it is difficult for women to compete with their male counterparts. Lack of training and coaching opportunities, particularly in rural and remote areas, is a great hindrance for girls from rural background to join civil service. Women officers mainly come from families which can afford expensive education in private schools. Education, financial, and administrative background help girls to take up competitive examination.

In families with limited resources, girl's education is viewed as a liability and boys are given preference because education for them is considered as an investment. The girl's education is viewed as a liability because the parents have to give dowry for their wedding. Parents often feel that their daughters should get married at the right age, hence most of the time they do not encourage the girls to avail of the chances because civil service examination is lengthy, time-consuming, and cumbersome. Even after qualifying, it is a problem for parents to find a suitable match because of the prevailing societal norms such as groom should be more qualified and in a better job, and marriage should take place within the caste/*jati*, as pointed out by Srinivas (1978). Lack of quality schools and state scholarship for girls are also obstacles for women to join the civil service. Girls born in rural families whose dependence on agriculture and low rate of geographical mobility are obstacles in way of girl's education.

ADMINISTRATIVE BARRIERS TO GENDER MAINSTREAMING

Service conditions involving postings in distant cadres, taxing field duties, balancing family commitments with demands of the job, and sexual harassment at workplace are some of the administrative factors responsible for discouraging women to join the civil service. Public perception that for women domestic responsibilities take precedence over the workplace also pressurizes them to accord low priority to their professional advancement. Sexual harassment committees at work places are not very effective, partly for the reason that very few cases are reported to the committees and partly because of the tendency to settle disputes through mutual compromises. One can notice some kind of contradiction in the behavior of the government. The government has often expressed the desire to recruit more women in the civil service. But it does not appear to be very serious in taking actions against male officials sexually harassing women at work places. The case of Rupam Deol Bajaj, Special Secretary, Department of Finance, who complained against K.P.S. Gill, DGP, Punjab, for committing a series of serious misdemeanors against the aforesaid female officer is an example of government apathy in cases of sexual harassment. Bajaj brought it to the notice of the Governor who proposed actions on the advice of J.F. Rebeiro which were termed as soft by Bajaj. Even after 6 months of the incident, no concrete action was taken against Gill (Maswood 1989).

Gender stereotyping of posts has resulted in the denial of important postings to women. In the last 65 years, there have been no women Secretaries of Home, Finance, Defence, Personnel, and Cabinet Secretary. They are considered unfit because they lack different masculine skills required for these important departments. The "glass ceiling" effect has dissuaded the promotion of a woman officer to the senior posts in international institutions like the World Bank or IMF. Certain kinds of work are considered to be "women's work" and others as men's, but more important is the fact that whatever work women do they get lower wages and are less valued, e.g., nursing and teaching are predominantly female professions. Feminists point out that this "feminization" of teaching and nursing is because such work is seen as an extension of nurturing work that women do within the home (Menon in Bhargava and Acharya 2008, p. 226). Women who join civil service are expected to serve "soft ministries/departments" like Ministry of Women and Child Development, Department of Posts, and Indian Foreign Service due to stereotypes about their sensitive nature, nurturing, and diplomatic skills.

Political Barriers to Gender Mainstreaming

Politicization of civil service has become rampant in India, especially since the seventies. Refusal to succumb to the wishes of the political bosses often results in frequent transfers of the civil servants. The women officers feel it is difficult to handle political leaders. They remain under constant threat of victimization if they do not toe the political line. This holds true especially in recent years due to increase in the criminalization of politics. Expected close political proximity with political bosses is possible only through compromises in decision-making as well as in ethical standards. There is considerable corruption at the operating levels. This discourages women from taking up civil service or to opt for voluntary retirement during their service.

Two recent developments have focused on the relationship between political executives and public servants. In 2013, Prime Minister Manmohan Singh urged that if there was no evidence of wrongdoing, there should not be any presumption of criminality. He also said that section 13(d)(iii) of the Prevention of Corruption Act would be removed. This section extends the corruption to any loss to the government by the action of public servants. Second, the Supreme Court of India, on a public interest litigation plea by several retired senior civil servants, ruled in favor of greater order and transparency in transfers and posting. It directed the formation of a Civil Services Board of senior civil servants to decide on transfers and postings and a fixed tenure for postings. It also directed civil servants not to accept oral orders from their superior officers or Ministers, and to ensure that the orders are reduced in writing before they are carried out.

However, the following disjoints in governance should be kept in mind: First, the Prime Minister's assertion at the anti-corruption seminar on November 2013 that a loss to the government and the country does not necessarily constitute wrongdoing indicates the direction of future political decision-making. If this is the mind-set, there is no way the Supreme Court judgment will change the behavior or attitude of those in power. Second, fixity of tenure in lucrative jobs, as promised by the court, is but a guarantee to continue to exploit the benefits of the position. It will become a double-edged sword. If there is collusion between the interests of the political executive and the civil service, the Supreme Court judgment will result in an increase in wrongdoing, not a curb on it. There is enough evidence at all levels of administration that this is true. Lastly, there is the ultimate question of accountability. As long as wrongdoing goes unpunished, the politician will continue to believe that getting voted back to power is sufficient proof of innocence and that the civil service should not be a bottleneck. The vertical hierarchy of notes and orders prevalent in India shifts responsibility in a manner that makes accountability difficult—it is time to change that (Narayan 2013). Civil Service Board is also required to set up a cell exclusively to deal with women's issues and grievances.

SOCIAL BARRIERS TO GENDER MAINSTREAMING

A patriarchal system which excludes women from decision-making, early marriage or marriage at the age when a woman is preparing to enter the civil service, lack of education and financial resources, family attitudes favoring the male child's higher education are some of the social barriers responsible for discouraging women from joining civil service. Families which already had a government servant provided more motivation and encouragement to girls of their families to take up civil service. Family members influenced them to become a bureaucrat since it saved the parents from payment of dowry and solved the marriage problems of their daughters.

Urban residence and education are essential for women preparing for civil services. In India, female education has not only followed male education but an intimate link exists between female education, marriage, and caste. One consideration of relevance is that a girl ought not to be more educated than her husband. The pressure to get women educated is part of the process of securing good husbands. Parents want their daughters to get only that much education as will give them the utmost advantage in the marriage market including waiving of dowry. Colleges and universities provide respectable waiting places for girls who wish to get married. Since girls could not be kept idle at home till they were married, they were sent to school and colleges. Now, girls are encouraged to qualify the civil services examination regarded essential for obtaining a good groom.

Due to mental conditioning and socialization from early childhood, boys and girls are trained in appropriate, gender-specific forms of behavior, play, dress, and so on. Thus, feminists argue that sex-specific qualities and the value that society attributes to them are produced by a range of institutions and beliefs that contextualize social behavior of boys and girls differently. In addition, societies generally value "masculine" characteristics more highly than "feminine," while at the same time, ensuring that men and women who do not conform to these characteristics are continuously disciplined into appropriate behavior. The process of gender socialization itself is a violation of basic human rights as it attempts to control women's autonomy and independence of thought and action: obstacles that operate to keep women away from decision-making positions, thus depriving them of rights and opportunities that are presently available to men.

The existence of patriarchy at the work place has proved to be a major challenge. Patriarchy refers to an overarching system of male dominance operating at every level—economic, political, cultural, and professional. Thus, individual woman may appear to hold some power, but it would be strictly within the limits set by patriarchal rules. Therefore, women in Indian Civil Service enjoy a very limited say in the decisions regarding their postings and assignments, which are largely decided by their male counterparts. Male colleagues usually do not prefer women to be posted in high powered ministries. It is thus clear that the present subordination of women arises from social and cultural values, ideologies, and institutions that ensure the material and ideological subordination of women. Feminist critiques point out that women are denied equal access to resources through the structured operation of patriarchal ideology which endorses distinction between sex-specific qualities, e.g., bravery and confidence as masculine and sensitivity and shyness as feminine. It creates an artificial dichotomy between "public" (relating to profession and career) and private (relating to family) and encourages gender-based division of labor where women are primarily responsible for reproductive work related to the family and men for productive work.

Concluding Observations

Gender equality is a far more complex aspiration and requires the intervention of community organizations and policy-oriented efforts by the state as well as nongovernmental organizations. History proves that societies where men and women have played equal roles have been more balanced and prospered faster than those which have either been patriarchal or matriarchal. Inclusion of women in large numbers will provide a strong foundational administrative grid to the steel frame. More diverse civil service will contribute to a more wholesome diversity in negotiating complex policy environments. For a system to permit room for multiple choices and corrections, a sufficiently diverse civil service is imperceptive.

Inclusive governance must include good management practices. "Good management in the context of government refers to the budgeting, measurement and organizational system and processes that ensure the most effective and efficient use of public resources to ensure public missions and outcomes-without good management, we have infective governance at best" (The Woodrow Wilson International Center for Scholars 2014). According to the *Second Administrative Reforms Commission 2005*, "Governance is admittedly the weak link in our quest for prosperity and equity." Thus, improvement in the quality, performance, and effectiveness of the civil services will have a positive impact on the quality of governance which requires adequate representation of women in civil service. There are examples of women bureaucrats who have refused to fall in line with the wishes of their political masters. Durga Shakti Nagpal, the feisty officer who took on the Utter Pradesh sand mafia is a case in point.

A steady increase in a number of women appearing and joining civil services over the years appears to be a silver lining in this so-called male bastion. Men have accepted without protest women as their bosses in government offices, schools, colleges, and universities. The career woman in India is very visible, and it is significant that the society at large has readily accepted women's assumption of new roles.

Although prejudiced mind cannot be reformed overnight even by applying most stringent coercive measures, one has to constantly attack the sources of prejudice by evolving simultaneously alternative thought processes seeking to bring about changes in the wider social, economic, and political environment.

This is not a battle between two biologically divided sections of society, but a tussle between two diametrically opposite *weltanschauung*: one for change and the other for status quo. Since it is struggle against a mind-set, it cannot be exclusively gender-driven, but an encounter involving various sections of society which are persuaded to believe that gender equality is not a charity, but is a key to human progress, and hence, the sooner it is accomplished, it is better for a society reeling under well-entrenched prejudices, depriving half of India's population of equality and fairness. Inclusive governance demands that adequate representation of all sections of society, including women will help in enhancing the glitter of the steel frame and ensure that its shine does not fade away with passage of time.

An institutionalized policy toward the representation of women will surely be an impetus toward creating a space for gender equality, although this cannot be adequate to root out prejudices against gender equality. There should be an awareness that women's reproductive and productive roles were closely linked to economic, social, cultural, and political conditions constraining women's advancement, and that factors intensifying the economic exploitation, marginalization, and oppression of women emanate from chronic inequalities in the family and community at national and international levels (Jha 2003).

NOTE

1. Available at http://timesofindia.indiatimes.com/india/Women-on-top-in-UPSC-results-but-fail-to-break-male-stranglehold-in-overall-merit-list/articleshow/47967077.cms, accessed October13, 2016.

REFERENCES

Alexander, P. C. (1998). Civil service: Continuity and change. In Hiranmoy Kalekar (Ed.), *Independent India: The first fifty years*. Delhi: Oxford University Press.

Barik, R. K. (2004). Social background of civil service: Some depressing trends. *Economic and Political Weekly, 39*(7), 625–628 (Feb 14–20).

Beteille, A. (1988). *The idea of natural inequality and other essays.* Oxford: Oxford University Press.

Bhargava, R., & Bhargava, A. (2008). *Political theory: An introduction.* Delhi: Pearson Longman.

Bhattacharya, M. (2000). *New horizons of public administration.* New Delhi: Jawahar Publishers.

Jain, B. (2015). *Women on top in UPSC results, but fail to break male stranglehold in overall merit list.* Accessed October 13, 2016, from http://timesofindia.indiatimes.com/india/Women-on-top-in-UPSC-results-but-fail-to-break-male-stranglehold-in-overall-merit-list/articleshow/47967077.cms.

Jeanne, M. (1988, April). Women in public administration and management: Trends, analysis and training. *Indian Management, 35.*

Jha, M. (2003). *Women representation in decision-making bodies in India: A comparative study of government institutions in some select states, Unpublished.* Ph.D. thesis, Department of Political Science, University of Delhi.

Maswood, A. A. (1989). Women and civil services. *Economic and Political Weekly, 24*(5), 214 (Feb 4).

Mohanty, M. (2000). *Contemporary political theory.* New Delhi: Samskriti.

Morris-Jones, W. H. (1964). *The government and politics of India.* London: Hutchinson University Library.

Najiullah, S. (2006). Representation of minorities in civil services. *Economic and Political Weekly, 41*(8), 688–689 (Feb 25–March 3).

Narayan. (2013, November 15). A question of accountability. *The Hindu.*

Patel, A. (2014). *Why so few Muslims are IAS officers: Poor participation in civil service exams.* Accessed October 13, 2016, from http://www.firstpost.com/blogs/why-so-few-muslims-are-ias-officers-poor-participation-in-civil-service-exams-1359787.html.

PTI. (2013). *Kerala girl Haritha V Kumar tops civil services examination.* Accessed October 13, 2016, from http://indianexpress.com/article/india/latest-news/kerala-girl-haritha-v-kumar-tops-civil-services-examination.

Srinivas, M. N. (1978). *The changing position of Indian women.* New Delhi: Oxford University Press.

Woodrow Wilson International Center for Scholars. (2014). *Women leading public service and political participation in South Asia: New and emerging developments.* Washington: The Women in Public Service Project.

CHAPTER 11

Limits of Inclusion: Women's Participation in Nepalese Civil Service

Narendra Raj Paudel

The feminist approach stresses that the development of a nation will be incomplete in the absence of either sex's participation in public organizations. The voice and interest of either gender who cannot be represented in an organization will be silenced. Thus, initiatives have been taken worldwide to ensure the participation of women in different areas of society, economy, and polity. Conceptually, women's participation means not only women's involvement in decision-making and its implementation but also sharing of benefits. Although women have made progress in higher education, labor market participation, and wages in recent decades, they remain underrepresented in top positions in corporations, civil service, and politics (Bowling et al. 2006). For example, women occupied only 16.9% of all Fortune 500 board director positions in 2013, 18.5% of seats in the US Congress in 2014, and 29% of OECD senior civil service positions in 2010. Across the globe, 60% of countries have adopted alternative forms of quota which have advanced women's representation in governance at national, provincial, and local levels (The Woodrow Wilson International Center for Scholars 2014).

N.R. Paudel (✉)
Tribhuvan University, Kirtipur, Nepal
e-mail: narendra.radharam@gmail.com

© The Author(s) 2018
N. Ahmed (ed.), *Women in Governing Institutions in South Asia*,
DOI 10.1007/978-3-319-57475-2_11

In South Asia, on average, the representation of women in the national parliament varies from six to 33%. But the representation of women in the national civil service is still low. The major barriers that obstruct women's representation include lack of female aspiration, lack of qualified women, and socio-cultural factors. It is often argued that women are interested in looking after their homes and children; they may be reluctant to compete especially with males. Women are also observed to be less competent in laboratory experiments (Gneezy et al. 2003). Contrary to these arguments, proponents of women's participation observe that greater economic stability and growth occurs when more women hold senior positions. Women's representation accelerates the decision-making process in order to bring about a fundamental shift in the gender balance in positions of influence. Then, men and women [of Europe] can have an equal voice in working together toward a better future (EU 2010).

This chapter examines the role of women in the civil service of Nepal. It tries to identify the status of women in the civil service and explores measures that have been taken to include women in greater numbers. The paper also identifies the gap that exists between the policy of inclusion, which appears to be forward-looking and praise-worthy, and the reality on the ground.

Notwithstanding the adoption of different measures for inclusion, the rate of representation of women remains low. The paper explores reasons that underlie the 'poor' representation of women in the civil service. It argues that the creation of an 'enabling' environment leads to enhancement of the capability of women. Eventually, they achieve success in the civil service examinations. This paper tries to identify the extent to which an 'enabling' environment has been created in the case of Nepal and the extent to which women in Nepal have been able to reap benefits from it.

Structure of Civil Service in Nepal

Civil service is an organization that carries out different functions on behalf of the government. The role of the civil service has changed with time. It is more diversified in nature now than in the past. Not only do civil servants share policy functions with politicians; they are also involved with almost every function of the government. These functions can be categorized into four groups—governance, economic, social, and infrastructure (MoGA-UNDP 2014, p. 9). The governance functions include administrative services, logistics management, internal security and peace, foreign relations, and human resource management. The economic activities include economic planning, creation of investment climate and promotion of macro-economic stability. It also includes the mobilization of resources for the generation of income and employment. Moreover, civil service provides social services such as health, education, drinking water, sanitation, and social security to enhance the quality of life of the people. Civil service also focuses its attention on building infrastructure needed for sustainable economic and social development such as transportation, communication, energy supply, and environmental management.

The Civil Service of Nepal has thirteen categories of services. They are as follows: General Administration, Agriculture, Auditing, Economic Planning and Statistics, Education, Engineering, Forestry, Health, Justice, Parliament, Foreign Affairs, and Miscellaneous. Nearly half of the civil servants belong to general administration, while the health service employs about one-fifth of total civil servants. Engineering and forestry services are placed in third and fourth positions respectively. Other services like economic planning and statistics, education, parliament, and auditor general have a smaller proportion of civil servants (Table 11.1). The Government has opted for the policy of increasing decentralization and placing services closer to the people, with the result that more field

Table 11.1 Structure of civil service (by category)

Categories	Number	Percentage
General administration	37,044	46.30
Agriculture	4925	6.16
Auditing	327	0.41
Economic planning and statistics	369	0.46
Education	1644	2.05
Engineering	7961	9.95
Forestry	4829	6.04
Health	16,418	20.52
Justice	3028	3.78
Parliament	221	0.28
Constitutional	52	0.06
Foreign affair	210	0.26
Miscellaneous	2973	1.53
Total position	80,001	100

Source Department of Civil Personnel Record, MOGA (2013)

offices have now been established. The duties and responsibility of central government's organizations are formulation of basic policy, macro-level planning and monitoring, and evaluation, whereas the responsibility for implementation of these policies rests with departments and regional- and district-level organizations.

THE POLICY OF INCLUSION

Nepal made its commitment to amend the country's rules and regulations in line with international conventions and laws, mostly those framed by the UN, with a view to encouraging more women to be active participants in the governing process. The need for the involvement of women has been recognized in different documents. The Government of Nepal (GoN) expressed its commitment to reform legal instruments to remove barriers to women's participation in different sectors of the economy and society (Paudel 2006). In fact, Nepal has already enacted as well as amended many statutes and provisions of law to improve the status of women—important among them are The Gender Equality Act 2006, Human Trafficking and Transportation Control Act 2007, 12th amendment of Country Code (that criminalizes witchcraft and recognizes it as a crime against state), and Domestic Violence Control Act 2008. Measures have also been taken to replace the Country Code 1963.

The government of Nepal amended the Civil Service Act of 1993 in 2007 and introduced the quota system in the Nepalese Civil Service. The Election Act of 2007 provided for reserving one-third of seats for women in the National Parliament. The present Constitution of Nepal, passed in 2015 by the Second Constituent Assembly, made several provisions for guaranteeing the rights of women. Article 38 provides that every woman has equal lineage right without gender-based discrimination. Women also shall have the right to safe motherhood and reproductive health. They shall also have the right to participate in all bodies of the state on the basis of the principle of proportional inclusion (GoN 2015a, b). The Constitution further states that women have the right to obtain special opportunities in education, health, employment, and social security on the basis of positive discrimination. Finally, the spouse shall also have the equal right to property and family affairs (GoN 2015a, b). The GoN is thus constitutionally committed to ensure a favorable environment for women's improvement and participation.

The Civil Service Act of 1993 (4th Amendment) made a special provision for women in case of recruitment to the civil service. It provided for reserving 45% of the total seats (as quota) for women, Dalits, Madhesi, the disabled, backward areas, and ethnics. Assuming 45% of seats as hundred percent, 33% of the seats are reserved for women. It means that only 15% of seats out of both open and inclusive categories are reserved for women. In case of age limit, there is also provision for relaxation of age limits for women. The maximum age limit for men is 35 years, whereas it is 40 years for women. No age limit applies to women who have worked for more than five years continuously in the development sector; they can apply for a position in the civil service whenever they want.

Women also have less probationary period after they join the service—six months; in contrast, the probationary period for men is one year. Women also become eligible for promotion one year earlier than men. It is 3 years at the non-gazetted level and 5 years at the gazetted level for men to be eligible for promotion. This implies that women will have a natural advantage over men in case of promotion. It is rare to find this kind of 'extreme' positive discrimination in any other country of the world. Women also get 98 days delivery leave twice during the whole service period. Also, women get special leave on the occasion of Teej, Rishipanchami, and International Women's Day. The adoption of such positive discrimination measures is expected to create a favorable environment for women to join and build a career in the civil service.

WOMEN IN THE CIVIL SERVICE

The share of women in the Nepalese Civil Service is quite low. Women constituted only eight percent of the total civil servants in 2003; this increased to 15% in 2010 and to 18% in 2015. Most of the women work at lower levels; their participation at the policy level is extremely negligible (less than 3%). No woman has ever held any top level position in the civil service. These senior positions mostly remain the preserve of men. Table 11.2 shows that the highest share of women's participation is observed at the non-gazetted level. For example, the percentage of women holding non-gazetted level positions increased from 11 in 2003 to 22 in 2012; it thus doubled in ten years. The percentage, however, decreased to 21 in 2015. Those holding these non-gazetted positions are

Table 11.2 Women's share in Nepalese civil service

Rank	2003			2010			2015		
	Male	Female	Female share (%)	Male	Female	Female share (%)	Male	Female	Female share (%)
Special class	41	1	2	67	2	3	63	2	3
Gazetted I	304	4	1	416	13	3	429	29	7
Gazetted II	1399	52	4	2474	113	4	3119	163	5
Gazetted III	4909	304	6	7129	593	8	12,451	1698	12
Non Gazetted	38,596	4224	11	34,813	7632	22	32,686	8774	21
Class less	23,885	1432	6	20,366	1446	7	19,175	1518	7
Total	69,134	6017	8	65,265	9799	15	67,923	12,184	18

Source Civil Service Department, Ministry of General Administration 2015

mostly expected to assist officers (gazetted and special position holders) in discharging their functions.

There existed no policy of inclusion for women before 2007. Social and cultural impediments also did not allow many women to do any outside work; they were expected to remain at home and do only household chores. Job-seeking by women in Nepal is relatively a new phenomenon. However, despite the state's effort to narrow down gender gap in the civil service, the situation is still not very encouraging. Women constituted only 15% of the total civil servants in 2015. Reasons are many; the following appear to be important.

- The inclusion policy adopted for the civil service is still at the initial stage and it may take a few more years for the figures to go up.
- Those who have joined civil service have little career-development opportunity and move up through performance-based promotion system.
- No attraction for competent women outside bureaucracy to join high-level civil service positions through lateral entry system as provided for in the Act (Awasthi and Adhikari 2012, p. 30).

However, one encouraging feature is that the number of women applying for civil service positions has increased over the years; their success
rate has also increased. In contrast, although the number of male candidates has also increased, they have had a lower success rate than women.
Table 11.3 provides a comparative account of the nature of competition between men and women for civil service jobs in Nepal. Table 11.3
shows that the number of female applicants increased significantly
between 2007 and 2012. In 2007, there was 39% of female applicants,
whereas the males accounted for 61%. The number of female applicants
continued to increase in successive years, reaching up to 47% in 2012.
The main reason underlying the increase in the number of women applicants is due to the implementation of the policy of inclusion. The inclusive policy encouraged women to apply for jobs in the civil service. On
the other hand, the percentage of male applicants decreased from 61
to 53, although their number increased considerably (from 107,687 in
2007 to 195,387 in 2012).

One thing to be mentioned here is that although the number of women
applicants has increased substantially, the rate of women appearing in civil
service examinations is low. More than one-third of the applicants did not
actually appear in the examination in 2010–2011. Awasthi and Adhikari
(2012, p. 26) have identified three reasons that account for this gap.
They are lack of confidence [of candidates], lack of time to prepare for the
examination, and long distance between the examination centers and their
homes. The rate of success of women candidates compared (with male
applicants) is found to be very low; it varied from 6 to 12% between 2007
and 2012. Notwithstanding the adoption of a policy of inclusion, women
still trail far behind men in passing civil service examinations. As a result,
many seats reserved for women remain vacant. According to estimates by
Public Service Commission, about 250 positions reserved for women could
not be filled due to lack of appropriate candidates. Several reasons account
for this state of affairs, of which the following are important:

- It takes around 18 months to complete the PSC cycle—from advertisement to making final recommendations. Many candidates thus
  cannot wait for such a long period of time.
- Lack of availability of appropriate candidates.
- Lack of availability of candidates for technical positions (in particular).
- Inability on the part of candidates to secure pass marks (Awasthi
  and Adhikari, p. 27).

Table 11.3 Success rate of men and women in civil service examinations

Number of applicants passed rate on the basis of sex

FY	Female				Male				Total	Total passed nos.	Both Nos and passed percent
	No. applied	%	No. passed	%	No applied	%	No. passed	%	Nos.		
2007/08	67,435	39	366	9	107,687	61	3647	91	175,122	4013	100
2008/09	32,457	38	117	6	53,711	62	1747	94	86,168	1864	100
2009/10	139,963	47	495	11	160,500	53	4030	89	300,463	4525	100
2010/11	110,307	44	367	11	141,344	56	3298	89	251,651	3665	100
2011/12	113,785	42	398	11	157,792	58	3194	89	271,577	3592	100
2012/13	173,418	47	617	12	195,387	53	4461	88	368,805	5078	100
Total	637,365		2360		816,421		20,377		1,453,786	22,737	100

Source Annual Report of Public Service Commission (2008, 2009, 2010, 2011, 2012, 2013, 2014)

Those who have agrarian background, studied in community colleges, and belong to educated Brahmin and Chhetri family succeed in greater number in Public Service Commission's examinations (Paudel 2014).

EXPLAINING VARIATIONS IN REPRESENTATION

As stated above, women candidates generally trail behind their male counterparts in civil service examinations. Notwithstanding the introduction of several measures for mainstreaming gender in the civil service, the response is not satisfactory. Women have apparently failed to take much advantage of the measures taken for improving their representation in the civil service. This section tries to explore the reasons for the under-representation of women by seeking answers to a few questions:

- Is the examination conducted by Public Service Commission fair?
- Why do some castes fare better than others?
- Does the present legal provision give a sense of justice to Nepalese women aspiring to enter into the Nepalese Civil Service?
- What are the factors responsible for entry into civil service in Nepal?

Two methods were used to collect data to answer these questions: First, macro-level data on civil servants for 12 years—from 2003 to 2015— were gathered from the Civil Service Department and grouped gender-wise, while the share of women aspirants (2007–2012) was gathered from Public Service Commission, a constitutional body responsible for recruiting civil servants. Second, 227 candidates, 182 males and 45 females, were approached to collect primary data through closed-ended questionnaire from seven districts (Dhanusa, Dhankuta, Dhangadi, Gorkha, Accham, Dailekh and Kathmandu). 28 key informants who were organizational heads/chiefs of concerned offices were interviewed. Questions about the impartiality and effectiveness of the PSC and the level of performance of civil servants were included in the questionnaire. Reasons for specific caste domination, domination of agrarian rather than urban people, and domination of graduates from community colleges rather than private ones were also explored in the study.

The Impartiality of Public Service Commission

As per the Constitution of Nepal, 2015, the duty of the PSC is to conduct examinations for selection of suitable candidates to be appointed to vacant positions in the civil service (GoN 2015a, b, p. 163). The assumption of this study is that the share of women in the civil service will increase if the selection process of PSC is impartial and effective. No one can enter into the civil service without crossing the PSC door. Therefore, the question, in this study, was about whether the selection of civil servants by PSC was impartial and effective. The findings of the study showed that 95% of the respondents readily agreed on the impartiality and effectiveness of PSC in selecting appropriate candidates. No major difference in the opinion of the two categories of respondents could be noticed (Table 11.4).

Most of the candidates also observed that the different types of test used by the PSC to judge the suitability of candidates—written test, interview, IQ, language test, practice test—were also impartial and effective (Table 11.5). In an interview with the author, an organization head opined: 'The selection process of PSC is based on scientific methods; it is always alert to make the process error-free and totally merit-based.'

One thing to be noted here is that although both groups of applicants agreed that the impartiality of the PSC was beyond any question, nearly one-fifth of female respondents did not consider it to be totally impartial. Part of the reason was that the advertisement made by the PSC inviting applications was not easily accessible to many women living in remote areas. Some women applicants also alleged that the policy of inclusion

Table 11.4   Role of Public Service Commission

Variables	Male ($N_1 = 182$)		Female ($N_2 = 45$)		Total
	Yes (%)	No (%)	Yes (%)	No (%)	N = 227
Impartiality of Public Service Commission	95	5	93	7	95
Effectiveness of PSC to select appropriate candidates	84	16	79	21	83

Source Field study (2014)

Table 11.5 Perception of respondents on PSC examination

Variables	Male (N₁ = 182)		Female (N₂ = 45)		Total (N = 227)
	Bad (%)	Good (%)	Bad (%)	Good (%)	Good (%)
Written test	2	98	9	91	97
Interview	6	94	9	91	93
I.Q.	7	93	14	86	92
Language test	6	94	11	89	93
Practical test	7	93	11	89	93

Source Field Study (2014)

was not implemented properly. One of the male respondents also criticized the selection process in the following way: According to him:

> PSC did not identify the role of section officer, under-secretary, joint-secretary in each service. There must be different standards of questions and the evaluation method for each position be different. PSC has used the same selection methods such as written test, interview and so on [for each category].

It is to be mentioned here that there are 11 services in Nepal. Nine services are governed by Civil Service Act, 1993 and separate acts exist for the health service and the parliamentary service. In general, the process of selection of candidates is considered to be effective as well as impartial. A study undertaken by Central Department of Public Administration of Tribhuvan University also found the PSC was that the most trusted public institution in Nepal. Such trustworthiness mostly stems from the policy of impartiality and effectiveness that the PSC has followed in the selection process. The findings of the study showed that more than four-fifth of the respondents observed that the policy pursued by PSC was just. Most of them found that it was open to all and adopted an inclusive policy. No discrimination was noticed; the screening process of PSC was extremely impartial. Comparatively, more women perceived the PSC policy as 'just.' However, one respondent opined that:

> Despite an increase of women aspirants, the real competition remains confined to 'elite' women. University degree is a pre-condition to apply for

Table 11.6   Perception of respondents on justice from PSC

| | Gender | | Total N = 227 |
	Male (N₁ = 182)	Female (N₂ = 45)	
Yes (%)	81	87	82
No (%)	19	13	18

Source Field Study (2014)

PSC exams. Middle class women and women belonging to lower income groups lag behind the others in respect of getting access to the university. The rate of literacy for women is also lower than the corresponding rate for men. Thus, not many women can apply for vacant posts published by PSC mostly because they lack university degrees. Besides, an examination of social background of women who have been selected shows that they are either the sister of a civil servant or wife or sister-in-law etc. In fact, most of them are relatives of civil servants. It means that the real benefit [of the policy of inclusion] goes to families whose members are already in the civil service.

Much of what the respondent had said was, as the discussion in the next section shows was true (Table 11.6).

FAMILY ORIENTATION AND EDUCATION

PSC invites applications for prescribed positions as per demand of the Ministry of General Administration (MOGA), a central personnel agency in Nepal. It publishes its calendar to conduct service-wise and position-wise examinations throughout the year. PSC has also changed the procedure of submitting application—from the manual to the on-line system. It is now easier to apply and the PSC, which used to remain over-crowded [with applicants] in the past, now can work almost undisturbed. To some extent, this can be seen as an important factor accounting for an increase in the number of applicants for civil service jobs. However, the success rate of female candidates still remains low. Table 11.7 shows reasons that candidates attributed to their success.

Almost all except a few female civil servants observed that family orientation was critically important for their success in the civil service examination (97%). A slightly lower percentage (94%) of male candidates

Table 11.7 Reasons for the success of PSC examination

Variables	Male (N$_1$ = 182)		Female (N$_2$ = 45)		Total (N = 227)
	Agree (%)	Disagree (%)	Agree (%)	Disagree (%)	Agree (%)
Family orientation	94	6	97	3	95
Much secured job in civil service	96	4	93	7	96
More laborious	96	4	93	7	95
No reliable alternative other than civil service	88	12	93	7	89
More educated	97	3	91	9	96
Nepali language as mother tongue	90	10	88	12	90
State has discriminated	27	73	46	54	31
More economic benefits in civil service	38	62	44	56	39

Source Field Study (2014)

agreed to what the female civil servants had said. While analyzing the social background of women who were successful in the PSC examination, it was found that most of them had (one of the) parents, brothers, or husbands in the civil service. Only a very few women who had no family members in civil service achieved success. This shows that family members' support (in the form of coaching and/or supplying reference materials) for the preparation of examination matters a lot. In case of male candidates, the findings show that many of them worked hard to prepare themselves for the examination. They found neighbors and relatives very helpful.

Most of the civil servants (96% male and 93% female) were attracted to the civil service because of the guarantee of the security of job. Government service in Nepal is preferred to a private-sector job because the salary and other benefits provided by GoN are fixed and have more certainty, while these are uncertain in the private sector. Government servants enjoy the security of tenure. The government cannot easily terminate anyone; it can only dismiss a civil servant from office in case he/she is proved guilty of corruption or murder. Otherwise, the job is safe. It is for security of tenure and higher social status, and not for economic benefits, that graduates prefer jobs in the civil service.

The way candidates prepare themselves for civil service examination is an important factor determining their success (or failure). Those who labor hard can expect to succeed. Extra labor often causes stress and this is noticeable among both male and female civil servants, although it is slightly more noticed among the latter. Both found the civil service as the main source of employment. Since no reliable alternative (source of employment) exists, there is extra demand for jobs in the civil service. Since there is an oversupply of candidates for a limited number of jobs, competition becomes acute. This, in turn, puts extra-pressure on the candidates.

97% of the male civil servants and 91% of the female civil servants emphasized the importance of 'good' education as one of the important keys to success in the PSC examination. More male civil servants, however, emphasized the importance of 'quality' education than female civil servants. In Nepal, the literacy rate of women is about 57%, whereas for males, it is 75%. Only a small percentage of women get the opportunity for higher education; this, in turn, disadvantages them in the competition for civil service jobs. Without university education, people cannot compete for gazetted posts. For non-gazetted posts, the minimum education required is higher secondary graduation.

Overall, three major factors—family orientation, education, and labor for the examination—play a crucial role in the selection of candidates in the PSC examination. Women trail behind men in almost every respect; hence, they have a lower rate of success in the examination conducted by the PSC.

Conclusion

This chapter has explored the status of women in the civil service in Nepal. Available evidence shows that notwithstanding the introduction of a policy of inclusion, women remain underrepresented in the civil service. Their number in absolute terms has improved over the years, but the rate of improvement is slow, especially compared with men. The rate of success for women in the civil service examination is much lower than it is for men. Among the reasons accounting for underrepresentation, education, and family orientation appear to be crucially important. In Nepal, the rate of literacy for women is very low. Socially, a daughter was considered to be a liability until recently. Nepal has had a son-preference culture. Therefore, women generally did not get any real opportunity for education in the past. Culturally, they were also confined within the household in the past due to the prevalence of patriarchal values and prejudices. The policy of inclusion introduced in accordance with the provision of the new Constitution has had some effect in creating a favorable environment for women. But the process of change is very slow. Nepal will probably have to wait longer than many of its neighbors to mainstream gender in the civil service for reasons mostly unique to Nepal.

REFERENCES

Awasthi, G. D., & Adhikari, R. (2012). *Changes in Nepalese civil service after the adoption of inclusive policy and reform measure.* Kathmandu: Support to Participatory Constitution Building in Nepal (SPCBN/UNDP).

Bowling, C. J., Kelleher, C. A., Jones, J., & Wright, D. S. (2006). Cracked ceilings, firmer floors, and weakening walls: Trends and patterns in gender representation among executives leading American state agencies, 1970–2000. *Public Administration Review, 66*(6), 823–836.

EU. (2010). *More women in senior position: Key to economic stability and growth.* Belgium: European Union.

Gneeezy, U., Niederle, M., & Rustichini, A. (2003). Performance in competitive environment: Gender difference. *Quarterly Journal of Economics, 118*(3), 1049–1074.

GoN. (2015a). *The constitution of Nepal.* Kathmandu: Law Books Management Board.

GoN. (2015b). *The constitution of Nepal, 2015.* Kathmandu: Government of Nepal.

MoGA–UNDP. (2014). *The Nepal civil service and re-structuring of the State.* Kathmandu: Ministry of General Administration and United Nations Development Program.

Paudel, N. R. (2006). *Changing gender status in Nepal: Achievement and challenges,* Unpublished Report. Kathmandu: University Grants Commission.

Paudel, N. R. (2014). *Development management.* Kathmandu: Sirjina Pahari.

PSC (Public Service Commission). (2008). *The 48th Annual Report of Public Service Commission.* Kathmandu: Public Service Commission.

PSC (Public Service Commission). (2009). *The 49th annual report of public service commission.* Kathmandu: Public Service Commission.

PSC. (2010). *The 50th annual report of public service commission*. Kathmandu: Public Service Commission.

PSC. (2011). *The 51st annual report of public service commission*. Kathmandu: Public Service Commission.

PSC. (2012). *The 52nd annual report of public service commission*. Kathmandu: Public Service Commission.

PSC. (2013). *The 53rd annual report of public service commission*. Kathmandu: Public Service Commission.

PSC. (2014). *The 54th annual report of public service commission*. Kathmandu: Public Service Commission.

The Woodrow Wilson International Center for Scholars. (2014). *Women leading public service and political participation in South Asia: New and emerging development*. Washington, D.C: The Woodrow Wilson International Center for Scholars.

CHAPTER 12

Women in Pakistan Civil Service

Nighat Ghulam Ansari

The history of women in the formal workplaces of Pakistan generally and in the managerial positions specifically, is not very long owing to social constraints and a very low literacy rate of Pakistani females (about 47%) (GoP 2015). However, the situation is improving at least in urban areas where girl students now outnumber the boy students in higher education and are also entering the job market in great numbers. The female participation in the total workforce of the country as a ratio of their population shows an improving trend: from 13.6% in 2001–2002 to 22.1% in 2012–2013. The share of female vulnerability ('at risk of lacking decent work' as per UNDP definition) amounts to 75% as compared to 54.3% for males, which implies that a majority of females is working on the jobs of lesser quality and stability than those of their male counterparts (GoP 2014). This chapter discusses the females' representation in the civil bureaucracy of Pakistan and delineates how they cope with various challenges and professional demands in a bid to sustain and succeed in their professional career.

N.G. Ansari (✉)
Institute of Administrative Sciences, University of the Punjab,
Lahore, Pakistan
e-mail: ngansari@yahoo.com

© The Author(s) 2018
N. Ahmed (ed.), *Women in Governing Institutions in South Asia*,
DOI 10.1007/978-3-319-57475-2_12

CIVIL SUPERIOR SERVICES (CSS)

The Civil Service in Pakistan comprises twelve occupational groups collectively known as Civil Superior Services (CSS)—the largest public sector organization covering almost all the spheres of public service from civil administration to foreign services to inland revenues to police service and also the information services and office management positions of the secretariat. The origin of the CSS Pakistan can be traced far back to the colonial period. The British developed a well-organized civil service system to rule over India. It was initially manned by people recruited from Britain. However, when the need for associating Indians with administration became imperative, the British sought to ensure that those who joined the civil service were what Lord Macaulay once called: 'Indians in blood and color, but English in tastes, in opinions, in morals, and in intellect.'

At the top of the hierarchy of different categories of services (All-India, Central, and Provincial) was the Indian Civil Service (ICS). The ICS had a very prestigious and elite connotation, and the objective was to serve the rulers contrary to the present concept of being accountable to the public. This elitism persisted in the civil service even after the independence of Pakistan in 1947 when the ICS cadre was re-designated as PAS (Pakistan Administrative Service), and subsequently as the CSP (Civil Service of Pakistan). There were two All-Pakistan Services, the CSP and PSP (Police Service of Pakistan), and eleven Central Superior Services. The CSP enjoyed an elitist status with reservation of key posts, financial benefits, and prestige. A class distinction in the civil service was introduced by the Islington Commission in 1912, where Class-1 officers held the position of the executives or administrators and Class-11 officers held posts of operational level; this was subsequently expanded to class-111 (mostly the clerical jobs) and class-IV (peons and messengers). This classification and elitism of CSP continued after the independence of Pakistan but evoked a strong resentment and reaction from the public and members of other superior services, which eventually resulted in 1974 reforms. The reforms focused on eliminating the hegemony of the CSP, which was viewed as the direct successor of the ICS, hence entailing a colonial heritage. CSP was renamed as District Management Group (DMG) after the 1974 reforms, and effort was made to bring all services on an equal footing.

The civil service of Pakistan has been subjected to a number of administrative reforms and mostly by the commissions of foreign experts who gave numerous recommendations. Finally, the reforms were announced by Prime Minister Bhutto on August 20, 1974. By virtue of these reforms, all the services and cadres were merged into a unified graded structure and the earlier classification was abolished in favor of 22 grades; which were applicable to all Ministries and Departments of the Government where grade 1 was the lowest grade and grade 22, the highest. In order to emphasize professionalism in the field of administration, the 'occupational groups' were also constituted which at present are 12 in number and include Commerce and Trade Group (C & TG), Customs and Excise Group (C & EG), District Management Group (DMG) renamed as Pakistan Administrative Service (PAS), Foreign Service of Pakistan (FSP), Inland Revenue Service (IRS), Information Group (IG), Military Lands and Cantonment Group (MLCG), Office Management Group (OMG), Pakistan Audit and Accounts Service (PAAS), Police Service of Pakistan (PSP), Postal Group (PG), and Railways Group (RG).

Pakistan is a federal state where, as per the constitution of 1973, the Federal Government in the name of the President exercises executive authority of the Federation. Prime Minister is the Chief Executive of the Federation and exercises the authority of the Federal Cabinet. The subjects to be dealt with by the Federal Government and those to be dealt with by the Federal and Provincial Governments concurrently are stipulated, while the remaining matters are the jurisdiction of the Provincial Governments. Federal Government handles its matters through Federal Secretariat comprising several ministries/divisions and their attached departments. Currently, there are 46 ministries and 220 attached departments in the Federal Government. Each ministry is headed by a minister (an elected politician), who is assisted by a federal secretary (BPS 21/22) for performing the administrative duties. The Federal Secretaries are the most senior civil servants mostly from DMG and OMG cadre who are assisted by the Additional or Joint Secretaries (BPS 20). A division is divided into a number of sections. A Deputy Secretary (BPS 19) is in charge of a group of sections. Each section is headed by a Section Officer (BPS 17 & 18). Similar grouping and structure exists in the provinces for administration of provincial matters.

CSS is considered a generalist cadre, where recruitment is made on the basis of general education of the candidate up to the Master's or

Bachelor's degree. The candidates are selected on the basis of a combined competitive examination, which is held every year by the Federal Public Service Commission (FPSC), and consists of a written examination, psychological test, medical test, and a viva voce. The candidates thus selected are then allocated to various Occupational Groups on the basis of the order of merit obtained by a candidate, his/her domicile (for provincial quota), and his/her own preference for the Occupational Groups. Pre-service training of about 6 months is imparted to the selected candidates before they are sent to the specialized training institutes for the specific requirements of their allocated Occupational Group. Later on, in-service training is also provided to the officers of various grades as a refresher course in order to keep them up-to-date on the latest trends in public administration experiences. The system may be termed as 'Rank Oriented System,' as the recruitment is made for a specific career or rank in an Occupational group and not for a specific job (Khan, 1987). The incumbents of these groups are mobilized horizontally for various different jobs of the same rank.

Representation of Women in Federal Civil Service: Trends and Patterns

Although the rights of citizens are protected under Article 27 of the Constitution of Pakistan stating that 'no citizen otherwise qualified for appointment in the service of Pakistan should be discriminated against in respect of any such appointment on ground of sex, caste, or creed' (Khosa, 1992), yet women's entry into the civil service was restricted to some select groups only until the administrative reforms of 1974. Women were considered eligible to compete for Pakistan Audit and Accounts Service, Pakistan Military Accounts Service, Customs Service, and Income Tax or Inland Revenue Service but deemed incongruent for physically strenuous and rigorous jobs of the CSP and the Police Service of Pakistan (PSP) (Khurshid, 2011). The Administrative reforms served to remove this barrier and allowed women to compete for all occupational groups of the federal civil service.

However, there are some anecdotal reports of gender streaming and subtle discriminatory practices against women at the time of recruitment, via more subjective recruitment tools such as viva voce and/ or the psychological testing that is used to determine the suitability of the candidates for various occupational groups. These tools being more susceptible to gender stereotyping are considered liable to skewing the female ratio in the occupational groups that are considered more prestigious and/or attractive in terms of better career growth and more chances of reaching the top positions of the civil service hierarchy (Jabeen, 2013). Reservations also exist for the field postings of lady officers, especially in District Management Group (now PAS), where the District Magistrate (DM) or Deputy Commissioner (DC) has to perform in the capacity of the CEO of the district, maintaining law and order, collecting revenue, monitoring social and economic development, and supervising multiple executive duties, for which male incumbents are considered more suitable than the females.

Despite the reservations, however, there are instances where female officers have opted for and been assigned the field postings of DMG and they proved quite effective and successful in their career. Women have been competing for the CSS groups on merit without reservation of seats or quota until 2008 when a fixed quota of 10%, in addition to open merit, for each CSS group was introduced to ensure their due representation in bureaucracy. This affirmative action has been proved a catalyst for triggering a consistent increase in the number of women officers, from an average of five and 25 each year to 81 in the 37th common batch of 2009 as Table 12.1 shows.

Henceforth, a phenomenal growth in the number of female employees in the Civil Service is recorded each year, as per the statistical bulletin of Federal Government employees published by the Establishment Division of the Government of Pakistan, showing a number of 639 women officers in 2010–2011 and 797 in 2012–2013. The representation of women in various unconventional occupational groups such as PAS and PSP has also improved a great deal as reflected in the (Table 12.2), showing the density of females in various groups, however, women still tend to crowd in some groups such as IRS, IG, and C & EG. The Information Group (IG) has the maximum representation of women (26.14%) followed by IRS (18.5%), C & EG (18.12%), and Commerce and Trade (16.32%).

The larger presence of women in these groups is attributed to their 'self-selection' of such occupational options, which are perceived as more congruent and socially acceptable and also more manageable along with their family and care responsibilities. The most preferred groups are the ones that have the least incidence of mobility in terms of postings and/

Table 12.1 Total number of female officers in each common training program (CTP)—from 13th CTP to 37th CTP

CTP	Year	No. of female officers	CTP	Year	No. of female officers
13th	1985	11	26th	1998	27
14th	1986	10	27th	1999	24
15th	1987	9	28th	2000	24
16th	1988	9	29th	2001	24
17th	1989	9	30th	2002	28
18th	1990	4	31st	2003	25
19th	1991	14	32nd	2004	23
20th	1992	6	33rd	2005	40
21st	1993	8	34th	2006	27
22nd	1994	18	35th	2007	36
23rd	1995	16	36th	2008	53
24th	1996	26	37th	2009	81
25th	1997	20			

Source Khurshid (2011)

Table 12.2 Federal government employees by their gender and occupational/functional group (2012–2013)

Sl. no.	Name of group	Females	%	Males	%	Total
1	Commerce and Trade	39	16.3	200	83.7	239
2	Pakistan Customs Service	87	18.1	393	81.9	480
3	Pakistan Administrative Service	111	14.1	679	85.9	790
4	Economists	7	15.9	37	84.1	44
5	Foreign Service of Pakistan	68	15.0	384	85.0	452
6	Inland Revenue Services	173	18.5	762	81.5	935
7	Information	69	26.1	195	73.9	264
8	Military Lands and Cantonment	6	9.7	56	90.3	62
9	Office Management	49	10.9	398	89.1	447
10	Pakistan Audit and Accounts	92	12.6	638	87.4	730
11	Police Service of Pakistan	17	2.5	660	97.5	677
12	Postal	27	13.1	179	86.9	206
13	Railways	18	14.9	103	85.1	121
14	Secretariat	34	6.7	474	93.3	508
Total		797	13.4	5158	86.6	595

Source Statistical bulletin of Federal Government employees, Establishment Division, Government of Pakistan

or trainings so as to avoid disturbing their families. This attitude evidently converges with the assertion in the literature that 'parenthood &

self-selection' constitutes a significant barrier in the female professional life (Issac et al. 2012).

The groups with a greater incidence of women officers are apparently favored by the potential female candidates due to the presence of role models who are surviving and are successful in their career; so it works as a feedback on these groups for aspiring women officers. On the contrary, the groups with lesser number of women such as PAS and PSP are the ones that are perceived as difficult to manage due to the requirement of field postings and/or public dealing, which in turn is considered incongruent with female role in terms of societal dictates. Also, women in unconventional groups, owing to their 'token' presence, have to perform extra hard to prove their worth and compete with their male colleagues for promotions. In the words of Kanter (1977), 'women having a token presence in a profession have to carry the burden of representing their category (gender) whereby they not only try to "overachieve" but also attempt to lose their unavoidable "visibility" by way of toning down their feminine attributes and adapting to the mannish attitudes.'

The successful female officers of PAS visibly strive for this adaptation and are duly acknowledged and admired by their male colleagues for 'acting like a man.' Nevertheless, the recent venturing of women into the unconventional groups of CSS and their successful performance therein have indeed served to open new avenues for the aspiring female officers by way of creating an acceptance of their role and recognition of their valued contribution not only by the Service but the society at large.

The self-selecting behavior of women is also manifest at the time of field postings where they avoid the frequent rotation and opt for the secretariat assignments at the cost of losing mainstream and are eventually rendered deficient in the vital ingredient of exposure and experience required for career advancement. It also serves to reinforce the stereotype that women are less career-oriented and have lesser motivation to endure and move ahead in their careers thereby contributing to creating and/or strengthening the glass ceiling both at the time of entry as well as progression in their career.

If we notice the comparative statistics of career progression of males vs. females in terms of their ratio in the lower, middle, and highest levels of civil service (Table 12.3), we do not find a huge difference across genders as far as their percentage reaching the highest echelon of the Service is concerned i.e., 4.4% for females as opposed to 5.22% for males. This interesting pattern appears to arise out of an off-the-cuff approach of performance evaluation system at CSS, which under the influence of the

Table 12.3 A comparison of female and male ratios at various levels (2013–2014)

Level	Grades	Male		Female	
		Number	Percentage	Number	Percentage
Lower level	17 & 18	2953	57.2	574	72.0
Middle level	19 & 20	1936	37.5	188	23.6
Top management level	21 & 22	269	5.2	35	4.4

collectivist societal traditions does not approve of writing a bad report and having the responsibility of rendering someone jobless. Evidently, the performance evaluation process that does not record or report a deficiency in the employees' job performance, whether a male or a female, has a minimum or may be no contribution at all in creating a glass ceiling for the females in their career advancement; rather it may somehow be supporting them by not allowing a medium for the stereotypes about female performance to surface even if perceived as such.

PERCEPTION OF OFFICIALS ON REPRESENTATION OF WOMEN IN THE CIVIL SERVICE

An acquiescence of the female inclusion in various civil service groups for the sake of representing about 52% population of the country is clearly palpable in the minds of both male and female officials of the Service. However, a deep-seated stereotypical conviction about 'suitable' and 'decent' professions for women is still inexorable. A very strong verdict of some male officers was revealed during the course of in-depth interviews (Ansari, 2014) regarding the demarcation of professions in terms of their suitability for the females. The majority of male officials believed very strongly that females should opt for teaching and medical professions only, as the rest of the vocations, especially the ones where they have to interact with males and deal with general public, is not quite suitable for them. Even some women officers corroborated such opinions about the suitability or lack there of of some professions/occupational groups while talking about their opting for certain CSS groups.

The conventional incongruity of certain professional demands imposes women to select themselves out of certain groups and avoid certain tasks/assignments thereby endorsing the stereotypic belief about their lack of motivation for a professional career. Self-selection by the women is exercised at the time of giving options for the groups where they consciously try to opt for the groups that are perceived more 'acceptable' or 'decent' by the society and/or are more manageable for themselves in view of their domestic responsibilities. Another point of self-selection in CSS is encountered when women using certain exemptions in the service opt out of field postings and choose secretariat (office) jobs for their convenience. This type of mind-set is in line with the sex-role identity theory of Chusmir and Koberg (1991), according to which, women feel discomfort while crossing over to the masculine sex-typed jobs. A study by 2009 (Ceci et al. 2009) revealed that the factors impacting women's career 'spill over into the family or the reverse, the family spills over into the job.'

The female officers' self-selection at the time of field postings generates a criticism from their male counterparts who seem to harbor strong reservations about women joining the profession on equal footing, drawing equal remunerations and then claiming exemptions out of the difficult situations. Such perceptions, in the long run, can prove quite damaging for the female professional careers in multiple ways. Firstly, women by refusing the field postings and opting out of the mainstream are always at the risk of being sidelined at the time of promotions for not having adequate experience or exposure of the field. Secondly, this practice serves to endorse the stereotypes about female workers of having lesser orientation, seriousness, and motivation to sustain and succeed in their career. Finally, it serves to undermine their value as a useful human resource by way of creating an administrative issue for the Service to find enough vacancies in the big cities, an issue which is going to become even graver in view of an expanding number of women joining the service.

The perception of an extra baggage of female employees in the shape of their domestic responsibilities goes beyond affecting the career of an individual woman and tends to have an adverse impact on the prospects of all aspiring candidates at the time of entering or joining a profession. They are likely to be ignored in favor of a male candidate who is perceived more serious for a professional career, hence more eligible; thus subjected to a 'disparate impact,' in terms of Burgess and Borgida (1999). The disparate impact is largely responsible for producing the dismal statistics of females' workforce participation in Pakistan.

As per the evidence in the literature, the agentic/communal divide between men and women constitutes a major ingredient of the stereotypic 'difference barrier' between genders which in turn is the most conspicuous panel of the 'glass ceiling' that women have to encounter and tackle while progressing upward in their professional careers. This division, however, seems blurred in the context of CS, Pakistan, where the agentic and communal traits in men and women are overlapping and indistinct, apparently due to the collectivist influences (Ansari, 2014) and have served to weaken the perception of 'difference barrier' and ultimately the glass ceiling in the Civil Services of Pakistan. Women in CSS are visibly able to circumvent the barriers and reach the highest echelons of service (Table 12.3) if they are able to manage their 'family /societal issues.'

GENDER MAINSTREAMING IN PAKISTAN CIVIL SERVICE: IMPEDIMENTS AND SUPPORT

Various reforms coupled with the affirmative action aimed at improving the female representation in the country's civil bureaucracy have proved successful to the extent of facilitating their entry into the service, which is clearly reflected in the given statistics. However, encompassing them into the mainstream of this typically masculine profession so as to ease their sustenance is a challenge that might not be realized unless some basic changes in the administrative and cultural fabric of the Service are initiated.

The concept of a career woman is still quite novel in the society of Pakistan and the working women have to endure a dual challenge of proving their credibility in their chosen career and maintaining the image of a 'good woman' to the tune of societal prescriptions dictating the duties of a female toward her family and governing her social conduct. The 'Asian' society of Pakistan prescribes a clear-cut division of gender roles where the woman has to assume the household duties including taking care of her husband, children and the extended family as her primary role; her desire to pursue a career is tolerable only on the condition that her primary duty to her family and the household is not compromised. This automatically relegates her professional role to a secondary position in contrast to a man whose career assumes his primary obligation.

This primary/secondary division becomes quite explicit in the workplaces where women giving priority to their domestic duties compromise on their career front and become deficient to compete with their male counterparts who expend their primary duty of a career unencumbered by any extra baggage of domestic responsibilities. The primary/secondary split creates an inherent bias in the professional performance of male and female employees as is explicit in the following discussion of the impediments in the job performance of females in the Civil Service, Pakistan, examined in terms of two main societal doctrines: the duties of a female toward her family and the social conduct of women.

Despite the enactment of various laws for limiting the maximum work hours, working beyond the stipulated hours is the norm in most of the professions in most of the countries around the world, especially at the managerial level jobs. Although it is considered an issue of work-family life balance for all the employees in general, it is specifically regarded a major obstacle for women aspiring for higher positions in their career. Coser and Coser (1974) termed professions such as law, medicine, or laboratory science, and also the top civil society jobs as the 'greedy institutions' due to their characteristic of more-than-full-time ethos. It is evident in the literature that an important 'reason for women's lack of career success is that women, even when in full-time employment, usually retain the major responsibility for caring and domestic work' (Harkness 2003 cited by Crompton and Lyonette 2011, p. 233).

CSS, like most other professions, practices the 'beyond full-time ethos' or 24/7 norm as a 'gender-neutral' practice which nonetheless imposes a major challenge for females who are unable to work beyond office hours due to what is termed as their 'family issues.' Since they cannot sit late in the office just like men do, they are not considered as useful a human resource as men and relegated to a lesser evaluation in spite of having equal or sometimes superior professional capabilities. The same family issues impel women officers to resist job postings to remote areas of the country in their bid to remain in big cities and in turn culminate into depreciating their value as a resource, or in some cases, decreeing them a burden on the Service.

The CSS criteria of promotion to the next grade stipulate a variety of experience and exposure, which the females tend to miss due to their restricted rotation in their job and preference to remain in a few selected positions. They miss out the experience that they could avail through field/foreign postings and also lose their professional development, which could have been gained through the training opportunities. By opting for the secretariat jobs over field postings, they tend to skip the mainstream and become sidelined or marginalized which ultimately limits/delays their prospects of moving ahead or upward in their career.

The second doctrine of the society seems to constrain the performance of women officers in unconventional or incongruent groups such as PAS, PSP, and Foreign Service where they need to interact with general public mainly comprising male members. This limitation for females can be viewed in conjuncture with their tendency of avoiding field postings and can be attributed to the societal values which do not allow, rather censure a liberal interaction of males and females. Women officers, having internalized these values, are understandably deficient to handle interactions involving public dealing.

Similarly, professional networking is considered a valuable tool for gaining success in career and reaching the top echelons. Evidence, however, shows that working women usually face more difficulty in creating or joining social networks than men do. According to Ibarra (1993), it has been found in the analyses of social networks that men have more extensive social networks that include influential organizational members than do women. The literature also reports working women facing more difficulty in establishing mentoring relationships in their organizations than do men because of the possibility of having more men in the mentoring capacity (Ragins and Cotton 1991). This impediment of constrained or limited capacity to networking by professional women is further aggravated in the Asian culture of Pakistan, where the interaction of male and female is restricted and rather frowned upon by the society. So this limitation actually works to 'out-group' women in their organizations and by limiting their potential to accumulate social capital, works to halter their progress toward the desired levels of their career.

The above restraints in females' professional performance actually exert a two-pronged effect on their career prospects. First, it impacts them on an individual level where it obstructs their career on account of falling short on the requisite criteria for promotions. Second and more pronounced effect is evident in terms of creating and reinforcing the conventional stereotypes about the suitability (or lack thereof) of the whole feminine gender for formal jobs. Professional women do not only have to perform for themselves on the jobs but they also have the burden of representing their whole gender. Most of the stereotypes that are held with conviction by the employers seem to be generated out of the above-stated limitations and constraints of the female incumbents.

There are, however, instances where women have been able to circumvent these barriers and reach the highest echelons and coveted positions of the Service, which brings us to the discussion of 'support mechanism' for female officers. Family support, by way of giving relaxation in household duties as well as social conduct, acts as the strongest moderator for females' performance and their success in the professional career. Besides that, there is an evidence of 'cultural and systemic support' that provides an important relief to female careerists (Ansari, 2014). A strong tradition of collectivism in Pakistani society (Hofstede, 1984), where helping someone in a problem situation is considered a duty of the other members of collectivity, entails an accommodating attitude of the bosses and colleagues in the workplaces presenting a source of ample support for the working women. The bosses may 'crib about' the female employees' issues but they do not document it in their Performance Evaluation Reports.

The collectivist approach is also manifest in the systemic support in the form of various exemptions for the female officers from late sittings as well as postings to the remote or insecure areas of the country. The 'wed-lock policy' of the system, acknowledged and appreciated by most lady officers, is a great support for the married women where they can get posted at the posting place of their husband and keep their family together. Another informal way of accommodating the family issues of female officers is evident where they are allowed to have a relaxed posting (with lesser workload) at the time of raising their children.

It may, however, be pertinent to note here that the above systemic support specific to women officers, although providing them a much-needed relief in the short term, evidently contributes to their losing visibility, being marginalized and losing mainstream in the long run, hence impeding their career progression. Moreover, the systemic support or exemptions may be possible in the current scenario where women are in small numbers and have a token presence only, but once this number increases, as it is already manifest in the statistics, such provisions may not remain practicable.

Toward an Assessment

The situation of female careerists in Pakistan seems more like endorsing the notion of 'labyrinth' presented by Eagly and Carli (2007), rather than the 'glass ceiling' alone. A number of snags and catches are evident at various stages of the journey of women aspiring to join and succeed in the paid employment. For a start, girls do not enjoy equal opportunities in education, especially in the lower-income families. Boys' education takes preference over girls' because of the societal norms that consider paid jobs the domain of males and household duties the sphere of females, leading to the belief that the girls do not need education as they do not have to secure a paid job. This scarce opportunity for education creates the primary and most insurmountable hurdle that restricts the entry of girls in the workforce. Fortunately, the situation has much improved in the urban areas of the country where girls are getting educated in large numbers and not only outnumber boys in higher education but outsmart them also in terms of merit.

Secondly, strict demarcation of gender roles by the collectivist Asian society of Pakistan prohibits the females to opt for paid employment at the cost of neglecting their primary duty of domesticity and care; so even after getting a professional education (e.g., medicine, engineering and MBA), females can join the workforce only if permitted by their fathers and brothers before marriage and after marriage it is up to the husband and in-laws whether they allow her to adopt a career or not. This phenomenon has actually resulted in a burning debate in the country about allowing girls to compete for professional colleges on open merit because girls are more competitive than boys in terms of educational grades and merit and therefore are more likely to get admitted in these colleges (currently girls constitute about 50–70% of the classes in higher education).

It is argued that since there is no certainty that girls would join the workforce after getting these degrees, their enrollment in these colleges not only deprive the boys from the opportunity of getting professional education but the subsidy given by the government on such education also goes wasted. A number of female doctors not practicing after attaining their degrees are quite a popular example most frequently cited in the debate about equal opportunities for both sexes. Unfortunately, this phenomenon is portrayed and used against feminine gender as if it is a matter of their own choice rather than the result of a socially constructed barrier.

Thirdly, even when women are allowed to join a career they are under close scrutiny by the society about not only their social conduct outside their homes but also in terms of fulfilling their primary duties of domesticity and care. Due to this, career women are always under a lot of stress to not only maintain a 'respectable' social reputation but also create a balance between their professional duties and domestic responsibilities, where the family responsibilities assume a primary role as against the career requirements, which are relegated to a secondary position. Such attitude of females in fact constitute a major barrier in their career progression as it entails making a lot of sacrifices on the career front in terms of denying the important field duties, skipping the training opportunities, and taking career breaks for accompanying spouses on their postings and keeping family together. This attitude of sacrificing on account of familial duties not only costs women to lose development and progression in their own career, but it also serves to perpetuate the stereotypes about the lack of seriousness and career motivation for the whole feminine gender, which in turn, serve to restrict their entry as well as advancement to the higher echelons.

Family factors assume the role of a very significant moderating variable in the female performance where it can both propel and impede their career progress. While some familial aspects seemingly create a lag in the female career, there are others that actually contribute a great deal in the success of career women. Joint family system, where the married couples reside with their parents and siblings, is still in vogue and encouraged in the Pakistani society which, if the family is cooperative and have good relations, can lend a great support to working women. She can leave her children in the care of her mother or mother-in-law and perform her professional duties with a peace of mind. Besides, there is a strong tradition of hiring domestic help in Pakistani homes even when women are housewives. Domestic chores are thus not that much of an unmanageable burden. The working females cite family support as their main strength in the successful pursuance of their career (Ansari 2014).

Gender-neutral practices in the words of Acker (1992) visualize the worker as 'disembodied abstraction of an ideal worker' whose characteristics and attributes are more similar to male than those of a female who is quite encumbered with her family responsibilities in terms of time and commitment. The impact of so-called gender-neutral practices of full-time availability and an extensive job rotation in the civil service is definitely not that neutral in case of female officers who, in their quest to fulfill their professional commitments within the parameters of afore-mentioned societal prescriptions, face an automatic exclusion from the mainstream.

CONCLUSION

Diversity of workforce, defined by Equal Employment Opportunity Commission (EEOC) as differences in gender, racioethnicity, and age, no longer remains an option but has become the fact of life in today's fast-paced global world. The phenomenon of diversity, specifically gender diversity, is fast becoming an inevitable reality for the organizations as an increasing number of female workers are joining the formal workforce both in the developed and in the developing world. Failing to respond to this unavoidable change and maintaining a status quo in the policies and practices of organizations could result in the loss of productivity as well as profitability due to the costs associated with 'diversity mismanagement' as documented in the extant literature. A reported higher rate of absenteeism and turnover among the female employees as compared to their male counterparts may be an apparent consequence of an unwelcoming and unsupportive climate in the organizations, which ultimately costs organization in terms of substituting a well-developed and trained human resource.

The policy initiatives like Equal employment Opportunities and Affirmative Action have paved the way for workforce diversity by encouraging the inclusion of marginalized sections, including females, in the formal employment. However, these interventions have been subjected to a lot of criticism for having a sole focus on 'normative and structural' changes and not targeting the 'cultural models dominant within organizations' (Meyerson and Fletcher, 2000), which continued to favor masculine gender in formal workplaces. The fragmented nature of these interventions has achieved the target up to a limited level where they have succeeded to open the doors for the new entrants; however, the climate of the organizations has evidently remained unchanged and for the most part unwelcoming for the new variety of workers. It has been noted in the literature that improving the influx of diverse sections in organizations cannot reap the fruits of diversity unless it is complimented by a holistic improvement in the management practices for catering a diverse workforce in organizations (Groeneveld and Verbeek, 2012).

In the context of the Civil Service of Pakistan, the administrative reforms and affirmative action of introducing quota system for females in the occupational groups have definitely improved the influx of female officers in the Service; however, the practices and policies in vogue for the traditionally masculine Service remain unchanged in the name of 'gender neutrality' and both male and female officers are subjected to the same treatment and requirements which sometimes result in automatic exclusion/alienation of the latter. The predominant practice of '24/7 presence,' for an instance, is considered a gender-neutral practice but it works to exert undue stress on female employees who unlike 'unencumbered' male employees have multiple responsibilities to meet and expectations to serve.

The 'face-time system' (Poggio, 2010), attaching more value to physical presence in the workplace as compared to meetingperformance targets, is seemingly considered a remarkable feat in the context of CSS, which is more likely to be accomplished by male employees as compared to their female counterparts; ultimately alluding aspersions to the comparable worth of the latter as a useful human resource. Alarmingly, both male and female officers of the Civil Service consider the beyond-full-time practice as 'normal,' in the name of gender neutrality, and therefore no challenge and protest as such are forthcoming from the female officers who somehow try to meet this demand, with extra hardship of course, and try to act at par with their male counterparts (Ansari, 2014).

It may be concluded from the above discussion that in order for the diverse perspectives and capabilities of a heterogeneous workforce to turn into a competitive advantage, the organizations need to incorporate a gradual and incremental change in their overall policy as well as cultural framework whereby the 'Gender neutrality' of organizational practices and discourses is replaced with 'Gender sensitivity.' Only then the unwelcoming and unsupportive workplaces could be transformed into such conducive and empathetic settings wherein the heterogeneity of human capital is properly catered and flourished and diversity is not only tolerated but valued for its contribution.

References

Acker, J. (1992). Gendering organizational theory. In A. J. Mills & P. Tancred (Eds.), *Gendering organizational analysis*. Sage: Newbury Park, CA.

Ansari, N. (2014). *Female Career Advancement in the Workplace: A Performance Perspective* (Available at dspace.library.uu.nl).

Burgess, D., & Borgida, E. (1999). 'Who women are. *Who Women Should Be: Descriptive and Prescriptive Gender Stereotyping in Sex Discrimination'*, Psychology, Public policy and Law, 5, 665–692.

Ceci, S. J., Williams, W. M., & Barnett, S. M. (2009). Women's under-representation in science: Socio-cultural and biological considerations. *Psychological Bulletin, 135*, 218–261.

Chusmir, L. H., & Koberg, C. S. (1991). Relationship between self-confidence and sex role identity among managerial women and men. *Journal of Social Psychology, 131*, 781–790.

Coser, L., & Coser, R. (1974). The housewife and Her Greedy family. In L. Coser & R. Coser (Eds.), *Greedy Institutions: patterns of undivided commitment*. New York: Free Press.

Crompton, R., & Lyonette, C. (2011). Women's career success and work–life adaptations in the accountancy and medical professions in Britain. *Gender, Work and Organization, 18*(2), 231–254.

Eagly, A. H. and Carli L. L. (2007). 'Women and the labyrinth of leadership,' *Harvard Business Review, 85*.

Groeneveld, S., & Verbeek, S. (2012). Diversity policies in public and private sector organizations: An empirical comparison of incidence and effectiveness. *Review of Public Personnel Administration, 32*(4), 353–381.

Hofstede, G. (1984). *Culture's Consequences: International Differences in Work-Related Values* (2nd edn.), Beverly Hills CA: Sage.

Ibarra, H. (1993). Personal networks of women and minorities in management. *The Academy of Management Review, 18*(1), 56–87.

Issac, C. A., Kaatz, A., & Carnes, M. (2012). Deconstructing the glass ceiling. *Sociology Mind, 2*(1), 80–86.

Jabeen, N., & Jadoon, M. Z. I. (2013). Civil service system and reforms in Pakistan. In M. Sabharwal & E. M. Berman (Eds.), *Public administration in South Asia: India, Bangladesh, and Pakistan*. New York: CRC Press.

Kanter, R. M. (1977). *Men and women of the corporation*. New York: Basic Books.

Khan, J. R. (1987). *Government and administration in Pakistan*. Islamabad: Pakistan Public Administration Research Center.

Khosa, A. S. K. (1992). *The constitution of Pakistan, 1973*. Lahore: A. N. Sohail.

Khurshid, K. (2011). *A Treatise on the Civil Service of Pakistan: The Structural— Functional History (1601–2011)*, Faisalabad.

Meyerson, D. E., & Fletcher, J. K. (2000). A modest manifesto for shattering the glass ceiling. *Harvard Business Review, 78*(1), 126–136.

Government of Pakistan. (2014). *Pakistan Employment Trends 2013*, Islamabad: Pakistan Bureau of Statistics. Available at www.pbs.gov.pk.

Government of Pakistan. (2015). *Pakistan Economic Survey 2014–2015*, Islamabad Ministry of Finance. Available at www.finance.gov.pk/survey.

Poggio, B. (2010). Vertical segregation and gender practices: Perspectives of analysis and action. *Gender in Management, 25*(6), 428–437.

Ragins, B. R., & Cotton, J. L. (1991). Easier said than done: Gender differences in perceived barriers to gaining a mentor. *Academy of Management Journal, 34*, 351–939.

CHAPTER 13

Women in Administrative Service in Sri Lanka

M.A.F. Anwara Nilmi and Darshi Thoradeniya

Sri Lankan women have achieved remarkable successes in the spheres of education, healthcare, economy, and sports over the decades. The literacy rate of women in Sri Lanka today is 98.6%, which is much higher than any other country in the South Asian region. Women have joined the Sri Lankan Administrative Service (SLAS) in larger numbers than men; in fact, they now constitute 64.49% of the total civil servants in Sri Lanka (unpublished data collected and compiled by Ministry of Public Administration for internal Purpose only). In terms of women's employment, Sri Lanka compares favorably not only with its neighbors and other developing countries but also with many middle-income countries. Why and how such metamorphosis has taken place, the extent to which this increase is related to the wider issue of women empowerment, how do women administrators perceive their responsibility as civil administrators, and the extent to which women are capable of handling civil administration effectively despite various limitations

M.A.F. Anwara Nilmi (✉)
University of Peradeniya, Peradeniya, Sri Lanka
e-mail: fanwara@gmail.com

D. Thoradeniya
University of Colombo, Colombo, Sri Lanka
e-mail: dnthoradeniya@gmail.com

© The Author(s) 2018   229
N. Ahmed (ed.), *Women in Governing Institutions in South Asia*,
DOI 10.1007/978-3-319-57475-2_13

they face in the public sphere are some of the important questions that need to be empirically explored to understand the real essence of the higher presence of women in public offices. In general, the status and role of women in the Sri Lankan Civil Service have remained a neglected field of academic inquiry. This chapter seeks to fill this void.

The objectives of this chapter are fourfold: firstly, to examine the level of representation of women in the civil service; secondly, to identify the role women civil servants play in the administrative service; thirdly, to explore how the stakeholders such as heads of departments and offices, male colleagues, and service recipients view women's presence in civil administration and evaluate their services; and fourthly, to explore whether women face any challenges in delivering administrative services as civil servants. The chapter is mostly based on the information collected from primary and secondary sources. The authors interviewed 10 officials of Sri Lankan Administrative Service (SLAS) of grades I, II, and III (executive and senior executive categories) in 2016 with the intention of exploring their views on different issues, particularly to know how they perceived their role and how their male colleagues looked upon them and their activities. In addition, 25 undergraduate students of the University of Peradeniya were interviewed to explore their views on joining the SLAS in the future.

WOMEN IN SRI LANKA

Sri Lanka was under the Western colonial rule for nearly four and a half centuries until independence was granted by the British in 1948. The Portuguese (1505–1656) and the Dutch (1656–1796) held only the coastal areas, but the British ruled over the entire island from 1815 to 1948. By the 1900s, railways, roads, and harbors were developed by the British government in order to facilitate rapid development of the tea plantation economy.[1] Simultaneously, a new social consciousness among the colonized people gradually developed. Due to the tea plantation economy and increased educational facilities, an urban and a rural petty bourgeoisie class came into shape by the late nineteenth century. Following India's lead, the Ceylon National Congress was formed in 1919. Other mass social movements including the Social Service League, founded in 1915, addressed health issues and promoted welfare thinking. By the late 1940s, British colonial administrators and constitutional reformers such as Sir Charles Jeffries (permanent undersecretary at the Colonial Office from 1945 to 1947) identified Sri Lanka as a 'model colony' due to the strength of its civil society, the political maturity, and sophistication of its leaders, and above all, for the fact that it had granted universal adult suffrage in 1931 (de Silva 1982).

Sri Lanka's rapid progress toward political modernity was understood to be in part the result of its educational infrastructures that served both boys and girls. These infrastructures were initially built by the Baptist and Methodist missionaries from the American Mission and the Church Missionary Society. These missionaries began to establish schools for Sri Lankan girls from the 1820s. Local languages (Sinhalese and Tamil) were the medium of instruction in schools for the poor and English for the economically privileged (Jayawardena 2003, p. 118; Jayaweera 2002). The Ceylon Medical College was inaugurated in 1870 in Colombo, and the first female student was admitted in 1892. The English Training College for teachers was opened in 1902, and the first woman was admitted in 1908 (Jayawardena, p. 111). The welfare policy followed by the colonial government, especially in the education and health sectors, was also crucially important in promoting women's education and health. By the 1950s, Sri Lanka became a model to be emulated by other nations of the region while developing their public healthcare systems (Myrdal 1968, p. 1419). Western demographers became interested in studying Sri Lanka in the 1950s because it was able to successfully bring down mortality rates.

Influenced by British, American, and Canadian women's rights advocates, and taking the example of Indian women activists, a group of Sri Lankan middle-class, western-educated women came together to fight for women's rights and social reforms. The Women's Franchise Union was formed in 1927 by a group of Sri Lankan professional women, many of whom were wives of nationalist and labor party leaders. The first meeting of the Women's Franchise Union was presided over by Lady Dias Bandaranaike (mother of S.W.R.D. Bandaranaike, Sri Lanka's Prime Minister from 1956 to 1959) (Jayawardena, p.128). These pioneering women, members of these social and political movements, were doctors, teachers, and lawyers. As stated earlier, Sri Lankan women had the opportunity of school education provided by Baptist and Methodist missionaries at the American Mission and the Church Missionary Society from the 1820s. By the early 1900s, there were a significant number of qualified upper-class women in Sri Lanka eager to engage in social work. Missionary education, especially in boarding schools, disciplined and molded the careless, restless bodies and the inattentive, obstinate minds of native girls (de Alwis 1997). Women's education, first introduced in missionary schools and later in national schools established by the Theosophical Society in Sri Lanka, was a progressive step toward women's emancipation. Despite being dated, Dharmapala's concepts such as '*Gedara Budun*' are still taught in the school curriculum of Sri Lanka.

Contesting the notion of emancipation, Jayawardena (p.120) argued that women's education perpetuated and reproduced patriarchal ideology by limiting women's curriculum to needlework, home economics, cookery, drawing, and piano music. The general perception was that 'girls needed only limited education, just enough to make them presentable house wives' (Jayaweera 1989; Jayaweera (ed.) 2002). Even though female literacy rate in Sri Lanka is a commendable 97% today,[2] women are still educated, as Jayawardene pointed out, within an ideological framework of patriarchy. Since women's education is more geared toward producing presentable housewives—to fulfill a necessarily social reproductive role—education does not equip women with essential tools to think 'beyond' this reproductive role that they are traditionally bestowed with. In fact, female education in Sri Lanka has become a double-edged sword. On the one hand, female literacy rate, which is high when compared with other countries in the region, is often seen as a measure of women's empowerment. On the other hand, women's education has a strong emphasis on social reproduction. The empowerment that women are supposed to achieve through education is entangled with the aim of training for social reproduction.

Table 13.1 shows that women occupy far less positions than men as managers, senior officials, and legislators (Government of Sri Lanka 2016, p. 18). Jayasinghe (2004, p. 127) identified a number of reasons for the low participation of women in managerial positions. These are as follows: reluctance by women to work for longer hours (after normal working time), lack of preparedness to do any extra work during the weekends or holidays, and unwillingness to work outstations when required by management. These were acknowledged by the management as hindrances to the promotional possibilities of women in employment (Jayasinghe, p.127).

The Labor Force Survey of 2015 shows that women constitute 65.8% of the professionals. The professional group consists of 'teachers, nurses, doctors ….etc' (Government of Sri Lanka 2016, p.18). However, according to the same survey, 64.1% of the total female population remains economically inactive. This is an outlier situation with regard to women's education and labor force participation in Sri Lanka. In other

Table 13.1   Employment in Sri Lanka (by occupation and gender) 2015

Occupation	Total	Gender		% Contribution of female to the total employment
		Male	Female	
Total	100	100	100	34.9
Managers, senior officials, and legislators	6.1	7	4.6	25.9
Professionals	6.5	3.4	12.3	65.8
Technical & associate professionals	6	6.3	5.6	32.3
Clerks and clerical support workers	4	2.9	5.9	51.8
Services and sales workers	10.9	11.5	9.8	31.3
Skilled agricultural, forestry, and fishery workers	18.6	18.9	18	33.8
Craft and related trades workers	16.2	16.3	15.8	34.2
Plant and machine operators and assemblers	8.6	11.3	3.5	14.3
Elementary occupations	22.6	21.6	24.3	37.7
Armed forces occupations	0.5	0.7	0.2	12.6

Source Government of Sri Lanka (2016)

words, even though women graduates are high in number, a large percentage of them are economically inactive due to the social reproductive role that they are bestowed with. Following an introductory note on the origin and development of Ceylon Civil Service in the next section, the Chapter will look at how women in Sri Lankan Administrative Service have fared against this larger picture on women's education and labor force participation in section three. Section four identifies the factors accounting for the increase in the number of women in the adminsitrative service, while Section five explores the issue of gender mainstreaming. Section six examines the attitude of men and women in the adminsitrative service toward each other, while Section seven concludes the Chapter.

Origin and Development of Ceylon Civil Service

The British colonial government introduced the Ceylon Civil Service (CCS) in 1802, under Governor Frederick North in order to establish a stable administration in the country. The failure of the Madras Civil

Service introduced in 1796 in the Maritime Provinces compelled the British to establish a separate civil service (Warnapala 1974, p. 32). In 1833, following the Colebrooke–Cameron reforms, Ceylon had to do away with the administrative divisions based on the ethnic and cultural lines and came under one uniform administrative system based on the five provinces, namely Northern, Eastern, Southern, Western, and Central provinces (Wickramasinghe 2006, p. 29). Together with the indigenous feudal administrators, a handful of British officials who had access to the Secretary of State initially entered the CCS and ruled the country. The Colonial Office decided to introduce a system of competitive examination in 1856 and allowed the university graduates with liberal education to enter the civil service. The Northcote–Trevelyan reforms implemented in Britain in 1854 largely influenced the decision to introduce open competition in the CCS. However, it was only in 1870 that a merit-based open competitive selection was introduced, and Ceylonese candidates were also permitted to sit for the examination (Nanayakkara 2015, p. 80).

After independence in 1948, recruitment to the CCS took place through a competitive examination for Sri Lankan graduates in the age group of 22–24 (Somasundram 1997, p. 5). The interview, which carried 25% marks, was an important component of the selection process. The interview board was composed of the Vice-Chancellor of the (only) University of Ceylon (now Peradeniya), Secretary of the Treasury, and three other senior secretaries. Only five to eight candidates were selected for appointment every year. Those who failed the CCS examination were given lower-level positions in the civil service. However, with the change of government in 1956—from the right-wing capitalist UNP to left-wing socialist SLFP—a new situation emerged. There was a need for reducing the gap between the elite civil servants and the rural masses. With the gradual increase in the number of *Swabasha* elites, the gap was reduced to a significant extent. On the first day of May 1963, CCS was replaced by Ceylon Administrative Service (CAS) (Somasundram, p.340). The first advertisement for recruitment to the newly formed CAS was for men only (Endagama, p. 97).

The Sri Lanka Examination Department conducts a competitive examination to select the civil servants. The competitive examination is held every year under two categories: open and limited. The minimum qualification required for entering into SLAS is a degree from the University Grants Commission approved universities. Newly passed

Table 13.2   Gender composition of Sri Lankan Administrative Service

Batch	Percentage of civil servants	
	Male	Female
1980–1985	68.18	31.82
1986–1990	70.41	29.59
1991–1995	71.09	28.91
1996–2000	63.44	36.56
2001–2005	61.89	38.11
2006–2010	41.56	58.44
2011–2015	35.51	64.49

Source Unpublished data collected and compiled by Ministry of Public Administration for internal purposes only. It was supplied at the special request of the first author by Deputy Director of Ministry of Public administration

university graduates under the age of 28 can apply for the open competitive examination. A graduate is eligible to sit twice for the open examination. However, those who are already working in the administrative service can apply for the limited examination. The upper age limit for the limited examination is 50 years. This examination is held in a particular period of time for the whole Island and is conducted in all three languages (Sinhala, Tamil, and English).

To qualify in the written examination, each candidate is required to secure at least 50 marks in each of the following subjects: General Intelligence, Global Trends, Aptitude for Management, Analytical, Creative and Communication Skills, Social, Economic, Political Background, and Trend in Sri Lanka. Those who qualify in the written examinations are called for a formal 100-mark interview which is intended to check the applicant's personality, skills, and abilities. The candidates are selected on merit, i.e., on the basis of marks obtained both in written and in viva voce. Those who are selected have to undergo training for 6 months at the Sri Lankan Institute for Development Administration (SLIDA).

WOMEN IN SRI LANKAN ADMINISTRATIVE SERVICE

CAS was made open to women in 1965 as a result of the pressure exerted by the All Ceylon Women's Conference. At the beginning, a 10% quota was reserved for women, which was increased to 25% in 1975.

Table 13.3 Men and women in Sri Lankan Administrative Service

Year	Class I			Class II/I			Class II/II			Total		
	Total No.	Women No.	Women (%)	Total No.	Women No.	Women (%)	Total No.	Women No.	Women (%)	Total No.	Women No.	Women (%)
1979	165	3	1.8	345	19	5.5	1035	95	9.2	1545	117	7.6
1984	162	6	3.7	327	47	14.4	1141	138	12.1	1630	191	11.7
1988	178	12	6.7	274	59	21.5	1147	185	16.1	1599	256	16.0
1993	445	56	12.6	477	63	13.2	777	171	22.0	1699	291	17.1
2003[a]	675	143	21.2	307	92	30.0	721	224	31.0	1703	455	26.7
2006[a]	716	183	25.6	171	47	27.5	833	311	37.3	1720	541	31.5
2007[b]	706	192	27.2	127	41	32.3	1043	431	41.3	1876	664	35.4

Sources Changing Role Of Women in Sri Lanka, 1997
Handbook on Sex-disaggregated Data: Sri Lanka: 2003, 2003
[a] http://www.pubad.gov.lk
[b] The Sri Lankan Woman: Partner in Progress, 2007

This resulted in a gradual increase in women in the CAS, later renamed Sri Lankan Administrative Service (SLAS). The quota system was, however, abolished subsequently (Endagama 1985, p. 97). Table 13.2 shows the male–female ratio in the civil service from 1980 to 2015.

Table 13.2 shows the male domination of the SLAS from 1980 to 1995. Since then (1995), there has been a steady decline of men and a corresponding increase in the number of women. One reason for the decline of men in SLAS may be due to the growth of jobs in the information technology field; these are mostly male-centric jobs. Women, however, mostly hold lower-level positions in the civil service, although Sri Lanka produces more women graduates than men. More women hold class II positions than class I positions (Table 13.3). This probably implies that notwithstanding an increase in the number of women in the civil service, breaking the 'glass ceiling' still remains a formidable task.

EXPLAINING THE INCREASE IN WOMEN IN CIVIL SERVICE

As stated above, women now fare better than men in the competition for jobs in the SLAS. Several reasons account for this, of which the following are considered to be important. Firstly, as mentioned earlier, members of the SLAS are selected through a rigorous competitive examination. The selection process generally takes a year. Many male graduates consider this long wait as wastage of time. They want to start working immediately after graduation mostly for pragmatic reasons. Most of the male graduates have family responsibilities, and some also do not like to depend on their parents. Because of the breadwinner idea that still exists in Sri Lankan society, men find it hard to wait for the SLAS examination, although female graduates do not mind the wait. Most of the women respondents confided that they liked to do a government job because of the (job) security that is attached to the government sector.

Secondly, male graduates dislike working in a defined structure. They often prefer jobs that require traveling, while women prefer to be stationed at one place. One important reason is that it provides an important opportunity to women to balance work and home roles. Men generally do not bother about this kind of balance; they prefer jobs that require field visit and/or offer greater freedom. Women usually do not like field posting, as it may cause difficulties for them to balance multiple roles they are required to play.

Thirdly, men prefer private-sector jobs as these are both challenging and rewarding (in terms of financial benefits and other facilities). On the other hand, many women prefer job security to higher financial incentives as a safety valve, as field posting or work beyond office hours may create personal and family problems that are not easily amendable to resolution. Moreover, having a secure job means one is able to support herself/himself. On the other hand, private-sector jobs lack security of tenure, and hence, many women do not opt for jobs in this sector.

Fourthly, SLAS has apparently lost its glamor. Unlike in the past when SLAS was considered to be a source of honor, prestige, power, and social reputation, many graduates, especially male ones, nowadays do not find it very attractive as it cannot offer satisfactory remuneration or other financial benefits. Nor can its members exercise the power and discretion they could in the past. Graduates are keen to look for private-sector jobs as these offer better incentives. Male students interviewed for the purpose of this study observed that government jobs are very sensitive and risky; they are held responsible for each action. Thus, males do not prefer to get tied down to such a responsible job when they have opportunities to engage in a side business and earn quickly.

Fifthly, an increase in the migration of male graduates can be seen as a positive factor for women to join the SLAS in greater numbers. As stated earlier, men usually want to have a job as soon as they graduate. But the government cannot offer jobs to every graduate. Moreover, there always remains a gap between the demand for jobs and the capacity of the government to respond to graduates' demands. Besides, since securing a job in the public sector is a lengthy process, many graduates cannot wait. They go overseas to continue their postgraduate studies because in Sri Lanka they cannot find a job with good salary after graduation. While staying abroad, they can study as well as earn money by doing part-time jobs. After completing their studies, they mostly stay there and try to find a better job; some may even permanently stay there and apply for citizenships. But most of the female graduates wait for a job in SLAS.

Barriers to Gender Mainstreaming in Sri Lankan Civil Service

There are different types of social, political, and cultural barriers to gender mainstreaming in the SLAS. Gender biases in the civil service can be noticed in a number of ways. For example, according to SLAS

Minutes, applicants have a common age limit, but there are no gender requirements. Applicants may be a male or a female (Government Gazette 2013). The Ministry of Sri Lankan Public Administration generally fills out available vacancies opened in different administrative offices in different ministries in the island by selecting officers on the basis of merit. However, when they actually start their work, gender rather than ability becomes a major criterion. For example, jobs requiring extensive field works are often offered to male officials; this is one way of undermining the ability of female officials. However, many women SLAS officers generally prefer working in offices mainly in urban areas mostly for fulfilling family responsibilities and also for lack of security and facilities in non-urban areas. It also reflects traits of Sri Lankan culture. It has been noticed in recent years that because of the short supply of male officials, women officials are assigned functions that may require working at night. Many women officials in the SLAS considered it as a challenge.

An administrator, irrespective of sex, has huge responsibilities. But a woman official has some additional responsibilities that she can rarely delegate to others. A woman plays different important roles in a society other than an administrative one. She may have to play the role of a mother, a wife, and a daughter. She has to handle all responsibilities of different types and try to balance them equally. She has to patiently bear all responsibilities with more stress than a man. A woman with a difficult administration job will thus find it hard to excel in balancing both home and work roles.

During their 6-month stay (for training) at SLIDA, all SLAS officers are given training in management, communication, and problem identification and resolution. They, however, learn a lot of things through practical work and experiences. It is often found that women find it difficult to handle different types of work, partly because of lack of skills and different socialization (than men). Strain and stresses caused by the inability to balance different tasks may also influence the way women officials work. These may call for adopting strategies aimed at capacity building of women officials as well as reducing stress that are, however, not easily forthcoming. All women officials in the sample suggested that facilities such as housing, day care centers, or family support should be given mainly to female officers; lack of these facilities may be seen as a hindrance to gender mainstreaming in the civil service.

MEN AND WOMEN IN THE SRI LANKAN ADMINISTRATIVE SERVICE

Interviews with both male and female officials of SLAS reveal that male officials have a very positive view about women and their role in the civil service. Generally, male officials accept that all the women are not biologically equal to men, but they do have enough capabilities to do a work. They are also really hard workers. They respect their occupation equally to their personal life. Studies on Sri Lankan culture reveal that women behave in a more democratic manner [than men] and have an inclination to consult other officers before taking important decisions. Whenever a woman accepts some responsibility, she tries to do it at her level best. Women also have the reputation of achieving higher targets even at the risk of sacrificing many important things. Male officials also believe that many women are interested in studying new things related to their field of work or specialization and often practice what they learn. Many male officials also appreciate the contribution women officials make to the development of the nation through providing effective administrative services and are also sympathetic to problems they face.

On the surface, female officers can be seen as a kind mother, a good wife, an obedient daughter, and a helpful sister. Women officials interviewed for the purpose of this study observed that the society expects that they should manage both administration and family in an equal manner. A woman should be able to balance both. But in practice, it is difficult for an Asian woman to live up to this expectation. Women officials observed that they are often engaged in 'silent struggles,' particularly when they have young children. They have to simultaneously try to be an active and efficient officer, a good mother, and a wife. It is an 'internal struggle that male officers do not have to fight.'

Female officers were happy that more women were joining the SLAS; many also took pride in being a member of the SLAS. Some of the sampled women officials observed that they had enough capabilities to handle any difficult situation in a patient and efficient manner. However, while expressing some kind of satisfaction as successful SLAS officers, many of them were still found blaming themselves for not 'properly' taking care of their family members including children and also for not being able to spend time with them. Many women officials thus observed that they got fed up for not being able to balance the two spheres—public and private. Some observed that they could not take part in school programs as well as in family functions. Some women officers were thus sad and frustrated, with a few even expressing some kind of guilty feeling. Overall, this kind of feeling causes stress and may have some kind of negative impact on their work performance. However, interviewees, both male and female, said that Sri Lanka should have a representative SLAS where men and women should be represented equally.

CONCLUSION

This study shows that the representation of women in Sri Lankan Administrative Service is very high, at least compared to other countries in the region. The increase in the number of women in SLAS is mainly due to several reasons, particularly free education and high rate of economic growth and development. Moreover, the study demonstrates that women play an equal vital role in the SLAS as men though they face various difficulties. Both male and female officers perceive women as capable, efficient, and committed and duty bound. However, women feel that they do an internal struggle to balance their roles in public and private spheres, and in some cases, women are pushed into disadvantaged positions while working at top levels. Such situations create frustration and guilty feelings in women's mind. Therefore, many female officers suggest initiating some family support systems. Both male and female officers suggested that the Sri Lankan government should introduce measures to have gender balance in the SLAS at all levels.

NOTES

1. According to the *Ferguson's Ceylon Directory*, by 1921, 1,093,000 acres were under plantation, while 798,000 acres were used to grow rice.
2. http://www.accu.or.jp/litdbase/policy/lka/index.htm (Accessed on the March 9, 2012).

REFERENCES

de Alwis, Malathi. (1997). Motherhood as a space of protest: Women's political participation in contemporary Sri Lanka. In Amrita Basu & Patricia Jeffrey (Eds.), *Appropriating gender: Women's activism and the politicization of religion in South Asia*. London: Routledge.

de Silva, K. M. (1982). The model colony: Reflections on the transfer of power in Sri Lanka. In A. J. Wilson & Dennis Dalton (Eds.), *The states of South Asia: Problems of national integration*. London: C. Hurst & Company.

Endagama, K. (1985). Impact of the UN decade for women in Sri Lanka. Colombo: Women's Bureau of Sri Lanka.

Government of Sri Lanka. (2016). *Labor force survey—Annual Report 2015*. Colombo: Department of Census and Statistics.

Jayasinghe, V. (2004). *A new vision: A feminist perspective in Sri Lanka*. Pace Printers: Rajagiriya.

Jayawardena, K. (2003). *Feminism and nationalism in the third world*. p.120, London: Zed books Ltd.

Jayaweera, S. (1989). Women and education. In Swarna Jayaweera (Ed.), *The UN decade for women: Progress and achievements of women in Sri Lanka*. Colombo: CENWOR.

Jayaweera, S. (Ed.). (2002). *Women in post-independence Sri Lanka*. New Delhi: Sage.

Myrdal, G. (1968). *Asian drama: An inquiry into poverty of nations* (Vol. II). New York: Pantheon.

Nanayakkara, V. K. (2015). Sri Lanka Administrative Service (1963–2013): A fifty year legacy. *Sri Lanka Journal of Development Administration, 5, 79–93*.

Somasundram, M. (Ed.). (1997). *The third wave: Governance and public administration in Sri Lanka*. Colombo: ICES.

The gazette of the Democtratic Republic of Sri Lanka Part 1 : Section 1, (2013, December 23). Retrieved fromhttp://www.pubad.gov.lk/web/images/stories/slas/Service_Minite/pg1884(e).pdf.

Warnapala, W. A. (1974). *Civil Service Administration in Ceylon: A study in bureaucratic adaptation*. Colombo: Department of Cultural Affairs.

PART III

Women in Local Government

Women's Representation and Participation in Local Government in Bangladesh: New Openings and Remaining Barriers

Maheen Sultan

Participation of women in local government bodies in Bangladesh is not a new phenomenon, with women entering through reserved seats from 1976. What is, however, new is the emergence of *Mahila* members (as women members are called) who are more visible now than in the past and who have proved their worth as public representatives, responding to interests and wishes of their constituents in no less effective manner than their male counterparts. In other words, their presence matters, although its scope and extent may vary depending upon various factors. There is thus now less debate about whether there should be women in the local government bodies as it has become a given but there is still debate about what roles they can and should play there. Those who are dismissive of what women can and should do as public representatives feel that they are there out of sympathy, as a front for their male family members or as a formality because of government provisions that

M. Sultan (✉)
BRAC Institute of Governance and Development
BRAC University, Dhaka, Bangladesh
e-mail: sulthuq@bol-online.com

© The Author(s) 2018
N. Ahmed (ed.), *Women in Governing Institutions in South Asia*,
DOI 10.1007/978-3-319-57475-2_14

245

require a certain number of seats needed to be filled by women. Others who would like to see local governance reform with greater participation and power in the hands of local representatives see the women as untainted by corruption, unspoilt by politics, and closer to their constituents. The reality is probably somewhere in the middle, with the women representatives being shaped by the culture and society they belong to and influenced by the political practices that surround them.

As various authors have argued, representation does not equal participation (Goetz and Hassim 2003; Panday 2008). The Bangladesh Government is proud to cite the figures of the number of women who are now in local government bodies [General Economics Division GOB (2013a, b), Ministry of Women's Affairs (2014)]. As a result of the reservations made for women representatives, the numbers are quite impressive, although how much voice and influence they have and/or whose interests are they representing are issues that need further analysis and review. Even in the areas where projects and national NGOs are working, the elected women representatives and their constituents are still operating in a patronage model of politics The idea that the mandate for local government action might come from the constituency is unfamiliar to the UP representatives or other actors in the system, whether male or female: voters expect them to deliver projects or benefits for them—this is still the prevailing culture of local government (Hossain and Akhter 2011, p. 3).

Various studies have shown that elected women representatives are increasingly participating in an effective manner in the affairs of the local government bodies, making their presence felt and their voices heard. They are participating in the UP meetings, in various public forums, and also raising different issues concerning budgeting and planning; women's concerns; project implementation; and scheme selection (Panday 2008; 2013). However, it is also important to know the processes being followed and how far they are able to influence decisions and how they do so. Another aspect that various studies have shown is that women elected representatives have a special role in representing women's interests and responding to their needs, which is acknowledged by their constituents and themselves. This is highlighted by Panday (2008, 2013), Nazneen et al. (2014), and Khan and Mohsin (2008).

This chapter will explore why women chose to become public representatives at the local government level and what processes they went through to gain the acceptance of their constituents and family. It will explore how women function while in office, in terms of dealing with other UP members, the Chair, and also various government functionaries. It will also analyze why they choose to continue or discontinue their political careers. The hypothesis is that women in local government bodies are political actors who exercise agency and can influence structures, processes, and people to bring about change or make decisions in their favor. This chapter will show that women are in fact strategically considering various options and making decisions and are able to take various initiatives to gain greater control and influence within the constraints in which they operate.

This chapter will argue that women representatives have gendered routes to power which are related to their gender roles of caring for family members and community members by providing for their needs and promoting peace and harmony in the family and community through problem solving and dispute resolution. Their gendered route to power also is related to their past experience of public dealings where their previous experiences of social work, community services, and working for NGOs have made them familiar figures and built up their reputation as credible, trustworthy, and capable of solving problems for others.

A similarity with male politicians is seen in the case of the women who belong to political families where they have learned the rules of the game by watching family members practice politics, and they are able to use the family networks and connections to come into the public domain and make a place for themselves there. Johansson (2006) also concluded that they are gendered by different pathways to power in different "welfare states" reflecting "the way that different welfare states are gendered." This also points to the phenomenon that there is an influence of different political and cultural contexts on the way political leadership is gendered.

In the Bangladesh context, it was found that women have alternative strategies of exercising power, which are also related to their past gendered experiences and also possibilities open to them, which are also different from those of men. Women's participation is also affected by various changes which have taken place in the overall context. Women's literacy and education levels have increased as have their mobility and participation in the labor force. With increasing access to the media, mobile phones, and the Internet, women's (as well as men's) access to information and communications with others has increased. News and opinions travel faster. On the other hand, political parties have increased their penetration to both rural areas and urban slums, and political actors and events are present at village and "moholla" (neighborhood) levels. This enables women to witness and participate in local level politics more than before.

While the above function as enabling factors for women to participate in public life more effectively, some of the barriers that have been previously identified persist. These include the dominance of money and muscle where women are relatively disadvantaged in having less financial resources of their own as well as well less access to volunteers who can exert force or intimidation. Another barrier, that is, valid for men as well is the lack of authority and power of local government bodies, with power being concentrated in the hand of the UP Chair. As argued by Ahmed (2016), even the power and authority of the UP Chair are limited as decentralization is limited and local government bodies such as the UP, have more responsibilities than authority. It is observed that most women do not contest a second time for UP elections, which would seem to indicate that they become discouraged by the barriers and constraints they experience once in office.

This chapter will also review the considerations of such women members in depth. This too is not specific to Bangladesh. Other researchers have also found that once elected women find the environment and culture of local government to be inimical and intimidating, with men showing aggression and resistance when they cannot cope with the women (Beck 2001; Drage 2001; Irwin 2009). Australian research with women councillors by the Department of Women (2000) in New South Wales found that women felt isolated when they are a minority on the council and that women are more often subject to bullying and other inappropriate behavior than are male councillors. It is important to recognize that the structures and processes of local government bodies are not neutral and are gendered and more attuned to male ways of working and being than to female ways. This paper is based on an in-depth qualitative study undertaken by the author under the Sharique program on local governance mandated by SDC and implemented by Helvetas Swiss Intercooperation (HIS) and BRAC Institute of Governance and Development (BIGD), which investigated experiences of women who have been elected in the UPs at least once and also women who have decided not to run for elections. It also explored the relationships between women in local government bodies and local political parties, local level UP representatives (UP Chair, members), and other civil society groups such as NGOs and women's organizations. The methodology used for the research consisted of desk review and primary data collection.

As the purpose of this study was to explore in depth the experience of women in local government and not to generalize the study findings, fieldwork was conducted in six (6) unions in two adjacent Upazilas in one division in order to control for the context (i.e., socioeconomic conditions) as much as possible. We selected unions that have reelected women members. The local level research site was in the Sharique program sites of Rajshahi (Mohanpur and Tanor Upazilas) where some unions have reelected women representatives. Field research included key informant interviews (KIIs) at both national and local levels. In each union, we interviewed three incumbent women members (which included reelected members); one woman who was elected once and not currently a serving member; the UP Chair; one male member; and one CSO representative and one political leader. We also interviewed one UNO (a Upazila executive officer). In total, we had 47 interviews from six unions, of whom 22 were women elected representatives and 12 were male elected representative. Secondary data were collected through review of existing literature and are available as the Stocktaking Report on Women's Participation in Local Government. Secondary sources have included academic and policy literature on local governance, relevant government documents and consultancy reports. National level interviews of academics and civil society experts were also carried out.

From Marginal Representation to "Critical Mass"

The Union Parishad, Upazila Parishad, Zila Parishad, Municipalities, and City Corporations are the local government bodies (LGBs) under the Local Government Division of Ministry of Local Government, Rural Development, and Cooperatives. Local Government Units are Zila Parishads (Districts Councils—64), Upazilas/Thanas (Subdistrict—487), City Corporations (11), Pourashavas (Municipality—323), and Union Parishads (Rural—4573). In the three Hill Districts, the local government bodies are the Regional Council, the Hill District Councils, the Upazila Parishad, Union Parishad, and Pourashavas. The Pourashava is the local government institution for municipalities/urban areas. Union Parishads, Upazila Parishads, Municipalities, and City Corporations are elected bodies.

Article 11 of the Constitution of Bangladesh confirms that the "Republic shall be a democracy in which ... effective participation by the people through their elected representatives in administration at all levels shall be ensured." The Constitution is quite unique in including detailed provisions for local government (Chapter 111, part IV Articles 59 and 60) ensuring that "every administrative unit shall be entrusted to bodies composed of persons elected in accordance with law" (Article 59) and outlining their functions and conferring power to collect taxes, prepare budgets, and maintain funds. Women's rights are guaranteed in the Constitution and women have equal rights in all spheres of the State and public life [Article 28(2)]. Article 9 further advances the principle of special representation of women in all local self-governing bodies.

Women's representation in the UP was promoted through two presidential ordinances: the Local Government Ordinance of 1976 and Municipal Ordinance of 1977, which for the first time provided for the nomination of two women members in the UP. The Union Parishad Ordinance of 1983 further made a provision for nomination of three women members. However, direct election to the reserved seats for women in the Union Parishad was first made in the Local Government (UP) (Second Amendment) Act of 1997. It allows for direct election of one chairperson and twelve members to the Union Parishad, with three seats reserved for women members. Each woman member represents three wards (each ward constituted by several villages). The three women seats are reserved for direct election. In addition to three reserved seats, women can take part in direct elections for general seats. The Act is considered a milestone toward increasing women's participation in politics and promoting their political skills through direct elections. Nevertheless, the Act was not able to address the confusions regarding the role and responsibilities of women members. The quotas were introduced in a way that women's seats were added on so that they do not disturb existing competition for electoral wards or constituencies. However, by having direct elections to these reserved seats as was introduced in 1997, their legitimacy as representatives is enhanced. This has been documented by various researchers (Khan and Mohsin 2008; Nazneen and Tasneem 2010). The number of women representatives has also increased substantially over the years as shown in Tables 14.1 and 14.2.

Table 14.1 Participation in union parishad (by sex)

Category of representatives and year of election

	Chairman				Member			
	2008		2011		2008		2011	
	Number	%	Number	%	Number	%	Number	%
Men	4477	99.53	4132	99.47	40,339	74.74	38,036	75.66
Women	21	0.47	22	0.53	13,637	25.26	12,236	24.34
Total	4498	100.00	4154	100.00	53,976	100.00	50,272	100.00

Source GoB (2013a, b)

Table 14.2 Participation in upazila parishad (by sex)

	Chairman					
	2009		*2010*		*2011*	
	Number	%	Number	%	Number	%
Men	452	99.56	473	99.37	473	99.37
Women	2	0.44	3	0.63	3	0.63
Total	454	100.00	476	100.00	476	100.00

Source Same as Table 14.1

THEORETICAL APPROACHES

A concept critical for those working on women's representation in politics is that of "critical mass" to explain that a significant number of women are needed before they can make a difference to processes and outcomes. This concept was first introduced by Kanter (1977) and Dahlerup (1988) who analyzed the experiences of women forming small minorities in the corporate and political spheres. Both were concerned with the dynamics of marginalization in situations where women were minorities, speculating on how this experience would change if numbers increased. The critical number was proposed as 30%, at which level women are expected to be able to make a substantial difference in politics (Dahlerup 2006). This concept has been supported and used by many researchers and academics (Mansbridge 1999; Lovenduski 2001;

Choudhury 2002). However, other research suggests that lower number of women working together in the legislature can also affect political change (Childs and Krook 2008). Some also argue that we should look more closely at parliamentary and electoral systems instead of critical mass (Tremblay 2006; Grey 2006).

The idea that having a sufficient number of women in local government bodies to form a critical mass may have influenced those carrying out local government reform to try to provide a minimum of one-third seats for women in bodies at each level (three seats for women versus nine general seats in the UP, which in fact comes to 25%). That there was a strong enough support for such as proactive measure is significant in itself. As Mahmud and Nazneen (2014, p. 17) have pointed out: "the support for and various other measures taken to increase women's presence and (...) elected bodies are themselves the result of negotiations between different social and political actors (political parties, their leadership, women within the parties, other influential party factions, women's movement, etc.). What influences the action taken by the actors are: the actual and perceived interests these actors have in promoting women's representation; the context within which opportunities for promoting women's representation arises; the strength i.e., resource of these actors to negotiate and influence other actors and the gender discourses that influence actions of these actors."

The research results show that while the number of women present in each UP does make a difference to the women by giving them greater confidence and voice, and allowing them to form alliances among themselves, they still face other cultural and structural constraints that limit their voice and agency. Voice and accountability are also important concepts to understand women's presence in politics and how this can turn into effective participation. Goetz and Hassim show that it is important to understand the mutual determinations of voice and accountability to understand how women can effectively participate in political institutions where "women's political effectiveness is understood as the ability to use 'voice' to politicize issues of concern to women, to use electoral leverage to press demands on decision makers, to trigger better responsiveness from the public sector to their needs, and better enforcement of constitutional commitments to women's equal rights" (2003: 29). The authors show how "voice" does not automatically lead to better outcomes for women because public institutions can have strong gender biases which counteract the impact of women's voice and presence in public. Many of the constraints to women's "voice" are due to their gender roles and relations such as their responsibility for family welfare, their lesser human and financial resources compared to men, and the way their sexuality is controlled by society. The latter translates into lesser physical security in public spaces and the fact that their sexuality is a matter of public discussion and attacks when they are in public life.

Pathways to Political Power at the Local Level

It is important to supplement achievements in terms of number of women in politics and in local government with an understanding of the trajectories of the women who have decided to enter the sphere of politics, including their motivations and entry points as well as barriers and obstacles. Formerly, women's agency in deciding to enter local government and politics was denied and it was assumed that they were proxy candidates for men who would exploit their wives, sisters, and daughters to be able to access the advantages and resources allocated for such posts. While such considerations have not fully disappeared, their importance relative to the women's own motivation has diminished. They too have their own ideas of why they are interested and what they can gain, both as individuals and for their families.

Although it is often said that women have less exposure than men to politics and therefore less experience and skills in this area, a few studies have highlighted that they may have experience and skills which are relevant to their roles and responsibilities as public representatives and they too have various personal, family, professional, and political networks that they can put to use. Some have experience of "how to do politics" through voluntary and welfare work and in other informal spaces. Some women have used their families to build their constituencies and political networks and also to address the needs of their constituents. Nazneen et al. (2014) show that political apprenticeship starts at home and in informal spaces. Their family members had been involved in politics or social activities and/or the women have been involved in student politics and/or professional work. They actively build relationships and constituencies, using their family connections, social networks, and also relationships with development agencies and women's organizations.

Learning to do Politics and Deciding to Contest Elections

For the women interviewed for the study, "serving society" was the key motivation mentioned for competing in the UP level elections. The reasons they mentioned included firstly, having the opportunity to serve the community; secondly, people's love and respect; and thirdly, that people would continue to remember them as a member and treat them with respect. Several factors encouraged women to contest the UP elections. Family background played a significant role for women to be involved in elections. If family members such as husband, father, brother, and in-laws are known to the community or have served as community leaders, this gives the women an advantage. In most cases, the women themselves did not have a political party affiliation before standing for elections but once elected, they joined a party or openly declared their allegiance to a party to facilitate interactions and their work in the UP. About half of the women opted to support the political party that other family members supported but for the other half, they chose to support the party in power or the UP chairman's party, out of strategic considerations.

In a number of cases, it was the women themselves who were known in the community through their social engagements. Ten of the women interviewed worked as health workers (2), domestic workers (1), midwife (1), NGO worker (2), school teacher (3), or even as a domestic worker or office staff. All these jobs entail a great deal of interaction with the community and are often seen as serving the community. Such social interactions with community members also serve as a training ground for political activities. The community gets to know about the women and gains respect for them, which encourages some women to contest elections.

The desire of family members such as husband, father-in-law, other family members' to see women of their families in the UP, or community members' requests could play a crucial role in making women interested. Another factor that illustrates the importance of the family relations is that if a woman married within her natal community and her in-laws and father's family live in the same constituency, it is easier for her to contest elections (being both a daughter and daughter-in-law of the community). Although expectations of monetary benefit from the post were not mentioned explicitly by the women, it became clear in the course of the interviews that all of them do a cost-benefit analysis and often complain about their earnings and allowances being inadequate. This seems to indicate that financial considerations are a hidden reason for contesting elections.

In general, there are a number of barriers for women to contest general seats which make it more sensible from their point of view to contest reserved seats. These barriers include having to face more competitors for general seats; expenses being therefore higher (also men spend more for elections as they have easier access to money than female candidates); women facing mobility constraints in canvassing votes; and lacking political experience and skills compared to male contestants.

PEOPLE'S PERCEPTIONS OF WOMEN UP MEMBERS

Some characteristics are identified by the community as important for someone who would wish to be a public representative, which are as follows:

- Mobility and familiarity in the community which would give her the opportunity to work with people and serve them as needed, i.e., NGO worker, teacher, health worker, and insurance worker.
- Known as a social worker who provides services such as birth attendant and match maker for marriages.
- Good natured and helpful, e.g., can mix with people and provide advice, help with dispute resolution, etc.
- Engaged with the community and its activities.

According to the FGDs respondent and other key informants, there are mixed feelings about women candidates and elected representatives in UPs. Firstly, as mentioned above, mobility is seen as an important qualification to succeed in local politics. However, they are perceived to be less mobile than men. Secondly, they are seen to be socially and economically disadvantaged. UP chairman, members, local political leader, and NGO key informants observed that most of the female candidates came from "comparatively lower class of the society" who wanted to get respect and monetary benefit from the post. They also believed that better off or educated families did not like the idea of their daughters or wives working with common people for a minimum honorarium, little respect, and insignificant tasks to do. Men in the community even went so far as to say that women candidates and elected members have questionable moral characters (since they are active in the public sphere where they interact with male UP members and the general public). Women community members did not mention this issue but they stressed that they felt that they were better represented in the UP by a woman.

There are, however, many prejudices against, and resistances to, women's participation in politics. Male FGD participants felt that society still does not approve of women participating in elections or politics. Some referred to Bangladesh being a Muslim country and women's activities in recent times do not reflect that. Some of the general people seem to have an unreasonable suspicion about the "moral" character of the female members though they do not have evidence of that. For others, the women representatives are not important or significant. "We don't give much thought about the female members. They are like optional subjects in a syllabus (4th subject)" (Talondo Male FGD).

Women Councillors: Roles and Responsibilities

The Union Parishad Act 2009 states that the Union Parishad shall be composed of a chairman, nine general members, and three members to reserved seats. Clause 10.3 mentions that three seats will be reserved for women and will be called reserved seats and women will be elected directly to these seats. This Act also provides for 13 Standing Committees which generally consist of four members, relevant government service providers, and various co-opted persons (e.g., school teacher). Each UP member is supposed to Chair at least one Standing Committee. The 2009 Act mentions that Chair of the Standing Committees will be selected from among the elected members, and the women elected to the reserved posts will Chair at least one-third of the Standing Committees (Section 45.3). The Act sets out guidelines for the functioning of the Standing Committees, which are to be supplemented by bylaws. In addition, there are several General Committees concerned, for example, with disaster management, water and sanitation, and selection and distribution of relief and welfare.

The 2009 Union Parishad Act adds the requirement to form ward assemblies which shall meet at least twice per year and mandates that both planning and budgeting should be participatory from 2010 for all UP. The ward assemblies organized by the ward member are required to identify priorities for action, raise awareness of local issues, monitor lists of beneficiaries of social welfare programs, and motivate participation in open budget and planning meetings. The elected women representatives on the reserved seats are to be advisors to the ward assemblies (clause 5.5). The Act also requires each UP to hold an open budget meeting (OBM) to seek public approval of the UP budget.

The UP Act, however, does not clearly define the functional jurisdictions for the women councillors in the Union Parishad nor mention that it is the same as that of the general members. On the other hand, it is given a separate status by the statement that these would be referred to as "reserve seats for women." This sets the women aside as a separate category in the councils leaving scope for the interpretation that when the general seats are mentioned it is not applicable for the reserved seats. The Chairs and male members have been using this major oversight in the law to discriminate and often exclude the women councillors from participating in UP activities.

Initially, when the first batch of women was elected to the UPs in 1997 on the basis of the new law, women were denied a role in project planning, implementation, budget making, financial management, preparing list, and distribution of VGD and VGF cards under the food security schemes. Women were also denied the right to provide citizenship, character, and other certificates usually issued by male representatives. The women were also reported to be often excluded from meetings and important decisions of the UPs. The ministry then responded positively to the complaints from the elected women members and the concerned civil society organization including the media. It issued circulars and orders from the Local Government Division of the Ministry of Local Government, Rural Development, and Cooperatives, specifying some roles and positions that have to be provided to women reserve seat members.

In addition, the Chairs and the male members continued to resist implementing these orders from the government and no action was taken for non-compliance. In many places, the women members approached the UNOs and other Upazila officials seeking intervention for the chairmen to comply with the orders but with no success. Thus, although the sociocultural and economic barriers to women's participation in the political institution of the UP were overcome to some extent by women's elections, this anomaly in the law prevented the removal of the institutional resistances to their incorporation in the UP functions.

Like men, the newly elected women members are not aware of the legal framework of the UP and for their rights and responsibilities. Although training is provided from various sources, they mainly learn the functioning on the job. There are examples of women who benefit from the training and the study of the various documents available and are able to use that to ensure that the procedures are followed and that they are given their due. An example is given in the next section.

ROLE OF WOMEN COUNCILLORS IN LOCAL COUNCIL DECISION MAKING

The structure of the Union Parishad is such that the chairman has a disproportionate role in decision making, and the general ward members or women of the reserved seats play a secondary role. Procedurally, ward assemblies or Standing Committees can make recommendations to the council and the council makes the decisions. However, in the case of decision making in the council, the chairman is the final authority. In regard to the issues like dowry, divorce, and violence against women, which are issues perceived of as related to women, the opinion of female members is valued. In the case of land-related disputes, female members' opinion does not get importance (Interview 0101FM3). When asked, the female members stated that it is the chairman who decides about the Chairs of Standing Committees. It is the Chair who represents the UP in government meetings and at the next level up, in the Upazila Parishad.

The chairman is the chief executive of a Union Parishad. He decides on all matters. He assigns work, approves sanctions of development works, and presides over all meetings, committees. Without his support and favor, nothing is possible and both male and female members have to maintain good working relations with the chairman. Although the elected women members interviewed said that they have good relations with the chairman, probing revealed a different reality with the women members having to strategize to influence decision making.

If a woman member has strong political connections, ties with the administration, or family status, then it is easier for her to get chairman's support, cooperation, and favor. For example, Puspa Rani had a strong connection with the ruling party and she was the Secretary of Krishok (farmers') League at district level (Interview 0102FM2). The chairman used her political influence to clear bills from government offices and obtained allocations from MP's personal fund. As the chairman was not from the political party in power, he needed her assistance in these issues. She would receive her share of money for making his work easy. Puspa Rani was therefore in a strong position to be able to negotiate with the UP Chair. Social status is also a factor in gaining favor from the chairman. Fayzunnahar who is the wife of the *Pramanik* (village head) said that "I use my social power to influence chairman's decision." Other interviewees mentioned that other members and the UP Secretary respected her as wife of *Pramanik* (village head). She was not willing to attend all meetings: "if they need my consent or signature, the chairman will send the papers by *choukidar (nightguard)* or Secretary will bring them and I will sign these." This was done as a sign of respect for her and acknowledgment of her influence and position. Fayazunnahar also felt capable of pressurizing the UP Chair which she does through other political leaders. Also if she did not agree with the UP council, she refused to sign the papers (0102 FM1).

Not all the women members were able to influence the UP chairman. In the case of Champa Begum (0101FM1), she had an argument with the chairman about the distribution of VGD cards as she thought she should get more than the male members as she was elected from three wards. But the chairman allegedly misbehaved with her, told her to never set foot in the Union Parishad again and did not allow her to attend meetings. In case of Josna Begum (0102FM3) when she asked for more information about some project and refused to sign a resolution without checking it, the chairman misbehaved with her and she was unofficially barred from the Union Parishad.

Khairun Begum (0201FM1) a reelected member described how she relentlessly fought for her rights in the UP. Although she was elected with the support of BNP (the Bangladesh Nationalist Party) and the chairman and six male members are supporters of BNP as well, it was not easy to get what she deserves. Most of the time, the chairman provided false information about the allowance cards and even tried to avoid including female members in the projects and programs like LGSP. Since she was active and gathered information from different sources, she could confront him and ensure she obtained her share of UP allocations.

Most of the examples of dispute between the chairman and women members result in the chairman prevailing over the woman member. Therefore, most of them do not opt for open confrontation or disputes. They choose alternative strategies. For example, Shabana Akhter (0101FM3) keeps a manual of UP regulations with her. When she has any doubts about the chairman's decisions, she suggests that they consult the manual. There are others who choose not to be confrontational. Raihana Begum (0202FM3) described how she did not bother the chairman in his wrong doings. When asked why she did not complain against the chairman, she said she did not want to be in bad terms with the chairman. Since she is from a solvent family, she did not need money and she was happy with whatever she got from the programs that she ran. She said that the decision-making processes are quite well conducted and Open Budget, Ward Meetings, and Standing Committee meetings are held regularly in the UP. Thus, she gets the opportunity to share her ideas in those meetings. But most of the time she, along with the other members, keeps quiet and does whatever the chairman suggests.

Although Champa Begum (0101FM1) later entered into a confrontation with her UP Chair, she had mentioned a strategy of the women members coming together. She described how female members had started forming what she called "syndicates," i.e., coalitions in order to establish their demands and opinions. She felt that earlier women members had little or no opportunity to express their opinions as their male colleagues did not value their opinions. But, now the scenario had changed and women can have their say and give their suggestions. The importance of women members coming together was also mentioned in the neighboring union, Ghasigram. Rahela Begum (0103FM3), in the Ghasigram Union, also felt that male members and chairman come together to act as a team to serve their own benefit and always try their best to keep female members away from important works. More or less, important decisions are taken without consulting the female members. Another strategy mentioned by some of the women was using emotions and appealing to men by showing that they were weaker and needed help. Sometimes female members would cry in front of chairman and secretary to get their sympathies (0101FM2). Some women showed their anger in front of chairman and others sometime walked out from the meeting. As a result, the chairman called them back and tried to solve the problems.

MEN AND WOMEN COUNCILLORS: ADVERSARIES OR ALLIES

The interviews with women members show that to function effectively in the UP, they needed to have the male members and/or the chairman as their allies, although structurally and culturally there were more reasons for them to be adversaries. Once elected, women find the environment and culture of the UPs, unfamiliar and uncomfortable. Men are often aggressive, some use abusive language (slang and swearing), and women may be subject to bullying and inappropriate behavior. This may include personal attacks, inappropriate jokes, and putting down because of their inexperience, age, or gender. This is not a phenomenon limited to Bangladesh or even South Asia (see Irvin 2009).

Some of the women might be called "Apa" (older sister) as a term of respect or "Bhabi" (sister-in-law) which might also be a sign of respect or a means of othering—relating to the woman through her husband and not as an individual. In general, male members do not treat women members as equals and do not want to include women members in day-to-day activities so that they can take benefit without creating scope of involvement for female members. This came out clearly in both male and female UP members' interviews.

Kinship often hampers the working relationship between the male and female members. Male members try to dominate female members which the female member may not like. Having male relatives interested in contesting elections has already been mentioned as a reason why women would choose to contest for reserved seats so as not to compete with male family members. Sometimes they create artificial crisis—for example, Binu Begum, an ex-member (0102EFM) explained:

> My uncle and I were from the same constituency. My uncle wanted to exercise all the power. When we got a project jointly he never involved me in the project and never gave my share. He always wanted to prove that I couldn't do anything without his help. To prove this he always created false crisis like when I try to solve any dispute he opposes me behind the scenes and creates another dispute.

Women members try to motivate the male members to work together with them. Female members have to keep good relations with male members in their three wards to work together to distribute VGD, old age allowance, etc. They try to work closely with their male counterparts to avoid complications. Women who can "manage" the male members can work freely and smoothly in the UP. Champa Begum (0101FM1) stated "Togetherness is a good thing to complete any task. But, it doesn't function properly all the time. Most of them, male members form a 'syndicate' or their own coalitions." However, male members also recognized the cooperation between women and male members as an effective strategy (0101MM).

The conflicts between women and men elected representatives are often over allocations and resources. Although Shabana Akhter (0101FM3) was an AL supporter and presided over the committee for the distribution of widow allowances, when she selected a widow who was a BNP supporter, the male AL member refused to sign the card. There are also social norms which restrict interactions between women and men which also complicate relations between male and female UP members. If men and women are seen together, people will start gossiping about both of them. In fact, men in the FGDs conducted had expressed the opinion that the elected women were of "dubious character." Some male citizens said that they try to maintain a distance from the female members. They prefer not going to a female member even if they need to. The reason is that if a male citizen is seen with a female member more than once, people will start talking about them. So the male citizens try not to go to a female member even if they need for avoiding such situations.

Assessing the Role of Women in Local Government

This chapter has attempted to understand the trajectories of elected women representatives in local government to understand the pathways through which women gain access to political power and develop their political voice and agency. With a change in the socioeconomic context, the increased education levels of women, and their previous experience of social and community work, women are more effectively playing their roles as public representatives. The concept of critical mass helps us understand how the increased numbers of women in public office have lead to their gaining greater recognition and importance, while the concepts of voice and agency help us understand how individual women and their coalitions have negotiated the various barriers and constraints to develop more effective participation.

Women often take gendered routes to power and also have alternative strategies of exercising power, which are related to their gender roles of caring for the family and community and providing services to them. While the women and men both strategize and negotiate with various persons, parties, and institutions to overcome opposition and achieve their goals, compared to the men, the women are less experienced and skilled at this. Peer-to-peer learning and support can help the women to be more conscious and strategic. For example, they learned by example that complaining to the UNO about the UP Chair would have a negative impact and the other women members chose not to complain after the experience of Josna Begum (0102 FM3). Also, the study found that in some of the unions, the women had been able to develop solidarity between themselves and support each other when they faced problems. Where they were isolated from each other, the UNO, Chair, and members were able to dominate them more easily.

Various UP structures and process provide the opportunity for women members to play a leadership role and develop their management and leadership skills. These include the Chairing of Standing Committees, Project Implementation Committees, and being advisors to ward shobhas. These have a contribution in giving the women specific tasks and responsibilities but their functioning is influenced by the actions of the UP Chair, the secretary, and other male members. The differences in authority between the Chair and members mean that the Chair takes the final decisions and the members cannot go against his decisions. In order to ensure the smooth functioning of the Standing Committees, or the projects, the women members have to make compromises and "manage" the male members, the Chair, and also the political party activists nominated to the various committees. While it is essential to emphasize the implementation of the existing legal provisions, it is important to understand the constraints the women have to work within to make these functional.

In conclusion, in spite of the various constraints and barriers, we can see that women are strategic actors who decide to contest general or reserved seats based on an assessment of the context and the factors in their favor or disfavor. They function in the UP through making compromises and alliances with the UP Chair and male members and also political activists appointed to various Standing Committees. They use their political party allegiances and alliances to support their case or the UP Chair. They seek to exert influence and power when and where they can and strategically decide not to do so when the costs are too high or the possibility of a positive outcome are remote. Some of the women have suffered in the process of confronting the UP Chair, political party, or government officials but at least they have tried to make their views heard. The overall picture emerging is of a more conscious, vocal and capable group of women leaders and public representatives who cannot be discounted.

REFERENCES

Ahmed, T. (2016). *Bangladesh: Reform agenda for local governance*. Dhaka: Prothoma Prokashan.

Beck, S. A. (2001). Acting as women: The effect and limitations of gender in local government. In S. Carroll (Ed.), *The impact of women in public office*. Bloomington: Indiana University Press.

Childs, S., & Krook, M. L. (2008). Critical mass theory and women's political representation. *Political Studies, 56*(3), 725–736.

Chowdhury, N. (2002). *The implementation of quotas: Bangladesh experience – dependence and marginality in politics*. Stockholm: International Institute for Democracy and Electoral Assistance.

Dahlerup, D. (1988). From a small to a large minority: Women in scandinavian politics. *Scandinavian Political Studies, 11*(4), 275–297.

Dahlerup, D. (2006). The story of the theory of critical mass. *Politics and Gender, 2*(4), 511–522.

Department of Women. (2000). *Hands up for women's councils!*. Sydney.

Drage, J. (2001). *Women in local government in the asia and the pacific. Comparative analysis of 13 countries*. Bangkok: United Nations Economic and Social Council for Asia and the Pacific.

Goetz, A. M., & Hassim, S. (2003). Introduction: Women in power in Uganda and South Africa. In A. M. Goetz, & S. Hassim (Eds.), *No shortcuts to power: African women in politics and policymaking*, London: Zed Books.

Government of Bangladesh (GoB). (2013a). *Gender statistics of Bangladesh 2012*. Dhaka: BBS.

Government of Bangladesh. (2013b). *The millennium development goals: Bangladesh progress report 2012*. Dhaka: General Economics Division, Bangladesh Planning Commission.

Grey, S. (2006). Numbers and beyond: The relevance of critical mass in gender research. *Politics & Gender, 2*(4), 492–502.

Hossain, N., & Akhter, S. (2011). *Gender, power and politics in Bangladesh: A baseline study for the Upazila support project, (draft)*. Dhaka: UNDP.

Irwin, R. (2009). *Dancing in the lion's den: Women leaders in local government*, Ph.D. thesis, Southern Cross University.

Johansson, V. (2006). Gendered roads to mayorrship in diffferent welfare states. In H. Back, H. Heinelt, & A. Muguier (Eds.), *The European mayor: Political leaders in the changing context of local democracy.* Wiesbaden: Publisher for the Social Sciences.

Kanter, R. M. (1977). Some effects of proportions on group life: Skewed sex ratios and responses to token women. *American Journal of Sociology, 82*(5), 965–990.

Khan, Z. R., & Mohsin, A. (2008). Women's empowerment through local governance: Emerging issues and debates. Paper presented at Pathways of Women's Empowerment RPC Mid Term Review Conference, Cairo, January, 20–24.

Lovenduski, J. (2001). Women and politics: Minority representation or critical mass? *Parliamentary Affairs, 54*(4), 743–758.

Mahmud, S., & Nazneen, S. (2014). *Gendered politics of securing inclusive development.* Dhaka: BIGD.

Mansbridge, J. (1999). Should blacks represent blacks and women represent women? A contingent yes. *The Journal of Politics, 61*(3), 628–657.

Nazneen, S., & Tasneem, S. (2010). A silver lining: Women in reserved seats in local government in Bangladesh. *IDS Bulletin, 41*(5), 1–7.

Nazneen, S., Ehsan, I., & Hasan, B. (2014). Exceptional women: Reserved councillors in municipal corporation in Bangladesh. In Mariz Tadros (Ed.), *Women in politics: Gender.* Power and Development. London: Zed Books.

Panday, P. K. (2008). Representation without participation: Quotas for women in Bangladesh. *International Political Science Review, 29*(4), 489–512.

Panday, P. K. 2013. Impact study on women empowerment through effective, transparent and inclusive local governancereport prepared for shariquelocal governance program.

Tremblay, M. (2006). The substantive representation of women and PR: Some reflections on the role of surrogate representation and critical mass. *Politics & Gender, 2*(4), 502–511.

CHAPTER 15

Proxy or Agency? Women in Rural Local Government in India

Prakash Chand

People's participation in the governance process of a nation is the essence of democracy. Such participation is possible only when powers of the state are decentralized to local bodies where people can sit together, discuss their problems and concerns, and formulate as well as implement their developmental policies and programs. Local self-government is critical not only for restoring the self-esteem of the villagers, but also for reducing the burden of the state government. It also helps in mitigating the alienation of the rural people as they become aware of the fact that they are being consulted and their voice is being heard in the governance of their own affairs by the state and the center (Chandrasekhar 2011, p. 1). Decentralization of power and authority is the primary essence of local governance. It is a process as well as a mechanism through which democracy becomes truly representative, responsive, and accountable to the people. In this way, local governance becomes a source of empowerment of the grassroots people.

India has one of the oldest traditions of local governance as the village councils have existed here since ancient times. Local governments

P. Chand (✉)
Dyal Singh Evening College, University of Delhi, Delhi, India
e-mail: pcka120872@yahoo.com

© The Author(s) 2018
N. Ahmed (ed.), *Women in Governing Institutions in South Asia*,
DOI 10.1007/978-3-319-57475-2_15

in independent India have been formalized under the Panchayati Raj (PR), a three-tier system with elected bodies at the village, block, and district levels. The modern system is based in part on the traditional panchayat governance, in part on the vision of Mahatma Gandhi, and in part on the suggestions of various committees to harmonize the highly centralized Indian administration with a degree of local autonomy. The initiative was intended to facilitate greater participation of the people in the local government through effective implementation of rural development programs.

The participation of women in all spheres of life has become a significant issue in the discourse of social and economic development. The entrance of elected women representatives into the grassroots polity through elections to the PR Institutions (PRI) in massive numbers is a relatively new political phenomenon in India. Since 1993, when the 73rd Constitution Amendment providing, among other things, for the reservation of one-third of seats at each PR level for women came into force, women have moved forward and demonstrated their ability to hold such positions and fulfill the mandate of their constituents. With every succeeding panchayat election, women have been able to enlarge their representation beyond the minimum 33% prescribed by the Constitution. While speaking in the Lok Sabha on December 16, 2015, the Union Minister of State for Panchayati Raj Nihal Chand shared the information that women formed 46% of the total 1.341 million elected representatives (ERs) in PRIs across the country (TIE 2015, p. 8). This implies that some kind of metamorphosis has taken place in respect of representation of women at the local level.

This chapter attempts to examine the extent to which women's higher presence makes any difference in local government's policymaking process. It tries to analyze the effectiveness of legislative weapon for empowerment of women and highlights issues and challenges that confront women panchayat members. It also looks into the dynamism of the process whereby women empowerment is achieved through legislation and seeks to analyze whether political participation of women does in fact translate into concrete women empowerment—a state where women are able to carve a niche for themselves in the traditional male bastion and successfully find a forum for effective redressal of gender issues or whether increased political participation of women is just an eyewash. This chapter will try to explore the ground realities in light of the case studies and experiences of some of the Indian states.

LOCAL GOVERNMENT IN INDIA: HISTORICAL PERSPECTIVE

Local self-governing institutions have a long history in India, with the earliest evidence from the Rig-Veda texts dating to 1200 B.C. Over a period of time, these self-governing *sabhas*, or councils, evolved into panchayats or councils of five people. These councils, usually controlled by upper-caste men, were responsible for governing village affairs and managing land and taxes. They also existed to monitor social conduct and ethics of members as well as their occupational affairs (Sekhon 2006, p. 105). These bodies enjoyed a substantial amount of autonomy in terms of organization, functions, and finance bestowed upon them by village communities. The uniqueness of this form of governance was that it was absolutely a spontaneous development and no external authority had ever devolved power and authority on these bodies. Moreover, there was no uniform pattern of this form of governance as different village communities had no uniform pattern of organization (Srivastava 2002, p. 7). The vibrant tradition of local democracy in India remained almost unaffected and self-sufficient despite the vicissitude of political empires at the central level. Thus, in India, from the distant past there existed a well-organized system of village self-government, the pertinacity of which was so well described by Lord Metcalfe in 1830 in the following way:

> They seem to last where nothing else lasts. Dynasty after dynasty tumbles down, revolution succeeds revolution, Hindu, Pathan, Mughal, Mahratta, Sikh, English are all masters in turn, but, the village communities remain the same. (Metcalfe as quoted by Mallik 1929, p. 36)

The British colonial state, as part of its housekeeping functions, had adopted several measures to streamline local self-government. Notable among them were the Ripon Resolution (1882), the Bengal Local Self-Government Act (1885), and the Bengal Village Self-Government Act (1919). Out of the said measures, the Bengal Village Self-Government Act of 1919 may be regarded as the beginning of local self-government in India, providing a two-tier structure—union boards at the bottom level and district boards at the higher level. However, those self-governing structures were neither self nor local as those bodies were marked by the perennial resource crunch, over-bureaucratization, and dominance of local landed gentry. They remained as mere appendage of provincial government (Chakrabarty and Chand 2012, p. 271).The underlying objective was solely to serve the interest of the Empire.

The centralizing tendencies that were set in motion during the British rule continued during the first decade of independence. Independence had brought about a shift in power structure, but not in the attitude regarding grassroots governance. Although the independence leaders debated the issue of village self-governance, there was no unanimity on it. The first major step toward institutionalizing the panchayats was made in the late 1950s when the government introduced, on the basis of the recommendations of the Balwantrai Mehta Committee, a three-tier system of rural local government—i.e., a village panchayat at the village level, a panchayats samiti at the intermediate level, and a Zilla Parishad at the district level. The panchayats samiti was given greater recognition than the other two bodies. The issue of women's participation in the panchayat was first proposed in 1959 when the Mehta report recommended that two women be appointed to panchayats. At that time, the women appointed often came from rural elite families.

The Ashok Mehta Committee, appointed subsequently to inquire into the working of PRIs and to suggest measures to strengthen them, felt that a combination of factors such as an unsympathetic bureaucracy, absence of political will, lack of involvement in planning and implementation on a substantial scale, and the domination of local institutions by the economic and social rural elite was likely to undermine the PRIs, (Desouza 2002, p. 371). The Mehta Committee recommended a more radically decentralized system of panchayats with strong decision-making powers, as well as the inclusion of women and other disadvantaged groups such as the lower-status castes and tribes in it. It underscored the functional necessity of decentralization and recommended a two-tier system, with the Zilla Parishad and Mandal Panchayat as the administrative setup for panchayats.

The committee also recommended that the district should be the basic unit since it was a viable administrative unit for which planning, coordination, and resource allocation were feasible and for which technical expertise was available. The Ashok Mehta Committee also demanded the constitutional recognition for panchyats. The committee even drafted a model bill, which they appended to the report, seeking an amendment to the Constitution along these lines (Kumar 2006, p. 23). But due to the change in the political power at the center, the recommendations of the Ashok Mehta Committee could not be implemented. No major change in local government occurred until 1993 when the 73rd constitutional amendment was made, to which reference has been made earlier.

STRUCTURE OF RURAL LOCAL GOVERNMENT
AND CONSTITUTIONAL QUINTESSENCE

As stated earlier, a three-tier structure of rural local government, with a Zilla Parishad at the top, a panchayat samiti (PS) in the middle, and a village panchayat at the bottom, was introduced in most of the Indian states following the recommendations of the Balwantrai Mehta Committee. In most of the cases, these PRIs became moribund and non-functional in subsequent years. Elections were not held, and the panchayats did not assume any active role (Ghatak and Ghatak 1999). Several reasons accounted for the weaknesses of the PR system. These include lack of proper funding, political interference, upper caste-class domination, absence of participation of women, irregular elections, lack of uniform structure, and non-constitutional status of local self-governing institutions. One of the important ways to overcome the problems was to accord constitutional recognition to local government and to recognize panchayats as the 'third tier' of federal government.

The Seventy-Third Constitutional Amendment Act, 1992, is considered as an important landmark in the history of local government in India. It can be seen as an important step to salvage the age-old traditional local government system. The Act provided for several important changes aimed at making different PRIs representative and empowering them to undertake a range of functions that differed significantly with the past. The main features of the 73rd Amendment Act are as follows:

- It provided for a three-tier Panchayati Raj system, with a Zilla Parishad at the top, a Panchayat Samiti at the intermediate level, and village panchayats at the bottom.
- It provided for devolving power, authority, and responsibilities to rural local bodies to enable them to function as institutions of self-government.
- It made elections to PRIs mandatory for every 5 years. In case of early or premature dismissal of PRIs, elections are to be held within a period of 6 months, with the newly elected members serving out the remainder of the 5 year term.
- It provided for reservation of one-third of seats at all panchayats level for women, of which one-third is to be reserved for the women belonging to schedule caste and tribes,

- A state-level Election Commission is to be constituted for a period of 5 years to ensure free and fair elections in local bodies.
- A state-level Finance Commission is to be set up every 5 years to review the overall financial position of local bodies,
- Schedule XI (Art 243G) has been added providing a list of 29 functions to be performed by PR institutions.

It is evident from the above that several radical provisions were incorporated in the 73rd Amendment Act. These range from granting constitutional status to PRIs, empowering the socially and economically disadvantaged groups, i.e., Dalits, Adivasis, and women, and ensuring free, fair, and regular elections, to fixing the terms of local councils, empowering PRIs to formulate and implement policies, and addressing financial issues of local bodies. Overall, the Act provided for a significant degree of fiscal, administrative, and political decentralization from the state to local levels. The new Act can thus be regarded as a path-breaking legislation, providing a democratic framework for the governance of local government institutions in rural India.

WOMEN IN RURAL LOCAL GOVERNMENT: FROM MARGINAL REPRESENTATION TO 'CRITICAL MASS'?

One of the most significant features of the 73rd Constitution Amendment Act is the institutionalization of women's participation via reservation of seats in the local bodies. Womenfolk in India, especially in rural India, have been subject to a systematic and systemic exploitation of the patriarchy. They have been systematically 'excluded' from the corridors of power. The Act has substantially elevated the status of Indian women from a subjugated status to a self-reliant one. The Act has stipulated in categorical terms that 'not less than one-third of the total number of seats to be filled by direct election in every panchayats shall be reserved for women'. Earlier, participation of women in PRIs was questioned in terms of the substance and effectiveness of representation. Social and political backwardness prevented them from taking part in decision making. Local committees insufficiently represented women. Women rarely headed any panchayat. Thus, rural women did not get their due share in development process in the past. The 73rd Amendment Act has tried to alleviate all these weaknesses.

A quota for women in local government bodies is justified on a number of grounds. Firstly, it is a matter of justice that women be included in political structures, as they constitute 50% of the population and should not be absent from spheres of power. Secondly, elected women will bring 'women's interests' to the formal political sphere. Because men do not understand 'women's interests', male-dominated political institutions either leave them off of the agenda, or act in a manner that indirectly or directly damages women's position. Thirdly, elected women will transform the very culture of politics. Finally, there is a symbolic relevance to women's reservations. The quotas dismantle the status quo and let women feel, and *be seen as*, represented in the formal decision-making process (Philips 1995).

There was no opposition to the 73rd constitutional amendment bill providing for reservation of seats for women. Nor was there any serious demand, especially from women's organizations, for any such reservation. In fact, 'reservations in India did not emerge out of a typical historical pattern, nor did the Indian women's movement push the formal political sector for the quotas. Indeed, the women's movement in the early 1990s was primarily mobilizing around issues of dowry, rape/sexual harassment, and prohibition' (Jain 1998). Politicians moved and supported the amendment mostly in self-interest than for empowering women in the real sense. Several reasons have been cited. While some politicians looked upon the women's reservation as an opportunity for women in their families and kin groups, and also as a welcome chance to reduce bitter factional conflicts at the local level, others did not consider PRIs as centers of power and authority, hence they did not care if women occupied one-third of the seats in these bodies (Baviskar 2003). Jain (1998) argues that 'the majority of (if not all) political parties supported quotas for women because they did not expect women's participation to be empowering; instead, perhaps they assumed that women would take on a passive, subdued role in the formal political sector.' This weak presence would enable parties to easily dominate the representative and forward their own agendas through them (Jain 1998).

Experience, however, shows that there has been a huge surge in women's interest in getting elected to local councils. Numerically, today India can actually boast that there are more elected women representatives (EWRs) in India than the rest of the world put together. As stated earlier, nearly half of the EWRs at the local level are women. Several states/union territories (UTs), for example, Assam, Andhra Pradesh,

Bihar, Chhattisgarh, Madhya Pradesh, Maharashtra, Rajasthan, and West Bengal, have reserved half of the seats in PRIs for women. Among the five states/UTs which have reported higher EWRs include Jharkhand, Rajasthan, Uttarakhand, Chhattisgarh, and Karnataka with 59.18, 58.29, 57.83, 55.14, and 53.40% representation, respectively (TIE 2015, p. 8)

PRIs operate in a complex socioeconomic environment. Caste, class, and gender hierarchies have a crucial bearing on institutional process and democratic practices. Generally, participation in panchayats in India is affected by the apathy of women. This indifference has its roots in the long historical background of their non-participation in governance because of entrenched caste, class, and gender hierarchies. The dominant political culture noticed since independence has also been one patronage and it has certainly not encouraged the participation of women in the institutional process. Low level of education and sociocultural norms also forbid women to enter into politics. Conservative attitude of the family members and the system of patriarchy prevailed in society also account for their backwardness. To some extent, poverty and lack of financial independence often make women dependent on men. Since they do not have independent decision-making power in the family, they often show their apathy toward politics (Gochhayat Artatrana 2013).

It was a very bold step for the rural women to come out of their homes and enter into the political domain that was previously monopolized by the male folk. The elected women leaders have tried to overcome these problems by different ways. They now try to be regular in panchayat meetings and keep themselves updated. They also participate actively in discussion at village level to overcome constraints problems. The training programs launched by the government have also helped them become confident and face the day-to-day issues/problems in a better way.

There are still some inherent snags in the present system. One of such is the rotational reservation system. First of all, only a very small percentage of first time women members get elected for the second or third time. Secondly, as male members previously held all these seats, they often manage to fix these up in favor of one of their women relatives. Hence, it is generally found that most women representatives scarcely possess the previous experience of being associated with political or social organizations; the majority of ERWs get elected to seats previously held by their family members. A study report of the Government of India (2008) shows that 41.7% of the female pradhans and 41.8% of the female ward members drew their inspiration for contesting panchayat elections from their spouses. Community groups such as Mahila Mandals and self-help groups motivated 23.3% of women to take a plunge, while political parties ranked a poor third motivating only 6.9% of the women representatives and that too only in the states of West Bengal, Sikkim, Tripura, and Kerala.

Thirdly, women candidates are rarely nominated for unreserved seats. In rural local bodies, only 10.8% of the women get elected from unreserved seats. For male contestants, however, this figure is 49% (Government of India 2008). Women that have got in simply through family connections are also not effective in asserting themselves and bringing about meaningful change. The process also entails a huge wastage of resources on the part of state governments as with every election they have to start the process of training and other related activities ab initio for the women members (Jain and Singh 2015). Thus, the rotational system of reservation begets a short-term gain mindset, leading to a lack of accountability among the PRI members.

Women Councillors: Roles and Responsibilities

As per the provision of the 73rd Amendment Act, panchayats are authorized to prepare plans for economic development and social justice and also to execute them. To facilitate this, states are supposed to transfer 29 functions and provide funds to execute these responsibilities. Most of the functions of panchayats are carried out through different standing committees. Each of the members remains in charge of a committee, while the overall responsibility rests with the chairperson of the panchayat. The panchayats are supported by a host of local officials in the formulation as well as implementation of their policies. Apart from funds received from the government under the recommendation of the Finance Commission, panchayats also receive grants for executing the schemes, such as poverty elevation programs, employment schemes, and rural development programs. They are also authorized to raise funds by imposing taxes, fees, penalties etc.

Some states have made special provisions for women's empowerment. The state of Kerala can be seen as a role model. It has earmarked 40% of the budgetary allocation for the panchayats. The planning board has been entrusted with the task of implementation of a People's Plan for Panchayat development. Gender dimensions have received special priority. A number of steps were taken in this direction. First, special instruction was given to ensure greater participation of women in the gram sabha meetings. Second, women-related issues were an important theme for discussion both at gram sabha meetings and also at the training programs conducted for the resource persons. Third, panchayats are mandatorily required to make a gender impact statement while making cost–benefit assessment of the projects. Fourth, the local bodies were advised to set apart 10% of the grant-in-aid under women component plan for projects directly targeting women (Radha and Chowdhury 2002, p. 56).The women component plan during its operation in last one decade has many achievements to its credit.

For the first time, development of women was brought into the agenda of each local body. Women were treated not as mere beneficiaries but as partners in the development process. With WCP, there was a quantum increase in the benefits given to women. Within this broad context, the disadvantaged groups such as widows, separated women, and families with unmarried girls were given more weightage while selecting beneficiaries for various projects. These initiatives helped in enhancing the confidence of women and improved their decision-making capacity.

Role of Women Panchayat Members in Decision Making

Reservation of seats for women in Panchayati Raj Institution has facilitated the empowerment of women. It has ensured their participation in the policymaking process. Now, they can take decisions, influence decisions, and have power over values, ideas, and resources. They are bringing transformation in politics by challenging the existing hierarchies of power. Several studies have explored the impact of reservation on the empowerment of women in India. A study carried out in Orissa by Hust (2007) has found that women have gained in many respects. They have acquired a legitimate space in rural political institutions. The elected women take part in the local meetings, interact with officials, and participate in the decision-making process. The study has concluded that reservation, as a strategy to empower women, has been successful.

Other studies have also observed that women leaders are making a difference in rural India. A study carried out by Chattopadhayay and Duflo (2003) in Birbhum in West Bengal has found that women now invest more in goods that are relevant to the needs of local women, i.e., water and roads. The study suggests that given the difficulty of targeting public transfers to specific groups in an otherwise decentralized system, reservation may be a good tool to ensure not only adequate representation but also adequate delivery of local public goods to disadvantaged groups (Chattopadhyay and Duflo 2011, p. 242). Women leaders make a difference on the ground. It also suggests that rectifying imbalance in the political system does result in improving in the other spheres as well.

Women leaders are also playing an important role in promoting girl's education and challenging the corrupt officials in Rajasthan. In Bhadsiya village, 115 km from the district headquarters of Nagaur in the heart of Rajasthan, girl students in a higher secondary school used to skip classes and lug heavy buckets of water from a hand pump outside the compound to the kitchen, where their mid-day meal was prepared. This was a daily chore the girls had to perform dutifully. Those who did not want to do it simply absented themselves from school on the days allocated to them. When sarpanch (head of village panchayat) Radha Devi came to know of this, she became furious. Not only did she reprimand the principal for getting the students to do work that was outside their curriculum; she also motivated the young girls to attend school regularly. In another case in Ekran gram panchayat of Bharatpur district, it was due to the diligent efforts of sarpanch Anguri Devi that the numbers of girl students in the local high school could be boosted (Kumar 2013, p. 56). Thus, the vigilant women heads of panchayats in Rajasthan are working hard to ensure proper schooling to girls, besides seeking ways to make their villages more gender friendly.

The above case studies make it evident that women are making a difference in the local governance. They are playing an important role in the decision-making process, giving more importance to social development activities such as health, education, sanitation, old-age pensions, and social welfare. The active participation of women representatives in local affairs has enhanced their confidence that has motivated other women to come forward. Reservation has been fruitful in two ways: firstly, it has facilitated women empowerment; and secondly, it has also been proved to be an effective tool to ensure adequate delivery of local public goods to the disadvantaged groups.

MEN AND WOMEN MEMBERS OF PANCHAYAT: ADVERSARIES OR ALLIES?

The attitude of men toward women's entry into politics has begun to change from that of total rejection to limited encouragement and, in some cases, even to active support and motivation. However, there is still a common complaint that women's power is being misused by their relatives, especially their husbands. They are being portrayed as proxies or puppets. Strulik (2003) rejects such castigations. He believes that it reflects a male-centered perspective denying women's agency and rational. To quote Strulik (2003):

> By focusing on women's dependency on their husbands, it is often ignored that men also depend heavily on their own support systems. Also, men have to rely on both female and male support structures. Men have their mothers, daughters and spouses, so that they can neglect bothering about reproductive work. They have, of course, their circle of male friends, where they discuss village matters, where they shape their ideas, and where they can draw support from different patron-client type relations. Still nobody suggests that they are puppets or proxies for someone, whereas the influence other people may have on their decisions, and their dependency on these sources of support, may just be more hidden and subtle.

Similarly, women can also utilize their support system. They can also take the help of their relatives including their husbands. The study by Strulik reveals that in many cases husbands were the biggest aides of their wives in helping them to enter a completely new arena. Though in the initial phase there might have been an intention to manipulate the women, but very often these processes developed their own dynamics and gradually the women extended their scope of action. Ultimately, the whole process has empowered the women. Thus, women, according to Strulik, are not proxies, but are transforming the way the political field is constructed, and are reshaping their field of action in the political arena.

Another study (Nielson ORG-MARG) on the issue of proxy has also made similar conclusions. It observes that there is a reason to be optimistic on this count as this practice is diminishing and women are depending lesser on their sarpanch *patis* (husbands) for decision making. It suggests that a good way of reforming this practice is to make training compulsory for all elected representatives (whether male or female) of PRIs in order to help them discharge their duties more effectively (CDHR, 2015).

The issue of 'surrogate participation' of women is one of those popular notions that just refuse to fade away. Yes, in some circumstances, where cultural and the social environment is highly patriarchal, proxy participation continues. However, in circumstances where surrogate participation is seen the actual situation might be that man might be playing a nurturing and consulting role, assisting the new woman entrant into the panchayats. Further, while surrogate participation might exist for the first elected term of the woman, quite often we come across situations where women have increasingly asserted themselves, once they have gained confidence—even winning the next election on their own worth, rather than as symbols of their male backers (Tiwari 2012). There is a need to bring about an attitudinal change in both men and women. The common perception that women are only meant for household activities and childrearing needs to be transformed into a feeling of equal partnership. To inculcate this attitudinal change, there is a need to impart education and awareness to both men and women members.

Assessing the Role of Women in Local Government

Reservation of seats for women in PRIs has acted as a catalyst in the process of women's political empowerment. A study by Mohanty (2001) highlights some significant transformation due to reservation of women in panchayats. According to the study, about 80–90% of women members attend panchayat meetings regularly, implying that democracy has become more participatory than before at the grassroots level. This argument becomes strengthened because the socioeconomic background of these women shows that the majority of them come from the lower income groups, particularly at the village panchayat level. Women not only seriously take up issues relating to basic needs—drinking water and availability of doctors and teachers in the villages, which is dear to them— but also want to undertake basic developmental activities. Mohanty's study also reveals that women in panchayats weave many dreams and their self-perception changes when they realize the immense potential of the public sphere. Due to their active participation in different activities, villagers also recognize their potential. Their respect in family has also increased which is linked to their empowerment.

As a result of the implementation of the policy for reservation of seats for women in local bodies, more than one million women have become involved in active (local) politics, while another three million are involved in the political process and have become aware of the grass-roots institutions. So, a ground has been created to mobilize the women of rural India to seek gender justice in a more vigorous way (Mohanty 2001, pp. 5–8). Mohanty's study clearly indicates that women's presence in PRIs has had a very positive impact. It has engendered development process at the grassroots level; there is an enhancement of women's self-respect in family as well as in society; and there is an active mobilization of women in the political life at the grassroots level. Another study (Singla 2003) points out that a large majority of the respondents feel that it is beneficial to have women in the decision making as it would facilitate representation of matters concerning them which are generally forgotten in the meetings.

Overall, the impact of women's participation in rural local bodies has been very positive. It has helped the rural women to become empowered not only politically but also socially, culturally, and economically. Now, they are more confident about their rights and responsibilities in the society. Women's participation in public sphere has emerged as a potent tool of social transformation. To quote Baviskar (2003, p.9):

> Shubhatai of village Vitner in Maharashtra looks more confident, and her husband has stopped battering her, thanks to her enhanced status in the family and community after she got elected in panchayats. Even, many men have given up drinking. More significant is the improvement in the self-image of women and their increasing confidence and experience in public life. They no longer obey orders from males unquestioningly

Perhaps, the most important impact is the recognition of the value of education by women. New panchayat members experience many handicaps due to lack of education. This makes them keen to educate their daughters. There is no doubt that female literacy and education will improve in the near future, partly due to women's participation in panchayats. It is likely that the next generation of women panchayat leaders will be better educated and, therefore, better equipped to govern local affairs.

The above observations are not intended to idealize the role of EWRs in PRIs. Many EWRs still face different problems. Barriers to women's political empowerment are still widely noticed. Women's participation in PRIs often remains confined to their representation and reservational participation only. Many factors are responsible for this, of which two—psychological and low level of education—are important. The psychological factor that inhibits active participation of women in the rural local government system is their shyness and submissiveness, and their lack of understanding of roles and responsibilities; their low level of education compounds this problem.

The infamous '*pradhan-pati*' syndrome is still widely seen, especially in northern India. In this typical phenomenon of proxy participation, male members of the women candidate wield power on her behalf. In some cases, women have been used as rubber stamps. Actual decisions are being taken by their male partners. Thus, the elected women representatives have reportedly been reduced to proxies of their male relatives and are under the control of male-dominated political party system. Often, men do not accord women the respect and regard that are their due. Officials take advantage of their inexperience and poor education. Effective devolution is so uneven and inadequate that oftentimes, even the most able women are crippled for want of the rightful allocation of functions, finances, and functionaries. A Ministry of Panchayati Raj report observes that although the womenfolk participate in the gram sabha meetings, they remain hesitant to interact officials.

Notwithstanding difficulties as stated above, women members in panchayats have generally performed well throughout the country. The process has brought a positive change in improving the status of women, empowered them socially, politically, and economically, and helped them to emerge as political leaders. Women are now more aware about their rights and are more responsive to issues of drinking water, health, education, economic empowerment, and the issue of alcohol abuse. There is a new awakening and consciousness among women as a result of their active involvement in the grassroots governance.

CONCLUSIONS

The 73rd Amendment has created an opportunity for a large number of rural women to take an active part in the PRIs. It has made Indian democracy participatory as well inclusive in its true sense. In many places, women have been functioning well and have engendered the development process. The family has accepted the new role, and even the relationship between husband and wife has been altered. The initial hostility of men toward the change is on the decline. Now, men have accepted the change and are trying to use women to their own advantage. The new process has democratized the local self-government and made people at the grassroots aware of the value of substantive democracy.

There is no denying that in an unequal patriarchal society like India, reservation of seats for women has invariably uplifted the status of women. However, it should not be taken as the only way of empowering women. It is only a step toward empowerment, not empowerment in itself. Therefore, women members of panchayats need to be educated and informed about politics, their rights, the nature of Indian democracy, and policies and programs for women and the underprivileged section of society. Social organizations can serve as a catalyst to mobilize women to address their issues. As far as the role of women in local governance in India is concerned, we can say that participation and representation are clearly different from empowerment. An elected woman representative needs the requisite social space in order to effect the changes that she desires. Also, the onus is on political parties who must motivate and integrate more women in the political process. Empowerment as a process is slow, but self-perpetuating. Providing women with opportunities and support systems through reservations and other affirmative action has the potential to put into motion a sustainable process for a change in gendered power relations allowing them to slowly but steadily break the shackles of existing boundaries. Thus, a combination of constitutional provisions, governmental efforts, social action programs, and self-awakening among rural women is needed to eventually facilitate the Indian women to become an active part of the mainstream political system.

References

Baviskar, B. S. (2003). Impact of women's participation in local governance in rural India. Retrieved September 30, 2016, from http://www.sapcanada.org/wp-content/uploads/2014/06/SAP-WE-Workshop-Baviskar.pdf.

Chakrabarty, B., & Chand, P. (2012). *Public administration in a globalizing world: Theories and practices.* New Delhi: Sage.

Chattopadhayay, R., & Ester, D. (2003). The impact of reservation in the panchayati raj: Evidence from a nationwide randomized experiment, Nov 2003, IIM Calcutta and MIT. Existed at https://poverty-action.org/sites/default/files/panchayati.pdf.

CDHR. (2015). Women's empowerment through panchayati raj. Available at: http://www.cdhr.org.in/womens-empowerment/womens-empowerment-through-panchayati-raj/.

Desouza, P. R. (2002). Decentralization and local government: The 'Second Wave' of democracy in India. In Zoya Hasan, E. Sridharan, & R. Sudarshan (Eds.), *India's living constitution: Ideas, practices, controversies.* Delhi: Permanent Black.

Ghatak, M., & Ghatak, M. (1999). *Grassroots Democracy: A study of the panchayat system in West Bengal, (Mimeo).* Calcutta: Development Research Group.

Gochhayat, A. (2013, Oct). Political Participation of Women in Gram Panchayat Elections in Odisha: A Case Study of Hindol Block in Dhenkanal District. *International Journal of Rural Studies, 20*(2).

Government of India. (2008). Study on elected women representatives in panchayati raj institutions. New Delhi: Ministry of Panchayati Raj.

Handrasekhar, L. (2011). *Undermining democracy: Parallel governance in contemporary South India.* Lodon: Rutledge.

Hust, E. (2007). Political representation and empowerment: Women in the institutions of local government. In Satyajit Singh & Pradeep K. Sharma (Eds.), *Decentralization: Institutions and politics in rural India.* New Delhi: Oxford University Press.

Jain, S. (1998). Redefining the politics of presence: The case of Indian women in panchayati raj institutions. Retrieved August 18, 2016, from http://www.swaraj.org/shikshantar/papers_politics_presence.html.

Jain, S., & Singh, A. (2015). Women in panchayats. Academike, Marh 27. Retrieved September 15, 2016, from http://www.lawctopus.com/academike/women-panchayats/.

Kumar, G. (2006). *Local democracy in India: Interpreting decentralization.* New Delhi: Sage.

Kumar, R. (2013). Women Sarpanches keep a sharp eye on girls. Retrieved September 11, 2016, from http://www.wfsnews.org/thp-20%20years%20of%20empowerment-2013.html.

Mallik, S. N. (1929). *Local self-government in India.* New Delhi: Sage.

Mohanty, B. (2001). The daughters of 73rd Amendment [online] New Delhi, Indian Institute of Social Sciences. Available from: http://www.onlinewomeninpolitics.org/india/bidyut73rd.pdf.

Phillips, A. (1995). *The politics of presence.* New York: Oxford University Press.

Radha, S., & Balu Roy, C. (2002). *Women in local bodies.* Discussion paper no. 40, Kerela Research Programme on Local Level Development, Centre for Development Studies, Thiruvananthapuram.

Sekhon, J. (2006). Engendering grassroots democracy: Research, training and networking for women in local self-governance in India. *NWSA Journal, 18*(2), 101–122.

Singla, P. (2003). Women's Participation in Panchayati Raj Institutions, Nature and Effectiveness. New Delhi: Rawat Publications.

Singh, S., & Sharma P. K. (eds.). (2007). Decentralization: Institutions and politics in rural India. New Delhi: Oxford University Press.

Srivastava, R. (2002). *Evaluation of anti-poverty programs in Uttar Pradesh: Study report.* New Delhi: Planning Commission.

Strulik, S. (2003). *Against the notion of proxie: Women pradhans in Himachal and Uttar Pradesh.* New Delhi: Institute of Social Sciences.

(TIE) The Indian Express. (2015). Women constitute 46 percent representation in panchayati system. New Delhi. December 17.

Tiwari, N. (2012). Women and panchayati raj. *Yojana.* June.

CHAPTER 16

Gender and Local Governance in Pakistan

Nasira Jabeen and Umm-e-Farwa Mubasher

No nation can rise to the height of glory unless your women are side by side with you. We are victims of evil customs. It is crime against humanity that our women are shut up within the four walls of the houses as prisoners. There is no sanction anywhere for the deplorable condition in which our women have to live.
Muhammad Ali Jinnah, Father of the Nation (Speech at a meeting of the Muslim University Union, Aligarh, March 10, 1944).

A wide range of governance and administrative reforms has been initiated in different parts of the world in the last four decades to bring in more efficiency, more effectiveness, better responsiveness and improved performance of institutions, specifically public sector institutions. Since the implications of governance for progress are commonly accepted and good governance is viewed as an imperative for development, the

N. Jabeen (✉)
Institute of Administrative Sciences, University of the Punjab
Lahore, Pakistan
e-mail: director.ias@pu.edu.pk

U.F. Mubasher
Institute of Administrative Sciences, University of the Punjab
Lahore, Pakistan
e-mail: umm-e-farwa.ias@pu.edu.pk

© The Author(s) 2018
N. Ahmed (ed.), *Women in Governing Institutions in South Asia*,
DOI 10.1007/978-3-319-57475-2_16

285

concept is at the heart of recent governance and management reforms. Therefore, a key emphasis of the reform initiatives remains largely on various dimensions of good governance as identified by the World Wide Governance Indicators (WGI) such as devolution, political stability, partnership, participation, accountability and rule of law (Christensen and Laegreid 2007; UNDP 2007; World Bank 1992).

The latitude of governance goes far from the above, encompassing other values such as public empowerment, cooperative accomplishment, shared negotiations and communal countenance. It comprises "the manner in which power is exercised in the management of a country's economic and social resources" (World Bank 1992) and the exercise of economic, political and administrative authority to manage a country's affairs at all levels. Despite the normative and descriptive variations in the above views, they all consider public empowerment and involvement, gender parity, transparency, accountability, efficiency and bottom-up approach to decision-making as core dimensions of governance. The rigid boundaries among public, business and civic society sector get blurred in the new mode of governance as all three are considered as partners and imperative players in the process.

An equal and full participation of all stakeholders irrespective of gender is extremely important in decision-making for uniform human resource development, effective governance and sustainable development. Gender-responsive and gender-sensitive governance has also received global attention. Both gender equity and equality of opportunities are recognized as key strategies for development and adopted as part of development framework by the international development organizations (ADB 2008; DFID 2007). It is widely acknowledged that women constitute half of the world's population and it is unfair and unreasonable to not include this half of the human race in the process of development. Gender representation and participation at various levels have thus received considerable attention, resulting in expanded roles for women in various echelons of governance. This phenomenon has taken place not only in developed countries but also in developing countries including Pakistan where women have been allocated an increased share in political governance. At local level alone, they have been provided 33% of representation through a system of Devolution of Power Plan 2001 to enhance their political participation in governance (NRB 2006; Bari 2000).

Local governments throughout the world serve as the basic component of democracy and provide the stage for public to be part of formulation, execution and implementation of local-level policies and civic provisions. Local governments help communities in organizing their efforts at the grassroots level and enable them to voice their concerns in power corridors. They are well thought out to be a platform to develop sound political leadership and a nursery for good governance. An analysis of the local governance system in Pakistan suggests that although the Constitution of the Islamic Republic of Pakistan provides for equality, participation, right to vote and protection against discrimination (Articles 25, 27, 34), no major effort was made to improve the participation of women at the local level in a true sense (Jabeen and Jadoon 2009). Article 25 of the constitution states: "All citizens are equal before law and are entitled to equal protection of law and there shall be no discrimination on the basis of sex alone," while Article 27 offers shield from discrimination in employment and states: "No citizen otherwise qualified for employment in the services of Pakistan shall be discriminated against on the basis of race, religion, cast or sex" (Khosa 1992). Furthermore, Article 34 of the constitution indicates the state's pledge to guarantee the participation of women in different spheres of life and provides for assenting the state action in this regard (Khosa 1992).

Keeping in line with the above constitutional provisions, the previous constitutions of Pakistan (1956, 1962, 1970, 1973 and 1985) provided for the reservation of 5–10% of seats for women to promote their representation at the local level. But the Local Government Ordinance of 2001, in response to global trends, gender awareness and civil society backing, earmarked 33% of seats for women at all three tiers of local governance, i.e., District Council, Tehsil Council and Union Council through an affirmative action. The noteworthy representation of women in local governance at different levels was regarded as a turning point reform in the context of Pakistan that was projected to offer novel opening of prospects for Pakistani women to establish themselves at the grassroots level and express their concerns in the policy arena. Correspondingly, it was anticipated that such an opportunity would enable women to participate in political, fiscal and community decision-making arenas on equivalent footing and would help in eradicating gender prejudices and biases innate in Pakistani society (ADB 2008; UNDP 2007; World Bank 2005) (Fig. 16.1).

Much of the existing literature in this regard has focused on the issues, problems, obstacles and causes of low and limited participation

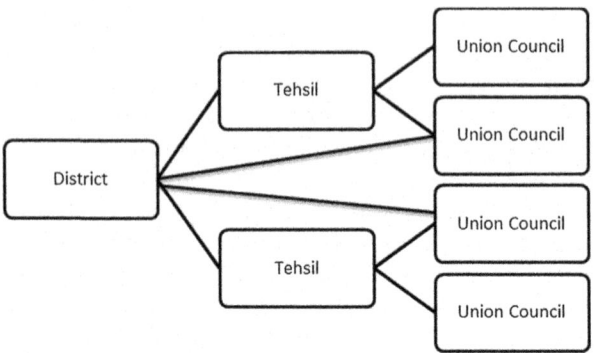

Fig. 16.1   Local government structure in Pakistan

of women in local governance process attributing them mainly to political, economic, social and demographic factors in Pakistan. Nevertheless, there is an emerging concern that to ensure full participation of women in local governance requires to turning the coin's side and evaluating roles, responsibilities, performance and effectiveness of women in line with the shift from local government to local governance. This chapter explores the role of women local councillors in Pakistan. It focuses on a number of issues such as the content of different legislation on local government and the context of their implementation, roles and responsibilities of local councillors, problems they face while performing functions and the attitude of men and women councillors toward each other. The paper makes an overall assessment of the role of women local councillors in Pakistan.

Trajectory of Local Government and Governance in Pakistan

The history of local government structure in Pakistan can be traced back to the All India Municipal Act of 1850 which established the base for local government legislature at a larger scale. Afterward, several acts and resolutions were made during the colonial rule to reinforce the structure together with the Lord Mayo's Resolution in 1870 on administrative and financial devolution and Lord Ripon's Resolution in 1882 on local self-governance which permitted provinces self-sufficiency and authority to structure legislature on local government systems (NRB 2006). The colonial local government structure was mainly designed to oblige the colonial interests such as collection of land proceeds and preservation of law and order. Bureaucratization, elitism, centralization, command and control and state dominance over local institutions were the main features of the then local government structure (Jabeen and Jadoon 2009).

At her independence from the British rule in 1947, Pakistan inherited a system of local government which was characterized as an amalgam of British colonialism and Indian origin with unstable institutions and unbalanced progress. It continued in the early years of the post-colonial period. Regardless of the realization and need for having an indigenous local government system appropriate to the local requirements of the soil, numerous acts and laws such as the Land Revenue Act, 1967; Police Act, 1861; and Criminal Procedure Code and Pakistan Penal Code, 1860, persisted to be executed as in the colonial period, and a status quo was maintained concerning supremacies of the officials, i.e., commissioners, deputy commissioners, assistant commissioners, police officers and civil servants of other ranks.

Over the years, every initiative to bring local democracies closer to people through changing laws, policies, acts and manuals actually created more distance and increased gap among the masses, elected officials and administration. For instance, in 1956 and 1962, an effort was made to introduce constitutional changes in the prevalent local government system and the basic democracies system was introduced in 1959 through the promulgation of Basic Democracies Ordinance 1959. The Municipal Administration Ordinance was introduced in 1960. However, both of these ordinances could not be implemented due to the rise in political disturbance and instability in the country. Basic democracies system (1959) was introduced by the military regime of General Ayub Khan after disbanding the previous system of local government as part of the government's efforts to promote people's participation in local affairs. All necessary arrangements were made to implement the new system. However, after the fall of Ayub Khan's government in 1969, the system could not be executed as designed (Local Government Department, Sindh, 2004). Similarly, an altogether new system of local government was designed by the first democratically elected government of the country in 1975 through promulgation of people's Local Government Ordinance 1975. It also remained unimplemented due to the postponement of local government elections. Thus, bureaucrats and politicians maintained their control over local institutions throughout the period (Jabeen and Jadoon 2009).

The existing local government system, which owes its origin to the Devolution of Power Plan 2001 was envisaged by the military government of General Pervez Musharraf and introduced in the country on August 14, 2001, through the promulgation of Local Government Ordinance 2000. National Reconstruction Bureau (NRB), a federal agency specifically established for this purpose, was given the responsibility to design, develop and lead the plan. NRB formulated the devolution of power plan which provided a conceptual and legal framework for the new system of local governance for each of the four provinces of Pakistan: Punjab, Sindh, Khyber Pakhtunkhwa and Baluchistan. The official goals of devolution included: devolving political power to elected politicians, decentralization of administrative authority, distribution of resources to districts, deconcentration of management functions and diffusion of power–authority nexus for transparency and checks and balances in the system through oversight by citizens.

In other words, the system of Devolution of Power Plan 2001 emulated the transformation in development thinking over time, reflecting a paradigm shift that took place from local government to local governance by the year 2000. A marked change noted in this shift was inclusiveness and integration, involvement of people in the process of development, based on the realization that all development should be ultimately people oriented, and without their engagement in the process, no goals can be achieved as desired. Keeping in line with this gradual shift in development thinking, the Devolution of Power Plan 2001 clearly defined the functions of each of the three tiers of local governance, i.e., districts, tehsils and unions. In order to ensure involvement of various groups, it provided for the reservation of 33% of seats for women and 20% for workers/peasants at all levels of local government. Nevertheless, devolution, after the completion of its first term, has taken the next terms in 2005 and 2013 (only in Punjab and Sindh provinces), but is still facing many institutional, organizational and human resource challenges.

WOMEN IN LOCAL GOVERNMENT: FROM MARGINAL REPRESENTATION TO "CRITICAL MASS"?

Women comprise 49.2% of the total population of Pakistan.[1] Women's representation and participation in political forums of Pakistan have never been so promising. For a long time, they were either absent or marginally represented in formal political forums, from parliament to local government level. Throughout the history of Pakistan, their representation in National Assembly was no more than 2.2%. During the years 1947–2000, the representation of women could not be more than 1.0%. Their participation was further lower in Senate and the National Assembly as there had never been any reserved seat for women at that level till the year 2000. It was late in the year 2000, when 17% quota was earmarked for women in National Assembly and the Senate. The situation was not different in the case of Provincial Assemblies. The local government was the level that witnessed the most vulnerable women's representation at various levels. However, trends have changed gradually, and this lowest tier has also started receiving attention in studies for its significance, influence and shifting pattern with regard to women representation and participation as exhibited in Table 16.1.

The metropolitan and village local government is a three-level administration structure (Union Council, Tehsil/Town Council and District Council). Excluding the Union Councils, the associates of all the supplementary councils are circuitously designated. The designated councillors

Table 16.1 Women's representation in local government in Pakistan

Time Period	Regime	Representation
1958–1962	Ayub Khan	No special representation under Basic Democracies
1971–1977	Zulfiqar Ali Bhutto	No special representation was provided
1977–1985	Zia-ul-Haq	Two seats at UC and 10% for other tiers except NWFP
1988–1990	Benazir Bhutto	Local government elections were not held
1990–1993	Nawaz Sharif	10.4%
1994–1996	Benazir Bhutto	Local government elections were not held
1997–1999	Nawaz Sharif	12.7% in Punjab 25.8% in Balochistan, 2.9% in NWFP and 23% in Sindh
1999–2008	Pervez Musharraf	33% at all levels

Source Adapted from Aurat Foundation (2001)

Table 16.2   Status of women in local government in Pakistan

Local government level	No. of seats reserved for women	No. of elected women
Union Council	36,066	32,222
Tehsil Council	1749	1675
Town Council	161	161
District Councils	1988	1905
Total	39,964	35,963
Women elected on reserved seats for Minorities		126
Women elected on Nazim/Naib Nazim seats		16
Total No. of elected women		36,105

Source Adapted from Rayes (2002)

at the union level form the Electoral College for all elections for the Tehsil/Town and District Councils. It was a common apprehension of the Local Government Ordinance 2001 that women would probably be reluctant to compete for the local government polls or their partaking would be restricted by ethnic and societal barricades. Reality, however, falsified this apprehension. Women ventured into local governments arena in large number and substantiated 90% of the seats reserved for them, and their fringe representation headed to the trend of becoming a critical mass. This silent revolution was replayed again and again in all local government elections. As Table 16.2 shows, women contenders fared well in the local elections and chairs earmarked for women in the Union Council were occupied every single time.

With reference to the summary profile of designated women councillors who were likely to lead the planned transformation in the social and political setting of Pakistan, the prevailing statistics echoed that the mainstream of women (60%) was comparatively beginners and younger (age was less than 45 years), 75% had never been elected before, 73.7% were housewives and half of them were uneducated (Bari 2000; Social Audit 2004–2006). In standings of socioeconomic rank of elected women, the ADB (2004) report stated that 52% of the elected women were underprivileged or monetarily reliant on, 32% coming from working or middle class, 13% from the upper middle class and only 3% belonging to the landlord or elite class (Asian Development Bank 2004).

Recently, the local body elections on a non-party basis were held under the supervision of the Election Commission of Pakistan. The first phase of local elections was held in two major provinces of Pakistan,

Table 16.3 Seat distribution in Punjab for local government elections 2015

Category of seats	District councils	Metropolitan corporations	Municipal corporation	Municipal committees	Union councils	Total
Chairman/ Vice Chairmen	3281	274	460	–	–	
General	19,686	1644	2760	3587	–	
Women	6562	548	920	657	6562	
Peasants & Workers	3281	274	460	–	–	
Youth	3281	274	460	182	3281	
Non-Muslims	3281	274	460	222	3281	
Total seats	39,372	3288	5520	4863	16,405	69,448

Source Election Commission of Pakistan (2015)

Punjab and Sindh, on October 31, 2015. There were thousands of candidates of different parties who had participated in the local government elections. In Punjab, the main rivalry was between the two major political parties, i.e., Pakistan Muslim League Nawaz (PLMN) and Pakistan Tehrik-e- Insaf (PTI). In Sindh, the Pakistan People's Party (PPP) was the dominant party. The elections were held to disperse administrative and financial authority to local governments in order to ensure good governance at the grassroots level. Seats were reserved for women in Zila Council[2], and it was the responsibility of the Election Commissioner to organize and conduct elections fairly. Tables 16.3 and 16.4 show, among other things, the nature of the representation of women in local elections in Punjab and Sindh, respectively.

While preparations for local government election were made and seat distribution was planned in the province of Khyber Pakhtunkhwa, no such effort was made in the province of Baluchistan (Table 16.5).

PATHWAYS TO POLITICAL POWER AT THE LOCAL LEVEL

Women in Pakistan have taken different pathways to reach to the highest political forum of decision-making over time. Since the independence of Pakistan, the trajectory of women participation in policymaking indicates that women till 2000 were not able to mark a visible entrance in the man subjugated realm of politics. As per Gender-Organization-System (GOS)

Table 16.4 Seat distribution in Sindh for local government elections 2015

Category of seats	District councils	Metropolitan corporations	District Municipal corporation/ Municipal corporation	Municipal committees	Town committees	Union committees	Union councils	Total
Chairman/Mayor Vice Chairman/Deputy Mayor	48	02	18	72	296	702	2350	
General	1175	209	351	605	984	1404	4700	
Women	389	69	116	201	332	702	2350	
Peasants & Workers	58	10	19	40	148	351	1175	
Youth	58	10	19	40	148	351	1175	
Non-Muslims	58	10	19	40	148	351	1175	
Total seats	1786	310	542	998	2056	3861	12,925	22,478

Source Election Commission of Pakistan (2015)

Table 16.5 Seat distribution in Khyber Pakhtunkhwa for local government elections 2015

Category	District councils	Tehsil councils	V/N councils	Total
General	978	978	23,111	25,067
Women	329	335	6678	7342
Peasants/Workers	59	85	3339	3483
Youth	59	85	3339	3483
Minority	59	85	3339	3483
Total	1484	1568	39,806	42,858

Source Local Government, Elections and Rural Development Department, Government of Khyber Pakhtunkhwa. http://lgkp.gov.pk/wp-content/gallery/lg-elections-2015/Seats-distribution-in-KP-for-LGE-2015.png

approach, they were facing different systematic (legal, political, cultural), organizational   (gender composition, opportunities for training and development, participation in decision-making, mentoring and network-ing, gender-friendly policies and practices), personal (familial, education, skill development, self-confidence, socialization, domestic responsibili-ties) and environmental factors as impediments to their entry into the political arena (Jabeen 2001). The state enabled them to represent and participate at that level through legitimate electoral reforms (i.e., quota/representation of seats through affirmative action). While the social, political, cultural and economic environments are stirring in contradic-tion to women's administrative partaking and representation, then the state becomes responsible to take measures through the means of leg-islative as well as administrative restructurings to facilitate the process of transformation in favor of gender parity in governmental arrangements and courses.

In line with the above, the government of Pakistan established distinct departments, ministries and bodies to address women concerns, review existing laws and policies and reform legislation on status of women such as National Commission on Status of Women, 2000; Gender Reform Action Plans (GRAPs), 2004; and Women Development Department, 2012. More recently, Provincial Commissions on Status of Women 2015 have been established to brace enactment of policies and incorporation of gender in governance reforms. Besides the above, numerous strategies and policies, i.e., National Policy for Development and Empowerment of Women, 2002; the National Plan of Action, 1998; and the 10 Year

Perspective Plan (2000–2011), integrated the state's pledge to endorse involvement of women in all domains of life. After the 18th amendment in the Constitution of Pakistan, provinces have been accorded more responsibility to craft and ensure execution of reforms. All partners in governance including public, private, civic society establishments and community are making concerted efforts to promote as well as facilitate women participation in politics and decision-making forums at par with men (Jabeen and Jadoon 2009). The rising trends in local governance partaking and working practices of women councillors in Pakistan endorse that legislative, electoral and administrative reforms through an affirmative action and gender quota are the pathway to women's entry and progression at the local level.

The literature on defining political career progression of women can be broadly classified into traditional and newer pathways; nevertheless, regardless of the paths, all trails continue to be slender and insufficiently defined. A brief discussion in this regard is presented below:

The "traditional pathways" into political affairs normally comprise of a long-lasting participation with the political party and practice on the local level, for instance, presiding an electorate party, performing as party representative or, most frequently, sedentary as a local councillor. At present, there is a certain deviation in these traditional pathways together with: *"the political activist," "the trade unionist"* and *"the civic activist"* as follows:

1. *The political activist*: The profile of many candidates who currently are representatives reveals their pathways into politics. It began in their childhood with their blood relations and kinfolks' political participation.

2. *The trade unionist*: Trade unionism remained a predominantly significant track for numerous members into politics, e.g., the Pakistan People Party (PPP, a political party founded by Zulfiqar Ali Bhutto) and other parties. Trade unions are deliberated to be the key path through which working-class individuals collect backing and counseling that stand essential to turn out to be councillor and at that juncture a fellow of assembly/parliament/government later.

3. *The civic activist*: A number of legislators point out the ways some particular occasions encouraged them to catch up with politics. Other representatives discourse about exactly how specific

concerns driven their participation in politics, for instance, gender equality Gender equality rights, association with human rights or civil society organizations Civil Society Organization (CSO).

The new pathways usually include working involvement in policymaking, college or university training, specialized achievement, participation in activism or an interest group, specific expertise set and/or personal self-belief, passion and motivation for public service, etc. It may also be drawn from professional involvement, for instance, the activism and analysis abilities of an advocate, education of public administration or politics education and training. Thus, novel pathways contain the undergraduate candidate, the specialized representative, the personal motivation centered politician and the politics enabling professionals. *"New pathways"* are undoubtedly further exclusive. University training and proficient experience specifically in the field public administration and policymaking ought to become the prominent features of present politicians. To conclude, new pathways as compared to traditional pathways are more diverse and flexible requiring multiple skill sets which encourage educated, skilled and professional people to join the process of local governance.

WOMEN COUNCILLORS: ROLES AND RESPONSIBILITIES

The last four decades of the twentieth century have witnessed a substantial transformation in the roles and responsibilities of women in terms of their representation and participation in governmental, fiscal, societal and managerial arenas. While women around the world have extensive roles to play in different spheres of life, differences are there in terms of their contribution, input and fully fledged performance from area to area and state to state. The yardstick of the progress of nations today is determined on the basis of women's partaking in politics, governance, decision-making bodies and power corridors of societies. Keeping in line, the roles and responsibilities of women councillors need to be revisited in the context of Pakistan.

It is manifested from different research studies and reports that women leaders generally possess a considerable association and cooperative style that are considered as effective to encourage the performance of the subordinates. Moreover, women add further comfort to the work environment through their particular and natural tendencies of collaborating and resolving issues. Women leaders have the benefit of being intensely attentive on associations, contented with effective ways of communication, functioning on networks and assimilating anything they discern at workplace and family. The review of local government reports and documents suggests that women councillors frequently make use of indigenous strategies, set working principles and premises and show concerns for the effectiveness of their administrations. Women are involved in strategic planning aimed at the development of the entire community with wider prospects. They define the fiscal policy and allocate funds through committee budgets. They contribute toward backing wide-ranging issues concerning their communities and play their effective role in improving inter-governmental relations at different tiers of local governance and establishing alliances and agreements with other partners, i.e., corporate sector and civil society organizations. The review of local government research reports and documents also endorses the above characteristics relating to women's roles and responsibilities at that level:

> Women councillors are vocal in raising issues of public interest, they asked questions regarding financial irregularities during the sessions, staged walk outs, held press conferences and organized protest rallies on the issues of their concerns. There are number of stories of courage that women councillors were able to tell, how they fought for the political space and the financial resources in the local government. How they managed to mobilized resources for social welfare of their communities. Women councillors were particularly active in facilitating the poor to access safety nets such as Zakat[3] and Bait-ul-Mal fund[4]. They helped their community members in arranging funds for dowry, marriages, children's admission in schools, and getting identity cards. Also women councillors played a role in facilitating local communities to interface with the line departments and were able to mediate needs of their constituents with the government. (GoP 2010)

Women are thus managing the administration of public resources quite effectively, accepting their new challenging roles willingly and paving ways for other women for public partaking.

MEN AND WOMEN COUNCILLORS: ADVERSARIES OR ALLIES?

There is a general saying that women and men are like two wheels of the same cart. Only if both of them are balanced and stable enough to perform equally better, only then the cart may run well. Likewise, no cart can run with one wheel or sufficiently small wheel as compared to the other. The same applies to the role and status of men and women in society. A society can develop and progress only if all of its members fully participate in all spheres of life. However, research studies and reports illustrate that mainstream of female councillors often faces male opposition for their administrative partaking in the local government (Aurat Foundation 2005).

The male supremacy in local structures, particularly on higher seat of authority such as that of the position of *Nazim* and common male-controlled mentality of the public representatives, is commonly cited as fundamental obstacles in the way of smooth functioning of women councillors. Traditions of purdah, gender segregation, rigid role divisions on the basis of gender, negative politics and *thana kacheri*[5] culture restrict women to come up with their fullest potential in constituencies and impede their efforts. Political parties with male dominance become the gatekeepers in the entry of women in politics. Women party fellows are treated by means of inferiority, and important decision-making positions are not allocated to them in their particular party.

Women are not professed equally prospective contenders to win, henceforth differentiated in the allotment of party ticket. Women councillors are often not informed of the time and venue of the conferences/meetings/summits organized at various forums. On the other hand, if they get invited and go for attending the meeting, they are not supplied with any sort of agenda or schedule. It is realized that the *Nazims* and male councillors deliberately discount women since they do not consider it indispensable for women to be participative in the decision-making practices. At times, women are tormented with unrelated queries and comments throughout the meetings, for example, topics of "*Pardah*" (veil) and wearing jewelry, makeup and dressing.

Their testament is to be considered as half, and their status is determined as per traditional societal norms and customs and ascribed as lower than that of their male counterparts. Some reports also point that women councillors are humiliated by male members when they demand for traveling allowance or daily allowance, resources and conveyance facility. Women are ridiculed by male councillors for their dearth of information concerning the meeting decorum. Several *Nazims* and men fellows treat women kindly, nonetheless not as per their equivalent counterparts. It also has been observed that when *Nazims* and men fellows require backing from women councillors and their effort, they at that moment treat them cordially and deal with reverence and assistance (GoP 2010).

On the other hand, a record number of studies of women councillors via different NGOs (Aurat Foundation 2005; Bari 2000) as referred
earlier indicate that female councillors did not accept the state of affairs
submissively. They objected on biased behaviors and arrogant attitudes
of *Nazims* and other influential position holders. They performed walk
outs, staged protests in public and press meetings to convict *Nazims'*
unfair conduct in allocating development resources. A few vocal ones
also claimed on checking the execution of their development schemes
(Aurat Foundation 2005).

Assessing the Role of Women in Local Government

Traditional cultural norms in Pakistani society are based on male domi-
nancy rules and division of roles and responsibilities for women and
men. While men are assigned more prominent roles in the public arena,
women are assigned roles that largely confine them to domestic sphere.
Women roles in politics in the past restricted them largely to the promotion of political parties and convincing womenfolk to come out of their
homes and casting vote in elections. Their starring role in the party was
restricted to the association of females section, organization of females in
courtesy of party and encouraging women for campaigning and marches.
These roles restricted women's full representation and participation in
social, economic, community and political arenas and even affected their
occupational aspiration.

Despite having twice elected the women Prime Minister, Ms. Benazir
Bhutto in Pakistan, women representation in politics remained very low
and limited till late 2000 as discussed earlier. It was only in 2001 that
women were allocated a visible representation of 33% in local governance of the country through an affirmative action under the Devolution
of Power Plan system. The substantial representation of women at local
level was pathbreaking in the history of Pakistan which ultimately set
the basis for making their way through the complex contextual traditions and accepting challenging public and political roles with changing
trends (Jabeen and Jadoon 2009). The participation of women in direct
polls facilitated a more open culture, empowerment and egalitarian roles
for women and men in Pakistani society. An unprecedented number of
women (36,105) were elected as representatives of local governance at
different levels, i.e., district, tehsil and union as a result of 2000–2001

elections. The elected women councillors belonged to diverse social, economic and political background which ultimately proved to be very helpful in forming the critical mass to organize women of all strata of society and voicing their community-specific concerns in the policy arena.

There were certain apprehensions regarding the performance of elected women in the local councils and their contribution in the newly established system. How the elected women would conduct themselves and cope with certain challenges in the system was another area of concern which proved to be false by the ending time of their electorates. All of them did not get comparable prospects and trials in the first term of local government and faced numerous challenges at systemic, organizational and personal level regardless of their large representation in quantitative terms. Overall, women proved themselves to be capable in terms of their competency and received marvelous recognition and pride from their superiors, peers, relatives and communities. Their participation and support too directed the approval of numerous bits of pro-women legislation and strategies by the federal and provincial government. Some of these women were groomed into energetic public workers, social activists and supporters of community concerns. Even after the completion of the term of their local governments, many of them continued to be the dynamic members in their societies providing for administrative and financial sustenance of their community fellows. A large number of women who initiated their political career as councillors at the Union Council level took part in 2008 and 2013 general election and became the participants of Provincial Assemblies.

The report on Social Audit of Governance and Delivery of Services, CIET 2004, noted the following findings about women councillors:

The satisfaction of general public with the local government institutions at Union Council increased in 2004 (54%) as compared to 2002 (48%). It was noted that in the case of women councillors, the level of satisfaction was higher. Health and Education were mentioned as two areas where quality of service delivery was recorded as satisfactory particularly by women. During the same period there was 2% increase in enrolment in public schools particularly among girls from 2002 to 2004. On average 57% women approached women councillors for help in solving various problems. Although there was a general complaint among women councillors that they did not have the power to resolve people's issues, they were still seen making an effort to connect them to relevant institutions/ officials to resolve their issues. The accessibility of women councillors and their supportive attitude toward their constituents earned them respect and social status. (GoP 2010, p.11)

The above findings and discussion revealed that women performed a significant role in bringing problems of violence, health, education, environment and governance on agenda for discussion and finding solutions using all possible measures and governmental ways. They adapted the learning philosophy, enhanced their understanding of the rules, regulations and policies, actively participated in dialog by questioning things, holding over cues and calling attention notifications.

CONCLUSIONS

To conclude, decentralization and good governance set the basis for bringing women into the mainstream politics and decision-making in Pakistan. It became evident that when women come into the public sphere of policymaking by means of affirmative action or legislation, they encountered certain challenges and constraints mainly by the patriarchal mind-set of the society. However, a review of the performance of women councillors at the end of the first term of Devolution of Power Plan 2001 revealed that women performed their roles and responsibilities considerably well by making their mark, creating an enabling environment in institutions and paving ways for fellow women members of their communities for their contribution. At the same time, dearth of political understanding, specific expertise, knowledge of the local government functioning, leadership and decision-making skills among councillors in common and women councillors in specific were recognized as the key areas of intervention by the government, civil society and donor organizations to enhance the capacity of the members at that level.

After the 18th amendment to the Constitution of Pakistan and the National Finance Commission (NFC) award, more responsibility has been assigned to provinces and districts to improve upon their governance, education and health provision which highlights more a prominent role for local-level governance. Keeping in view, specific reforms and interventions in this direction may include provision of essential information of local government framework, laws, policies and regulations, increasing specific governance, public administration and management education, coalitions, networking and partnership opportunities among the key partners at the district level along with gender sensitivity training, institutional association and support, capacity building for devolution administration, leadership, decision-making and human resource skills to enhance effectiveness of women councillors.

NOTES

1. Pakistan Bureau of Statistics, http://www.pbs.gov.pk, 2016.
2. A Zila Council consists of all Union Nazims (Nazim is the title in Urdu of the chief elected official of a local government in Pakistan, such as a district, tehsil, union council or village council) in the district, which consists of members elected on the reserved seats. These seats are reserved for women, peasants, workers and minority community. The Zila Council has its Secretariat under the Naib (the word Naib in Urdu literally means "assistant" or "deputy") Zila Nazim and has a separate budget allocation.
3. Zakat "that which purifies" is a form of almsgiving treated as a religious tax and/or religious obligation in Islam.
4. Pakistan Bait-ul-Mal (PBM), "an autonomous body set up through 1991 Act. PBM is significantly contributing toward poverty alleviation through its various poorest of the poor focused services and providing assistance to destitute, widow, orphan, invalid, infirm & other needy persons, as per eligibly criteria approved by Bait-ul-Mal Board" http://www.pbm.gov.pk/pbm.html.
5. Thana culture is deeply rooted within the policing system. This includes rude behavior of the police, torture, corruption, misuse of power, illegal detention and inefficiency to use it according to one's desire.

REFERENCES

ADB (Asian Development Bank) (2008). ADB Supporting Implementation of Gender Reform Action Plans In Pakistan, www.adb.org/prf.

Aurat, Foundation. (2001). *Citizen's campaign for women representation in local government.* Islamabad: Aurat Publication and Information Service Foundation.

Aurat, Foundation. (2005). *Citizens' campaigns for women's participation in local government election 2001 and 2005: backdrop, glimpses of the campaigns, overall results.* Islamabad: Aurat Publication and Information Service Foundation.

Bari, F. (2000). *Local government elections.* Islamabad: Ministry of Women and Development.

Christensen, T., & Lægreid, P. (2007). Regulatory agencies—The challenges of balancing agency autonomy and political Control. *Governance, 20*(3), 497–519.

Department for International Development (DFID). (2007). *Gender equality action plan 2007–2009: Making faster progress to gender equality.* London: DFID.

Election Commission of Pakistan (2015) Report on Local Government Elections 2015, http://ecp.gov.pk/Documents/LG%20Elections/LGE2015_Report.pdf.

Government of Pakistan. (2010). *Study on local bodies system and its impact on women.* Islamabad: National Commission on the Status of Women.

Jabeen, N. (2001). Gender, organization, system: A framework for research on women in management. *Asian Profile, 29*(6), 93–101.

Jabeen, N., & Jadoon, M. Z. I. (2009). Gender and local governance in Pakistan: Representation vs. Participation. *International NGO Journal, 4*(5), 264–276.

Khosa, A. (1992). *The constitution of Pakistan.* Lahore: Kausar Brothers.

National Reconstruction Bureau (NRB). (2006). *The local government system, 2001.* Islamabad: Government of Pakistan.

UNDP. (2007). *Gender parity report.* New York: UNDP.

World Bank. (1992). *Governance and development.* Washington, D.C: The World Bank.

World Bank. (2005). *Pakistan country gender assessment.* Washington, D.C: The World Bank.

CHAPTER 17

Testing the Politics of Presence: Women's Representation in Local Government in Sri Lanka

Kamala Liyanage

The Constitution of Sri Lanka (1978) guarantees both women and men the fundamental rights to equality. Article 12(2) of the Constitution states: "No citizen shall be discriminated against on the ground of race, religion, language, caste, sex, political opinion, place of a birth or any one of such grounds." Sri Lanka has ratified the International Covenant on Civil and Political Rights (1966) and the Convention on the Elimination of All Forms of Discrimination against Women (1981), which stress the equal rights of men and women in all sphere of life. Moreover, Sri Lanka has guaranteed women's rights by issuing the Women's Charter (1993). Achievements of Sri Lankan women in terms of literacy, education, health, physical quality of life, and life expectancy are remarkable. Sri Lanka has a high Human Development Index for women which is praiseworthy and is often cited as a model for developing countries (Handbook on Sex Disaggregated Data—Sri Lanka, 2003). Sri Lanka produced the first woman prime minister (1960).

K. Liyanage (✉)
University of Peradeniya, Peradeniya, Sri Lanka
e-mail: imiyakamala@yahoo.com

© The Author(s) 2018   305
N. Ahmed (ed.), *Women in Governing Institutions in South Asia*,
DOI 10.1007/978-3-319-57475-2_17

Two topmost positions of the government—the presidency and the premiership—were held by two women at the same time (1994–2004). However, notwithstanding this commendable achievement, women generally remain seriously underrepresented in politics, both at local and national levels. The percentage of Sri Lankan women's representation in the Parliament has been below six since 1977, and in Provincial Councils, less than 5% since its inception in 1987. The percentage of women's representation in local governments was 1.9% in 1997, 1.8% in 2004, and 1.9% in 2011.

This chapter explores the reasons underlying the low representation of women in local government in Sri Lanka. It will also try to analyze the results of the last (2011) local elections, focusing specially on the strategies adopted by winning and non-winning male and female candidates. The paper will also seek to identify the challenges faced by women in Sri Lankan local politics. It is expected that understanding the lack of representation of women in local governments in Sri Lanka will help us better understand their underrepresentation at the two upper tiers—provincial and national levels. The information for this study was gathered immediately after the 2011 local elections were held. Interviews were conducted with 26 female candidates (7 successful, 13 unsuccessful, and 6 rejected applicants), 19 male candidates (14 successful and 5 unsuccessful), 6 administrators, 4 journalists, and 9 civil society activists. Besides, sixteen case studies were done on 11 women local representatives and five defeated women candidates. Focused Group Discussions (FGDs) were held in 15 *Pradesheeya Sabhas* (Village Council) between February 2010 and July 2011. The FGDs consisted of male and female councilors of local governments, candidates, rejected applicants, local administrators, local party leaders and activists, Women's Development Officers, religious leaders, election monitoring officers and local election officers, journalists, community leaders and members of Village Women's Society's, and some voters.[1]

POLITICAL REPRESENTATION OF WOMEN: FEMINIST ARGUMENTS

The lack of adequate representation of women in public life reflects a significant loss of human resources to the nation. It raises serious questions about the validity and reliability of the decision-making process. Several arguments have been put forwarded by feminist political scientists to justify the equal representation of women in public bodies. The presence of women in elected bodies is evidence of the existence of equality between men and women and hence strengthens the legitimacy of equal rights and opportunity. It also will promote participatory democracy, democratic political systems, good governance, and peace. It is a matter of distributive justice that women should have a share in positions of power and authority commensurate with their demographic weight or their contribution to society. It also will guarantee equal citizenship and rights to women. It is a matter of social utility that the pools of talents from which public bodies are recruited should be effectively doubled and that the decision-making process should be enriched by, e.g., the nurturing experience of women. Besides, by participating at decision-making levels, women will be able to make qualitative changes in their lives and to develop their leadership skills.

It also provides role models for individual women by making them more satisfied with their leadership role and their contribution to the nation. Moreover, women's participation in politics will give them more confidence to work with society at large. It is important for women as a group, distinguished by their reproductive role (whether potential or actual), to be represented by those who share such a role so that they will protect their interests. The increase in the number of women in political institutions can create positive attitudes toward conventional politics. Democratic, sincere, flexible, committed, hardworking, thrifty and less corrupted women can create more women-friendly political institutions and processes. This will contribute to the change in the nature of political institutions and the political culture (Currel 1973; Vallance 1979; Kohn 1980; Norris 1987). Both women and men should be given opportunities to plan and implement development strategies. Then only a country can achieve sustainable development (Boserup 1970).

WOMEN IN SRI LANKAN LOCAL GOVERNMENTS

Local governments are considered as training grounds for future political leaders. The Municipal Council in Sri Lanka—Colombo—was established under the Municipal Council Ordinance of 1865 by the British colonial rulers. Sanitary Boards, Local Boards, and Village Councils were established in the late nineteenth century and the beginning of the twentieth century. In 1920, the Village Council Ordinance was introduced and changes were made to the old Village Councils. But women were not given the right to vote; they did not have any representation in different local bodies. Although the provision for universal adult suffrage was introduced in Sri Lanka in 1931 by the Donoughmore Constitution, no measure was taken to operationalize it for several years. Local government elections on the basis of universal suffrage were conducted 6 years after its introduction.

There existed four types of local governments—Municipal Councils, Urban Councils, Town Councils, and Village Councils at the time of independence (Warnapala 1993). In 1981, Gramodaya Mandala was introduced in the village areas but it was not a successful experiment. In 1987, Provincial Councils and *Pradesheeya Sabhas* were introduced and the government decided to retain the existing Municipal and Urban Councils. Though the local government system changed from time to time, the role of women was minimal. The first female representative in local government in Sri Lanka was Dr. Mary Rutnam who was elected to the Colombo Municipality in 1937. In 1949, Ayesha Rauff was elected to the Colombo Municipal Council and she continued her political life by contesting several times to the Municipality. She later became the Deputy Mayor of the Colombo Municipality. In 1979, Chandra Ranaraja became the Deputy Mayor and later the Mayor of Kandy municipality. Nalin Thilaka Herath too was elected as the Mayor to the Nuwara Eliya Municipality in 1996. R.E. Jayathileke, Nirupa Karunarathne and Kanthi Kodikara served as Chairpersons of Urban Councils.

No major change in the representation of women can be noticed in recent years. Of the 4552 local council representatives elected in 2011, 4465 (98%) were men. Only 87 women managed to win the elections; it is the lowest percentage among South Asian countries. The highest number of women (30) was elected by the Western Province. The Northern Province followed the Western Province, electing 11 members. The Central Province and the Eastern Province each elected nine women, Southern Province had seven women, North Western had six and North Central, Sabaragamuwa and Uva Provinces each had five women representatives. Among them, one woman was selected as the Chairperson of an Urban Council (UC), and another woman as the Vice Chairperson of another UC. Eight women were selected as Chairpersons of *Pradesheeya Sabhas.*

Thus, local governments do not appear to be a good training ground for women politicians in Sri Lanka to learn the "art" of politics. As Robert Kearney pointed out, "Prospects for service in local government bodies are so limited for women almost to the point of non-existence ...."

The small number of women in local government is a significant impediment to women's access to national politics" (1981, p. 81). Several studies (Kiribamune 1994; Liyanage 2002, 2003, 2004, 2005 Thambiah 2002; Leitan and Gunasekera 1998; Kodikara 2009) have identified major obstacles that discourage women from taking part in local politics. These are lack of confidence of women regarding their political leadership, lack of political experiences, and training mainly due to the gendered socialization process, lack of support of the political parties, media, community and voters, violence against women and character assassination of women candidates, financial problems mainly due to high cost of elections, attitudes of the society toward women's political leadership and patriarchal values and cultural taboos, and the weakness of the proportional representative system.

REDRESSING THE IMBALANCE: INITIATIVES BY GOVERNMENT AND NGOS

The issue of under-representation of women in local politics has been highlighted both by government and NGOs. After the 1970s, some women's NGOs and activists sought to influence the political parties to take necessary actions to increase women's representation. In 1994, 12 women's organizations jointly issued a Women's Manifesto which called for the introduction of a quota system, reserving one-third of seats in local governments for women. This Manifesto was presented to major parties at general elections of 1994, 2000, 2004, and 2010; every time, these parties promised to nominate more women, although the reality was completely different. No exception can be found; even the Sri Lanka Freedom Party (SLFP) did not remain an exception, Women who were elected benefitted from family connections and had/have no genuine desire to help women.

Recently, some NGOs and few government organizations have organized awareness raising and leadership training programs for aspiring women to run mainly for local elections. In 1985, the Center for Training of Rural Leaders—*Embilipitiya*—conducted leadership programs for the youth including women. In the early 1990s, several organizations such as the Department of Rural Development, Local Government Training Centre, Sri Lanka Institute of Local Governance, South Asia Partnership Sri Lanka, Center for Women's Research,

Friedrich—Ebert Stiftung, Konrad Adenaur Stiftung, and Muslim Women's Research and Action Forum also organized some women leadership programs. In the late 1990s, the Sri Lanka Foundation Institute and Asia Pacific Forum on Women, Law and Development organized several workshops to give political training to women. The National Committee for Women, Women's Bureau, *Sinhala Kanthabivurdhi Sanvidhanaya*, Agromat, National Peace Council, and National Democratic Institute too trained some women mainly for local elections (Liyanage 2004; Kodikara 2009). Some other organizations conducted training programs for women activists in rural areas in the late 2000s.

However, most of these programs were short-term and covered a range of sessions, such as the concept of gender, women's rights, good governance, advocacy and lobbying, media and campaigning, networking, building leadership skills, and national and local government structure of Sri Lanka. Some of these organizations organized visits to local government and party offices with the objective of giving some understanding of the functioning of them to these trainees. Some organized media and poster campaigns to raise the awareness of the public on this issue. But the outcome of such programs cannot be considered to be satisfactory.

THE NECESSITY OF WOMEN'S REPRESENTATION IN ELECTED BODIES

The majority of the FGD respondents (95%) emphasized the necessity of women's representation in all levels of elected bodies. The reasons given by them were women constitute half of the Sri Lankan population, they have different needs, interests, and experiences to represent, they are given equal citizenship and voting rights, and they view social issues from different perspectives.[2] Many respondents of FGDs and interviewees felt that women mostly raise issues that are related to access to drinking water, garbage, public toilets, day-care centers, domestic violence, drugs, alcohol, and security, and they are more sensitive to such issues. Therefore, it is important to have women in local governments. A PS Chairman said "there is only one female member in our *sabhawa* and she often discusses the issues related to drinking water, garbage, public toilets, day-care centers, domestic violence, drug, alcohol, and security. Before that, we rarely paid attention to such issues."[3]

Many (86%) interviewees claimed that most of the functions of the *Pradesheeya Sabhas* are connected to the lives of women and children. But many rural women suffer more than men due to the lack of infrastructure facilities, poverty and violence, etc. These women need the support of female leaders. Moreover, since women in Sri Lanka have gained achievements in various areas, many interviewees (73%) felt that it is high time that they are given a chance to be part of decision-making bodies.

A female Provincial Councilor observed:

> Women have different biological and social roles. ... they are more sensitive to the issues related to women and children and it is not only their rights but also their duties to represent their needs and interests. Then only their status can be improved.[4]

The majority of the respondents of the FGDs feel that the different characteristics and behavior patterns of a woman can be of assistance to change the nature of the political culture of the country. More than 50% of the interviewees claimed that the presence of a woman in a local elected body can create a more "decent" and less violent atmosphere. Also, many emphasized that women are protectors of the family, society, and the nation and thus, their contribution to politics is important. One PS chairman said: "When a woman is in the *sabhawa*, our men behave decently ... one woman can change the whole atmosphere of the *sabawa* ... we may have less corruption, less thuggery and more democracy in the *sabawa*, if we have more women."[5]

A PS Chairman pointed out that "women are more committed to and thrifty in doing rural social welfare activities and many CBOs are led by them. Therefore, I believe that they can represent PS easily."[6] According to another Chairman "I believe that about 80% of my votes are given by women. ... Since women can speak to other women's hearts, can read their minds easily, can behave openly with them, have closer relations with them, they can represent their problems better than men do."[7]

CHALLENGES FACED BY WOMEN IN LOCAL ELECTIONS

The majority of women applied for election nomination in 2011 stated that difficulty in obtaining the nomination was the main obstacle to expose their skills in politics. Both men and women find it difficult to obtain nominations mainly due to nepotism. Women are, however, pushed into more disadvantaged positions because of their gender status. A female candidate, who applied for nomination in 2011, observed:

> I have been with the Sri Lanka Freedom Party (SLFP) for more than three decades and supported Madam Bandaranayake during her difficult times in politics. In 1978, I was imprisoned due to my political activities but I did not give up ... However, the party rejected my applications for nominations at seven local and provincial council elections ... I heard this time that my name was included in the nomination list and I even went to Temple Trees to sign nomination papers where I was shocked to hear that my name was subsequently removed by the party organizer.[8]

A female PS councilor also had similar experiences:

> "I gave my service to the United National Party (UNP) for long 18 years. I worked as the President of *Lak Vanitha* in my area. The nomination [selection] board appreciated my performance and activities when I appeared before it. However, due to conflicts of the party organizer with a female Provincial Councilor with whom I have close relations, my application for nomination was turned down ... Nomination was finally given to the organizer's sister."[9]

Two women candidates, who challenged their party decisions, observed that they witnessed major problems in obtaining nominations and faced violence during their campaign. One of them observed:

> Both of us are active supporters of the party since our younger days. Hence, the party leaders motivated us to run for local elections ... When we heard that the selected nominees were asked to sign the nomination papers. We rushed to the party office but found that our names were not included in the list ... We joined an independent group. But unfortunately we were not allowed to organize meetings ... Our posters were destroyed and supporters were threatened ... Our agents (representatives) at the polling centers were chased away by thugs of a powerful minister of the area.[10]

Another female candidate who challenged her party expressed her anger in the following way:

> I worked for the SLFP for 17 years and served as the secretary to the *Kantha Bala Mandalaya* in my electorate. During the presidential, parliamentary, and provincial elections I took the leadership to establish women's groups to increase the voter base of the party. The party organizer promised to give me nomination and I applied for it during the last provincial council elections. But the organizer informed me that his brother who returned from Japan should be given the chance. I applied again for the Municipal election, and then he told me that his second brother who had returned from Italy should be nominated.[11]

Another female aspirant for a local council seat explained her frustration in the following way:

> I have been working actively for the SLFP since 1996, helping to establish women's groups in many villages, and to organize meetings ... I also accompanied the candidates to thousands of houses during the last national and provincial elections. Several ministers and our electorate organizer encouraged me to run for local elections ... I submitted 15 files to the nomination board, documenting my records of social activities for which I was given the highest marks ... I was advised to collect some funds and to plan my campaign by the board ... Finally, I was told that due to high competition, my application for nomination was rejected.[12]

Another female candidate observed: "Our organizer is an authoritarian fellow ... he gave the first preference to his son; and three other close associates followed him. The nomination list was filled by including "dummies" because he just wanted to make his son the chairman of the PS."[13]

Many male interviewees also expressed similar views. As one male chairman of a PS observed

> I applied 11 times but got nomination only this time. There are many vicious things and under cuttings which happen during the nomination procedure ... so one must be patient and should not leave politics after such failures, but should continue social work and gain the popularity, build the leadership and establish closer relations with the party leaders.[14]

Many interviewees and members of the FDGs claimed that women were often defeated as they had no experience in politics and found it difficult to invest their time and energy on gaining popularity, and recognition in society. They felt that women could be successful only if they started from the grassroots level and played the role of a leader in political organizations, and trade unions, etc.[15]

A male PS councilor argued: "Women are not courageous, nor are they committed enough; they just enjoy their subordinate positions in this patriarchal culture and confine their lives to families/homes. They must take the challenges to win the elections and to survive in the political world."[16]

Many members of the FDGs (75%) and interviews emphasized that many women could not win the elections due to lack of support and mentoring of senior women leaders. A male party official also held similar view. He thus observed:

> Women in the parliamentary (except one) arena do not pay any attention to this issue... They just want to enjoy the privileges they are entitled and are not much worried about other women.. Most of the male leaders are groomed by senior party leaders, but that is not the case with women.[17]

According to many members of the FDGs and interviewees (73%), the violent political culture has become a serious impediment to women's success during elections. A former Secretary to the Ministry of Women's Affairs elaborated the problem in the following way: "I find Sri Lankan political culture as the biggest impediment to women's political success. Violence, threats, male domination and lack of willingness of party organizers to give nominations have negatively influenced women's representation." Almost all of the women candidates referred to the nature of violence they had faced during elections. One female candidate elaborated: "I was threatened by a very powerful politician in that area who first asked me to withdraw my nomination, failing which he advised [me] ... not to organize any political meeting. Two of his followers [hence men] used a bike to follow me whenever I got out of my home. It really scared me."[18]

In the present Sri Lankan culture, the voters expect material support such as food, clothes, money, household items, and agricultural equipment from the candidates and their (candidates) popularity improves or declines depending upon their ability to distribute such patronages. Nine out of ten respondents observed that since women lacked the ability to distribute such materials among the voters on a wide scale partly because of their financial handicap, they do not appear to be as popular as they should be. Many voters sold their votes for Rs. 1000, or for a packet of rice and a tea-shirt. Some male candidates spent between 1.5 and 2.0 million LKR (Sri Lankan Rupee) for campaign, but only a few women could afford it. Generally, women cannot spend such a large amount of money.[19]

Another factor hindering the prospect of the election of women candidates, according to many respondents, is their inability to distribute alcohol among the supporters and voters. As elaborated by a female candidate: "There are many men around a male candidate ... they are treated with alcohol and food. Such candidates become more popular among voters."[20] A PS Chairman observed: "When I go from one house to another during my campaign, I am always accompanied by 20–25 supporters to demonstrate my power, strength and popularity. To obtain this support one has to treat them generously ... I know, it is difficult for a woman to do so."[21] Character assassination of women is also seen as a serious factor which may negatively influence the electoral outcome. Seven women candidates had faced such problems. According to a PS chairman: "In our culture, generally men are free to have sexual relations or extra marital affairs ... But women are not ... When political women maintain close association with men, their competitors often spread various rumors to malign them ... In such a situation, women try to limit their activities. It is a huge disadvantage to them."[22]

All of the women interviewed for the purpose of the study and a majority of FGD respondents considered the proportional representative system, introduced in 1978, as one of the major barriers to the success of women in elections. The system requires a candidate to cover [at least] a district during the election campaign. A female candidate said that:

> It is very difficult even for a man to cover the total area of the electorate as it requires huge funds and a solid manpower to do so. Although some male candidates are able to do it, women candidates lacking experience, skills, networking and patron-client relationships find it hard to compete.

A male PS chairman said: "Under the PR system, inter and intra party competition is rigorous even for a man. ... Men who can organize processions with at least 50–60 vehicles and demonstrate their power during the nomination day are the winners. Many women cannot do it or they do not like to do it due to their womanly–thrifty nature."[23]

A male journalist emphasized that: "The Sri Lankan culture has created a weak and flexible (*siyumeli*) woman ... the media shows programs

on cooking and beauty culture and never portraits women as leaders ...
The family, school and many religious leaders push women into subordinate positions. Therefore, women confine themselves to the so-called
feminine jobs."[24]

Data from the field show that women candidates also get less support
from families compared to males. A PS member said:

> My family members were very supportive ... my brothers played a key role
> in organizing meetings ... My wife, a teacher, went from house to house
> and was able to collect many votes ... My mother and daughters often
> cooked dinner at least for 25-30 men ... Many women may not have such
> advantages.[25]

Five aspiring women who were not allowed by the male members of
their families to apply for nominations and another four who applied for
nomination without considering the objection presented their negative
experiences. The husband of one such candidate remarked: "A was a nice
wife ... ours was a love marriage ... But after she entered politics she
does not respect me, she returns home late ... I have to cook for children. She does not feed and clean children ... Even she does not give me
my dinner plate which she did her for many years."[26]

Another woman said "It is my duty to feed my children and give
them a hot meal/rice ... My son has commented that if *amma* (mother)
wins the election, people will win; if *amma* is defeated, we will win. This
disturbs me and I have to give priority to my family."[27] This statement
shows that some women do not like to change their traditional roles and
consider these as their natural duties.

Winning Local Elections: The "Male" Methods

The majority of the male candidates (90%) winning elections stated that
they sought to build trust and confidence among the voters in their constituencies by working with them for a long period of time. They succeeded in generating funds from various sources, and building wells and
toilets and distributing materials among the school children. Many male
candidates felt that it was an effective strategy to win the trust of those
who had a low income, e.g., pavement vendors, three-wheeler drivers,
and *Samurdhi* grantees. Some candidates built houses for the poor and
helped them improve their living conditions and won their votes. Some

Muslim male candidates revealed that they used their ethnic identity to gain more votes in the Muslim-populated areas.

Establishing close relationships with the national as well as local party leaders was another important strategy used by many candidates to get elected to local councils. Many respondents (67%) felt that the "blessings of the leader" were very important. Having a good relationship with leaders, particularly with the electorate organizer of the party, is extremely essential. They (leaders) must be invited to public events, and candidates must attend the meetings that they participated in, and must praise their leadership. It is only then that the person will be considered an eligible candidate. Pre-campaign plans are essential to win an election. Some winning male candidates shared their experience in strategizing, viz. collecting funds, identifying issues in the area, and preparing attractive pamphlets even before receiving nominations. Getting the support of the youth is crucially important.

Some male candidates used new technology to get elected. Some candidates (34.1%) said that the youth helped them by circulating messages through SMS and Internet. Several male candidates considered that their "humble" and "kind" characteristics had made them popular among the voters. Nevertheless, 2 religious leaders, 2 human rights activists, 3 local journalists, 12 party supporters, and 16 voters who attended the FDGs pointed out that some male candidates used violent ways, viz. threatening and chasing out the agents of other candidates, giving alcohol and other material rewards to election and police officers and bribing counting officers as strategies to win elections. Six PS councilors and two chairpersons too mentioned about such strategies and emphasized that without using such devices it was difficult for them to win the elections.

NARRATING SUCCESS BY FEMALE CANDIDATES

Women who won the 2011 local elections used strategies similar to those used by their male colleagues. All 7 female candidates who won the 2011 elections in the Central Province said that the most effective strategy was taking part in the activities of their society and helping out the people. This strategy helped to gain the trust of the people. From providing funds to giving them space to do what they wished for their political campaign, the families remain supportive and encouraging. This gave confidence to the women and thus helped them win the elections. Due to the support of the family, some successful female candidates were able to develop a close relationship with the leaders of the party as well. This proved to be helpful because, as it was mentioned by some male candidates, developing a good relationship with party leaders was important to win an election. Pre-campaign planning was another successful strategy used by the winning female candidates. They made the planning months before the election and thus gained the trust of the people who voted for them and made them win.

CONCLUSION

This study shows that women have not been recognized as equal to men in the political representation. They face more difficulties than men to win the local elections. Although a very few trained community leaders in the Central Province have been empowered to challenge the age old patriarchal setup of the political parties by crossing over parties and obtaining nominations, the study illustrates that it was hard for them to win the 2011 election. However, women who have been elected to the local governments show that due to their established popularity and leadership in the community through their long-term social, cultural, and economic activities and the closer relationship with some party leaders, support given by the family and pre-planned campaign movement they won the elections.

When compared to men, it is obvious that the factors which help to win the elections for both men and women are quite similar, but due to the sociocultural and individual factors and lack of opportunities the men are at an advantage. If the trained women were given the nominations by the major parties, the result would be different. Therefore, it can be concluded that without having a structural policy for women to obtain nominations, the political training and other forms of support will solve only a part of the problem. Remedies such as greater awareness and political training for women will not produce quick results. But quotas will help to solve that part of the issue. The Parliament of Sri Lanka passed the 2012 No. 22 Local Elections (Amendment) Bill on February 9, 2016, and it states that one-fourth of members of local governments (MC, UC, and PS) should be women. According to this, a political party or independent group is required to submit two nomination lists for a local body, one for the purpose of electing members and the other to nominate women in respect of wards. According to the percentages of votes, a party/group received the women members selected from the second list.

For example, if one party receives 50% of total votes by its general list, it gets 50% members from women's list. Before 2015, Sri Lanka elected 4465 local councilors, and according to the 2016 amendment, the total number will be 6619 (70% (5092) simple majority system and 30% (1527) PR system—total elected 6619) and 2206 women members will be nominated.[28] The Act has not given a specific criterion for selecting women to this nomination list and it may be used by parties to include their women family members and relatives to local elected bodies. However, since the government has been planning to conduct local elections based on this amendment in the middle of 2016, it is yet hard to predict its results. The best way to fill the gap between men and women's representation in the local government of Sri Lanka is by introducing actual elected quotas and not just including nominated women into local bodies. However, it is noteworthy to mention that on one way at least by granting women to function as nominated representatives of local bodies, they will be able to learn the game and can develop their political skills to run for future local elections. Also, by incorporating women in local bodies, the recognition of their representation and legitimacy of women's presence in elected bodies will be strengthened. However, the quota itself will not solve the problem and the awareness raising of voters, leadership building of women candidates, supporting them in election campaigning, and giving them more opportunities for networking also should be taken into serious considerations.

NOTES

1. Interviews and FGDs were based on five questions: Is it necessary to have women representatives in the local governments? Why many women candidates were defeated? What were the strategies used by successful male/female candidates? What strategies should be used by female candidates to win the elections?
2. Information—FGD—Yatinuwara PS division—April 05, 2010.
3. Information—FGD—Akurana PS—December 07, 2010.
4. Interview—female Provincial (Central) Councilor—March 10, 2010.
5. Interview with the Chairman—Wattegama *Pradesheeya Sabhawa*—December 07, 2010.
6. Information—FGD—Patha Dumbara—April 22, 2010.

7. Information—FGD—Ambagamuwa—April 29, 2010.
8. Interview—female applicant for nominations in 2011—Hatton—April 29, 2011.
9. Interview—female UNP activist, crossed over the party and won the election in 2011—Menikdiwela—April 30, 2011.
10. Interview—two female candidates—Udapalatha—April 28, 2011.
11. Interview—woman applicant for candidacy—Matale—April 20, 2011.
12. Interview—female candidate—Gangawata Korale—March 19, 2011.
13. Interview—female candidate—Maskeliya—March 22, 2011.
14. Interview—Chair Person—PS Ambagamwa—April 24, 2011.
15. Interview—Provincial Councilor—Kandy—March 12, 2011.
16. FGD—Central province—June 12, 2011.
17. FGDs—Central province—June 12, 2011.
18. Interview—woman candidate—Doluwa—March 23, 2011.
19. FGDs—Matale, Kandy and Nuwara Eliya—19th, 23rd, and 22nd respectively.
20. Interview—vice chair-woman—Kadugannawa UC—April 06, 2011.
21. Interview—a Chair-person—Wattegama PS—September 20, 2010.
22. FDG—Yatinuwara—March 26, 2011.
23. Interview—a Vice Chair-person—PS Lindula—April 02, 2011.
24. Interview—a journalist—March 29, 2011.
25. Interview—member—Kandy Municipal Council—March 19, 2011.
26. Interview—husband of a PS councilor—March 19, 2011.
27. Interview—female candidate—Akurana—March 19, 2011.
28. Author is grateful to Gayani Premathileke, Legal Officer, Ministry of Provincial Councils and Local government for giving me this information.

References

Boserup, E. (1970). *Integration of women in development*. New York: UNDP.

Currel, M. E. (1973). *Political women*. Beckenham: Croom Helm.

Government of Sri Lanka. (1978). *The constitution of democratic socialist republic of Sri Lanka*, Colombo.

Kearney, R. N. (1981). Women in politics in Sri Lanka. *Asian Survey, 21*(7), 324–347.

Kiribamune, S. (1994). Women in local government politics in Sri Lanka. *Women their Rights in Local Politics*. Bangkok: Friedrich Ebert Stiftung.

Kodikara, C. (2009). *The struggle for equal political representation of women in sri lanka, a stock taking report for the united nations development program*. Colombo: Ministry of Child Development and Women's Empowerment.

Kohn, W. (1980). *Women in national legislatures*. New York: Praeger.

Leitan, T. & Gunasekera, S. (1998). Women in Rural Politics: A Study on Women's Participation in Politics in Selected Rural Areas in Sri Lanka, Unpublished Report, Colombo: Social Scientists' Association.

Liyanage, K. (2002). *Women in local self-governance in Sri Lanka: Problems, dilemmas and challenges.* Paper presented at a seminar on Local-self Governance in South Asia, September 2–4, New Delhi: India International Centre.

Liyanage, K. (2003). *Strategies for training and capacity building for women in local self-governance in Sri Lanka.* Seminar paper presented at the South Asian Workshop on Women and Local Governance, India, Haryana: Center for Women's Development.

Liyanage, K. (2004). *Capacity building to improve participation of women in local governance: A comparative study.* Paper presented at the Ninth National Convention on Women's Studies, Colombo: CENWOR.

Liyanage, K. (2005). Women in local self-governance in Sri Lanka: Problems, dilemmas and challenges. In Morina Perera & Rasika Chandrasekera (Eds.), *Excluding women.* Social Scientists' Association: Colombo.

Ministry of Women's Affairs. (2003). Handbook on Sex Disaggregated Data: Sri Lanka, Colombo.

Norris, P. (1987). *Politics of sexual equality: The comparative position of women in western democracies.* Colorado: Boulder.

Thambiah, Y. (Ed.). (2002). *Women and governance in South Asia: Re-imagining the state.* Colombo: International Centre for Ethnic Studies.

Valence, E. (1979). *Women in the house.* London: Athlone Press.

Warnapala, W. (1993). *Local politics in Sri Lanka: An analysis of the local government election of May 1991.* Colombo: Lake House.

PART IV

Conclusion

CHAPTER 18

Does Inclusion Matter? Women in Governing Institutions in South Asia

Nizam Ahmed

Major institutions of governance in South Asia, as in other regions, are gendered institutions; these are dominated by men. However, this domination is not as entrenched as in the past. Some improvements in the representation of women can be noticed across the region. Drawing upon the research presented in this volume, this chapter explores the reasons that account for an increase in the descriptive representation of women and tries to identify its impact on substantive representation. Attempts will be made to identify how men and women working in an institution look upon each other's role and define inter-role relationships. This chapter begins by providing a comparative account of the nature of change that has taken place in women's representation in governing institutions, particularly, parliament, civil service and local government.

TRENDS IN WOMEN'S REPRESENTATION

Women in South Asia are more visible now than in the past. Unlike a few years ago when women had a very marginal 'public' presence, one can now notice a gradual improvement in their representation in almost all

N. Ahmed (✉)
University of Chittagong, Chittagong, Bangladesh
e-mail: nijamuddin_ahmed@yahoo.com

© The Author(s) 2018
N. Ahmed (ed.), *Women in Governing Institutions in South Asia*,
DOI 10.1007/978-3-319-57475-2_18

institutions of governance in South Asia. For example, women who now have more than one-third of representation in the higher civil service in Bangladesh mostly remained unnoticed before the 1990s. Women's representation in national parliament has also increased manifold over the years—from 5% in the first parliament (1973–1975) to 20.3% in the tenth parliament elected in 2014. Similar trends can also be noticed in Pakistan and Nepal; in the latter, the change can be seen as phenomenal. The percentage of women parliamentarians in Nepal increased from 2.9 in 1991 to 34.3 in 2014. The increase in parliamentary representation in Pakistan is not as phenomenal as in Nepal. Still, considering the conservative tradition of Pakistan, the change can be seen as very significant. The representation of women in parliament in Pakistan doubled between 1988 and 2008.

However, the change in representation has not followed any uniform pattern; it is more evident in some countries and in some institutions than in others. For example, no major change can be noticed in the parliamentary representation of women in Bhutan; it remains stable at 8.5% of the total in the two parliamentary elections held since the transition from monarchy to democracy. Similar trends can also be noticed in Sri Lanka. The parliamentary representation of women has changed only marginally—from 4.4% in 1994 to 5.8% in 2015. However, increase in the representation of women in the bureaucracy in both Sri Lanka and Bhutan has surpassed the records of most other countries in the region. Sri Lanka has recorded the highest increase in women's representation, and it has been followed by Bhutan and Bangladesh. Pakistan ranks the lowest in the region in terms of the representation of women in the bureaucracy. Bhutan and Sri Lanka, however, lag behind the others in respect of representation of women in local government; women have only negligible representation in local government in these two countries—1.8% in Sri Lanka and 12.9% in Bhutan. The change in the rate of representation is the lowest in Sri Lanka; it increased from 1.7 to 1.8% over the years. (Table 18.1)

On the other hand, the representation of women in Bhutanese local government has doubled over the years—from 6.7 to 12.9%. More women can be found in local governments in India, Bangladesh, Nepal and Pakistan. Women's representation in these countries varies from 24%

Table 18.1 Representation of women in governing institutions

| Country | % of women in different governing institutions | | | | | |
| | Parliament/lower house | | Civil service | | Local government | |
	Minimum	Maximum	Minimum	Maximum	Minimum	Maximum
Bangladesh	10.3 (1991)	20.3 (2016)	10.7 (1984)	35.6 (2015)	24.3 (2011)	25.2 (1997)
Bhutan	8.5 (2008)	8.5 (2013)	16.1 (1996)	35.3 (2016)	6.7 (2011)	12.9 (2016)
India	7.1 (1991)	11.4 (2014)	7.5	24.5 (2012)	27.7	46.0 (2015)
Nepal	2.9 (1991)	34.3 (2014)	8.0 (2003)	18.0 (2015)	NA	7.7 (1999)
Pakistan	11.1 (1988)	22.8 (2008)	4.7 (2006)	13.4 (2013)	10.9 (1990)	25.0 (2011)
Sri Lanka	4.4 (1994)	5.8 (2015)	31.8 (1985)	64.5 (2015)	1.7 (1991)	1.8 (2011)

Source Compiled by the editor based mostly on data reported in different country chapters

in Nepal to as high as 46% in India. In Bangladesh and Pakistan, women constitute a quarter of local council members. Reasons that account for variations in women's representation in different governing institutions in the region are discussed in the next section.

EXPLAINING THE TRENDS

Women in South Asia have followed two 'dominant' pathways to seek entry into different governing institutions—merit and quota. A third pathway of 'inheritance' for entry into public institutions is also noticed. Ascent by inheritance has happened in most South Asian countries, and Bangladesh may be seen as the most advanced among them. Many women (men, too) are getting the advantage of being related to incumbent leaders of elected bodies and are ushered in after their male partners die or are declared ineligible for elections. The parliament has several examples in which women with no experience have been elevated to the most powerful group of decision-makers.

Table 18.2   Quota provisions in South Asia

Country	Quota for women in different governing institutions		
	Parliament/lower house (%)	Civil service (%)	Local government (%)
Bangladesh	16.7	10.0	25.0
Bhutan	No quota	No quota	No quota
India	No quota	No quota	33.0 (Reserved seat)
Nepal	33.0 (Candidate)	15.0	40.0 (Candidate)
Pakistan	17.5	7.5	17.7
Sri Lanka	No quota	No quota	No quota

Source Compiled by the editor based mostly on data reported in different country chapters

However, formally, the provision for merit as a mode of (political and administrative) recruitment exists in every country of the region, although some have also made laws allowing a certain percentage of positions/seats to be filled on the basis of quota. The existence of the quota system in fact accounts largely for differences in the representation of women in different governing institutions. There is, however, no uniform pattern to be observed in different countries. While Bhutan and Sri Lanka do not have any provision at all for quota, others, for example, Bangladesh, Nepal and Pakistan, have made provisions for the quota-based recruitment in all three governing institutions. Provision for quota exists in local government in India, but recruitment to other two governing institutions—parliament and bureaucracy—is made only on the basis of merit (Table 18.2).

Most of the countries in South Asia have not faced any serious problem in introducing the quota system. In Bangladesh and Pakistan, provisions for quotas were introduced by martial law decrees; hence there was not any scope to oppose these measures. In India, as stated in Chap. 16 by Chand, several factors such as strong commitment from the government to enforce the quota rule, inclination of some politicians to extend family network in politics by nominating own people, and the assumption by some parties that they would be able to use 'weak' women members for their own and party benefits, helped the introduction of the quota system in local government. But the task of reserving any quota for women in parliament appears to be extremely difficult, almost impossible. Bills providing for the reservation of seats for women have been moved in parliament several times but without any success.

During the first stint of the Congress-led UPA government, the Rajya Sabha—the Upper House—passed The Constitution (One Hundred and Eighth Amendment) Bill, 2008, popularly known as Women's Reservation Bill, in 2010. But it did not pass the litmus test in the Lok Sabha because of the opposition of the allies. Various political parties have staunchly opposed it because they fear many of their male leaders would not get a chance to fight elections if 33.3% seats are reserved for women.[1] Opponents also argue that the provision for reservation would perpetuate the unequal status of women since they would not be perceived to be competing on merit; it would also restrict choice of voters to women candidates only.[2] The Bill has also been opposed by politicians from the socially and economically backward classes who argue that reservation would only help women of the elitist groups to gain seats, therefore causing further discrimination and underrepresentation to the poor and backward classes. It is also argued that the Bill in its present form would end up ensuring seats in parliament for the female relatives of those who are already in power.[3]

The issue of reservation of seats in parliament has been debated in different fora in Bhutan. As Chuki's account shows [Chap. 3 in this volume], the ruling party as well as the main opposition party promised to introduce quotas for women in all elective institutions including parliament on the eve of the 2013 elections. No step, however, has yet been taken to implement the promise. The number of directly elected women decreased in the second election in Bhutan. Sri Lanka has enacted a law providing for reserving a quarter of local council seats for women. But no election has yet been held under the new law, and as a result, the number of women local councillors remains very low. Nor is there any serious demand for reserving seats for women in the parliament. Lack of any provision for reservation of seats for women in Sri Lanka and Bhutan has contributed to what can be called a marginal representation of women in parliament, although it has not had a similar effect in India. India has the largest number of women parliamentarians elected on popular votes.

However, the way the lack of reservation has affected the representation of women in parliament in the three countries does not appear to have a similar effect on the representation of women in the bureaucracy. Notwithstanding the absence of any quota, women have continued to fare well in civil service examinations and improved their presence in the civil service in Bhutan, India and Sri Lanka. There has been a continual increase of women in the civil service; such increase has taken place in a much higher rate in Sri Lanka than in any other country in the region. Nilmi and Thoradeniya [Chap. 13 in this volume] provide some interesting explanations accounting for such a surge in women representation in the Sri Lankan bureaucracy. One of the important reasons is that compared with men, women have more options to wait and prepare themselves for tests and examinations; they have also less compulsions than men to seek jobs. Women also graduate in larger number than men; hence more women theoretically have the chance to sit for civil service examination.

The number of women civil servants has also increased significantly in India and Bhutan, although no provision for quota exists in either of these countries. Lhamu [Chap. 9 in this volume] observes that the enabling and non-discriminatory environment provided by the Constitution and the Civil Service Act of Bhutan, 2010, which provides for safe and healthy working conditions to perform duties and equal opportunities for employment in the civil service, mostly account for the increase in Bhutan. Improvement in girl's education that has followed the implementation of a large number of school development programs is also one of the important factors that has contributed to an increase in the number of women in the civil service. In India, Singh [Chap. 10 in this volume] observes that individual/family factors as well different 'positive' government policies have encouraged more women to join the civil service. In Bangladesh, the increase is quite significant. In fact, the number of women recruited on merit is two times higher than those recruited on the basis of quota (10%). Ahmed and Jahan [Chap. 8 in this volume] have explored the reasons accounting for an increase of women in the Bangladesh civil service. They have found that besides the existence of several laws and rules that are intended to ensure favorable work environment for women, the 'social prestige' associated with the service and the scope to exercise power have become a fatal attraction and enrolment in the civil service in Bangladesh [as well in India].

On the other hand, the existence of the provision for quota may be a necessary but not a sufficient condition to ensure that more women will automatically become interested to join the civil service. Paudel's data on Nepal [Chap. 11 in this volume] show that notwithstanding the provision of a 'liberal' policy of inclusion, many seats reserved for women often remain vacant. Lack of 'quality' education and rural orientation mostly account for the inability of women to join the civil service. In Pakistan also, notwithstanding the existence of the provision for quota, the number of women entering into the civil service is low. Part of the reason, as Ansari's account shows [Chap. 12 in this volume], is the existence of several subtle discriminatory practices used against women during viva voce and psychological tests.

ROLE OF WOMEN REPRESENTATIVES

Theoretically, both men and women have an equal opportunity to play a proactive role in the governing process. In practice, some are seen as 'more equal' than others. As the discussion in the text shows, some kind of improvement in descriptive representation has taken place in most of the parliaments of the region. The extent to which it has led to any change in substantive representation is difficult to ascertain. Discussion in different chapters shows that women in some parliaments have fared better than others in raising issues that concern women as a whole. Variations can be noticed in the performance of the two categories of elected representatives—general seat and reserved seat—both at national and at local levels.

For example, reserved-seat women members in the Pakistan parliament have moved many private members bills aimed at promoting and/or safeguarding the interests of women. They have also more frequently used other parliamentary mechanisms than their counterparts in other parliaments to bring the issues of gender discrimination to the limelight. In some respects, the performance of reserved-seat women MNAs in Pakistan compares favorably with that of their male colleagues as well as general-seat women MNAs whom one commentator has termed 'surrogate men' as they behave more like men when gender issues are raised and discussed in parliament. As Chowdhury's estimate [in this volume] shows, reserved-seat women MNAs in Pakistan moved 42 and 70% of private members' bills in the 12th and 13th National Assemblies, respectively. In fact, they have moved most of the bills related to political, inheritance, legal and reproductive rights of women and most importantly, they have succeeded in getting those bills passed. This unique achievement has stemmed from a number of factors to which reference will be made subsequently. Suffice it to mention here that, as Chowdhury observes, the reserved-seat women MNAs speak more and also speak better for women than the popularly elected women or male MPs on issues that concern women.

Women in some other parliaments also try to raise issues and problems confronting women. Nowhere, however, can they match the performance of the reserved-seat women MNAs in Pakistan in respect of promoting women's issues and interests. In Bangladesh, women MPs moved only four private members' bills; they, however, fared better in using other techniques to raise important issues in the House. In both Bangladesh and Pakistan, RSWPs have better record of promoting women's issues than the general-seat women parliamentarians and obviously male parliamentarians. What is important to note is that the latter even do not always agree to support RSWPs when they try to bring women's issues to the limelight. The usual argument made to support this contention is that general-seat women parliamentarians have to remain busy with promoting their constituents' needs and priorities and any effort to accord extra importance to one group may antagonize the others, a risk that they can rarely afford to take.

Empirical evidence, however, shows that reserved-seat parliamentarians do not always lag behind their general-seat women counterparts in raising constituency issues. In both Bangladesh and Pakistan, they have in fact fared better in raising constituency issues. Chowdhury [Chap. 6 in this volume] observes that women elected to general seats [in Pakistan] find it difficult to be publicly identify with women's issues because it might be detrimental to their future political career. This could be noticed in other cases also. For example, in Sri Lanka, as Liyanage account shows [Chap. 7 in this volume], there is more instance than one when women MPs did not readily agree to support issues in parliament that directly concerned women's interests such as abortion or domestic violence.

Dhal and Chakrabarty [Chap. 4 in this volume], however, provide accounts of women MPs' achievement in India in getting passed many 'social' legislation that are likely to benefit women more than others. Chuki [Chap. 3 in this volume] has also observed although the women MPs in Bhutanese parliament are cautious of promoting women's issues lest they be negatively termed feminist in the face of huge male dominance, they nevertheless have succeeded in moving several pro-women legislation such as legislation aimed at preventing domestic violence or rape. Chuki has observed that the first ten women parliamentarians [in the first parliament] were trailblazers who demonstrated a principled, feminine, political leadership in a masculine environment.

They contributed to Bhutan's development by enabling legislation which directly impacts on women and children (rape and domestic violence) in their first term. One of the main reasons for their success was that they sought and succeeded in securing support from their male colleagues to get legislation passed. Such achievements cannot be underestimated.

Several factors account for the difference in the nature of activism of women MPs in the region. As observed above, women MPs in Pakistan, particularly those elected from reserved seats, appear to be more active than their counterparts in other legislatures. One of the important factors underlying their success was the formation of an all-party parliamentary caucus on women and a woman Speaker providing guidance to the caucus. Chowdhury argues [Chap. 6 in this volume] that the caucus, besides providing a training ground for newcomers, also played a critically important role in the formulation and enactment of many women-related bills. Yadav [Chap. 5 in this volume] has also observed that an all-party caucus in the first Constituent Assembly in Nepal was instrumental in getting many important bills related to women's interests passed such as domestic violent punishment act, caste discrimination bill and untouchability bill. Women members were able to negotiate many important women's issues individually and collectively through the caucus. The women's caucus mattered a lot in promoting women's issues in the first Constituent Assembly.

A parliamentary women caucus also exists in Sri Lanka, but it does not appear to be very much active because of lack of party support and adequate number of members. There are only a few women MPs in Sri Lanka. On the other hand, the level of activism of women members in India and Bangladesh do not match that of their counterparts in Pakistan or Nepal, especially in the legislative field, although parliaments in both countries are now led by women. In fact, the leadership role of the Speaker in mobilizing women MPs and helping them promote women's issues in Bangladesh and India is virtually non-existent. Formation of an all-party women caucus appears to be extremely difficult—almost impossible—in Bangladesh. Since the leadership in the two major parties remains opposed to any kind of collaboration with each other, no party MP will probably dare to take any such initiative, not even the Speaker who mostly toes the party line. A USAID project once tried but failed to form an all-party caucus during the tenure of the ninth parliament (2009–2013). Even its effort to form separate caucuses—one for the ruling party and the other for the main opposition party—failed.

Several caucuses have been formed in the tenth parliament elected in 2014, but not a caucus on women. Parliamentary caucuses, however, do not provide a panacea; there are other factors such as party program and ideology, cultural norms and societal values that also may hinder the activities of women parliamentarians, as explained in a subsequent section.

Women in local governments in different countries of the South Asian region share some common attributes; their ability to play any proactive role is limited not because of their personal failings, but mostly due to the subordinate status of local government vis-a-vis central government. Different chapters in this volume have documented the achievements of women councillors in various countries, although it is difficult to make generalizations about their role and performance. Sultan [Chap. 14 in this volume] has observed that existing laws in Bangladesh have provided some opportunities for women councillors in Union Parishad (UP)— the lowest unit of rural local government—to play a leadership role. For example, one-third of standing committee chairs are reserved for women elected from reserved seats, and separate allocations are also earmarked for them that they can distribute according to their own choice. Their voice is 'more' heard while decisions are taken on women-related issues such as dowry, divorce and violence against women than in other cases. However, decision-making in the UP is highly centralized, with the chairman exercising 'unlimited' powers including the power to extend patronage. For a woman councillor (for any councillor) to be able to make her mark in local politics is to have good relations with the chairman; nothing moves, as Sultan argues, without his concurrence.

Women councillors in India play a far more important role now than before. As different studies show, women leaders make a difference on the ground. They are playing an important role in the decision-making process, giving more importance to social development activities such as health, education, sanitation, old-age pensions and social welfare [Chap. 15 in this volume]. Jabeen and Mubasher [Chap. 16 in this volume] have documented the scope and extent of the leadership role of women councillors in local government in Pakistan. Not only do they focus on issues that concern women and social sectors; as Jabeen and Mubasher [in this volume] observe, 'Women councillors define the fiscal policy and allocate funds through committee budgets ... they play their effective role in improving inter-governmental relations at different tiers of local governance and establishing alliances and agreements with other partners'.

These observations are not intended to idealize the role of women councillors. Many of the factors that discourage women at the national level to play a proactive role can also be found in local government in all these countries. The situation in Sri Lanka is different. Sri Lanka has what one commentator called a 'local government without women'. There is thus not much scope to explore the role women in local government in Sri Lanka as they have only a very negligible representation. Nepal has lacked any representative local government for nearly two decades.

WOMEN AND MEN IN GOVERNING INSTITUTIONS

It has been observed that the presence of women in different governing institutions matter. It is also now recognized that much of what women can do depends on many factors, of which the attitude of men is critically important. As evident from Table 18.1, men still constitute an absolute majority in all governing institutions; hence their opinion and ideas are likely to matter more than those of women when decisions are taken on different issues. The way elected women and men in different governing institutions look upon each other is crucially important.

The various chapters in this volume reveal that nowhere can one find men holding a very positive opinion regarding the role and participation of women. Although direct resistance to any policy aimed at women's empowerment is rare, everywhere men are often found adopting different strategies to make the life of women difficult. As Ahmed and Jahan observe [Chap. 8 in this volume], gender discrimination, sexual harassment and misbehavior of colleagues which are generally found in workplaces often create stress among officials in the civil service; those protesting such kind injustices are often victimized, among other things, by being posted to less important positions or are denied promotion and/or scope to participate in important training programs.

In Pakistan, as Ansari observes [Chap. 12 in this volume], male civil servants want women to be in the 'soft' professions such as teaching and medical than in professions carrying prestige and offering scope to exercise power and influence such as PAS or PSP. In India, male officials often have a tendency to consider women as less capable of holding important positions in important ministries; many also do not want to work under a female boss. Singh [Chap. 10 in this volume] observes that many male officials also have a tendency to believe that as women have to do multiple work, they often cannot pay proper attention to their civil service duties. Male officials in Sri Lanka apparently have a more positive view about the role of women officials; they readily appreciate the role played by women officials and are aware of difficulties that women face in workplaces and at home [Chap. 13 in this volume].

Men and women representatives in parliament and local government have a tendency to define their role in a mutually exclusive manner. Women often complain of indifferent attitude of the party leadership to their legitimate claims and demands. Reserved-seat women representatives remain doubly disadvantageous, although discussion in Chaps. 2 and 6 shows that they perform better than those elected on popular votes —male or female. In Bangladesh, reserved-seat MPs receive less allocation than their general-seat counterparts; they are also being discriminated against in the House [Chap. 2 in this volume]. General-seat women parliamentarians, rather than expressing solidarity with reserved-seat parliamentarians when the latter raise issues that concern women, often toe the line followed by their male counterparts. They do not easily want to identify themselves with women or women's issues and often have a tendency to assert that reserved-seat MPs have the main responsibility to promote issues concerning women. In fact, like their male counterparts, general-seat women MPs also tend to undermine RSWPs as someone having a 'second class' status in parliament as they lack popular mandate. The paradox, however, is that, as a comparative study of the nature of activism of the reserved-seat and general-seat women parliamentarians in different parliaments in Bangladesh (Ahmed 2013) shows, the former outdistance the latter in every respect, even in terms of raising constituency issues in the House. This issue needs further exploration.

Suffice it to mention here that the situation at the local level is somewhat different as all three categories of representatives—men and women elected from general seats and women elected from reserved seats—have popular mandate. Unlike the reserved-seat MPs who are elected only by popularly elected MPs, seats reserved for women in local government are filled in by direct elections. They enjoy greater legitimacy and also have better scope to assert themselves as their roles and responsibilities are prescribed in statutes/rules; in contrast, reserved-seat women MPs do not have any specific job description. Usually, reserved-seat local councillors are assigned responsibilities for dealing with women-related issues.

Some kind of division of labor can be found in local councils. Local councillors in India, however, have better opportunity to be proactive as they have separate constituencies like their male counterparts. Moreover, as Chand argues [Chap. 15 in this volume], women councillors do not face as much opposition as they witnessed in the past; the attitude of male councillors [as well as general public] has begun to change from total rejection to what Chand has called 'limited acceptance'. The scope of proxy participation, which was widely evident in the past, is gradually declining. However, male councillors still do not want to accept women representatives as equal. Women members are often not accorded the kind of recognition and respect they deserve. There is a tendency in India, as Chand has argued, to marginalize women members while taking decisions.

MAINSTREAMING GENDER IN GOVERNING INSTITUTIONS

Mainstreaming gender in governing institutions is a difficult task. Part of the reason is that since governing institutions exercise power, any attempt at mainstreaming gender will necessitate some kind of redefinition of power relations in these institutions, a task that is difficult to accomplish as the 'powerful' are likely to resist any attempt at power-sharing. The introduction of the quota system can be seen as one of the 'soft' ways of allowing power-sharing without posing any kind of threat to those who dominate different governing institutions. The 'quota women' are not considered equal to those who claim popular mandate; even in the bureaucracy, some kind of stigma is attached to those who enter as 'quota women'.

To be specific, 'quota women' generally lack strong bargaining power; general-seat representatives, constituting the majority, actually decide the 'rules of the game'. Since men still constitute the majority of power holders in different institutions, it is not unlikely that they will try to resist any kind of change that will require major power-sharing. Gender mainstreaming will thus require strong leadership capable of imposing some change that is not still in sight in most of the countries of the region. Although governments in half of the countries in the region have in recent years been led by women, no significant change has taken place in power relations in different governing institutions. Women leaders are probably wary of initiating any reform that may threaten their own positions in their parties and government. Minor proposals are even looked upon with suspicion. One reserved-seat woman MP in Bangladesh expressed her anger at the statement made by one of the senior (woman) party leaders in response to her request for some specific things: 'You've been made an MP; isn't that enough? What else do you want? Be satisfied with what you have been given'. Even reserved-seat MNAs in Pakistan, who appear to perform better than women MPs in other countries of the region, find it extremely difficult to go beyond a certain point where any effort to popularize certain issues risks becoming counterproductive.

Chowdhury [Chap. 6 in this volume] reports that proactive women MNAs are not only being reprimanded, one even lost her seat for being vocal on women's issues. Even the (former) Speaker of the Pakistan National Assembly—Fehmida Mirza—came under serious attack for supporting women's issues; she was even been labelled by some as a 'Women's Speaker' only. Chowdhury thus argues that both reserved-seat and general-seat women MPs face similar political context and reality. Cultural norms and societal values provide important impediments to making any kind of major change in power relations in different institutions including those charged with governing. Those who work in these institutions, especially women, often find it difficult to challenge these norms and values.

In Pakistan, as Chowdhury's account shows, pro-women legislators were seen as opposing pro-women legislation such as protection of women bill or a bill providing for the reservation of quota for women in federal public service, as well as supporting bills that were likely to negatively affect women such as the introduction of *Sharia* law in Swat Valley. Thus, politicians have to work within limits set by cultural norms and societal values which also influence political and party behavior. Cultural norms prescribing a time-honored division of labor is still practised, no matter whether women work at home or outside. One woman MP in Bangladesh expressed her anger/helplessness in the following way: 'He [meaning her husband] will not do anything at all ... will be willing to starve rather than cooking rice or fry an egg even when at home'.

An important problem working women, no matter whether they are in politics or are engaged in gainful employment, generally face is to identify ways to balance their home and work roles. As a strategy to balance the two roles, many women civil servants in Pakistan, as Ansari's account shows, avoid field postings or choose services that do not require posting outside the capital or main cities. This strategy, which solves immediate problems, however, causes stress subsequently as many of them find their career advancement blocked for lack of 'appropriate' experience. Maintaining the image of a 'good woman' as defined by social norms requires a delicate balance between home and work, a task many find difficult to attain. Many women, as Ansari observes [in this volume], thus have to relegate their professional role to a secondary position in contrast to a man whose career assumes his primary obligation.

Ansari, however, argues that female careerists in Pakistan often receive some kind of 'cultural and systemic support' such as exemptions from attending late meetings or posting to remote or insecure areas in the country, and/or experience accommodating attitude of bosses and colleagues; these may not be available to their counterparts in other countries. However, those who may succeed in adopting strategies aimed at easing tension between the two in the short run, as Ansari argues, may lose visibility, being marginalized and lose mainstream in the long run, hence impeding their career progression. This may create more problems in the long run. Moreover, family support, which has traditionally helped women balance work and home-related problems, is becoming uncertain mostly because of the high rate of family disintegration taking place, especially in urban areas. Lack of alternative reliable family support system compounds the problem.

Women working outside thus face a dilemma. There is no 'one best way' to resolve this dilemma. Moreover, the notion/image of a 'good woman'—societal prescriptions dictating the duties of a female toward her family and governing her social conduct [Chap. 12 in this volume]—does not apply only to a working woman; it equally applies to women who are involved in politics. Balancing politics and family requires at least as much skills and strategies as needed to balance work and home, although the way they may use these may vary from one context to another.

Overall, various country chapters in this volume reveal that more women can be found in different governing institutions in South Asia now than in the past. However, the rate of increase in representation can be seen as uneven, with some countries progressing at a much faster rate than the others. Part of the reason is the existence of a quota system that has contributed significantly to the improvement of descriptive representation of women, particularly in Bangladesh and Pakistan. The rate of increase of women's representation is slower in those countries where the system of quota does not exist, for example, Sri Lanka and Bhutan. Evidence shows that the increase in descriptive representation has a positive impact on the substantive representation of women in different countries. Those elected indirectly, referred to as 'quota women' in this book, do not always remain onlookers; in fact, 'quota women' in parliaments have fared better than those (women) elected on popular votes in almost every country in promoting issues that concern women. Differences in the nature of activism can be noticed not only between the two categories of women MPs in a single country, but also among women MPs in different countries, with Pakistani reserved-seat women MPs outperforming their counterparts in other countries, particularly in moving women-friendly legislation. Bangladeshi women MPs used different techniques other than legislation to promote various issues that concern them. Quota women in local governments also appear to be actively engaged in promoting women-related issues that generally do not interest male representatives.

Yet women lawmakers or local women councillors do not receive the kind of recognition they deserve. They often remain neglected and their contribution is less appreciated. Patriarchy is widely evident; examples of women being reprimanded for playing a proactive role are not rare. What is particularly noticed is the absence of a sense of comradeship among women representatives. Women do not always agree on women-related issues. In general, party restrictions discourage cross-bench collaboration; cultural norms and societal values compound this problem. Women in bureaucracies in different countries also remain disadvantaged, notwithstanding an increase in their representation over the years. In particular, glass ceiling is widely evident in different countries of the region. Moreover, very often women find it difficult to balance work and home roles. Experience shows that strategies adopted to make the two roles compatible in the short run often turn out to be counterproductive in the long run, thereby causing stress and strain among women officials.

One positive thing that can be observed is that resistance to women seeking entry into politics and bureaucracy and their advancement is not as widespread as in the past. Societal values regarding women are also changing. There is greater social acceptance of women in leadership roles now than in the past. Many even take pride in having daughters, sisters or wives in important positions in politics and administration; educated employed women are also seen as economic assets, especially in India. What is needed most is to adopt policies and programs aimed at turning different constraints to women's empowerment into opportunities, a task that seems to be difficult, although not impossible.

NOTES

1. What's the Women's Reservation Bill all about? *rediff News*, March 08, 2010. http://news.rediff.com/special/2010/mar/08/whats-the-womens-reservation-bill-all-about.htm. Accessed January 30, 2017.
2. 'Twenty Years Too Long: Women's Reservation Bill Continues to Languish in Lok Sabha', *The Wire*, September 16, 2016. https://thewire.in/66260/womens-reservation-bill-in-lok-sabha/. Accessed February 10, 2017.
3. Ayesha Sumbul, 'Women's Reservation Bill—A Critique', PCL Bulletin, August 2004. http://www.pucl.org/Topics/Gender/2004/womens-reservation-bill.htm. Accessed February 10, 2017.

INDEX

© The Editor(s) (if applicable) and The Author(s) 2018
N. Ahmed (ed.), *Women in Governing Institutions in South Asia*,
DOI 10.1007/978-3-319-57475-2